Lecture Notes in Computer Science 4364

Commenced Publication in 1973
Founding and Former Series Editors:
Gerhard Goos, Juris Hartmanis, and Jan van Leeuwen

Thomas Kühne (Ed.)

Models in Software Engineering

Workshops and Symposia at MoDELS 2006
Genoa, Italy, October 1-6, 2006
Reports and Revised Selected Papers

 Springer

Volume Editor

Thomas Kühne
TU Darmstadt
FG Metamodellierung
Hochschulstr. 10, 64289 Darmstadt, Germany
E-mail: kuehne@informatik.tu-darmstadt.de

Library of Congress Control Number: 2006939519

CR Subject Classification (1998): D.2, D.3, I.6, K.6

LNCS Sublibrary: SL 2 – Programming and Software Engineering

ISSN   0302-9743
ISBN-10   3-540-69488-9 Springer Berlin Heidelberg New York
ISBN-13   978-3-540-69488-5 Springer Berlin Heidelberg New York

Springer is a part of Springer Science+Business Media

springer.com

© Springer-Verlag Berlin Heidelberg 2007
Printed in Germany

Typesetting: Camera-ready by author, data conversion by Scientific Publishing Services, Chennai, India
Printed on acid-free paper   SPIN: 11969273   06/3142   5 4 3 2 1 0

Preface

Following tradition, MoDELS 2006 hosted a number of workshops and symposia. They provided collaborative forums for groups to conduct intensive discussions and complemented the main conference by focusing on important subject areas and enabling a high degree of interactivity.

MoDELS 2006 featured 11 workshops and three symposia during the first three days of the conference. In addition to the Doctoral and Educators symposia, which were already successfully held in 2005, a symposium on UML semantics was held for the first time at MoDELS 2006.

Keeping a time-tested tradition of the MoDELS/UML series, I formed an international workshop selection committee composed of the following researchers:

- Jean-Michel Bruel (University of Pau, France)
- Martin Glinz (Universität Zürich, Switzerland)
- Reiko Heckel (University of Leicester, UK)
- Jens Jahnke (University of Victoria, Canada)
- Hans Vangheluwe (McGill University, Canada)
- Jon Whittle (George Mason University, USA)

Out of 18 workshop proposals, we selected 11 workshops and the symposium on UML semantics. Because of the way the latter was organized we, as well as the symposium organizers, agreed that it fitted more appropriately under the heading of a symposium.

Six of the workshops have a history in the MoDELS/UML series and represented a continuation of ongoing discussions on established topics. The other five workshops featured new topics, further broadening the scope of MoDELS, beyond its traditional focus on UML. We believe this blend of established and innovative workshop themes made the MoDELS 2006 workshops and symposia a success worth attending. The summaries of all symposia and workshops plus revised versions of the two respective best papers are included in these proceedings.

I am grateful to the members of the Selection Committee who accepted my invitation and worked diligently to select the workshops with the maximum research relevance and highest potential of attracting participants. Gianna Reggio was an invaluable help in resolving organizational issues and my predecessor Jean-Michel Bruel immensely eased my work by generously sharing his experience.

November 2006

Thomas Kühne
Workshop Chair
MoDELS 2006

Sponsors

DISI, Dipartimento di Informatica e Scienze dell'Informazione, Università di Genova (`www.disi.unige.it`)

ACM Special Interest Group on Software Engineering (`www.sigsoft.org`)

IEEE Computer Society (`www.computer.org`)

Table of Contents

W4 – Quality in Modeling

W5 – Advanced User Interfaces

W6 – Real-Time and Embedded Systems

W7 – OCL

W8 – Integrating MDA and V&V

W9 – Model Size Metrics

W10 – Models@run.time

9th International Workshop on Aspect-Oriented Modeling

Jörg Kienzle[1], Dominik Stein[2], Walter Cazzola[3],
Jeff Gray[4], Omar Aldawud[5], and Tzilla Elrad[6]

[1] McGill University, Canada
[2] University of Duisburg-Essen, Germany
[3] University of Milano, Italy
[4] University of Alabama at Birmingham, USA
[5] Lucent Technologies, USA
[6] Illinois Institute of Technology, USA
joerg.kienzle@mcgill.ca, dominik.stein@icb.uni-due.de,
cazzola@dico.unimi.it, gray@cis.uab.edu, oaldawud@lucent.com,
elrad@iit.edu

Abstract. This report summarizes the outcomes of the 9th Workshop on Aspect-Oriented Modeling (AOM) held in conjunction with the 9th International Conference on Model Driven Engineering Languages and Systems – MoDELS 2006 – in Genoa, Italy, on the 1st of October 2006. The workshop brought together approximately 25 researchers and practitioners from two communities: aspect-oriented software development and software model engineering. It provided a forum for discussing the state of the art in modeling crosscutting concerns at different stages of the software development process: requirements elicitation and analysis, software architecture, detailed design, and mapping to aspect-oriented programming constructs. This paper gives an overview of the accepted submissions and summarizes the results of the different discussion groups. Papers and presentation slides of the workshop are available at http://www.aspect-modeling.org/.

1 Introduction

This report summarizes the outcomes of the 9th edition of the successful Aspect-Oriented Modeling Workshop series. The workshop took place at the Bristol Hotel in Genoa, Italy, on Sunday, October 1st 2006, as part of the 9th International Conference on Model Driven Engineering Languages and Systems – MoDELS 2006. A total of 11 position papers were submitted and reviewed by the program committee, 9 of which were accepted to the workshop. Approximately 25 participants attended the presentation session and took part in lively discussions. Papers, presentation slides, and further information can be found at http://www.aspect-modeling.org/.

2 Overview of Accepted Position Papers

Marcelo Sande from the Military Institute of Engineering in Rio de Janeiro, Brazil, described how he and his colleagues mapped AspectualACME, an architectural

T. Kühne (Ed.): MoDELS 2006 Workshops, LNCS 4364, pp. 1–5, 2007.
© Springer-Verlag Berlin Heidelberg 2007

description language, to UML 2.0 [8]. He presented why the base UML 2.0 modeling abstractions of component diagrams are not strong enough. One reason to this is that standard UML only allows to connect provided interfaces of components to required interfaces of other components. He explained how they made connectors first-order elements, and how they defined a special aspectual connector that can be used to connect the provided interface of a (crosscutting) component to both the provided and the required interfaces of another (base) component.

Natsuko Noda from the Japan Advanced Institute of Sciences and Technology in Nomi, Japan, presented a symmetric aspect-oriented modeling technique for aspect-oriented design [6]. In Noda's presentation, each concern of the system is modeled with aspects that are composed of class diagrams, object diagrams and state diagrams. Each aspect is self-contained. The connections between aspects are defined in aspect relation rules, which define how a transition change in one aspect can affect other aspects (i.e., by introducing events into other aspects).

Asif Iqbal from the Honeywell Technology Solutions Lab in Bangalore, India, works in the context of modeling of safety-critical systems. He talked about the issue of modeling temporal behavior, which usually crosscuts the functional model of a system [4]. In order to reason about concepts such as Worst Case Execution Time, time-depending behavior has to be explicitly represented in models. As an example, Asif mentioned the synchronization of local clocks with a global clock. He showed how this concern can be modeled with timed state diagrams, and how the crosscutting can be modeled using the AOSF framework with time extensions. However, state diagrams that are created using orthogonal composition run on a single clock, which is a problem that still needs to be addressed.

Thomas Cottenier from Motorola Labs in Chicago, USA, argued that reactive functionality of a system should be modeled using a reactive modeling formalism such as state diagrams [2]. He showed a small demonstration of the Motorola Aspect WEAVR, a tool for aspect-oriented composition of state diagrams. The Motorola models are executable (or transformable into executable code). Thomas argued that aspect-oriented modeling is more powerful than aspect-oriented programming: The join point model of state diagrams is better suited to express crosscutting reactive concerns than the classic join point model of aspect-oriented programming languages.

Sonia Pini from the University of Genoa, Italy, argued that current pointcut definitions require global knowledge of the base program by the developer in order to write meaningful pointcuts [1]. Hence, current join point selection mechanisms are fragile, because they fail to provide reusability and evolvability. In order to reason about the semantics of join points, she proposed a technique in which the join points are expressed at a higher level of abstraction (i.e., at the modeling level with sequence and activity diagrams). Furthermore, she presented a mechanism to map these high-level join point selections to program code.

Arnor Solberg from SINTEF/the University of Oslo, Norway, presented an aspect-oriented modeling technique based on sequence diagrams [7]. In this approach, aspect sequence diagrams are defined that represent a template of crosscutting behavior. To instantiate the aspects, the base model is annotated with tags that define where the aspects should be applied (i.e., instantiated). Simple aspects are inserted into the base sequence diagram at one specific point, whereas composite aspects are applied to regions within the base diagram (annotated with a tagged fragment). In order to allow fine-grained application of crosscutting behavior within this tagged fragment, a composite aspect defines several parts: begin/end parts that execute when the fragment is entered/exited, before/after parts that execute before or after every message invocation, and a body part that can alter the actual message sending.

Andrea Sindico from ELT Elettronica in Rome, Italy, presented an aspect-oriented modeling approach in which concerns are specified in an aspect diagram [3], which defines static crosscutting in the form of an inter-type declaration diagram, and dynamic crosscutting in the form of advice diagrams. Inter-type declaration diagrams are composed of two class diagrams. Advice diagrams are composed of pointcut diagrams and behavioral diagrams. In both cases, one diagram explains the context of the base program that is of interest, while the other shows what has to be added to the base context. Pointcut diagrams (comprised in advice diagrams), for example, define the set of join points to which an aspect is to be applied. In his work, Andrea suggests to specify them in the form of a UML activity diagram.

Thomas Cottenier from the Motorola Labs in Chicago, USA, also presented work on aspect interference at the modeling level [9]. He showed a demo of the Telelogic TAU tool, in which they implemented different dependencies in their aspect deployment diagrams: A «follows» B, which specifies that aspect A's behavior has lower precedence than B; A «hidden_by» B, which specifies that the behavior of aspect A is not activated when A and B apply to the same join point; and A «depends_on» B, which specifies that aspect A's behavior can only be applied where aspect B's behavior is also applied.

Roberto Lopez-Herrejon from Oxford University, UK, related Feature-Oriented Programming (FOP) to the approach of Aspect-Oriented Software Development with Use Cases (AOSD w/UC) [5]. He demonstrated how features can crosscut other features and how aspects can help to resolve this crosscutting. Roberto referred to the existing approach of AOSD w/UC and pointed out its limitations with respect to a well-defined composition mechanism. After that, he introduced the algebraic approach of FOP, which contains a formal composition model, but lacks an "intuitive" notation. Roberto proposed to combine FOP with AOSD w/UC to achieve mutual benefit.

3   Overview of Discussion Topics

Due to space limitations, this section offers a summary of the most interesting and significant issues that were addressed during the discussion sessions. These issues also emerged during the questions and comments in the presentation sessions.

Is AOM about visual representation? During the workshop, the participants expressed several opinions about the essence of AOM. The general idea of modeling is to make something simpler (i.e., more comprehensible). Very often, this goal is achieved by providing a visual notation. However, most of the participants agreed that a visual notation is not essential. Once the semantics of an abstraction are well-defined, finding a suitable graphical representation for it is only syntactic sugar. The discussion did not go into further details, unfortunately, about what precisely AOM should make simpler or more comprehensible other than "visual communication."

Is there a need to look at woven models? There has been a disagreement on whether developers need to have a look at woven models. Although some participants argued that this is necessary for comprehending the execution of an aspect-oriented program (or model) and for debugging, others claimed that, once the semantics of a given weaving mechanism is clear, developers do not care about (and do not need to look up) how these semantics are actually accomplished.

Does AOM meet its goals? One of the participants questioned if AOM actually meets its goals, such as an improved readability, comprehensibility, extensibility, and reusability of software (artifacts). The participant reported on a case study that was conducted in which aspect-oriented modeling techniques were used throughout the entire software development lifecycle. That is, each concern was separated all the way down from requirements elucidation to the pre-coding phase. In the end, the participant obtained a nicely separated set of concern specifications. However, this results in a full load of very complex composition specifications determining how those nicely separated concerns are supposed to work together. These composition specifications were not readable, comprehensible, extendible, or reusable.

What is the role of model composition specifications (join point selections, composition rules, etc.) in the software development process? Various participants were concerned about the relevance of model composition specifications (such as join point selections, pointcuts, composition rules, composition directives, or other kinds of dependency relationships between concern models) in the software development lifecycle. It has been stated that the gap between join points[1] in requirement specifications and join points in the corresponding code is huge. Consequently, the mapping of join point selections (composition rules) between different levels of abstraction is often problematic. One solution to this might be to introduce notions of join points at various levels of abstraction, such as architectural join points for architectural system descriptions, and map the join point notion of one abstraction layer to the join point notion of the layer beneath.

A statement from an industry participant suggested that AOM may help to keep concepts separated and consistent throughout the development process. However, AOM should also provide a means to indicate explicitly how those separated concepts interact with each other in order to document design decisions and tradeoffs. Furthermore, AOM should provide support for documenting the application of a particular policy in the general case and at the same time outlining under which circumstances a more specialized policy is used (e.g., in general, use password authentication, but in these and those special cases, use biometric authentication).

What is the target application context of AOM? Another question concerned the target application context of AOM and how AOM should support it. Industry mentioned that software projects rarely attack problems from scratch. Usually, existing software needs to be extended. Therefore, AOM should provide a means to support extensibility. Another point was that introducing aspects into industry should start with simple cases. Such simple aspects should be implemented by a small group of developers, which facilitates support for the larger group of "base program developers." Once the simple aspects are adopted, more elaborate aspects could be introduced. One problem that has to be solved concerns the fact that even simple

---

[1] or, more generally speaking, some kind of concern interaction points.

aspects can add an enormous amount of new possible states to a base program. Perhaps AOM can help in estimating the effects of an aspect onto a given base system. Another scenario mentioned concerns how AOM could be used to document design decisions and tradeoffs (see previous question).

4 Concluding Remarks

The 9th International Workshop on Aspect-Oriented Modeling in Genoa provided evidence that the AOM community has reached a state of maturity. Most participants were well aware of the fundamental ideas and key concepts of AOSD. Consequently, the focus of discussions shifted from "what are the right abstractions to use in AOM in general?" towards "how to use these abstractions and AOM in order to reach certain goals?" The participants from academia critically evaluated the existing modeling approaches with respect to certain claims and specific problems. Participants from industry expressed clear expectations of what they anticipate from AOM. These problems and expectations outline cardinal and substantial topics for future research on AOM.

Acknowledgements

We would like to thank the program committee members who have helped to assure the quality of this workshop: Mehmet Aksit, Aswin van den Berg, Thomas Cottenier, Robert France, Sudipto Ghosh, Stefan Hanenberg, Andrew Jackson, Jean-Marc Jézéquel, Kim Mens, Alfonso Pierantonio, Raghu Reddy, and Markus Völter. We also thank all submitters and workshop participants who helped to make this workshop a success.

References

[1] Cazzola, W., Pini, S., *Join Point Patterns: A High-Level Join Point Selection Mechanism*

[2] Cottenier, T., van den Berg, A., Elrad, T., *Model Weaving: Bridging the Divide between Elaborationists and Translationists*

[3] Grassi, V., Sindico, A., *UML Modeling of Static and Dynamic Aspects*

[4] Iqbal, A., Elrad, T., *Modeling Timing Constraints of Real-Time Systems as Crosscutting Concerns*

[5] Lopez-Herrejon, R., Batory, D., *Modeling Features in Aspect-Based Product Lines with Use Case Slices: An Exploratory Case Study*

[6] Noda, N., Kishi, T., *An Aspect-Oriented Modeling Mechanism Based on State Diagrams*

[7] Reddy, R., Solberg, A., France, R., Ghosh, S., *Composing Sequence Models using Tags*

[8] Sande, M., Choren, R., Chavez, C., *Mapping AspectualACME into UML 2.0*

[9] Zhang, J., Cottenier, T., van den Berg, A., Gray, J., *Aspect Interference and Composition in the Motorola Aspect-Oriented Modeling Weaver*

Modeling Features in Aspect-Based Product Lines with Use Case Slices: An Exploratory Case Study

Roberto E. Lopez-Herrejon[1] and Don Batory[2]

[1] Computing Laboratory, University of Oxford, England
[2] Department of Computer Sciences, University of Texas at Austin, USA
rlopez@comlab.ox.ac.uk, batory@cs.utexas.edu

Abstract. A significant number of techniques that exploit aspects in software design have been proposed in recent years. One technique is use case slices by Jacobson and Ng, that builds upon the success of use cases as a common modeling practice. A use case slice modularizes the implementation of a use case and typically consists of a set of aspects, classes, and interfaces. Work on *Feature Oriented Programming (FOP)* has shown how features, increments in program functionality, can be modularized and algebraically modeled for the synthesis of product lines. When AspectJ is used in FOP, the structure of feature modules resembles that of use case slices. In this paper, we explore the relations between use case slices modeling and FOP program synthesis and describe their potential synergy for modeling and synthesizing aspect-based product lines.

1 Introduction

A significant number of techniques that exploit aspects in the realm of design have been proposed in recent years [4]. One technique, proposed by Jacobson and Ng [15], is *use case slices*, which are modular implementations of use cases. Typically, the implementation of a use case slice consists of a set of aspects, classes, and interfaces. A similar structure appears when aspects are used to implement features [16][19], which are increments in program functionality, with *Feature Oriented Programming (FOP)* [10][11], a technology that studies feature modularity in program synthesis for product lines.

In this paper, we present a simple product line example and its implementation in AspectJ. This example helps us illustrate how use case slices can model features in aspect-based product lines and how features can be algebraically modeled for program synthesis. We analyze the relations between use case slices modeling and FOP program synthesis and describe how their potential synergy can serve as a foundation of a methodology for modeling and synthesizing aspect-based product lines.

2 Product Line Example

To illustrate the similarities between use case slices and features we use a simple product line based on the Extensibility Problem [17]. This problem has been widely

T. Kühne (Ed.): MoDELS 2006 Workshops, LNCS 4364, pp. 6–16, 2007.
© Springer-Verlag Berlin Heidelberg 2007

studied within the context of programming language design, where the focus is achieving data type and operation extensibility in a type-safe manner. Our focus is on designing and synthesizing a family of programs that we call the *Expressions Product Line (EPL)* [17]. Next we describe in detail this product line and its implementation using AspectJ.

2.1 Example Description

EPL supports a mix of new operations and datatypes to represent expressions of the following language:

```
Exp      : :       =     Lit          |        Add        |        Neg
Lit      : :       =           <non-negative                    integers>
Add      : :       =     Exp                "+"                      Exp
Neg      : : = "-" Exp
```

Two operations can be performed on expressions of this grammar:

1) `Print` displays the string value of an expression. The expression `2+3` is represented as a three-node tree with an `Add` node as the root and two `Lit` nodes as leaves. Operation `Print`, applied to this tree, displays the string "2+3".

2) `Eval` evaluates expressions and returns their numeric value. Applying the operation `Eval` to the tree of expression `2+3` yields 5 as the result.

An extra class `Test` creates instances of the datatype classes and invokes their operations.

A natural representation for EPL is a two-dimensional matrix [17]. Rows represent datatypes and columns specify operations. Each matrix entry is a feature that implements the operation, described by the column, on the data type, specified by the row. As a naming convention throughout the paper, we identify matrix entries by using the first letters of the row and the column, e.g., the entry at the intersection of row `Add` and column `Print` is named ap and implements operation `Print` on data type `Add`. This matrix is shown in Figure 1 where feature names are encircled.

A program member of this product line is composed from the set of features that are at the intersection of the set of operations (columns) and datatypes (rows) selected for the program. EPL is formed by all the possible combinations of selections of rows and columns. For instance, the program that implements `Print` and `Eval` operations on datatypes `Lit` and `Neg` is composed with features lp, le, np, and ne.

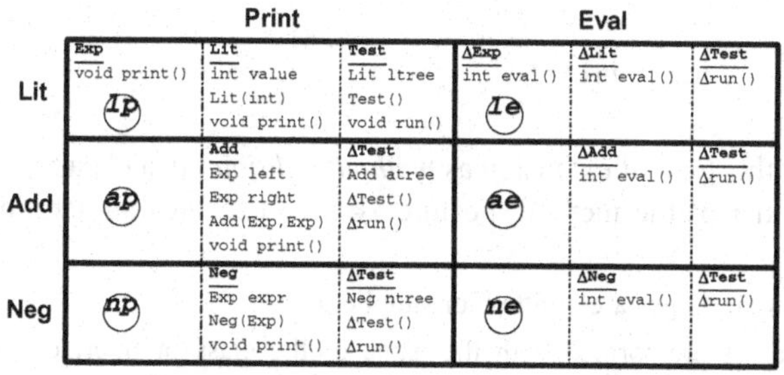

		Print			Eval	
		Lit	**Test**	**ΔExp**	**ΔLit**	**ΔTest**
Lit	**Exp** void print() (**lp**)	int value Lit(int) void print()	Lit ltree Test() void run()	int eval() (**le**)	int eval()	Δrun()
Add	(**ap**)	**Add** Exp left Exp right Add(Exp,Exp) void print()	**ΔTest** Add atree ΔTest() Δrun()	(**ae**)	**ΔAdd** int eval()	**ΔTest** Δrun()
Neg	(**np**)	**Neg** Exp expr Neg(Exp) void print()	**ΔTest** Neg ntree ΔTest() Δrun()	(**ne**)	**ΔNeg** int eval()	**ΔTest** Δrun()

Fig. 1. Matrix representation of EPL

2.2 AspectJ Implementation

Let us now analyze how the features of EPL are implemented in AspectJ [17]. Recall that feature 1p implements operation print on datatype Lit. Thus the implementation of this feature contains: a) interface Exp that declares method print, b) class Lit with a value field, a constructor, and the implementation of print method, and c) class Test with a field ltree of type Lit, a constructor that creates an instance of Lit and assigns it to ltree, and method run that calls method print on ltree. See entry 1p in Figure 1 for the short depiction of this feature's contents. 1p can be implemented as follows[1]:

```
//                    Exp.java
interface Exp { void print( ); }

//                    Lit.java
class  Lit  implements  Exp  {
  int                  value;
  Lit  (int  v)  {  value  =  v;  }
  void          print()         {
    System.out.print(value);
  }
}
```

```
//                    Test.java
class          Test              {
  Lit                       ltree;
  Test(   )   {   ltree   =   new
Lit(10);                        }
  void  run(  )  {  ltree.print(
);                              }
  void   static   main(String[]
args)                           {
    Test  test   =  new  Test();
    test.run();
  }
}
```

Feature 1p constitutes the base code in our product line because it contains only standard Java classes and interfaces which are used by all the other features of EPL.

Let us now consider the implementation of feature 1e. This feature implements operation eval on Lit datatype. It adds the definition of method eval to an existing interface Exp using an inter-type declaration as follows[2]:

```
//                                         Exple.java
aspect              Exple                           {
   abstract         int                    Exp.eval();
}
```

We refer to this as an *interface extension* [10][11] which we denote with ΔExp in Figure 1. Similarly, we refer to the additions to existing classes as *class extensions* [10][11], which are also shown in Figure 1 with symbol Δ prefixed to the name of the class. Feature 1e makes class extensions for classes Lit and Test. It adds a new method to class Lit as follows:

```
//                                              Litle.java
aspect              Litle                                {
   int      Lit.eval()          {     return    value;    }
}
```

We refer to this type of extension as *method addition* [10][11] and denote it in Figure 1 with the header of the method. Feature 1e also executes an additional statement in

---

[1] Class members privileges are omitted for simplicity.

[2] Aspect file names are formed with the name of the class or interface they are extending followed by the feature they help implement. This naming scheme was chosen to make the connection to the algebraic model described in Section clearer.

method run of class Test that calls method eval on field ltree. We call this a *method extension* [10][11] and denote it as Δrun() in Figure 1 . The implementation uses a pointcut that captures the executions of method run and gets a reference to the object target of the execution, and an around advice that contains the additional statement as shown below:

```
//                                                          Testle.java
aspect                          Testle                                {
    pointcut LPRun(Test t): execution(void Test.run()) && target(t);
    void          around(Test       t)      :      LPRun(t)          {
        proceed(t);              System.out.println(t.ltree.eval());
    }
}
```

Seasoned AspectJ programmers may wonder at this point why the contents of the three aspects are not aggregated (copied) into a single one. In previous work we showed that composing aspects in this way is not equivalent to their separate file definitions under the current AspectJ precedence rules [18]. Additionally, keeping classes and interfaces extensions into separate aspects improves program understandability [6] and simplifies the algebraic composition model described in Section 4.

As another example, consider the implementation of feature ap. First this feature implements operation print on the Add datatype as follows:

```
//                                                           Add.java
class           Add           implements           Exp                {
    Exp                       left,                        right;
    Add   (Exp  l,  Exp  r)   {  left  =  l;  right  =  r;  }
    void print(){ left.print(); System.out.print("+"); right.print();}
}
```

```
//                                                          Testap.java
aspect                                                        Testap{
    Add                                               Test.atree;
    pointcut APTest(Test  t):  execution(Test.new())  &&  target(t);
    void          around(Test       t)      :         APTest(t)       {
        proceed(t);      t.atree  =  new   Add(t.ltree,   t.ltree);
    }
    pointcut APRun(Test t):execution (void Test.run(..)) && target(t);
    void  around(Test  t)   :  APRun(t)  {  proceed(t); t.atree.print();}
}
```

Notice that Testap implements a *construction extension* denoted as ΔTest() in Figure 1. The implementation of the rest of the features is similar to the ones just described.

An EPL program is created by passing all the names of the files that implement its features to the AspectJ compiler or weaver ajc [5]. When several pieces of advice apply to the same join point an order of execution must be specified following AspectJ precedence rules as the order is in general undefined. For example, if in the program that implements both operations for Lit and Add (which we call LitAdd) we would like to execute the method extensions to run in order ap, followed by that in le, and ae, we would need to define a precedence clause in an aspect as follows[3]:

---

[3] In [18] we describe several compositional problems that precedence clauses cause.

```
aspect                        Ordering                              {
   declare      precedence      :      Testae,      Testle,      Testap;
}
```

The whole composition of `LitAdd` becomes:

```
ajc Exp.java Lit.java Test.java Exple.java Litle.java Testle.java
Add.java    Testap.java    Addae.java    Testae.java    Ordering.java
-outjar LitAdd.jar
```

With this example, we present how use case slices can be used to model EPL features.

3 Use Case Slices

Use cases are a common technique to capture system functionality and requirements using UML [21]. However the implementation of use cases using traditional object oriented languages and techniques typically breaks use case modularity as their implementation is scattered and tangled in the modules supported by the underlying OO languages. This is the observation that Jacobson and Ng exploit to make the connection with the work on aspects [15]. They propose *use case slices* as a modularization unit to address these problems.

A use case slice contains ([15] pages 111-112):

- **Collaboration**. A collaboration is a set of UML diagrams (interaction, class, etc.) that describe how a use case is realized.
- **Specific Classes**. Classes that are specific to a use case realization.
- **Specific Extensions**. Extensions to existing classes specific to a use case realization.

A use case slice is modeled as a special kind of package with stereotype << use case slice >>. The package has the following basic contents:

- Use case slice name.
- A collaboration symbol (a dashed ellipse) and its name.
- Specific classes. Denoted with the standard UML symbol for classes. These classes may have any relationships of standard class diagrams.
- Specific aspects. Denoted with a symbol similar to UML class. It has stereotype <<aspect>>. This symbol has two compartments, one for the pointcuts and one for the class extensions. Aspects may have the same relations between them as supported by AspectJ.

Let us illustrate a use case slice with feature ap as shown in Figure 2. Recall that this feature implements the print operation on the Add datatype. First, notice the name of the use case slice and its collaboration. Since ap adds new class Add, this class is represented using the standard class symbol. This feature also contains one constructor extension and one method extension to class Test. The pointcuts compartment of the Testap aspect contains the definitions of pointcuts APTest and APTRun. The class extensions compartment contains class Test as all the extensions that this aspect implements are for this class. In the attributes compartment of the Test class the atree field appears as it is introduced by the aspect. In the operations compartment, the method extension and constructor extensions are shown. The extensions are given names for reference, `apAtree()` and `apRun()`, and specify the type of advice (`around`), the pointcuts they apply to (`APTest` and `APRun`) and a denotation of their operations, `addf` and `testf` (names chosen arbitrarily) for adding and testing a field (in this case `atree`).

Use case slices have the same relationships as use cases, `extend`, `generalization`, and `include` with a comparable semantics. This relationship can be used to describe how a program of the product line can be composed. To the best of our understanding, use case slices do not provide modeling support for the variability entailed by a product line design, thus a use case slice diagram conveys the design of a single member of a product line. Use case slices can be further modularized into *use case modules*, where each slice modularizes a different model of the use case lifecycle: analysis, design, implementation, testing, etc. [15] (Chapters 4 and 10).

In this section we described the basic ideas of use case slices. However, they can provide more sophisticated modeling functionality . For instance, their pointcuts, classes, and class extensions can be parameterized, using UML templates, to allow extra design flexibility [15]. In next section, we present how EPL can be algebraically modeled with FOP.

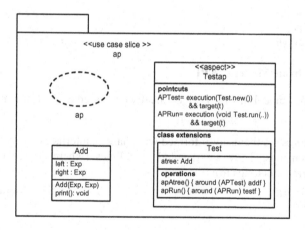

Fig. 2. Use case slice for feature `ap`

4   Feature Oriented Programming (FOP)

Feature Oriented Programming (FOP) is a technology that studies feature modularity and its use in program synthesis. FOP aims at developing a structural theory of programs to express program design, manipulation, and synthesis mathematically whereby program properties can be derived from a program's mathematical representation. In this context, a program's design is an expression, program manipulation is expression manipulation, and program synthesis is expression evaluation. *AHEAD (Algebraic Hierarchical Equations for Application Design)*, is a realization of FOP that is based on a unification of algebras and step-wise development [8][11]. FOP research predates the work on use case slices and aspects.

4.1 AHEAD in a Nutshell

An AHEAD model of a domain is an algebra that offers a set of operations, where each operation implements a feature. We write $M = \{f, h, i, j\}$ to mean model M has operations (or features) f, h, i, and j. AHEAD categorizes features as *constants* and *functions*. Constant features represent base programs, those implemented with standard classes and interfaces. For example:

```
    f           //      a      program     with      feature      f
 h              // a program with feature h
```

Function features represent *program refinements* or *extensions* that add a feature to the program received as input. For instance:

```
   i•x          //     adds     feature     i     to     program     x
 j•x            // adds feature j to program x
```

where • means function application. The design of a program is a named expression which we refer as a *program equation*. For example:

```
  prog1 = i•f          //   prog1   has   features   f   and   i
  prog2 = j•h          //   prog2   has   features   h   and   j
  prog3 = i•j•h        //  prog3 has features h,j,i
```

4.2 An Algebraic Model of EPL

The AHEAD model of EPL is algebraically expressed as a set of features:

```
  EPL = { lp, le, ap, ae, np, ne }
```

These features are themselves formed with classes, interfaces, class extensions, and interface extensions. They are denoted as follows (where subscripts identify the feature an element belongs to):

```
     lp = { Exp_lp, Lit_lp, Test_lp }      le  = {  Exp_le,  Lit_le,   Test_le }
     ap = { Add_ap, Test_ap }                         ae = { Add_ae, Test_ae
     }
     np = { Neg_np, Test_np }                                          ne =
     { Neg_ne, Test_ne }
```

Thus features are hierarchical modules that can contain any number of nested modules. Two features are composed by composing its elements by name (ignoring subscripts). The elements that do not have a match are simply copied to the result of the composition. For example, the composition of ap•lp is defined as follows:

```
    lp    = { Exp_lp, Lit_lp,              Test_lp                         }
    ap    = {               Add_ap,        Test_ap                         }
    ap•lp = { Exp_lp, Lit_lp, Add_ap,      Test_ap•Test_lp }
```

A similar composition scheme is only depicted throughout Chapter 4 in Jacobson and Ng's book [15], where it is denoted with symbol +, however its realization is not further described nor elaborated.

Features are implemented as hierarchies of directories and can contain multiple artifacts other than source code. Artifact types are distinguished by the names of the file extensions. Composition of non-code artifacts follows the same principles of source code composition [10] and feature elements are composed when they match both file name and extension. The *AHEAD Tool Suite (ATS)* provides tailored tools for different artifacts which are selected by ATS's composer tool according to the artifact type. Currently ATS supports composition of equation files, extended Java files, XML files, and grammar files [8]. Since AHEAD treats all artifacts from all life cycle stages equally, we find that the ideas of use case slides and use case modules are unified or indistinguishable in AHEAD.

Scalability is a prominent concern in any software project. We explain now how AHEAD addresses this concern. Normally, a program is specified in AHEAD by a single expression. By organizing feature models as matrices (or k-dimensional cubes), a program is specified by k expressions, one per dimension. This can drastically simplify program specification, from $O(n^k)$ to $O(nk)$ for k dimensions and n features per dimension [11]. This complexity reduction is key for the scalability of AHEAD's program synthesis. Such matrix (or cube) is called an *Origami Matrix*. An example is the EPL matrix in Figure 1. Each dimension of a matrix is represented with a model. In EPL, the dimensional models are:

```
Operation      =      {      print,         eval       }
Datatype = { Lit, Add, Neg }
```

Each model lists the features in each dimension. To specify a program, one expression is defined per dimension. For instance, a specification of program `LitAdd` is:

```
operation=        eval•print       =       Π_ξ(eval,print)Operation
datatype   = Add • Lit = Π_jξ(Add,Lit)DataType
```

where $\Pi_{i\xi x}$ denotes dot composition of a given sequence x of features. If we denote MLA as the projected EPL matrix that forms the intersection of Lit and Add rows on both columns, LitAdd program can be algebraically expressed as:

$$P \quad = \quad \Pi_{i\xi(eval,print)}\Pi_{j\xi(Add,Lit)}MLA_{operation,datatype}$$
$$= \quad ae \quad • \quad le \quad • \quad ap \quad • \quad lp$$
$$= \quad \{ \quad Add_{ae}, \quad Test_{ae} \quad \} \quad • \quad \{ \quad Exp_{le}, \quad Lit_{le}, \quad Test_{le} \quad \}$$
$$• \quad \{ \quad Add_{ap}, \quad Test_{ap} \quad \} \quad • \quad \{ \quad Exp_{lp}, \quad Lit_{lp}, \quad Test_{lp} \quad \}$$
$$= \{ Add_{ae}•Add_{ap}, Lit_{le}•Lit_{lp}, Exp_{le}•Exp_{lp}, Test_{ae}•Test_{le}•Test_{ap}•Test_{lp}\}$$

The algebraic representation of origami matrices has proven an useful abstraction to analyze matrix orthogonality, a property that guarantees that the same program is produced for any valid (conforming to design constraints [11]) composition order [9].

AHEAD has been successfully used to synthesize large systems (in excess of 250K Java LOC) from program equations [11]. Currently AHEAD does not support AspectJ, it uses a language called *Jak* that can express all the types of extensions required by EPL. We are working on extending and integrating an algebraic model of AspectJ [18] into ATS. Nonetheless, the composition model described for EPL still holds. Furthermore, FOP ideas have been used to implement an AspectJ version of the core tools of AHEAD which generates 207+KLOC of which around 30% is aspect code [19].

5 Integrating Use Case Slices and Features

The last two sections explore two seemingly disjoint facets of aspect-based product line development. The first proposes modeling aspect-based features with use case slices while the second describes an algebraic foundation of program composition and synthesis.

On closer inspection there are several similarities. Use case slices consist of classes, interfaces and their extensions implemented with aspects; which is identical to the structure of features. Both features and use case slices can be nested hierarchically and also aim at modularizing non-code artifacts. Similarly, both have relative strengths and drawbacks which we analyze next.

One one hand, we presume that use case slice notation may be easy to adopt for aspect modeling as UML is a popular modeling language. However, we believe the research on use case slices lacks a clear composition model to map use case slices models to concrete working implementations. In terms of source code, the translation to AspectJ is missing an important compositional issue, precedence management. Similarly for other artifacts, we find unclear how such modularization is actually realized (implemented).

On the other hand, the strength of AHEAD is its composition model that supports scalable composition of multiple artifacts. However, for programmers unfamiliar with algebraic notation it may be less intimidating to adopt a familiar modeling notation such as UML.

We believe that the differences and similarities described can be exploited for the development of an aspect-based product line methodology that profits from both lines of work. A feature modeling notation based on use case slices that can ease the adoption by programmers, and an underlying scalable and multi-artifact composition model for program synthesis.

Along the same lines, earlier work by Jacobson hints at the possibility of expressing use case models with a simple algebra of program extensions [14]. However this line of thought is not further pursued in the work of use case slices. We believe our work on AHEAD and FOP could provide a basis for an algebraic foundation for use case slices. We are unaware of any tools that support use case slices and generate AspectJ code from their models. In any case, such kind of tools would encounter the same sort of problems of program synthesis of multiple artifacts faced and solved by AHEAD.

6 Related Work

In UML 2.0 a collaboration is a set of class instances that play different roles [21]. In that sense it is closer to the notion of collaboration-based designs which are the origins of AHEAD [10]. Though use case slices also treat several types of UML diagrams as part of a collaboration.

A close line of work to use case slices is Theme [8]. A *theme*, is an element of design: a collection of structures that represent a feature [8]. Themes are classified into: *base themes* that share structure and behaviour with other themes, and *crosscutting themes* that correspond to aspects. Programs are built by composing themes with a set of binding specifications. Thus Theme and AHEAD classify features in a similar way, but their composition mechanism is significantly different.

Also, to the best of our knowledge there is no tool support for this approach. It would be interesting to explore if the composition mechanism of Theme could be expressed in an algebraic notation similar to AHEAD's.

Several extensions of UML to model product lines have been proposed. One example is *Product Line UML-based Software engineering (PLUS)* [13] which is a method that brings FODA [12] modelling ideas to the realm of UML diagrams. PLUS models features as packages of use cases that are stereotyped with the kind of feature they implement such as optional, alternative, etc. Another example is the work of Ziadi and Jézéquel that describes extensions to model variability in class and sequence diagrams and an algorithm for product derivation based on UML model transformations [23]. To what extent this line of work could benefit from aspect research and algebraic modeling is an open question.

There are several pieces of work on aspect-based product line engineering. Anastasopoulus and Muthig propose criteria to evaluate AOP as a product line implementation technology [3]. Alves et al. study product line evolution and refactoring techniques applied to mobile games [2]. Loughran et al. merge natural language processing and aspect oriented techniques to provide tool support for analyzing requirements documents and mining commonality and variability for feature modeling [20].

7 Conclusions and Future Work

In this paper we compare and contrast use case slices and FOP as complimentary facets in the modeling and synthesis of aspect-based product lines. We briefly sketched how these two lines of work can serve as the foundation of a product line methodology that exploits their synergy, feature modeling based on use case slices and program synthesis based on FOP.

We plan to explore how to model algebraically and implement advanced use case slices functionality such as parameterized pointcuts. A promising venue is the work on *Aspectual Mixin Layers (AML)* which allows extensions of pointcuts and pieces of advice using mixin technology [5]. AML provide some support for the parameterization of use case slices. Similarly, the work by Trujillo et al. could be used as a basis for the composition of UML diagrams that are part of a use case slice collaboration [22].

References

1. AHEAD Tool Suite (ATS). http://www.cs.utexas.edu/users/schwartz
2. Alves, V., Matos, P., Cole, L., Borba, P., Ramalho, G.: Extracting and Evolving Game Product Lines. SPLC (2005)
3. Anastasopoulus, M., Muthig, D.: An Evaluation of Aspect-Oriented Programming as a Product Line Implementation Technology. ICSR (2004)
4. AOSD Europe. Survey of Analysis and Design Approaches. Deliverable D11.
5. Apel, S., Leich, T., Saake, G.: Aspectual Mixin Layers: Aspects and Features in Concert. ICSE (2006)
6. Apel, S., Batory, D.: When to Use Features and Aspects? A Case Study. GPCE (2006)

7. AspectJ, http://eclipse.org/aspectj/
8. Baniassad, E.L.A, Siobhán, C.: Theme: An Approach for Aspect-Oriented Analysis and Design. ICSE (2004)
9. Batory, D.: Feature Oriented Programming. Class Notes. UT Austin. Spring (2006)
10. Batory, D., Lopez-Herrejon, R.E., Martin, J.P.: Generating Product-Lines of Product-Families. ASE (2002)
11. Batory, D., Sarvela, J.N., Rauschmayer, A.: Scaling Step-Wise Refinement. IEEE TSE, June (2004)
12. Czarnecki, K., Eisenecker, U.W.: Generative Programming: Methods, Tools, and Applications. Addison-Wesley (2000)
13. Gomaa, H.: Designing Software Product Lines with UML. From Use Cases to Pattern-Based Software Architectures. Addison-Wesley (2004)
14. Jacobson, I.: Use cases and Aspects — Working Seemlessly Together. JOT. July (2003)
15. Jacobson, I., Ng, P.: Aspect-Oriented Software Development with Use Cases. Addison-Wewley (2004)
16. Lopez-Herrejon, R.E., Batory, D.: Using AspectJ to Implement Product-Lines: A Case Study. Tech. Report UT Austin CS. TR-02-45. September (2002)
17. Lopez-Herrejon, R.E., Batory, D., Cook, W.: Evaluating Support for Features in Advanced Modularization Techniques. ECOOP (2005)
18. Lopez-Herrejon, R.E., Batory, D., Lengauer, C.: A disciplined approach to aspect composition. PEPM (2006)
19. Lopez-Herrejon, R.E., Batory, D.: From Crosscutting Concerns to Product Lines: A Function Composition Approach. Tech. Report UT Austin CS. TR-06-24. May (2006)
20. Loughran, N., Sampaio, A., Rashid, A.: From Requirements Documents to Feature Models for Aspect Oriented Product Line Implementation. MDD in Product Lines at MODELS (2005)
21. Pilone, D., Pitman, N.: UML 2.0 In a Nutshell. A Desktop Quick Reference. O'Reilly (2005)
22. Trujillo, S., Batory, D., Diaz, O.: Feature Refactoring a Multi-Representation Program into a Product Line. GPCE (2006)
23. Ziadi, T., Jézéquel, J.-M.: Software Product Line Engineering with the UML: Deriving Products. FAMILIES project research book. To appear in Springer LNCS.

Join Point Patterns:
A High-Level Join Point Selection Mechanism

Walter Cazzola[1] and Sonia Pini[2]

[1] Department of Informatics and Communication,
Università degli Studi di Milano, Italy
cazzola@dico.unimi.it
[2] Department of Informatics and Computer Science
Università degli Studi di Genova, Italy
pini@disi.unige.it

Abstract. Aspect-Oriented Programming is a powerful technique to better modularize object-oriented programs by introducing crosscutting concerns in a safe and noninvasive way. Unfortunately, most of the current join point models are too coupled with the application code. This fact hinders the concerns separability and reusability since each aspect is strictly tailored on the base application.

This work proposes a possible solution to this problem based on modeling the join points selection mechanism at a higher level of abstraction. In our view, the aspect designer does not need to know the inner details of the application such as a specific implementation or the used name conventions rather he exclusively needs to know the application behavior to apply his/her aspects.

In the paper, we present a novel join point model with a join point selection mechanism based on a high-level program representation. This high-level view of the application decouples the aspects definition from the base program structure and syntax. The separation between aspects and base program will render the aspects more reusable and independent of the manipulated application.

1 Introduction

Aspect-oriented programming (AOP) is a powerful technique to better modularize OO programs by introducing crosscutting concerns in a safe and noninvasive way. Each AOP approach is characterized by a *join point model* (JPM) consisting of the *join points*, a mean of identifying the join points (*pointcuts*) and a mean of raising effects at the join points (*advice*) [9]. Crosscutting concerns might be badly modularized as aspects without an appropriate join point definition that covers all the interested elements, and a *pointcut definition language* that allows the programmer of selecting those join points.

In most of the AOP approaches, the pointcut definition language allows the programmer of selecting the join points on the basis of the program lexical structure, such as explicit program elements names. The dependency on the program syntax renders the pointcuts definition fragile [7] and strictly couples an aspect to a specific program, hindering its reusability and evolvability [6]. The required enhancement should consist of developing a pointcut definition language that supports join points selection on a more semantic way [4]. To provide a more expressive and semantic-oriented selection mechanism means to use a language that captures the base-level program behavior and

T. Kühne (Ed.): MoDELS 2006 Workshops, LNCS 4364, pp. 17–26, 2007.

properties abstracting from the syntactic details. Several attempts in this direction have been done but none of these completely solve the problem. They focus on specific behavioral aspects such as execution trace and dataflow neglecting some others. Moreover, they still rely on name conventions and on the knowledge of the implementation code. We think that the problem could be faced and solved by selecting the join points on an abstract representation of the program, such as its design information.

In this paper, we propose a join point model with a pointcut definition language that allows the selection of the join points abstracting from implementation details, name conventions and any other source code dependency. In particular the aspect programmer can select the interested join points by describing their supposed location in the application through UML-like descriptions (basically, activity diagrams) representing computational patterns on the application behavior; these descriptions are called *join point patterns* (JPPs). The join point patterns are just patterns on the application behavior, i.e., they are not derived from the system design information but express properties on them. In other words, we adopt a sort of enriched UML diagrams to describe the application control flows or computational properties and to locate the join points inside these contexts. Pointcuts consist of logic composition of join point patterns. Thus, they are not tailored on the program syntax and structure but only on the program behavior.

The rest of the paper is organized as follows: in section 2 we investigate the limitations of some of the other join point models, in section 3 and section 4 we introduce our join point model and the weaving process respectively; finally, in section 5 we draw out our conclusions.

2   Limits of the Join Point Models

The join point model, in particular its pointcut definition language, has a critical role in the applicability of the aspect-oriented methodology. The pointcut definition language allows to determine where a concern crosscuts the code. Since the beginning, the pointcut definition languages are evolved to improve their expressivity, their independence of the base code and the general flexibility of the approach. The first generation of pointcut definition languages (e.g., AspectJ pre v1) were strictly coupled to the application source code because they allow of selecting the join points on the signature of the program elements. To reduce the coupling problem, the next generation of pointcut definition languages introduced wildcards (e.g., AspectJ v1.3, HyperJ), this technique reduces the coupling but introduces the necessity of naming conventions; a new problem raises since the naming conventions are not checkable by the compilers and their respect cannot be guaranteed. Recently, some aspect-oriented languages adopted *meta-data* or code instrumentation (e.g., AspectJ v1.5, AspectWerkz) to locate the join points. This approach decouples the aspects from the base program syntax and structure. The meta-data are used as a placeholder of sorting that can be triggered to get a customizable behavior. Anyway this technique does not resolve the problem as well, it just shifts the coupling from the program syntax to the meta-data syntax. Moreover, this approach breaks in an explicit way the *obliviousness* [5] property. To get the obliviousness the aspect programmer should be unaware of the base program structure and syntax to apply the aspects and vice versa.

In this situation, the aspect programmer must have a *global knowledge* of the base program to be sure that his/her pointcuts work as expected. Moreover, the JPMs based on these kinds of pointcut definition languages are suitable to select join points that are at the object interface level whereas badly fit the need of capturing join points expressed by computational patterns, such as inside loops or after a given sequence of statements.

Pointcuts definition heavily relies on how the software is structured at a given moment in time. In fact, the aspect developers subsume the structure of the base program when they define the pointcuts; the name conventions are an example of this subsumption. They implicitly impose some *design rules* that the base program developers have to respect when evolve their programs to be compliant with the existing aspects and to avoid of selecting more or less join points than expected.

In general, the previously described join point models are sufficient for most cases but there are situations where a more fine-grained, flexible and semantic join point model is required — more on the join point models limitations can be read in [7, 4, 6]. Therefore, the AOP potentialities are limited by the poorness of the join point selection mechanisms.

3   JPP Specification Language

Design information (UML diagrams, formal techniques and so on) abstracts from the implementation details providing a global, static and general view of the system in terms of its behavior and should permit to locate and select the join points thanks to their properties and to the context instead of name conventions and syntactic details [4]. In this respect, we propose to overcome the limitations of the pointcut definition languages by describing the join points position (i.e., by defining the pointcuts) as a *pattern* on the *expected* application design information rather than on the code.

The *join point patterns* are the basic elements of our pointcut definition mechanism (called *join point pattern specification language*). They describe where local or region join points could be located in the application behavior abstracting from the implementation details: when a join point is located in the application high-level representation it will be automatically mapped on its code. The interested behavior can be well described by using design techniques, such as UML diagrams, that provide an abstraction over the application structure. Thanks to this abstraction, the join point patterns can describe the join point positions in terms of the application behavior rather than its code. In other words, we achieve a low coupling of the pointcut definitions with the source code since the join point pattern is defined in terms of design model rather than directly referring to the implementation structure of the base program itself.

The join point patterns are graphically specified through a UML-like description. A visual approach is more clear and intuitive and makes more evident the independence from the program source code. Finally, this approach is not limited to a specific programming language but can be used in combination with many. At the moment, we are using the Poseidon4UML program for depicting the join point patterns but we are developing an ad hoc interface for that, and the Java as programming language.

In the application, there is a clear separation between the application structure (e.g., class declarations) and its behavior (e.g., methods execution) and the aspects can affect both the structure and the behavior. In this paper, we only focus on the behavioral join point pattern definition; since affecting the application structure simply consists on introducing and removing elements and can be faced as explained in [2].

3.1 JPP Terminology and Description

We borrowed the terms *join point*, *pointcut* and *advice* from the AspectJ terminology but we use them with a slightly different meaning. The *join points* are *hooks where new behaviors may be added* rather than *well defined points in the execution of a program*. In particular we consider two different kinds of join points, *local join points* that represent points in the application behavior where to insert the advice code, and *region join points* that represent portions of the application behavior that might be replaced by the advice code. The *pointcuts* are logical compositions of join points selected by the join point patterns rather than logical composition of queries on the application code. Whereas the term *advice* conserves the same meaning as in AspectJ.The *join point pattern is a template on the application behavior identifying the join points in their context*. In practice the join point patterns are UML diagrams of sorting, with a name, describing where the local and region join points can be located in the application behavior. A join point pattern is a sample of the computational flow described by using a behavioral/execution flow template. The sample does not completely define the computational flow but only the portions relevant for the selection of the join points, i.e., the join point patterns provide an incomplete and parametric representation of the application behavior. Each join point pattern can describe and capture many join points; these join points are captured together but separately advised.

Now, we will give a glance at the join point pattern definition language "syntax" by an example. Let us consider the implementation of the *observer pattern* as an aspect to observe the state of a *buffer*. The Buffer instances support only two kinds of operations: elements insertion (*put action*) and recovery (*get action*). The observer will monitor the use of these operations independently of their names and signatures.

The join point pattern depicted in Fig. 1 captures *all the method executions that change the state of the instances of the Buffer class*. The activity diagram describes the context where the join point should be found; more details are used to describe the context and more the join point pattern is coupled to the application code. The exact point matched by the «joinpoint» depends on which element follows the stereotype: if the «joinpoint» is located on a flow line between two swimlanes it matches a call of a method with the behavior expressed in the other swimlane; if the «joinpoint» is located on a flow line inside a swimlane it matches the execution of the next instruction, if the element has a «exactmatch» stereotype, or the execution of the next block if the element has a «block» stereotype, or the execution of the next method if the element has a «method» stereotype. The use of *meta variables* grants the join point pattern independence from a specific case, and they are useful to denote that two elements have to refer to the same variable of the same method. Meta variables permit to access variables, methods, fields and so on used into the implementation code without knowing their exact names, but exclusively knowing their role. At the contrary, if the aspect programmer want to couple the join point

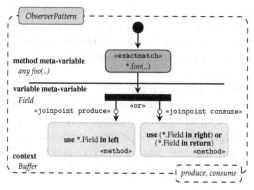

Fig. 1. The Observer JPP

pattern to the application code, they can use directly constant variable and method names (without declaring them as meta-variables).

In the example, foo and Field are meta-variables, respectively a *method meta-variable*, i.e., a variable representing a method name and a *variable meta-variable*, i.e., a variable representing a variable name. In the method meta-variables definition, the method signature is specified; if necessary, type meta-variables, i.e., a variable whose values range on types, can be used. Meta-variables got a value during the pointcut evaluation and their values can also be used by the advice. This permits to decouple the join point pattern from the code.

The behavior we are looking for is characterized by: i) the call to a method with any signature, ii) whose body either writes a field of the target object (i.e., a method belonging to the put family with any name and signature) or reads a field of the target object (i.e., a method belonging to the get family with any name and signature). This join point pattern explicitly refers to the concept of a method that changes the Buffer state rather than trying to capture that concept by relying on implicit rules such as naming conventions about the program implementation structure. In particular, in the caller swimlane, we look for the invocation of a generic method named foo(..)[1] whereas in the callee swimlane we look at the method body for the assignment to a generic field of the class (i.e., the behavior of a method of the put family) or, at either the use of generic class field into the right part of an assignment or the use of the field in a return statement (i.e., the behavior of a method of the get family). The former should be an exact statement match, I i.e., we are looking for exactly that call I whereas in the latter we are looking for a specific use of a field in the whole method body. This difference is expressed by using the following JPP syntax:

- a yellow rounded rectangle, called *template action*, indicates that we are looking for a meta-variable into a specific kind of statements in the searching scope, indicated by a stereotype; the «method» stereotype limits the search to the method body whereas the «block» stereotype to the current block;
- we can look for the use of a meta-variable in a left (left) or right (right) part of an assignment, in a boolean expression (booleanCondition), and in a generic statement (statement) or in their logic combination;
- a red rounded rectangle identified by the «exactmatch» stereotype, called (according to UML) *action*, indicates one or more statements, which must exactly match a sequence of code; the names used inside these blocks can be meta-variables, constant variable names (i.e., variable names used into the code) or if not useful to the pattern definition indicated as (i) with $i \in \mathbb{N}$.

---

[1] Note that foo(..) is a method meta-variable and its signature is not specified.

The join point possible location is indicated by the «joinpoint» stereotype attached to an arrow in the case of local join points and by the «startjoinpoint» and «endjoinpoint» stereotypes attached to the arrows to denote the borders of a region join points. All the searched join points name are listed in the window in the low-right corner of the join point pattern specification.

The join point pattern in Fig. 1 explicitly refers to the elements insertion and recovery behavior rather than trying to capture those behaviors by relying on naming conventions about the program implementation, such as put* and get*. Consequently, the point-cuts defined by using this pattern do not change when the base program evolves as long as the join points it has to capture still conserve the same properties; so if a new method inserting two elements in the buffer is added to the Buffer class it is captured by our join point pattern as well independently of its name.

We have adopted a loose approach to the description of the computational flow. In the join point patterns, based on activity diagrams, the lines with a solid arrowhead connecting two elements express that the first immediately follows the second, and the lines with a stick arrowhead (see Fig. 1) express that the first follows the second before or later, i.e., zero or more *not relevant* actions[2] could occur before the second action occurs, the number of actions that could occur is limited by the scope.

In most cases, the pointcuts refer to properties of individual join points in isolation without reference to contextual information. Our join point pattern definition language can express temporal relations between events and actions inside the join point pattern definitions. In particular, a join point can be selected only if a specific action is already occurred or will occur in the next future. The future prediction is feasible because the design description depicts all the behavioral information and therefore evaluated at compile time, if it does not involve dynamically computed values.

Our join point model is strictly based on the computational flow, so we do not need to differentiate between **before** and **after** advice but we can simply attach the «joinpoint» stereotype to the right position, i.e., before or after the point we want to advice. A special case is represented by the *region join points* which match portions of the computational flow instead of a single points; the whole matched portion represents the join point and will be substituted by the advice code.

3.2 Aspects That Use Join Point Patterns

A join point pattern simply describes where the join points can be found, to complete the process we must declare an aspect where the join point patterns are in association with advice code to weave at the interested join points.

The aspect definition, like in most AOP languages, includes pointcut and advice definitions and their relations. Moreover, it declares all the used join point patterns and which join points it imports from them. Both pointcuts and advices will use these information in their definition.

The following Observer aspect imports the produce and the consume join points from the ObserverPattern join point pattern (see Fig. 1). The join point patterns can define many join points but it is not mandatory to import all of them.

---

[2] These actions do not participate in the description of the join point position, so they are considered not relevant.

```
public aspect Observer {
  void notify() { ... }
  public joinpointpattern ObserverPattern(produce,consume);
  public pointcut p() : produce();
  public pointcut c() : consume();
  advice() : p() && c() {notify();}
}
```

The pointcuts are defined as a logical combination of the imported join point definitions.

4   Weaving in JPP

One central component in AOP is the weaver. Given a set of target programs and a set of aspects, the weaver introduces the code of the advices at the captured join points in the target programs during the weaving process. Our approach does not differ in that and the weaving process must be realized.

Notwithstanding the join point patterns are language independent, the weaving process strictly depends on the program it has to modify. At the moment, we have chosen the Java 5 programming language because its meta-data facility, by providing a standard way to attach additional data to program elements, has the potential to simplify the implementation of the weaving process. The weaving process in JPP consists of the following phases:

- *pre-weaving phase*: the abstraction level of the join point patterns and of the Java bytecode is equalized;
- *morphing/matching phase*: the matching is performed by traversing the model/graph of the pattern and the model/graph of the program in parallel;
- *join points marking phase*: when the pattern and the program models match, each captured join point is annotated at the corresponding code location;
- *advice weaving phase*: the annotated bytecode is instrumented to add the advice code at the captured join points.

Pre-Weaving Phase.   The target program and the join point patterns are at a different level of abstraction. To fill this gap and allowing the weaving, it is necessary to build a common representation for the target program and the join point patterns (the *pre-weaving phase*). Structured graphs [1] perfectly fit the problem; both program computational flow (through its control flow graph) and join point patterns can be represented by graphs and the structured graphs provide a graph representation and manipulation mechanisms at variable level of details. Relaxing the quantity of details used in the control flow graph it is possible to fill the gap with the join point patterns.

A structured control flow graph is generated from the control flow graphs of each method by using BCEL on the application bytecode and imposing a structure on that. Each instruction is a node of the structured flow graph and each method call is a macro-node, i.e., a node that can be expanded to the called method control flow graph. The structured graphs are stored in a special structure that separates the content from the layout saving the space and improving the efficiency of the navigation and of the layout reorganization (particularly useful on already partially woven programs). To simplify the matching of some join point patterns, an index has been built on the graph to provide access points that differ from the `main()` method.

Analogously, each join point pattern is stored into a structured graph. Since, the join point patterns already have a graph structure the conversion is less problematic. In this case the macro-structure provide a mechanism to navigate between different swimlanes and to skip some context details, e.g., in the case of a template actions.

Morphing/Matching Phase. The morphing/matching phase consists of looking for (matching) the join point patterns in the application control flow graph. Since, the basic elements of our pointcut definition language are expressed in a UML-like form, and the UML is a diagrammatic language, it is reasonable and promising to apply techniques developed in the graph grammar and graph transformation field to get our goal.

In particular, we have to solve a *graph matching problem* or better a model-based recognition problem, where the model is represented as a (structured) graph (the *model graph*, G_M), and another (structured) graph (the *data graph*, G_D) represents the program control flow graph where to recognize the model. In model-based pattern recognition problems, given G_M and G_D, to compare them implies to look for their similarities.

Graph and sub-graph isomorphism are concepts that have been intensively used in various applications. The representational power of graphs and the need to compare them has pushed numerous researchers to study the problem of computing graph and sub-graph isomorphisms. What we need is a inexact graph matching [8], or better a *sub-graph inexact matching* since one graph (the join point pattern representation) is smaller than the other (the program control flow graph representation).

Ours are attributed graphs, i.e., their vertices and edges contain some extra information, such as instructions (both for application and join point patterns actions), template actions and *loose connection* (stick arrows) for the join point patterns. Therefore, the type of our matching algorithm cannot be exact because the matching between corresponding parts of two graphs is possible even if the two parts are not identical, but only similar according to a set of rules involving predefined transformations. The inexactness implies that the join point pattern graph is considered matchable with the application one if a set of syntactic and semantic transformations can be found, such that the transformed join point pattern graph is isomorphic to a portion of the application graph.

During the morphing/matching phase, all the join point pattern graphs must be compared against the application control flow graph, the number of matching can be reduced by using the context information stored for every pattern. For each node of both graphs:

- if the current pattern element is a real Java instruction (i.e. it is from an *action* element), the algorithm tries to unify it with the current application node;
- if the current pattern element is a *template action*, the algorithm matches it with the current application node when there is a semantic transformation that transforms the first into the second node; if the match fails, the algorithm iterates on the next application node inside the scope defined by the scope stereotype.

In both cases, the unification process can fail or success with a set of variable bindings, known as a *unifier*. Found a match, the outgoing edge of the current pattern element gives to the algorithm information about how to continue the match: according to the kind of edge, the next pattern element should match exactly the next application node (solid arrowhead) or should match one of the next nodes not necessary the first (stick arrowhead). At the end of this process, the algorithm returns a set (that could be empty) of code locations for the captured join points.

Join Points Marking Phase. Each captured join point is marked directly in the bytecode by annotating its location. As already stated, Java 5 incorporates the concept of custom annotation that we could exploit in this phase. Unfortunately, Java annotation model permits of annotating only the element declarations, whereas we need to annotate the method body since the join points may be at every statement.

To overcome this problem, we have extended Java, codename @Java, to arbitrary annotate program elements such as blocks, single statements, and expressions. This work is partially based on the experience we have done in extending the annotation model of C# [3] that suffers of the same limitations. @Java minimally extends Java. The only real difference from the standard mechanism is related to the possibility of annotating a code block or an expression. In these cases, the annotation must precede the first statement of the block or the beginning of the expression to annotate and the whole block or expression must be grouped by braces to denote the scope of the annotation.

Every join point annotation, contains the join point pattern name, the join point name, the join point parameters, and when necessary, the run-time residual. Current implementation provides a compiler based implementation that does almost of the weaving work at compile time. This solves and then captures most of the join points at compile time and avoids unnecessary run-time evaluations and overheads. Some pointcuts, that needs run-time information to be evaluated, still cannot be completely evaluated at compile-time; in these cases the pointcut is reduced and a small residual for the not evaluated part is annotated at the potential join points waiting for the dynamic evaluation. Its evaluation will determine if the join point really has to be advised or not. However, the corresponding overhead is contained and the necessary residuals with our approach are less then in AspectJ. At the end of this phase the application is ready to be advised and to speed up the last phase an index on the captured join points is built.

Advice Weaving Phase. In this phase the bytecode application will be really modified. For every advice associated to a pointcut declaration we generate the bytecode of the advice by using the BCEL and in particular the `InstructionLists` structure. We retrieve the annotations associated to that pointcut to locate where the advice code must be inserted, then we use the `InstructionList.append()`, the `Instruction-List.insert()` or the `InstructionList.delete()` methods to insert the advice `InstructionList` into the application `InstructionList`. Finally, when the instruction list is ready to be dumped to pure bytecode, all symbolic references must be mapped to real bytecode offsets. This is done by a call to the `getMethod()` method.

5   Conclusions

Current AOP approaches suffer from well known problems that rely on the syntactic coupling established between the application and the aspects. A common attempt to give a solution consists of freeing the pointcut definition language from these limitations by describing the join points in a more semantic way.

This paper has proposed a novel approach to join points identification and to decouple aspects definition and base-code syntax and structure. Pointcuts are specified by using join point patterns expressed on the application expected behavior. More precisely, a join point pattern is a template on the application expected behavior identifying the join points in their context. In particular join points are captured when the pattern matches portion of the application behavior.

Compared with current approaches, we can observe some advantages; first of all, we have a pointcuts definition more behavioral. In the join point pattern definition we identify the context of the computational flow we want to match, and the precise point we want to capture. Notwithstanding that, we can still select the join points by using syntactic and structural specification, it is only necessary a more detailed join point pattern. The graphical definition of join point patterns is more intuitive and comprehensible for programmers. Moreover, it better demonstrates where and how an aspect can affect a program. Last but not least, our approach is quite general, it can be applied to every programming language (at the cost of adapting the weaving algorithm to the characteristics of the new language) and used to mimic all the other approaches to AOP.

There is also a drawback, the matching phase is very complex, and it demands time and space. Fortunately, most of the weaving phase is done once during the compilation and does not affect the performance of the running program.

References

1. M. Ancona, L. De Floriani, and J. S. Deogun. Path Problems in Structured Graphs. *The Computer Journal*, 29(6):553–563, June 1986.
2. W. Cazzola, A. Cicchetti, and A. Pierantonio. Towards a Model-Driven Join Point Model. In *Proceedings of the 11th Annual ACM Symposium on Applied Computing (SAC'06)*, pages 1306–1307, Dijon, France, on 23rd-27th of Apr. 2006. ACM Press.
3. W. Cazzola, A. Cisternino, and D. Colombo. Freely Annotating C#. *Journal of Object Technology*, 4(10):31–48, Dec. 2005.
4. W. Cazzola, J.-M. Jézéquel, and A. Rashid. Semantic Join Point Models: Motivations, Notions and Requirements. In *Proceedings of the Software Engineering Properties of Languages and Aspect Technologies Workshop (SPLAT'06)*, Bonn, Germany, on 21st Mar. 2006.
5. R. E. Filman and D. P. Friedman. Aspect-Oriented Programming is Quantification and Obliviousness. In *Proceedings of OOPSLA 2000 Workshop on Advanced Separation of Concerns*, Minneapolis, USA, Oct. 2000.
6. A. Kellens, K. Gybels, J. Brichau, and K. Mens. A Model-driven Pointcut Language for More Robust Pointcuts. In *Proceedings of Software engineering Properties of Languages for Aspect Technologies (SPLAT'06)*, Bonn, Germany, Mar. 2006.
7. C. Koppen and M. Störzer. PCDiff: Attacking the Fragile Pointcut Problem. In *Proceedings of the European Interactive Workshop on Aspects in Software (EIWAS'04)*, Berlin, Germany, Sept. 2004.
8. L. G. Shapiro and R. M. Haralick. Structural Descriptions and Inexact Matching. *IEEE Transactions on Pattern Analysis and Machine Intelligence*, 3(5):504–519, 1981.
9. N. Ubayashi, G. Moriyama, H. Masuhara, and T. Tamai. A Parameterized Interpreter for Modeling Different AOP Mechanisms. In D. F. Redmiles, T. Ellman, and A. Zisman, editors, *Proceedings of the 20th IEEE/ACM international Conference on Automated Software Engineering (ASE'05)*, pages 194–203, Long Beach, CA, USA, 2005. ACM Press.

Critical Systems Development Using Modeling Languages – CSDUML 2006 Workshop Report

Geri Georg[1], Siv Hilde Houmb[2], Robert France[1], Steffen Zschaler[3],
Dorina C. Petriu[4], and Jan Jürjens[5]

[1] Colorado State University
Computer Science Department
{georg, france}@cs.colostate.edu
[2] Norwegian University of Science and Technology
Computer Science Department
siv-hilde.houmb@telenor.com
[3] Technische Universität Dresden
Department of Computer Science
Steffen.Zschaler@tu-dresden.de
[4] Carleton University
Systems & Computer Eng. Dept.
petriu@sce.carleton.ca
[5] The Open University
Computing Department
j.jurjens@open.ac.uk

Abstract. The CSDUML 2006 workshop is a continuation of the series regarding development of critical systems using modeling languages. The report summarizes papers presented and discussion at the workshop.

1 Introduction

CSDUML 2006 was held in conjunction with the MoDELS 2006 conference in Genoa, Italy. The workshop took place on Sunday, October 1, 2006. Twenty-five people from both academia and industry attended the workshop. Six papers were presented during the day. However, the major part of our time was spent in discussions. The paper presentations were organized in four sessions, with discussions after the first, second, and fourth presentation sessions. The report summarizes the results of these discussions. The papers were structured into the following four sessions: 1) specification and analysis, 2) verification, 3) automatic system generation, and 4) case studies. The case studies contained results from some, but not all of the other categories. This report is structured according to the presentation sessions, summarizing the papers, discussion points, and outcomes.

Session 1: Specification and Analysis, Alexander Knapp Session Chair

The papers presented in this session covered modeling specification approaches and tool-support for their analysis. Two papers were presented in this session:

T. Kühne (Ed.): MoDELS 2006 Workshops, LNCS 4364, pp. 27–31, 2007.

1) Quality-of-Service Modeling and Analysis of Dependable Application Models, by András Balogh and András Pataricza, presented by András Balogh. The paper presents non-functional component and system property modeling and analysis to improve software quality and allow early recognition of possible problems.

2) Modeling an Electronic Throttle Controller using the Timed Abstract State Machine Language and Toolset by Martin Ouimet, Guillaume Berteau, and Kristina Lundqvist, presented by Martin Ouimet. The paper presents the Timed Abstract State Machine (TASM) language and toolset, to specify and analyze reactive embedded real-time systems. Non-functional properties including timing behavior and resource consumption can be specified, and their behaviors simulated for analysis purposes.

The session chair proposed a set of open research questions that still remain in light of the research presented in these papers. These questions stimulated the general discussion of critical systems specification and analysis. The discussion either reached conclusions or raised further points in the following three areas.

- Specification. Critical systems specifications are often cross-cutting, so aspect or other feature-oriented techniques may be applicable. These techniques must be able to specify the interference between QoS attributes, and allow for simple checks, refinement, and systematic overviews of particular properties. There is a difference between closed, predictable, embedded-style systems, and open, unpredictable business-critical systems. Interference between critical properties can be defined away in many closed systems, which greatly simplifies both specification and analysis. Open systems, by contrast, are subject to unpredictable interactions among critical properties.
- Analysis. Critical system property analysis varies between properties, so different tools are needed for each type of analysis. Additionally, many tools require model transformations prior to use. However, it is not clear how analysis techniques will scale to large system specifications. Traditional analysis tools may not be useful under all conditions. For example, trade-off analysis and prioritization must be done in light of the business domain. A typical strategy is to minimize hardware cost, as determined by complete cost of ownership (via supplier maintenance contracts). Analysis techniques still need to be integrated into newer specification techniques, such as aspect-specification techniques.
- Information dissemination. The need for a common platform for the dissemination and exchange of state-of-the-art research in languages and specification and analysis tools became clear in the discussions. Discussion included the ReMODD project and websites providing information on UML Case tools (http://www.jeckle.de/umltools.htm). As researchers, we should be using mediums such as these to enhance knowledge and discussion.

Session 2: Verification, Kevin Lano Session Chair

One paper in this session was presented. It concerned consistency checking of UML-based behavioral models:

1) Model Checking of UML 2.0 Interactions by Alexander Knapp and Jochen Wuttke. The paper describes a translation of UML 2.0 interactions into automata for

model checking to determine whether an interaction can be satisfied by a given set of message exchanging UML state machines.

The second discussion highlighted four areas.

- Consistency checking needs to occur across models and across critical system properties. In particular different types of models, e.g. deployment diagrams, static structure, and behavioral models, all need to be checked for consistency across the critical system properties. Workflow could be useful in supporting such checks. For example, when decisions are made regarding physical deployment, consistency checks need to occur to ensure that desired behavior still exists, and that critical properties are still present. The EU project Model Plex may have applicable work in this area with examples and techniques to trace model changes and verify run-time models.
- Techniques such as fault injection into state machines to check interactions could be used to verify critical system properties. Correctness by construction may also be a viable option during model transformations.
- An outstanding issue in verification is modularity. It isn't clear if UML model structure is sufficient. It also is not clear how to deal with hierarchical or incomplete models.
- Domain specific languages and profiles are two techniques leading to similar modeling results. Their use should be determined by domain experts. In general, the group considered profiles less work for the person creating them, but often more work for those trying to use them. This is particularly true when multiple, perhaps interacting profiles increases. An example is chip design, where 4-5 profiles are needed, which may or may not be very well aligned in terms of their use, interactions, and analysis tools. DSLs are more work to come up with, but may present a better language for developers to understand, and better aligned methods, techniques, and tools. An issue in this space is again the lack of disseminated knowledge and experience across the community.

Session 3: System Generation, Robert France Session Chair

The paper in this session covered the use of model-driven engineering technology for the generation of software for critical systems.

1) Automated Synthesis of High-Integrity Systems using Model-Driven Development by K. Lano and K. Androutsopolous. The paper describes the application of MDD to two areas of high-integrity systems: reactive control systems, and web applications. Semantic consistency analysis using two methods is also described.

Session 4: Case Studies, Geri Georg Session Chair

The two papers in this session presented case studies in the critical-systems domain.

1) Experiences with Precise State Modeling in an Industrial Safety Critical System by Nina Holt, Bente Anda, Knut Asskildt, Lionel C. Briand, Jan Endresen, and Sverre

Frøystein. This paper reports on experiences using statechart-driven UML modeling in the development of a safety-critical system at ABB.

2) Specification of the Control Logic of an eVoting System in UML: the ProVotE experience by Roberto Tiella, Adolfo Villafiorita, and Silvia Tomasi. This paper presents some of the issues and challenges faced during the development of an electronic voting machine, and how UML models were integrated in the development process. Some existing tools were extended to support the formal verification of the UML specifications.

The third discussion included the third and fourth session papers, as well as a general recap of topics discussed throughout the day. Conclusions and outstanding issues were drawn in five areas.

- Verification. Most verification work seems to be in state machines, using model checking. In part, this is due to the fact that verification of functional properties is more mature than for non-functional properties; it is harder to verify properties such as performance, timing, and security. There is some work going on using activity diagrams to perform quality constraint consistency checking. It may also be possible to check semantic consistency using OCL for verification, and reasoning over traces, pre- and post- conditions. It is also the case that deployment diagrams should be used since their information influences preserved properties in dynamic behavior models. Verifications need to be formal, but there are things we want to describe and there is no language to describe them; formalisms don't exist in these cases. Fault injection may be a technique we can use; based on state charts and fault states. We need to note however, that there is a difference between fault analysis and security analysis: faults can be simple, whereas attacks are usually quite complex – any real problem has infinite state space. Research should continue exploring the combination of model checkers and theorem provers to make the best of both worlds.

- Accidental Complexity. Using UML for critical system development is very complex. We discussed whether this is inherent in the nature of UML, or whether it is accidental – stemming from the way we use UML to develop these kinds of systems? If this complexity is introduced by our techniques and tools, it should be avoided whenever possible. Complexity definitely hinders acceptance by developers. Inherent complexity can perhaps be addressed through the use of domain specific languages. Profiles seem to make the problem worse.

- DSLs and representations. Domain experts have to restrict the use of UML notations, and have to present the subset in a way that can be useful; the language must allow engineers to be more effective without fundamentally changing what they do. In some sense they are like shortcuts, in fact it may be possible to derive DSLs from determining what shortcuts developers use. DSLs are necessary because while UML models capture what we mean, the diagrams are hard to create and sometimes understand – leading to complexity (accidental?). For example, in many cases text would be easier to create and understand than activity diagrams. An idea we might explore is to generate graphical representations from text, recognizing in some cases that the graphical representation might not be more intuitive than the text, and discarding it in that case. Some tools can synchronize text and graphics (e.g. SecureUML, which has an access policy DSL, and uses a graphical interface to generate this text.)

- Development Traceability. There must be a link between requirements and verification and changes made to models based on analysis results; the issue is that the traces have to be well defined and well understood.
- The results of case studies are problematic. They often do not produce any really new insights, or learnings that can be easily applied in other situations. It would be a good research topic to define how to go about performing a "perfect" case study – planning, what you want to find out, how to find it out, common problems, etc. The end result would be a template for running a case study that could be used by people setting up case studies, and people evaluating papers written about case studies, or evaluating the results of the case study, etc.

Modeling an Electronic Throttle Controller Using the Timed Abstract State Machine Language and Toolset

Martin Ouimet, Guillaume Berteau, and Kristina Lundqvist

Embedded Systems Laboratory
Massachusetts Institute of Technology
Cambridge, MA, 02139, USA
{mouimet, gberteau, kristina}@mit.edu

Abstract. In this paper, we present an integrated toolset that implements the features of the Timed Abstract State Machine (TASM) language, a novel specification language for embedded real-time systems. The toolset enables the creation of executable specifications with well-defined execution semantics, abstraction mechanisms, and composition semantics. The features of the toolset are demonstrated using an Electronic Throttle Controller (ETC) from a major automotive vendor. The TASM toolset is used to analyze the resource consumption resulting from the mode switching logic of the ETC, and to verify the completeness and consistency of the specification.

Keywords: Formal Specification, Modeling, Simulation, Real-Time Systems, Embedded Systems.

1 Introduction

In the design and development of embedded real-time systems, the design and specification problem is more challenging than for traditional interactive systems because both functional behavior and non-functional behavior are part of the system's utility and must be specified precisely and concisely [5]. Furthermore, the specification and analysis of system designs is often performed at various levels of abstraction [13]. The Timed Abstract State Machine (TASM) language was introduced in [17], as a novel specification language that removes the need to use many other specification languages. More specifically, TASM incorporates the specification of functional and non-functional behavior into a unified formalism. TASM is based on the theory of Abstract State Machines (ASM), a method for system design that can be applied at various levels of abstraction [3].

The TASM toolset implements the features of the TASM language through three main components - the editor, the analyzer, and the simulator. Those three components play a key role in gaining insight into the system under design during the early stages of development, and throughout the implementation of the system. The TASM toolset is well-suited to model and analyze the types of embedded real-time systems which are typically found in the automotive and aerospace industries.

In the automotive industry, many high-end car manufacturers use sophisticated electronics as an important sale point. For example, "drive-by-wire" systems [14] are becoming more commonplace in high end models. Drive-by-wire systems are composed

T. Kühne (Ed.): MoDELS 2006 Workshops, LNCS 4364, pp. 32–41, 2007.

of microcontroller units, sensors, and actuators to replace the direct physical linkage between the driver and the controlled elements.

In this paper, we present the TASM language and introduce the associated toolset by modeling a subset of a modern drive-by-wire system. More specifically, we focus on a fault tolerant electronic throttle controller (ETC) which is used at a major automotive company. The ETC allows the transfer function between the acceleration pedal and the throttle to be dynamically adjusted, according to various parameters, to optimize fuel consumption. The ETC is an industrial application that is well-suited for specification and analysis in the TASM language because it is safety-critical, it is embedded, it has hard timing constraints, and it contains concurrency.

This paper is divided into five sections in addition to this Introduction. The following section presents related work. The TASM language is presented in Section 3. Section 4 introduces the TASM toolset and its features. Section 5 describes the ETC model and details the analysis that has been performed on the model using the TASM toolset. Finally, the Conclusion and Future Work section, Section 6, summarizes the contributions of the paper and explains the additions that are to come in future development.

2   Related Work

In the finite state system family, model checkers have grown in popularity because of their automated analysis capabilities. The Uppaal [18] model checker has enjoyed popularity in the real-time system community. However, the formalism of Uppaal lacks structuring mechanisms and makes abstraction and encapsulation difficult to achieve [2]. Statecharts and the associated tool STATEMATE [10] augment automata with structuring mechanisms (superstates).

In the petri net family, a large number of variations on the traditional petri net model have been developed, including various models of time [6]. Non-determinism is an essential part of petri nets, which makes petri net unsuitable for the specification of safety-critical real-time systems [2]. Other popular languages include the Synchronous languages ESTEREL and LUSTRE [2], implemented in the SCADE tool suite. Those languages only apply to the specification of synchronous systems.

In the industrial community, especially in the aerospace and automotive industries, the Unified Modeling Language (UML) [15] and the Architecture Analysis and Design Language (AADL) [19] have come to dominate notational conventions. UML suffers from a lack of standardized formal semantics. AADL contains formal semantics but is still in the early development stages, so it could not be completely evaluated.

In the Abstract State Machine (ASM) community, various tools have been developed. The XASM language [1] and toolset extends ASMs with composition mechanisms. The XASM language does not include time nor resource specification and does not support concurrent ASMs. Other tools include ASM Gofer [20], the ASM Workbench [7], and Microsoft's AsmL [9] toolset. Aside from ASM Gofer, these tools do not support concurrent ASM specifications. Furthermore, these tools do not address time explicitly. The specification and execution semantics of resource consumption has not been addressed in the ASM community.

3   The Timed Abstract State Machine (TASM) Language

The TASM language was created as a language extending the ASM language to unify the specification of functional and non-functional properties. The TASM language comprises the ASM language, extensions to specify non-functional properties, and composition semantics [16,17].

3.1   Basic Definitions

The ASM language revolves around the concepts of an abstract machine and an abstract state. System behavior is specified as the computing steps of the abstract machine. A computing *step* is defined as a set of parallel updates made to global *state*. A *state* is defined as the values of all variables at a specific instant. A machine *executes* a step by yielding a set of state updates, called an *update set*. A *run*, potentially infinite, is a sequence of steps, that is, a sequence of update sets.

The term *specification* is used to denote the complete document that results from the process of writing down a system design. A basic abstract state machine specification is made up of two parts - an abstract state machine and an environment. The machine executes based on values in the environment and modifies values in the environment. The environment consists of two parts - the set of environment variables and the universe of types that variables can have. The machine consists of three parts - a set of monitored variables, a set of controlled variables, and a set of mutually exclusive rules. The *monitored* variables are the variables in the environment that affect the machine execution. The *controlled* variables are the variables in the environment that the machine affects. The set of rules are named predicates that express the state evolution logic by specifying how the variables in the environment are modified. For a complete description of the theory of abstract state machines, the reader is referred to [3].

3.2   Time

The TASM approach to time specification is to specify the duration of a rule execution. In the TASM world, this means that each step will last a finite amount of time before an update set is applied to the environment. At the specification level, time gets specified for each rule. The specification of time can take the form of a single value t, or can be specified as an interval $[t_{min}, t_{max}]$. The approach uses relative time between steps. The total time for a run is simply the sum of the individual step times over the run.

3.3   Resources

The specification of non-functional properties includes timing characteristics as well as resource consumption properties. A *resource* is defined as a global quantity that has a finite size. Power, memory, and bandwidth are examples of resources.

At the specification level, each rule specifies how much of a given resource it consumes, either as an interval or as a single value. The semantics of resource usage are assumed to be *volatile*, that is, usage lasts only through the step duration. For example, if a rule consumes 128 kiloBytes of memory, the total memory usage will be increased by 128 kiloBytes during the step duration and will be decreased by 128 kiloBytes after the update set has been applied to the environment.

The definition of an update set is extended to include the time and resource behavior of a step, in addition to the variable updates. The symbol TRU_i is used to denote the timed update set, with resource usage, of the ith step, where t_i is the step duration, RC_i is the set of consumed resources, and U_i is the update set: $TRU_i = (t_i, RC_i, U_i)$.

3.4 Hierarchical Composition

The composition mechanisms included in the TASM language are based on the XASM language [1]. In the XASM language, an ASM can use other ASMs in rule declarations in two different ways - as a sub ASM or as a $function$ ASM. A sub ASM is a machine that is used to structure specifications. A $function$ ASM is a machine that takes a set of inputs and returns a single value as output, similarly to a function in programming languages.

The execution semantics of auxiliary machines are *parallel*. For a given step that uses auxiliary machines, the duration of the step is the maximum of the durations of the steps of auxiliary machines. The resource consumption of the step will be the summation of individual consumptions of the steps of auxiliary machines, for each resource. The combination of two update sets $TRU_{1,i} = (t_{1,i}, RC_1, U_{1,i})$ and $TRU_{2,i} = (t_{2,i}, RC_2, U_{2,i})$ from two auxiliary machines invoked within the same step would yield a third update set TRU_i: $TRU_i = (max(t_{1,i}, t_{2,i}), RC_1 + RC_2, U_{1,i} \cup U_{2,i})$.

3.5 Parallel Composition

In the TASM language, parallel composition is achieved through the definition of multiple main machines. The semantics of parallel composition regards the synchronization of the machines with respect to the global progression of time. Machines execute one or more steps that can last any amount of time. A machine that executes a step that lasts longer than steps of other machines will be *busy* until the global progression of time reaches the end of the step duration. In the meantime, machines that aren't busy can keep executing steps. This definition gives rise to update sets no longer constrained by step number, but constrained by time. The synchronization of parallel machines is achieved through the step durations. For a complete description of the TASM language, the reader is referred to [16,17].

4   The Timed Abstract State Machine Toolset

The TASM toolset includes facilities for creating, editing, and composing TASM specifications through the TASM Editor. Furthermore, the toolset includes facilities for executing specifications through the TASM Simulator, to visualize the dynamic behavior of the system under design. Finally, the TASM Analyzer provides automated analysis capabilities to gain insight into the properties of the system being designed. These core components of the TASM toolset are explained in details in the following subsections.

4.1   The TASM Editor

The TASM Editor provides the facilities to define the three types of machines in the TASM language - main machines, function machines, and sub machines. The editor provides basic text editing and syntax highlighting functionality. Furthermore, the editor enables the creation of documentation into the Hyper Text Markup Language (HTML) format. The toolset can be used to import or to export a TASM specification in a well-documented format [16] expressed in the eXtensible Markup Language (XML) syntax. A screenshot depicting the TASM editor is shown in Figure 1.

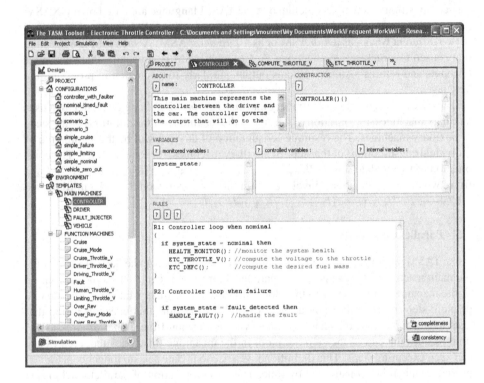

Fig. 1. Screenshot of the TASM Editor

4.2   The TASM Simulator

By definition, TASM specifications are executable. The execution semantics of the TASM language have been defined in [16,17]. The TASM Simulator enables the visualization of the dynamic behavior of the specification, in a step-by-step fashion. The visualization of the dynamic behavior includes time dependencies between parallel main machines, the effect of step execution on environment variables, and resource consumption. Resource consumption is graphed over time and statistics regarding minimum, maximum, and average resource consumption are compiled. Because time and resources can be specified using intervals, that is, using a lower bound and an upper bound, the simulation can use different semantics for time passage and resource consumption. For example, a given simulation can use the worst-case time (upper bound) for all steps, to visualize the system behavior under the longest running times. Other options include best-case time, average-case time, and using a time randomly selected within the specified interval. The same semantics can be selected for the resource consumption behavior.

4.3   The TASM Analyzer

The TASM Analyzer is the component of the TASM toolset that performs analysis of specifications. The analyzer can be used to verify basic properties of TASM specifications such as consistency and completeness [11]. In the TASM language, *completeness* ensures that, for a given machine and for all possible combinations of its monitored variable values, a rule will be enabled. If a specific combination of values of monitored variables is not covered by a rule, the specification is said to be incomplete and the analyzer gives a counterexample. In the TASM language, *consistency* ensures that, for a given machine and for all possible combinations of monitored variable values, one and only one rule is enabled. In other words, verifying consistency means verifying that the rules of a given machine are mutually exclusive. Future capabilities of the analyzer will include verifying worst-case and best-case execution times for TASM specifications, as well as verifying best-case and worst-case resource consumption. The Future Work section explains in more details the anticipated features of the TASM analyzer.

5   Modeling the Electronic Throttle Controller

The Electronic Throttle Controller (ETC) was initially modeled by Griffiths [8] as a hybrid system using Mathworks' Simulink and Stateflow. The main idea behind the throttle controller concerns optimizing fuel efficiency by controlling the amount of air and the amount of fuel that enter the engine. This is achieved by controlling the throttle angle and the fuel injectors.

Griffiths' Simulink model has two outputs – desired current and desired rate of fuel mass (dMfc). The angle of the throttle is controlled by the amount of current fed to the throttle servo. The desired current affects the position of the throttle and is determined based on the position of the gas pedal, vehicle speed, O_2 concentration in the exhaust, engine speed, and temperature. The other controller output is the rate of fuel mass (dMfc). The dMfc controls how much gas is sprayed in the combustion chamber. This value needs to be adjusted to maintain a stoichiometric combustion.

5.1   Components

We adopted the Simulink model into the TASM language by modeling the control of the desired current and the control of the desired fuel consumption as sub machines within a controller main machine. The specification makes use of auxiliary machines, both sub machines and function machines. The main steps of functionality have been divided using sub machines. For the throttle voltage calculations, under nominal operation, the main loop invokes 3 sub machines:

```
SET_MAJOR_MODE(); SET_MINOR_MODE(); CALCULATE_THROTTLE_V();
```

Table 1. List of machines used in the ETC TASM model for throttle voltage calculation

Name	Type	Purpose
ETC_CONTROLLER	Main	Main loop to calculate the throttle voltage
COMPUTE_THROTTLE_VOLTAGE	Sub	Calculates the throttle voltage
ETC_THROTTLE_V	Sub	Wrapper machine for the throttle voltage calculation
SET_MAJOR_MODE	Sub	Sets the major operating mode based on sensor values
SET_MINOR_MODE	Sub	Sets the minor operating mode based on sensor values
Cruise	Function	Determines whether the cruise control condition is enabled
Cruise_Mode	Function	Sets the cruise mode
Cruise_Throttle_V	Function	Returns the cruise throttle voltage
Driving_Throttle_V	Function	Returns the driving throttle voltage
Human_Throttle_V	Function	Returns the human throttle voltage
Limiting_Throttle_V	Function	Returns the limiting throttle voltage
Over_Rev_Throttle_V	Function	Returns the over revolution throttle voltage
Over_Torque_Throttle_V	Function	Returns the over torque throttle voltage
Over_Rev	Function	Determines if the over revolution condition is enabled
Over_Rev_Mode	Function	Sets the over revolution mode
Over_Torque	Function	Determines if the over torque condition is enabled
Over_Torque_Mode	Function	Sets the over torque mode
min	Function	Returns the smaller value of two floats
max	Function	Returns the larger value of two floats

This loop executes indefinitely until a fault is detected, the ignition is turned off, or the car gear is shifted out of the 'drive' position. Other core rules include the fault handling mechanisms and the rules to compute the desired fuel consumption. The calculations of throttle voltage and desired fuel mass are directly based on the mode of operation. Appropriate datatypes were defined to list the possible major and minor modes:

```
Binary_Mode     := {active, inactive};
Binary_Status   := {on, off};
Health_Status   := {nominal, fault_detected};
Mode            := {start-up, shut-down, driving, limiting};
```

The *Mode* datatype is used to set the major mode of operation. The *Binary_Mode* datatype is used to set the cruise, limiting, over revolution, and over torque minor modes.

5.2 Resources

The resources that are modeled in this example are power, to estimate the maximum power consumption of the throttle controller, and memory, to ensure that the memory used by the controller is adequately bounded. We make the assumption that the amount of memory available for the throttle controller is 512 kiloBytes. For power consumption, there is typically no upper bound, so we choose a large value, 1 Mega Watt.

The characteristics of the power utilization were estimated using the characteristics of the Xilinx Virtex II Pro implementation platform. This implementation platform was selected because it has been used in past research [4].

5.3 Complete Model and Simulation

The total list of machines used for the throttle voltage calculation is given in Table 1. For the rate of fuel mass calculation, a similar list of machines was used. This list is omitted here for brevity. The total model contains 29 machines (4 main machines, 8 sub machines, and 17 function machines). There are 21 environment variables, 4 user-defined types, and 2 resources. The complete model amounts to about 750 lines of TASM constructs.

5.4 Scenario Modeling

The electronic throttle controller reacts to changes in the state of the vehicle (speed, traction, altitude, failures, etc.) and operator inputs (gas pedal angle, break pedal angle, cruise control switch, ignition, gear, etc.). Various scenarios were devised to exercise the dynamic behavior of the throttle controller. The basic scenarios involved selecting a set of initial conditions that were not modified outside of the controller's behavior. The basic scenarios are useful in ensuring that the ETC behaves as expected for isolated conditions. More interesting scenarios were created by modeling driver behavior and plant behavior. Both the driver and the vehicle were modeled as main machines, composed in parallel with the controller machines. The driver and vehicle models enable the creation of more complex scenarios where the driver and vehicle can generate changes at prespecified times. The combination of driver and vehicle models injects dynamic state changes, and the controller behavior can be observed in response to these state changes.

5.5 Results

Creating a formal model of the ETC enabled the verification of consistency and completeness for the mode switching logic and throttle voltage calculation logic.

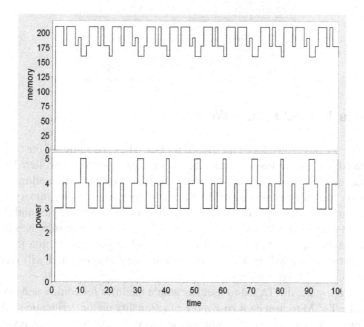

Fig. 2. Resource graph

Determining these properties was helpful during the early modeling stages to ensure that no cases were missed and that no cases were conflicting. This verification was established in isolation, by verifying completeness and consistency on a machine-by-machine basis. The ETC model was not overly complex and presented a good entry-level example to exercise the TASM toolset and to show the capabilities of the toolset. On the simulation side, the TASM toolset enables the creation of multiple simulation scenarios, using different initial conditions. Each scenario exercises the model in different ways and the toolset allows the visualization of resource consumption behavior over time. The TASM simulator presents graphical representation of timing behavior for main machines and of resource consumption behavior for all resources in the system design. Furthermore, it is also possible to visualize the state evolution of the environment and the internal state of the main machines. A sample graph depicting resource consumption for a sample run is shown in Figure 2. The top graph shows the memory consumption and the bottom graph shows the power consumption during a time interval.

Ten different scenarios were run for the ETC model, using the same set of components, but using different initial conditions. The results for scenarios which yielded different results are listed in Table 2. Throughout the scenarios, the maximum memory consumption was found to be 256 kiloBytes and the maximum power consumption peaked at 5 Watts. In certain scenarios, the system oscillated and reached a fix point after a number of states.

Table 2. List of Simulation Scenarios for the ETC model

Scenario	Fix Point	Peak Memory	Peak Power
1	13 steps	206 kBytes	3 Watts
4	10 steps	256 kBytes	4 Watts
5	6 steps	196 kBytes	3 Watts
9	11 steps	226 kBytes	5 Watts

6   Conclusion and Future Work

In this paper, we have introduced the TASM toolset. The capabilities of the toolset were demonstrated using an industrial example, an electronic throttle controller. The TASM toolset was used to model the mode switching logic, voltage calculation logic, and desired mass fuel rate calculation of the throttle controller. The preliminary results of the simulation show that the memory consumption peaked at 256 kBytes and the power consumption peaked at 5 Watts. The modeling of the throttle controller was helpful to verify consistency and completeness of the logic and to gain insight into the resource behavior. Future work will build upon this preliminary example and will incorporate more functionality into the toolset.

In its current state, the TASM toolset has ample facilities for editing and simulation. However, the TASM toolset could use more functionality on the verification side. In future versions of the toolset, we will enhance the analysis capabilities by mapping TASM specifications to Uppaal [18]. The aim is to be able to verify best-case and worst-case execution times between two states of a TASM specification. Furthermore, by using Uppaal, we will be able to verify the absence of deadlocks, and to verify the best-case and worst-case resource consumption behavior.

References

1. Anlauff M.: XASM - An Extensible, Component-Based Abstract State Machines Language. ASM 2000, International Workshop on Abstract State Machines (2000)
2. Berry G.: The Essence of ESTEREL. Proof, Language and Interaction: Essays in Honour of Robin Milner. MIT Press (2000)
3. Börger E., Stärk R.: Abstract State Machines. Springer-Verlag (2003)
4. Boussemart Y., Gorelov S., Ouimet M., Lundqvist, K.: Non-Intrusive System-Level Fault Tolerance for an Electronic Throttle Controller. Proceedings of the International Conference on Systems (ICONS 2006). IEEE Computer Society Press (2006)
5. Bouyssounouse B., Sifakis J.: Embedded Systems Design: The ARTIST Roadmap for Research and Development. Springer-Verlag (2005)
6. Cerone A., Maggiolo-Schettini A.: Time-based Expressivity of Time Petri Nets for System Specification. Theoretical Computer Science **216**. Springer-Verlag (1999)
7. Del Castillo, G.: Towards Comprehensive Tool Support for Abstract State Machines: The ASM Workbench Tool Environment and Architecture. Applied Formal Methocs – FM-Trends 98. LNCS **1641** Springer-Verlag (1999)
8. Griffiths P.G.: Embedded Software Control Design for an Electronic Throttle Body. Master's Thesis, University of California, Berkeley (2002)
9. Gurevich Y., Rossman B., Schulte W.: Semantic Essence of AsmL. Theoretical Computer Science **3** (2005)
10. Harel D., Naamad A.: The STATEMATE Semantics of Statecharts. ACM Transactions on Software Engineering and Methodology **4** (1996)
11. Heitmeyer C.L. Jeffords R.D., Labaw B.G.: Automated Consistency Checking of Requirements Specifications. ACM Trans. on Soft. Eng. and Methodology (TOSEM) **5** (1996)
12. Hessel A., Pettersson P.: A Test Case Generation Algorithm for Real-Time Systems. Proceedings of the Fourth International Conference on Quality Software (QSIC'04) (2004)
13. Jantsch A., Sander I.: Models of Computation and Languages for Embedded System Design. IEE Proceedings - Computers and Digital Techniques. **152** (2005)
14. Milam W., Chutinan A.: Model Composition and Analysis Challenge Problems. Smart Vehicle Challenge Problems (2005)
15. Object Management Group, Inc.: Unified Modeling Language: Superstrucure. Version 2.0. OMG Specification (2005)
16. Ouimet M.: The TASM Language Reference Manual, Version 1.0. Available from http://esl.mit.edu/tasm (2006)
17. Ouimet M., Lundqvist K.: Timed Abstract State Machines: An Executable Specification Language for Reactive Real-Time Systems. Technical Report ESL-TIK-000193, Embedded Systems Laboratory, Massachusetts Institute of Technology (2006)
18. Pettersson P., Larsen K.G.: Uppaal2k. Bulletin of the European Association for Theoretical Computer Science **70** (2000)
19. SAE Aerospace: Architecture Analysis & Design Language Standard. SAE Publication AS506 (2004)
20. Schmid J.: Executing ASM Specifications with AsmGofer. Technical Report. Available from http://www.tydo.de/AsmGofer (1999)

Model Checking of UML 2.0 Interactions

Alexander Knapp[1] and Jochen Wuttke[2]

[1] Ludwig-Maximilians-Universität München, Germany
knapp@pst.ifi.lmu.de
[2] Università della Svizzera Italiana, Lugano, Switzerland
wuttkej@lu.unisi.ch

Abstract. The UML 2.0 integrates a dialect of High-Level Message Sequence Charts (HMSCs) for interaction modelling. We describe a translation of UML 2.0 interactions into automata for model checking whether an interaction can be satisfied by a given set of message exchanging UML state machines. The translation supports basic interactions, state invariants, strict and weak sequencing, alternatives, ignores, and loops as well as forbidden interaction fragments. The translation is integrated into the UML model checking tool HUGO/RT.

Keywords: Scenarios, UML 2.0 interactions, model checking.

1 Introduction

Scenario-based development uses descriptions of operational sequences to define the requirements of software systems, laying down required, allowed, or forbidden behaviours. In version 2.0 [1] of the "Unified Modeling Language" (UML) a variation of High-Level Message Sequence Charts (HMSCs [2]) replaced the rather inexpressive notion of interactions in UML 1.x for describing scenarios. The scenario language of UML 2.0 not only contains the well-known HMSC notions of weak sequencing, loops, and alternative composition of scenarios, but also includes a peculiar negation operator for distinguishing between allowed and forbidden behaviour. The thus gained expressiveness would make UML 2.0 an acceptable choice to model high-quality and safety-critical systems using scenario-based techniques. However, several vaguenesses in the specification document have led to several, differing efforts for equipping UML 2.0 interactions with a formal semantics (see, e.g., [3,4]).

We propose a translation of UML 2.0 interactions into automata. This synthesised operational behaviour description can be used to verify that a proposed design meets the requirements stated in the scenarios by using model checking. On the one hand, the translation comprises basic interactions of partially ordered event occurrences, state invariants, the interaction combination operators for weak and strict sequencing, parallel and alternative composition, as well as a restricted form of loops, which can have potentially or mandatorily infinitely many iterations. On the other hand, besides these uncontroversial standard constructs, we also handle a classical negation operator [3], which avoids the introduction of three-valued logics as suggested by the UML 2.0 specification by resorting to binary logic.

The translation procedure is integrated into our freely available UML model checking tool HUGO/RT [5]: A system of message exchanging UML state machines together

T. Kühne (Ed.): MoDELS 2006 Workshops, LNCS 4364, pp. 42–51, 2007.

with the generated automaton representing a UML interaction for observing message traces is translated into the input language of an off-the-shelf model checker, which then is called upon to check satisfiability. Currently, we support interaction model checking over state machines with SPIN [6] and, partially, with UPPAAL [7].

The remainder of this paper is structured as follows: In Sect. 2 we briefly review the features of UML 2.0 interactions. In Sect. 3 we introduce our automaton model for interactions, and in Sect. 4 we describe the translation from UML 2.0 interactions into automata. Section 5 reports on the results of applying SPIN model checking with our approach. In Sect. 6 we discuss related work, and Sect. 7 concludes with a summary of the results and an outlook on future work.

2   UML 2.0 Interactions

UML 2.0 interactions consist of *interaction fragments*. The primitive fragments are *occurrence specifications*, specifying the occurrence of events within an object that is participating in the interaction. *Combined fragments* aggregate occurrence specifications into bigger interaction fragments. A combined fragment comprises an *operator*, defining the meaning of the particular fragment, and one or more *operands*. The operands are interaction fragments themselves, and can be guarded by an optional condition, limiting the possibilities for when this operand may be executed.

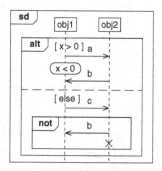

Fig. 1. Sample interaction

The example in Fig. 1 shows instances of the important aspects of a UML 2.0 interaction. The behaviour of two objects obj1 and obj2 is specified by message exchanges (sending and receiving occurrence specifications, denoted by arrow tails and heads) on their *lifelines*, object destruction (cross), state invariants (conditions in a rounded box), and combined fragments. Vertical juxtaposition of interaction fragments implies *weak sequencing*, such that in the second operand of the alternative the sending of c, *active* on obj1, comes before any event on obj1 inside the not fragment, and the receiving of c before any event on obj2. Both operands to alt are guarded by conditions, which determine which operands can be chosen at "runtime".

The primitive interaction fragments we consider are basic interactions, consisting of a set of event occurrences with a partial order [1, p. 410], and state invariants for a single or several lifelines that has to hold if the state invariant is reached. Of the interaction operators [1, p. 410–412], we consider weak (seq) and strict sequential composition, parallel composition (par), alternative (alt), weak and strict sequencing loop, ignore of messages not mentioned, and a binary negation (not).

3   Interaction Automata

We interpret a UML 2.0 interaction as an observer of the message exchanges and state changes in a system. Whenever the system under observation sends or receives a message or one of its objects terminates successfully, the observer is notified and can act accordingly by making a move accepting the event or by producing a failure. However, it may also refrain from doing so, if it does not deem the state change relevant. Taking such an observer to be an automaton accepting words of system changes, i.e. state changes or events, the acceptance conditions for finite and infinite runs can be rendered as the corresponding ones in finite state machines and Büchi automata [8].

Interaction automata, realising such an observer from an interaction by a state-transition system, are defined over an *interaction alphabet* (L, E, Σ) of a finite set of involved lifelines L, a set E of termination, send and receive events from messages exchanged between the lifelines, and a set Σ of system states. The transitions outgoing from a state define a set of events that, when occurring, enable the transition. Moreover, transitions may be guarded by conditions arising from the conditions in the interaction. In order to reflect weak sequencing of interactions, the events η and the guard g of a transition show a set of lifelines *lifelines*(η, g), which are active when making a move by this transition. Finally, an interaction automaton may also use and manipulate a set of counters V that allow to record how often lifelines in loops have executed. For the guards we assume a propositionally closed language $\mathscr{G}_{\Sigma,V}$; it should be expressive enough to capture system state queries on Σ and to compare counters in V. For the actions, we similarly assume a language $\mathscr{A}_V$ manipulating the set of counters V.

A *run* of an interaction automaton N starts from an *initial configuration* (i, v_0) where i is N's *initial state* and v_0 the valuation of the set of counters V to zero. A run of N proceeds by *steps* $(s, v) \xrightarrow{(\sigma, \zeta)} (s', v')$ with a system state $\sigma \in \Sigma$ and a set of events $\zeta \subseteq E$, if there is a transition outgoing from s with a set of events equal to ζ such that in σ and v the transition guard is satisfied and the valuation v is updated to v' according to the transition's action. N *accepts* a finite run, if this run reaches a state in the *accepting states* A of N, and it accepts an infinite run if this run reaches one of N's *recurrence states* R infinitely often.

It may be noted that although we define interaction automata to be finitely represented, the configuration space may be infinite due to unbounded increases of counters. However, for bounded interactions, in which no lifeline in a loop is allowed to proceed arbitrarily in advance with respect to another lifeline in the loop [9], the configuration space can be kept finite, and even for unbounded interactions, the system under observation may not produce runs that exhibit unbounded differences between counters.

4   Translation of UML 2.0 Interactions

We translate UML 2.0 interactions into interaction automata following the generally agreed upon semantics of basic interactions, state invariants, and the interaction operators seq, strict, par, alt, ignore, and, in a restricted form, loop [3,4]. Furthermore, we handle a binary logic not operator; not and loop are restricted to basic interactions.[1]

In contrast to other approaches (e.g. [10,11]) we propose not to generate one automaton for every object in an interaction, but to use only a single observing interaction

---

[1] For a more detailed account of the translation procedure we refer the reader to the unabridged version of this article in the proceedings of the workshop "Critical Systems Development Using Modeling Languages" 2006.

automaton for the entire interaction. This single automaton represents the property to be checked by a model checker. Our translation of basic interactions is a simplified version of the construction for Live Sequence Charts (LSCs) given by Brill et al. [12], the handling of weak sequencing cuts down techniques of Alur and Yannakakis for bounded MSCs [9].

4.1 Basic Interactions, Loops, and Negation

We first describe the translation of basic interactions, and loops and negations of basic interactions. These interaction fragments form the primitive blocks in our translation procedure and have to be represented as interaction automata directly.

Basic Interactions. The translation of basic interactions is performed by unwinding the partial order of events. For each event the partial order defines the prerequisite events, which must be unwound before that event can be unwound. The unwinding is performed in *phases* [12]. In every phase there exists a *history*, i.e., a set of events which have been unwound already. Given a phase, the function *ready* delivers the events which can be unwound in the next step, as inscriptions of transitions; we write *isAccepting*(*phase*) for *ready*(*phase*) = ∅. A function *nextPhase*, given a phase and a transition inscription, creates a new phase recording the additional event from the transition inscription in the history. The following algorithm *unwind* transforms phases directly into states of an interaction automaton *result*. Started for a basic interaction with the phase with empty history, the state returned by this call to *unwind* becomes the initial state of *result*.

1 *unwind*(*phase*, *result*) ≡
2 ⌈ *state* ← *addState*(*result*)
3   if *isAccepting*(*phase*) then *addAcceptingState*(*result*, *state*) fi

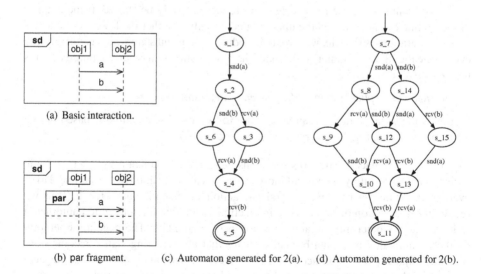

(a) Basic interaction.

(b) par fragment.

(c) Automaton generated for 2(a).   (d) Automaton generated for 2(b).

Fig. 2. Automata for a basic interaction and par (accepting states are doubly outlined)

```
4    for label ∈ ready(phase) do
5        addTransition(result, state, label, unwind(nextPhase(phase, label), result))
6    od
7    return state⌋
```

Figure 2(a) shows an example of a basic interaction, the interaction automaton in Fig. 2(b) shows the effects of unwinding its partial order. The branching in s_2 is due to the fact that the second event can be either the reception of a or the sending of b.

Loops. The UML 2.0 defines loops which have a lower and an upper bound for the number of iterations their operand has to perform; the lower bound has to be finite, while the upper bound may be infinity. We change this and also allow the lower bound to be infinity. However, we restrict loops to contain only a basic interaction.

For finite or infinite loops of a basic interaction the basic unwinding algorithm can be reused. As weak sequencing is used for loops, the lifelines in the underlying basic interaction can make different progress. Thus the history stored in a phase for a basic interaction becomes insufficient for loops, as not all prerequisite events for a given event will be present in the history if the lifeline's event is lagging behind the lifeline of one of its prerequisites. Thus we let *loop phases* also show a history, but the computation of the next events from a loop phase is changed: We introduce counters for recording the separate progress of each lifeline. Then, an event e on lifeline l is possible in a loop phase if the following condition is met: If e has a prerequisite e' on a lifeline l', either the counter for l' is greater than the counter for l, or the counters for l and l' are equal and e' is present in the history. Upon finishing a cycle through a lifeline the counter for this lifeline has to be increased in order to make real progress.

It remains to ensure that the number of iterations of the loops indeed is between its lower and upper bound. If the lower bound is finite, a phase becomes accepting if the counters for all lifelines are equal and greater than or equal to the lower bound. If the upper bound is finite a new cycle of a lifeline may only be started, if the counter of the lifeline has not reached the upper bound. Finally, if either the lower or the upper bound of iterations is infinite, we have to introduce a recurrent state which is run through every time the lifeline counters are equal. The introduction of a recurrent phase extends the *unwind* algorithm after line 3 by

if *isRecurrent*(phase) then *addRecurrentState*(result, state) fi

Figure 3 shows an example of an automaton for a loop. The example is based on the basic interaction in Fig. 2(a), wrapped into a loop $\langle 4, \infty \rangle$.

Negation. We replace UML 2.0's notorious negation operator neg by a binary logic variant not which simply accepts all those traces that are not valid for its operand. However, an algorithm for negating general interaction automata is out of reach. Thus we restrict the application of not to basic interactions, such that the interaction automaton to be negated is deterministic and does not involve counters. The negation operation on these interaction automata basically means that all accepting states become non-accepting states and all non-accepting states become accepting states in the negated automaton. A new recurrent state is added, and from all complemented states transitions to this accepting state are added to accept all events that were not accepted in the

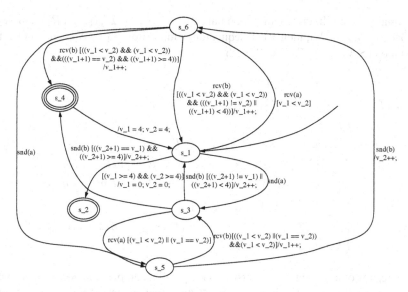

Fig. 3. The automaton for an infinite loop (recurrence states are triply outlined; transition annotations abbreviated)

corresponding state of the original automaton. This additional accepting state is also equipped with a self-loop accepting all possible events.

4.2 Interleaving, Sequencing, and Composition

We next describe the parallel (par) and weak sequential (seq) composition of two interaction automata N_1 and N_2 over a common interaction alphabet (L, E, Σ). We also give a brief account of strict sequential (strict) composition, extending this notion to introduce a general strict sequencing variant sloop of loops, and of alternatives (alt), ignore, and state invariants.

Parallel Composition and Weak Sequencing. The *parallel* composition $N_1 \| N_2$, accepting the trace $o_0 o_1 \cdots \in (\Sigma \times \wp E)^* \cup (\Sigma \times \wp E)^\infty$ by interleaving traces $o_0^{(1)} o_1^{(1)} \ldots$ and $o_0^{(2)} o_1^{(2)} \ldots$ accepted by N_1 and N_2 respectively, uses a construction very similar to the parallel composition of Büchi automata [8]. This construction only has to be adapted to cover the case that both or one of the interaction automata do not show recurrence states.

A slight modification of the construction for parallel composition can be used for obtaining the *weak sequential* composition $N_1 \mathbin{;_{\text{\tiny$\succeq$}}} N_2$ of N_1 and N_2: Also interleavings of traces $o_0^{(1)} o_1^{(1)} \ldots$ and $o_0^{(2)} o_1^{(2)} \ldots$ accepted by N_1 and N_2 are accepted by $N_1 \mathbin{;_{\text{\tiny$\succeq$}}} N_2$, but in the interleaving no $o_j^{(2)}$ is allowed to occur before an $o_k^{(1)}$ if their active lifelines overlap. Therefore, the states of $N_1 \mathbin{;_{\text{\tiny$\succeq$}}} N_2$ show an additional component of sets of lifelines, recording which lifelines have been covered by the interleaving of N_2.

Formally, given the interaction automata $N_1 = (S_1, V_1, T_1, i_1, A_1, R_1)$ and $N_2 = (S_2, V_2, T_2, i_2, A_2, R_2)$, their weak sequential composition $N_1 \mathbin{;_{\approx}} N_2$ is the interaction automaton $(S, V_1 \cup V_2, T, i, A, R)$ with

$$S = S_1 \times \wp L \times S_2 \times \{0, 1, 2\}, \qquad i = (i_1, \emptyset, i_2, 0)$$

$$(s_1, K, s_2, k) \in A \iff (s_1 \in A_1 \wedge s_2 \in A_2 \wedge k = 0)$$

$$(s_1, K, s_2, k) \in R \iff k = 2$$

$$((s_1, K, s_2, k), (\eta, g, a), (s_1', K', s_2', k')) \in T \iff$$
$$(((s_1, (\eta, g, a), s_1') \in T_1 \wedge s_2' = s_2 \wedge K = K' \wedge \textit{lifelines}(\eta, g) \cap K = \emptyset) \vee$$
$$((s_2, (\eta, g, a), s_2') \in T_2 \wedge s_1' = s_1 \wedge K' = K \cup \textit{lifelines}(\eta, g))) \wedge$$

$$k' = \begin{cases} k + 1, & \text{if } (k = 0 \vee k = 1) \wedge \\ & \qquad (s_{k+1}' \in R_{k+1} \vee (s_{k+1}' \in A_{k+1} \wedge R_{1-k} \neq \emptyset)) \\ k \bmod 2, & \text{otherwise} \end{cases}$$

The results of applying the construction for parallel composition and weak sequencing (using an optimised algorithm cutting off states that are unreachable from the initial state) to the interaction in Fig. 2(b) and Fig. 2(a) respectively, are shown in Fig. 2(d) and Fig. 2(c) and show the unrestricted interleaving in comparison with the restricted interleaving of weak sequencing.

Strict Sequencing, Alternatives, and Ignores. The *strict sequential* composition $N_1 ; N_2$ is achieved by building an automaton which appends N_2 at every accepting state of N_1. The simplicity of the strict sequencing construction for interaction automata also allows for the introduction of an unrestricted loop operator sloop, which enforces strict sequencing of the operand.

In alternative fragments all operands are guarded by either an explicitly given condition, or the implied condition [true]. We integrate the operand automata into a single automaton with guarded transitions from a new initial state to their respective initial states. A similar construction is employed for state invariants.

An ignore fragment specifies which messages are allowed to occur additionally in the traces generated from its operand. This is captured by adding self-loops to every state with the send and receive events from these messages, active for every possible sender or receiver, to the interaction automaton of the operand.

5   Model Checking UML 2.0 Interactions

We apply interactions as observers in model checking by translating the generated interaction automata into observing processes in the model checker SPIN. The system to be observed are message exchanging UML state machines. SPIN is called upon to check whether there is a run of the UML state machines that is accepted by the observer interaction automaton. The translation of UML state machines into SPIN, the translation from UML 2.0 interactions into interaction automata, and the translation of interaction automata into SPIN are integrated into the UML model checking tool HUGO/RT [5].

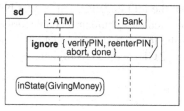 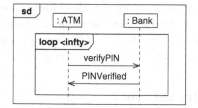

(a) PIN must have been verified   (b) Always give money to validated customers

Fig. 4. Two examples for the ATM case study

Implementation. We use SPIN's accept labels to capture the acceptance conditions of interaction automata both for finite and infinite traces. For infinite traces the accept labels are generated from the recurrent states, for finite traces a special accept label with looping transitions is produced from the acceptance states. The counters of an interaction automaton are represented as variables of the observing process. For recording events the system is instrumented to communicate with the observer via rendezvous channels: Each time a message is sent or received, or a state machine terminates successfully the observer is notified.

In order to keep the size of the SPIN code produced small state sharing is used in the algorithms for basic interactions and loops. Additionally, in the automata from parallel composition and weak sequencing unreachable states are cut off. These optimisations are done on the fly without constructing the product automaton. What is more, the *unwind* algorithm produces rather large automata, even with sharing: In the worst case for n independent events the resulting number of states will be 2^n. Thus it is beneficial to encode a phase not into the states of an interaction automaton, but to employ an external bit-array which encodes the progress of the phases and to use tests on this bit-array for checking whether an event can be accepted.[2]

Verification. Some examples for an automatic teller machine (ATM) case study [14] may show how the additions to interactions in UML 2.0 add to the expressiveness, and thus to the ease of specification and verification of interesting system properties. The two examples in Fig. 4 encode two important properties of the interaction between the system's components ATM and Bank: Figure 4(a) specifies a forbidden scenario; the state invariant that money is dispensed should not be reachable if no PINVerified (all other messages are ignored) has been sent. The interaction in Fig. 4(b) is a required scenario; it must be possible to take money from the ATM infinitely often, as long as the card is valid.

Having specified the interactions and state machines for the system components (see [14]) in the input language of HUGO/RT, the verification process itself is fairly straightforward. HUGO/RT translates the model into a set of SPIN processes and calls SPIN for finding acceptance cycles. For the interaction in Fig. 4(a) no such cycle is found, verifying that the interaction is indeed not satisfiable. For the interaction in

---

[2] For example, the error scenario in Fig. 15-9 of the telecom case study of Baranov et al. [13] with 19 messages on 5 lifelines amounts to 207 states and 476 transitions in the phase-based translation, but only 2 states and 39 transitions using a bit-array.

Fig. 4(b) an acceptance cycle is found showing that the infinite behaviour is possible. SPIN also produces an example trail, which is retranslated into a human-readable format of UML system states. For these simple examples the translation and model checking take about three seconds on an Intel® Pentium® 4, 3.2 GHz with 2 GB of memory.

6   Related Work

Over time there have been various approaches to formalising scenario descriptions in order to facilitate the analysis of requirements or specifications. Starting from MSCs, Uchitel et al. [15,11] specified semantics for HMSCs, and then developed an approach to synthesise behavioural models in the form of labelled transition systems. Their approach aims at preserving the component structure of the system. This causes their models to allow additional behaviours, which are not explicitly specified in the scenarios, and requires refinement steps to complete the specification [11].

Damm and Harel [16] developed LSCs as a more expressive extension of MSCs. They enrich their specification language with means to express preconditions for scenarios, and facilities to explicitly specify mandatory and forbidden behaviour. Klose [17] proposes an automaton-based interpretation of LSCs and gives an algorithm to create automata out of basic LSCs [17,12]. Bontemps and Heymans [18] formalise automata constructions for strict sequencing, parallel composition, and finite iteration of LSCs. Harel and Maoz [19] propose to port the semantics of LSCs to UML 2.0.

With CHARMY, Autili et al. [20] present a tool based on an approach similar to ours. The focus of CHARMY are architectural descriptions and the verification of their consistency. The semantics of interactions, given by their translation rules, however, deviates substantially from what can be gleaned from the UML 2.0 specification. Furthermore, in the program version we tested, combined fragments are not supported.

7   Conclusions and Future Work

We have presented a translation from UML 2.0 interactions into a special class of automata showing features of finite state automata, Büchi automata and counter automata. These interaction automata have been further translated into concrete programs for model checkers. Together with matching descriptions for UML state machines the approach has been used to model check consistency between the different system descriptions. In some examples we have shown the applicability of the translation procedures to check the satisfiability of scenarios by using the model checker SPIN. The added expressiveness allows the use of our approach to specify properties which before would have required formalisms other than UML interactions.

Since in the current implementation loop and not are restricted in terms of operands, one direction of future work will be to detail to which extent these restrictions can be removed. We also intend to integrate the remaining operators specified by the UML 2.0 specification, which we have disregarded so far. Furthermore, the specification patterns for scenarios described by Autili et al. [20] should be combined with our approach. Finally, we plan to integrate timing constraints and to enhance the translation of interactions into the real-time model checker UPPAAL.

References

1. Object Management Group: Unified Modeling Language: Superstructure, version 2.0. (2005) http://www.omg.org/cgi-bin/doc?formal/05-07-04[(06/07/18)].

2. International Telecommunication Union: Message Sequence Chart (MSC). ITU-T Recommendation Z.120, ITU-T, Geneva (2004)

3. Cengarle, M.V., Knapp, A.: UML 2.0 Interactions: Semantics and Refinement. In Jürjens, J., Fernandez, E.B., France, R., Rumpe, B., eds.: Proc. 3rd Int. Wsh. Critical Systems Development with UML (CSDUML'04), Technical Report TUM-I0415, Institut für Informatik, Technische Universität München (2004) 85–99

4. Runde, R.K., Haugen, Ø., Stølen, K.: Refining UML Interactions with Underspecification and Nondeterminism. Nordic J. Comp. **12**(2) (2005) 157–188

5. Hugo/RT website: http://www.pst.ifi.lmu.de/projekte/hugo[(06/07/18)] (2000)

6. Holzmann, G.J.: The SPIN Model Checker. Addison-Wesley (2003)

7. UPPAAL website: http://www.uppaal.com[(06/07/18)] (1995)

8. Clarke, E.M., Grumberg, O., Peled, D.A.: Model Checking. MIT Press (1999)

9. Alur, R., Yannakakis, M.: Model Checking of Message Sequence Charts. In Baeten, J.C.M., Mauw, S., eds.: Proc. 10th Int. Conf. Concurrency Theory (CONCUR'99). Volume 1664 of Lect. Notes Comp. Sci., Springer (1999) 114–129

10. Leue, S., Ladkin, P.B.: Implementing and Verifying MSC Specifications Using Promela/XSpin. In Gregoire, J.C., Holzmann, G.J., Peled, D., eds.: Proc. 2nd Int. Wsh. SPIN Verification System (SPIN'96). Volume 32 of Discrete Mathematics and Theoretical Computer Science., American Mathematical Society (1997) 65–89

11. Uchitel, S., Kramer, J., Magee, J.: Incremental Elaboration of Scenario-based Specifications and Behavior Models using Implied Scenarios. ACM Trans. Softw. Eng. Methodol. **13**(1) (2004) 37–85

12. Brill, M., Damm, W., Klose, J., Westphal, B., Wittke, H.: Live Sequence Charts. In Ehrig, H., Damm, W., Desel, J., Große-Rhode, M., Reif, W., Schnieder, E., Westkämper, E., eds.: Integration of Software Specification Techniques for Applications in Engineering. Volume 3147 of Lect. Notes Comp. Sci., Springer (2004) 374–399

13. Baranov, S., Jervis, C., Kotlyarov, V., Letichevsky, A., Weigert, T.: Leveraging UML to Deliver Correct Telecom Applications. In Lavagno, L., Martin, G., Selic, B., eds.: UML for Real. Kluwer (2003) 323–342

14. Schäfer, T., Knapp, A., Merz, S.: Model Checking UML State Machines and Collaborations. In Stoller, S., Visser, W., eds.: Proc. Wsh. Software Model Checking. Volume 55(3) of Elect. Notes Theo. Comp. Sci., Paris (2001) 13 pages.

15. Uchitel, S., Kramer, J., Magee, J.: Synthesis of Behavioral Models from Scenarios. IEEE Trans. Softw. Eng. **29**(2) (2003) 99–115

16. Damm, W., Harel, D.: LSCs: Breathing Life into Message Sequence Charts. Formal Meth. Sys. Design **19**(1) (2001) 45–80

17. Klose, J.: Live Sequence Charts: A Graphical Formalism for the Specification of Communication Behaviour. PhD thesis, Carl von Ossietzky-Universität Oldenburg (2003)

18. Bontemps, Y., Heymans, P.: Turning High-Level Live Sequence Charts into Automata. In: Proc. ICSE Wsh. Scenarios and State-Machines: Models, Algorithms and Tools (SCESM'02), Orlando (2002)

19. Harel, D., Maoz, S.: Assert and Negate Revisited: Modal Semantics for UML Sequence Diagrams. In: Proc. 5th Int. Wsh. Scenarios and State Machines: Models, Algorithms, and Tools (SCESM'06), ACM Press (2006) 13–20

20. Autili, M., Inverardi, P., Pelliccione, P.: A Scenario Based Notation for Specifying Temporal Properties. In: Proc. 5th Int. Wsh. Scenarios and State Machines: Models, Algorithms, and Tools (SCESM'06), ACM Press (2006) 21–27

3rd International Workshop on Metamodels, Schemas, Grammars and Ontologies

Jean-Marie Favre[1], Dragan Gašević[2], Ralf Lämmel[3],
and Andreas Winter[4]

[1] University of Grenoble, France
www-adele.imag.fr/~jmfavre
[2] Simon Fraser University, Surrey, Canada
http://www.sfu.ca/~dgasevic/
[3] Microsoft Corp., Redmond, USA
http://homepages.cwi.nl/~ralf/
[4] Johannes Gutenberg-Universität Mainz, Germany
http://www.gupro.de/~winter/

ateM-Workshop Series

In 2003 the ateM workshop series was established to discuss the use of *Schemas and Metaschemas* in reverse engineering (ateM is Meta reverse). ateM 2003, which was part of the 10th International Conference on Reverse Engineering held in Victoria, Canada, already dealt with *model driven approaches* to support program analysis and comprehension. Since models in reverse engineering mostly deal with documents written in certain programming or modeling languages, the extension of ateM towards grammars was a consistent step. Thus, ateM 2004, held at the 11th International Conference on Reverse Engineering, Delft, The Netherlands, viewed *Metamodels, Schemas and Grammars*. Nowadays model driven approaches are common in software engineering and furthermore, ontologies complement modeling technologies used today. So, the third ateM-workshop, which was part of the 9th International Conference on Model Driven Engineering, Languages and Systems in Genova, Italy, dealt with *Metamodels, Schemas, Grammars and Ontologies*.

The objective of ateM is to bring together researchers from *different communities* to study and compare the use of modeling approaches residing in different *technical spaces*. ateM 2006 is specifically focused on the meta technologies in a generalized sense of discussing the use of *language engineering* by Metamodels, Schemas, Grammars and Ontologies.

This view is generally consistent with model driven engineering (MDE) and modern software reengineering. It is specifically aligned with approaches for language engineering, grammarware engineering, domain specific language engineering, software factories and others. While plain MDE tends to assume that language descriptions are defined from scratch, ateM pays attention to the fact that language descriptions are often buried in software components, e. g. in grammarware such as transformation tools, documentation generators, or front-ends. Accordingly, it is important to better understand all means to continuously recover and describe language descriptions from arbitrary software artifacts.

T. Kühne (Ed.): MoDELS 2006 Workshops, LNCS 4364, pp. 52–55, 2007.
© Springer-Verlag Berlin Heidelberg 2007

ateM 2006: Metamodels, Schemas, Grammars and Ontologies

The language engineering approaches discussed at ateM 2006 addressed the grammar-based technical space (or grammarware, cf. [3]), the model and metamo-del-based technical spaces [1], and the ontology-based technical space [4]. According techniques include the definition and description of progamming- and modeling languages, the recovery of language descriptions as they are in-grained in existing software artifacts, the reuse, integration and transformation of language descriptions, as well as the use of language descriptions in a software reverse engineering and evolution context.

From 30 submitted papers, nine papers were accepted to be presented in Genova. All accepted papers showed important approaches and applications of language engineering by various techniques and led to interesting and fruitfull discussions during the workshop. The papers, not summarized in this proceed-ings, include:

- **Migrating a Domain-Specific Modeling Infrastructure to MDA Technology** by *Duncan Doyle, Hans Geers, Bas Graaf, and Arie van Deursen* explains experiences from migrating proprietary application models in domain specific languages (DSL) into MOF-compliant models.
- **Models for the Reverse Engineering of Java/Swing Applications** by *Joao Carlos Silva, Joao Saraiva, and José Creissac Campos* presents a modelbased approach to evaluate interactive applications.
- **Domain specific modeling, An approach for recovering business critical information** by *Carsten Bock and Detlef Zühlke* presents an ap-proach to integrate software engineering tools in a model driven tool chain.
- **A metamodel independent framework for model transformation: Towards generic model management patterns in reverse engineer-ing** by *Zinovy Diskin and Jürgen Dingel* presents an algebraic framework toward model transformation based on category theory.
- **A Unified Meta-Model for Concept-Based Reverse Engineering** by *Florian Deissenböck and Daniel Ratiu* combines technologies from meta-modeling and ontologies to bridge legacy software artefacts to real-world concepts.
- **Foundations for Defining Software Metrics** by *Rüdiger Lincke and Welf Löwe* shows an generalized approach to define software metrics based on the Dagstuhl-Middle Metamodel (DMM).

The workshop proceedings of the *ACM/IEEE 9th International Conference on Model Driven Engineering, Languages and Systems (MODELS 2006)* contain two extended versions of papers presented at the 3rd International Workshop on Metamodels, Schemas, Grammars and Ontologies:

- *Jürgen Rilling, Yonggang Zhang, Wen Jun Meng, René Witte, Volker Haarslev, and Philippe Charland* show in **A Unified Ontology-Based**

Process Model for Software Maintenance and Comprehension how reasoning techniques based in description logics are applied to analyse various software artefacts.

- *Miguel Garcia* presents in **Formalizing the well-formedness rules of EJB3QL in UML + OCL** experiences on applying class diagrams annotated by OCL constraints to define a metamodel for EJB3QL.

All papers presented at ateM 2006, are published in [2]. The proceedings are online available at http://planetmde.org/atem2006/atem06Proceedings.pdf.

The final discussions at ateM 2006 on the different approaches to define, analyse, and use languages in software (reverse) engineering concluded that currently the technical spaces *Grammarware, (Meta-)modeling,* and *Ontologies* are beneficially applied to various areas. Only little effort has been made to compare and combine these approaches. A general and systematic approach to defining mappings between grammar-based, (meta)model-based, and ontology-based technical spaces is still missing. Further reseach should investigate bridges between these spaces to provide space-spanning modeling techniques in model-driven engineering.

Acknowledgment

We, the organizers, thank the program committee and their coworkers who reviewed the submissions and provided useful feedback to the authors within a very short period of time:

- Jean Bézivin, University of Nantes, France
- Arturo Boronat, Polytechnic University of Valencia, Spain
- Ian Bull, University of Victoria, Canada
- Massimiliano Di Penta, University of Sannio, Italy
- Stéphane Ducasse, University of Berne, Switzerland
- Harald Gall, University of Zurich, Swizerland
- Mike Godfrey, University of Waterloo, Canada
- Jeff Gray, University of Alabama at Birmingham, USA
- Reiko Heckel, University of Leicster, UK
- Jürgen Ebert, University of Koblenz-Landau, Germany
- Elisa Kendall, Sandpiper Software, USA
- Nenad Krdzavac, University of Belgrade, Serbia
- Christoph Ringelstein, University of Koblenz-Landau, Germany
- Steffen Staab, University of Koblenz-Landau, Germany
- York Sure, University of Karlsruhe, Germany
- Jean Vanderdonckt, Université Catholique de Louvain, Belgium
- Arie van Deursen, Delft University of Technology, The Netherlands
- Daniel Varro, Budapest University, Hungary
- Chris Verhoef, Vrije University Amsterdam, The Netherlands

We also thank our authors for their papers and interesting talks, and our participants for intensive and valuable discussions. Our thanks also go to the organizers of MODELS 2006 for accepting ateM 2006 as part of their conference program. Furthermore, we thank our supporters, who helped in advertising and organizing ateM 2006:

- EVOL, the Software Evolution Working Group of ERCIM (European Research Consortium for Informatics and Mathematics)
- planetmde.org, the community web portal on Model Driven Engineering
- SRE, the German GI special interest group on software reengineering
- RIMEL, the French special interest group on Reverse Engineering, Maintenance and Software Evolution.

References

1. J. Bézivin, *On the Unification Power of Models, Software and System Modeling*, 4(2), 171-188, 2005.
2. J.-M. Favre, D. Gasevic, R. Lämmel, A. Winter: *3rd International Workshop on Metamodels, Schemas, Grammars, and Ontologies (ateM 2006) for Reverse Engineering*, Technical Report, Informatik Bericht 1/2006, Johannes Gutenberg-Universität Mainz, October 2006 (http://www.informatik.uni-mainz.de/370.php).
3. P. Klint, R. Lämmel, C. Verhoef, *Toward an engineering discipline for grammarware*, ACM Transactions on Software Engineering Methodology, 14(3), 331-380, 2005.
4. S. Staab, R. Studer, *Handbook on Ontologies*. Springer:Berlin, 2003.

A Unified Ontology-Based Process Model for Software Maintenance and Comprehension

Juergen Rilling[1], Yonggang Zhang[1], Wen Jun Meng[1], René Witte[1],
Volker Haarslev[1], and Philippe Charland[2]

[1] Department of Computer Science
and Software Engineering
Concordia University, Montreal, Canada
{rilling,yongg_zh,w_meng,rwitte,haarslev}@cse.concordia.ca
[2] System of Systems Section
Defence R&D Canada Valcartier,
Val-Bélair, Canada
philippe.charland@drdc-rddc.gc.ca

Abstract. In this paper, we present a formal process model to support the comprehension and maintenance of software systems. The model provides a formal ontological representation that supports the use of reasoning services across different knowledge resources. In the presented approach, we employ our Description Logic knowledge base to support the maintenance process management, as well as detailed analyses among resources, e.g., the traceability between various software artifacts. The resulting unified process model provides users with active guidance in selecting and utilizing these resources that are context-sensitive to a particular comprehension task. We illustrate both, the technical foundation based on our existing SOUND environment, as well as the general objectives and goals of our process model.

Keywords: Software maintenance, process modeling, ontological reasoning, software comprehension, traceability, text mining.

1 Introduction and Motivation

Software maintenance is a multi-dimensional problem space that creates an ongoing challenge for both the research community and tool developers. These maintenance challenges are caused in particular by the variations and interrelationships among software artifacts, knowledge resources, and maintenance tasks [3,20,22]. Existing solutions [10,20] that address aspects of these challenges are commonly not integrated with each other, due to a lack of integration standards or difficulties to share services and/or knowledge among them. The situation is further complicated by the non-existence of formal process models to create a representation that describes the interactions and relationships among these artifacts and resources.

There has been little work in examining how these resources work together for end users [13,20] and how they can collaboratively support a specific program maintenance task. Maintainers are often left with no guidance on how to complete a particular task

T. Kühne (Ed.): MoDELS 2006 Workshops, LNCS 4364, pp. 56–65, 2007.

within a given context. Our research addresses this lack of context sensitivity by introducing a formal process model that stresses an active approach to guide software maintainers during maintenance tasks. The process model, its basic elements and their major inter-relations are all formally modeled by an ontology based on Description Logic (DL) [2]. The process behavior is modeled by an interactive process metaphor. Our approach differs from existing work on comprehension models [3], tool integration [11, 20] and task-specific process models [8,19,20] in several aspects:

1. A formal software maintenance process model based on an ontological representation to integrate different knowledge resources and artifacts.
2. An open environment to support the introduction of new concepts and their relationships, as well as enriching the existing ontology with newly gained knowledge or resources.
3. The ability to reason about information in the ontological representation to allow for an active and context-sensitive guidance during the maintenance process.
4. Analysis of relationships among resources, e.g., the traceability between artifacts.

The process model itself is motivated by approaches used in other application domains, like Internet search engines (e.g., Google[1]) or online shopping sites (e.g., Amazon[2]). Common to these applications is that they utilize different information resources to provide an active, typically context-sensitive user feedback that identifies resources and information relevant to a user's specific needs. The challenge in applying similar models in software maintenance goes beyond the synthesis of information and knowledge resources. There is a need to provide a formal meta-model to enable reasoning about the potential steps and resources involved in a maintenance process.

For example, a maintainer, while performing a comprehension task, often utilizes and interacts with various tools (parsers, debuggers, source code analyzers, etc.). These tool interactions are a result of both, the interrelationships among artifacts required/delivered by these tools and the specific techniques needed to complete a particular task. Identifying these often transitive relationships among information resources becomes a major challenge. Within our approach, we support automated reasoning across these different information resources (e.g., domain knowledge, documents, user expertise, software, etc.) to resolve transitive relationships. Furthermore, our model can be applied to analyze and re-establish traceability links among the various resources in the knowledge base [1].

From a more pragmatic viewpoint, process models have to be able to adapt to ever changing environments and information resources to be used as part of the process itself. In our approach, we address this problem by providing a uniform ontological representation that can be both extended and enriched to represent any newly gained knowledge or change in the information resource(s). This knowledge will also become an integrated part of the process that can be further utilized and reasoned on.

The remainder of the article is organized as follows. The relevant research background is introduced in Section 2. Section 3 describes in detail the context-driven program comprehension process model, followed in Section 4 by its implementation and validation. Discussions and future work are presented in Section 5.

---

[1] www.google.com
[2] www.amazon.com

2 Background

Historically, software lifecycle models and processes have focused on the software development cycle. However, with much of a system's operational lifetime cost occurring during the maintenance phase, this should be reflected in both the development practices and process models supporting maintenance activities. It is generally accepted that even for more specific maintenance task instances (e.g., program comprehension, architectural recovery), a fully-automated process is not feasible [11]. Furthermore, existing models share the following common challenges:

- Existing knowledge resources (e.g., user expertise, source code artifacts, tools) are used to construct mental models. However, without a formal representation, these process models lack uniform resource integration and the ability to infer additional knowledge.
- Limited knowledge management that allows the extension and integration of newly gained resource and knowledge.
- These models provide typically only general descriptions of the steps involved in a process and lack guidelines on how to complete these steps within a given context (concrete software maintenance task and available knowledge resources).

In our approach, we provide a formal representation that integrates these information resources and allows reasoning and knowledge management across them. Furthermore, we address the issue of context-sensitive support, i.e., providing the maintainer with guidance on the use of the different information resources while accomplishing a particular task.

Research in cognitive science suggests that mental models may take many forms, but the content normally constitutes an ontology [8]. Ontologies are often used as a formal, explicit way of specifying the concepts and relationships in a domain of understanding [2]. They are typically specified using the standard ontology language, Description Logics (DL), as a knowledge representation formalism.

DL is also a major foundation of the recently introduced Web Ontology Language (OWL) recommended by the W3C[3]. DL represents domain knowledge by first defining relevant concepts (sometimes called classes or TBox) of the domain and then using these concepts to specify properties of individuals (also called instances or ABox) occurring in the domain. Basic elements of DL are atomic concepts and atomic roles, which correspond to unary predicates and binary predicates in First Order Logic. Complex concepts are then defined by combining basic elements with several concept constructors.

Having DL as the specification language for a formal ontology enables the use of reasoning services provided by DL-based knowledge representation systems. The Racer system [7] is an ontology reasoner that has been highly optimized to support very expressive DLs. Typical services provided by Racer include terminology inferences (e.g., concept consistency, subsumption, classification, and ontology consistency) and instances reasoning (e.g., instance checking, instance retrieval, tuple retrieval, and instance realization). For a more detailed coverage of DLs and Racer, we refer the reader to [2,7].

---

[3] Available online at http://www.w3.org/TR/owl-ref

3   Modeling a Software Maintenance Process

A model is essentially an abstraction of a real and conceptually complex system that is designed to display significant features and characteristics of the system, which one wishes to study, predict, modify or control [13]. In our approach, the software maintenance process model is a formal description that represents the relevant information resources and their interactions (Fig 1).

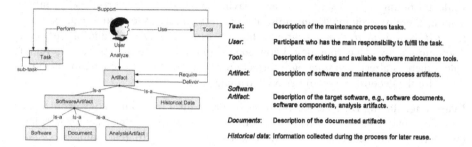

Fig. 1. Comprehension Process Meta-Model

In what follows, we describe in general: (1) the ontological representation used to model the information resources, (2) the ontology population and traceability among ontologies, and (3) the maintenance process and its management.

3.1   An Ontological Software Maintenance Process Model

Through the use of ontologies and DL, we formally model the major information resources used in software maintenance. The benefits of using a DL-based ontology as a means to model the structure of our process model are as follows:

Knowledge acquisition and management. As mentioned previously, program comprehension is a multifaceted and dynamic activity involving different resources to enhance the current knowledge about a system. Consequently, any comprehension process model has to reflect and model both the knowledge acquisition and use of the newly gained knowledge. The ontological representation provides us with the ability to add newly learned concepts and relationships, as well as new instances of these to the ontological representation. This extendibility enables our process model not only to be constructed in an incremental way, but also to reflect more closely the iterative knowledge acquisition behavior used to create a mental model as part of human cognition of a software system [3,8]. It is not realistic to expect all these sources to share a single, consistent view within a comprehension task. Rather, we expect disagreements between individual users and tools during an analysis. In our approach, we explicitly model those different views using a representational model that attributes information to (nested) contexts using so-called *viewpoints*.

An elegant model for managing (possibly conflicting) information from different sources has been proposed by [18]: Knowledge is structured into *viewpoints* and *topics*. Viewpoints are environments that represent a particular point of view (e.g.,information stemming from a particular *tool* or entered by a *user*). Topics are environments that contain knowledge that is relevant to a given subject (e.g., design patterns, architectural recovery). These environments are *nested* within each other: viewpoints can contain either other viewpoints or topics. A topic can contain knowledge pertaining to its subject, but also other viewpoints, e.g., when the subject is another user. These viewpoints create *spaces* that allow consistency to be maintained within a topic or a viewpoint, but at the same time, conflicting information about the same topic can be stored in another viewpoint. Therefore, knowledge can be collected while attributing it to its source, without having to decide on a "correct" set of information, thereby avoiding losing information prematurely. Viewpoints can be *constructed* as well as *destructed* through the processes of *ascription* and *percolation*. Ascription allows incorporating knowledge from other viewpoints (users, tools) unless there is already conflicting information on the same topic. Percolation is introduced for the deconstruction of nested knowledge.

Reasoning. Having DL as a specification language for a formal ontology enables the use of reasoning services provided by DL-based knowledge representation systems, by inferring knowledge through transitive closure across different ontologies. The DL-based ontology and reasoning services form the basis for both, the knowledge integration and retrieval used in our process model.

Building a formal ontology for software maintenance requires an analysis of the concepts and relations of the discourse domain. In particular, the outlined process model must be supported by the structure and content of the ontological knowledge base. Our approach here is twofold: We (1) created sub-ontologies for each of the discourse domains, like tasks, software, documents, and tools (Fig. 1); and (2) link them via a number of shared high-level concepts, like *artifact, task, or tool*, which have been modeled akin to a (simple) upper level ontology [16].

Having different knowledge resources modeled as ontologies allows us to link instances from these knowledge resources using existing approaches from the field of ontology alignment [17]. Ontology alignment techniques try to align ontological information from different sources on conceptual and/or instance levels. Since our subontologies share many concepts from the programming language domain, such as Class or Method, the problem of conceptual alignment has been minimized. This research therefore focuses more on matching instances that have been discovered both from source code analysis and text mining.

3.2 Ontological Representation for Software Artifacts

Software artifacts such as source code and documentation typically contain rich structural and semantic information. Providing uniform ontological representations for various software artifacts enables us to utilize semantic information conveyed by them and to establish their traceability links at a semantic level (Fig. 2b). In this section, we introduce our SOUND program comprehension environment [22], which was developed to establish the technical foundation for our ontological software maintenance process model.

The SOUND environment facilitates software maintainers in both discovering (new) concepts and relations within a software system, as well as automatically inferring implicit relations among different artifacts (Fig. 2a and 2b).

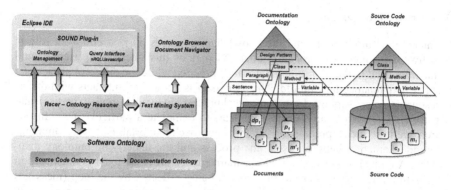

Fig. 2a. Overview of SOUND Environment   **Fig. 2b.** Linking Code and Documentation

Instances of concepts and roles in the software ontology can be populated by either our Eclipse plug-in or text mining system. The discovered instances from different sources can be automatically linked through ontology alignment [17]. Based on the software ontology, users can define new concepts/instances for particular software maintenance tasks through an ontology management interface. Text Mining (TM) is commonly known as a knowledge discovery process that aims to extract non-trivial information or knowledge from unstructured text. Unlike Information Retrieval (IR) systems, TM does not simply return documents pertaining to a query, but rather attempts to obtain semantic information from the documents themselves, using techniques from Natural Language Processing (NLP).We implemented our TM subsystem based on the GATE (General Architecture for Text Engineering) framework [4], one of the most widely used NLP tools [22].

The ontological reasoning services within the SOUND environment are provided by the ontology reasoner, Racer [7]. Racer's query language nRQL can be used to retrieve instances of concepts and roles in the ontology. An nRQL query uses arbitrary concept names and role names in the ontology to specify properties of the result. In a query, variables can be used to store instances that satisfy it. However, the use of nRQL queries is still largely restricted to users with a good mathematical/logical background due to nRQL's syntax, which, although comparatively straightforward, is still difficult for programmers to understand and apply. To bridge this conceptual gap between practitioners and Racer, we have introduced a set of built-in functions and classes in the JavaScript interpreter, Rhino[4], to simplify querying the ontology for users. The scriptable query language allows users to benefit from both the declarative semantics of Description Logics as well as the fine-grained control abilities of procedural languages.

In our previous work, we have already demonstrated an ontological model of source code and documentation supporting various reverse engineering tasks, such as program comprehension, architectural analysis, security analysis and traceability links [22]. We currently investigate its integration with work examining the requirements for software reverse engineering repositories [15] that deals with incomplete and inconsistent knowledge on software artifacts obtained from different sources (e.g., conflicting information delivered by source code and document analysis).

---

[4] Available online at http://www.mozilla.org/rhino/

3.3 Process Management

The interaction among users and the knowledge resources plays a dominant role in any software maintenance process model. As part of this interaction, users should become immersed in the program maintenance process, while the different phases of a particular maintenance task unfold. The user itself is active and interacts with different resources (e.g., support from tools, techniques, documents and expertise) and other users (e.g., system or historic user data) to complete a particular task. In this research, we introduce a process management approach that establishes the communication and interaction between users, the process and the underlying ontology manager [15]. A typical usage scenario of our maintenance process model is illustrated in Fig. 3. with the iterative nature of the process being reflected by the loop (messages 2-22). A user is completing a comprehension task and the process manager, ontology manager, reasoner and available resources are all working together to assist the user during the different phases of the software maintenance process.

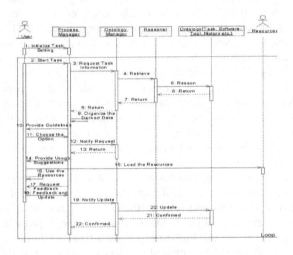

Fig. 3. Process Sequence Diagram

After each iteration, users will provide feedback and annotate briefly their experience with the resources and their success towards problem solving (Messages 18-22). The resulting feedback is used to further enrich the historical data stored in the ontology, as well as trigger the next step in the maintenance process.

In this research, we introduce an iterative process management approach that guides the communication and interaction between users, the process and the underlying ontology manager. A user is completing a comprehension task and the process manager, ontology manager, reasoner and available resources are all working together to assist the user during the different phases of the software maintenance process.

After each iteration, users will provide feedback and annotate briefly their experience with the resources and their success towards problem solving. The resulting feedback is used to further enrich the historical data stored in the ontology, as well as trigger the next step in the maintenance process. A more detailed description of the process manger can be found in [15].

4 System Implementation and Evaluation

In this section, we provide a general system overview of the implementation of our process model and a general overview of the ontological implementation used to model the knowledge base.

4.1 System Overview

The process itself is based on two main components, the process and the ontology manager.

Ontology Manager is used to manage the infrastructure of the process model, where the basic elements of the program comprehension process and their inter-relationships are formally represented by DL-based ontology. Our approach supports the addition of new concepts and their relations in a given sub-ontology, coordinates the reasoner with the ontologies, and controls querying and reasoning services across the sub-ontologies. A user can perform both pre-defined and user-defined queries. The ontology manager is an extension to our SOUND tool [22], an Eclipse plug-in that provides both ontology management (software ontology and document ontology have been developed) and inferences service integration using the Racer [7] reasoner. So far, the ontology management interface provides the following services: adding/defining new concepts/relationships, specifying instances, browsing the ontology, and a Java Script based query interface.

Process Manager is built on top of the ontology manager and provides users with both the context and the interactive guidance during the comprehension process. The process context is established by the process manager, depending on the user process interactions, the current state of the knowledge base and the resulting information inferred by the reasoner. For interactive guidance, the process manager utilizes different visual metaphors to establish a representation that allows users to immerse in the process context and, at the same time, provides an approach to analyze and utilize the inferred knowledge to provide guidance during the comprehension process itself.

4.2 Initial Evaluation

At the current stage, we have successfully implemented and used our SOUND ontology management and query tool to perform comprehension tasks such as impact analysis, design pattern recovery, and component identification [9]. In addition, we have defined an initial set of concepts and relations for the remaining sub-ontologies as the foundation for our process model. A more detailed description of the ontology implementation can be found in [15].

A set of frequently used queries has been defined in the system, e.g., identifying the coupling among classes, recovering the design pattern in a system. We are currently in the process of conducting a larger case study in collaboration with Defence Research and Development Canada (DRDC) Valcartier to explore and validate the applicability of our software maintenance process model. The system used for the case study is an open source software for the analysis and reporting of maritime exercises – Debrief [5]. As part of the ongoing Debrief case study, we are performing a specific component substitution task, in which a non-secure file access will be substituted by a client specific encrypted version. Feedback from the process and information resource usage will be collected for further refinement and enrichment of both the process model and the knowledge base.

5 Related Work

There exists only very limited research in applying Description Logics or formal ontologies in software engineering. The two major projects that are closely related to our ontological approach are the LaSSIE [6] and CBMS [21] systems. However, these systems are much more restricted by the expressiveness of their underlying ontology languages and they lack the support for an optimized DL reasoner, such as Racer in our case.

Current research in modeling software maintenance processes [10,19,20] typically describe only very generally the process and lack formal representations. Thus, they are unable to utilize any type of reasoning services across the different knowledge sources involved in the comprehension process. To the best of our knowledge, there exists no previous work that focuses on developing a formal process model to describe the program comprehension process.

Existing work on comprehension tool integration focuses either on data interoperability using a common data exchange format [20] or on service integration among different reverse engineering and software comprehension tools [11]. Our approach can be seen complementary to these ongoing tool integration efforts. Improving the overall capabilities and applicability of reverse engineering tools will help to enrich our tool ontology and therefore, directly/indirectly benefit the comprehension process model. However, our approach goes beyond just mere tool integration. It is the formal ontological representation that supports both reasoning across different knowledge sources (including tools) and context support during the comprehension process itself. Furthermore, our approach provides flexibility and extensibility required to support the evolution of the process model itself.

6 Conclusions

Our work promotes the use of both formal ontology and automated reasoning in software maintenance research, by providing a DL-based formal and uniform ontological representation of different information resources involved in a typical software maintenance process.

As part of our future work, we will conduct several case studies to enrich our current ontology and optimize the software maintenance process model for different maintenance tasks. We are currently in the process of developing a new visual process metaphor to improve the context-sensitive guidance during typical maintenance tasks.

Acknowledgement. This research was partially funded by Defence Research and Development Canada (DRDC) Valcartier (contract no. W7701-052936/001/QCL).

References

1. G. Antoniol, G. Canfora, G. Casazza, and A. De Lucia, "Information retrieval models for recovering traceability links between code and documentation". In Proceedings of IEEE International Conference on Software Maintenance, San Jose, CA, 2000.
2. F.Baader, D. Calvanese, D. McGuinness, D.Nardi, P.P.-Schneider, "The Description Logic Handbook". Cambridge University Press, 2003.
3. R. Brooks, "Towards a Theory of the Comprehension of Computer Programs". Int. J. of Man-Machine Studies, pp. 543-554, 1963.
4. H. Cunningham, D. Maynard, K. Bontcheva, V. Tablan. "GATE: A Framework and Graphical Development Environment for Robust NLP Tools and Applications." Proceedings of the 40th Anniversary Meeting of the ACL (ACL'02). Philadelphia, July 2002.
5. Debrief, www.debrief.info, last accessed 25/10/2006.
6. P.Devanbu, R.J.Brachman, P.G.Selfridge, and B.W.Ballard, "LaSSIE: a Knowledge-based Software Information System", Com. of the ACM, 34(5):36–49, 1991.
7. V. Haarslev and R. Möller, "RACER System Description", In Proc. of International Joint Conference on Automated Reasoning, IJCAR'2001, Italy, Springer-Verlag, pp. 701-705.
8. P. N. Johnson-Laird, "Mental Models: Towards a Cognitive Science of Language, Inference and Consciousness". Harvard University, Cambridge, Mass., 1983.
9. A. V. Mayhauser, A. M. Vans, "Program Comprehension During Software Maintenance and Evolution". IEEE Computer, pp. 44-55, Aug.,1995.
10. IEEE Standard for Software Maintenance, IEEE 1219-1998.
11. D. Jin and J. R. Cordy. "Ontology-Based Software Analysis and Reengineering Tool Integration: The OASIS Service-Sharing Methodology". 21st IEEE ICSM, 2005.
12. P. N. Johnson-Laird, "Mental Models: Towards a Cognitive Science of Language, Inference and Consciousness". Harvard University, Cambridge, Mass., 1983.
13. M. I. Keller, R. J. Madachy, and D. M.Raffo, "Software Process Simulation Modeling: Why? What? How?". Journal of Systems and Software, Vol.46, No.2/3, 1999.
14. U. Kölsch and R. Witte, "Fuzzy Extensions for Reverse Engineering Repository Models". 10th Working Conference on Reverse Engineering (WCRE), Canada, 2003.
15. W. Meng, J. Rilling, Y. Zhang, R. Witte, P. Charland, "An Ontological Software Comprehension Process Model", 3rd Int. Workshop on Metamodels, Schemas, Grammars, and Ontologies for Reverse Engineering (ATEM 2006), Genoa, October 1st, 2006, pp. 28-35.
16. Niles and A. Pease. "Towards a Standard Upper Ontology". Proc. of the 2nd Int. Conf. on Formal Ontology in Information System (FOIS), Maine, 2001.
17. N. F. Noy and H. Stuckenschmidt, "Ontology Alignment: An annotated Bibliography – Semantic Interoperability and Integration" Schloss Dagstuhl, Germany, 2005.
18. A. Ballim, Wilks, "Artificial Believers: The Ascription of Belief",Lawrence Erlbaum,1991.
19. C. Riva, "Reverse Architecting:An Industrial Experience Report", 7th IEEE WCRE, pp.42-52, 2000.
20. M. -A. Storey, S. E. Sim, K. Wong, "A Collaborative Demonstration of Reverse Engineering tools", ACM SIGAPP Applied Computing Review, Vol. 10(1), pp18-25, 2002.
21. C.Welty, "Augmenting Abstract Syntax Trees for Program Understanding", Proc. of Int. Conf. on Automated Software Engineering. IEEE Computer Soc .Press. 1997, pp. 126-133.
22. Y. Zhang, R. Witte, J. Rilling, V. Haarslev, "An Ontology-based Approach for Traceability Recovery", 3rd International Workshop on Metamodels, Schemas, Grammars, and Ontologies for Reverse Engineering (ATEM 2006), Genoa, October 1st, 2006, pp. 36-43.

Formalizing the Well-Formedness Rules of EJB3QL in UML + OCL

Miguel Garcia

Hamburg University of Technology, Hamburg 21073, Germany
miguel.garcia@tuhh.de
http://www.sts.tu-harburg.de/~mi.garcia/

Abstract. This paper reports the application of language metamodeling techniques to EJB3QL, the object-oriented query language for Java Persistence recently standardized in JSR-220. Five years from now, today's EJB3 applications will be legacy. We see our metamodel as an enabler for increasing the efficiency of reverse engineering activities. It has already proven useful in uncovering spots where the EJB3QL spec is vague. The case study reported in this paper involved (a) expressing the abstract syntax and well-formedness rules of EJB3QL in UML and OCL respectively; (b) deriving from that metamodel software artifacts required for several language-processing tasks, targeting two modeling platforms (Eclipse EMF and Octopus); and (c) comparing the generated artifacts with their counterparts in the reference implementation of EJB3 (which was not developed following a language-metamodeling approach). The metamodel of EJB3QL constitutes the basis for applying model-checkers to aid in assuring conformance of tools claiming to support the specification.

Keywords: Metamodel, OCL, Static semantics, EJB3QL.

1 Introduction

Language Engineering [1] is an increasingly important area which leverages basic results from Computer Science and a variety of tools developed over the years. Its main goals are (a) simplifying the generation of language processing tools and environments, as well as (b) offering guarantees about their conformance and interoperability. Progress around the first category (productivity) has benefited software practitioners facing the task of developing tooling for domain-specific languages in a cost-effective manner. The second category (correctness) has received less attention overall. Our findings confirm that metamodel-based language specifications are well-suited for both the "productivity" and the "correctness" categories.

Concrete examples of features under the "productivity" category include syntax-aware editors, support for visual syntax (either for editing or visualization only), and integrated software repositories (cross-artifact detection of inconsistencies, metrics). Support under the "correctness" category includes the model-checking of language processing algorithms to offer guarantees about the

T. Kühne (Ed.): MoDELS 2006 Workshops, LNCS 4364, pp. 66–75, 2007.

transformations they realize. Two basic desirable guarantees are: (a) that all output sentences belong to the target language [2], and (b) that the transformation function covers the whole input language for which it was designed [3]. Experience with current model-driven tooling shows that these basic requirements are not always met. Beyond these general requirements, guarantees specific to a transformation are also desirable. For example, that an optimized implementation outputs the same result as the non-optimized version.

The structure of this paper is as follows. Sec. 2 presents motivational examples of well-formedness rules and their formulation in the metamodel of EJB3QL. Sec. 3 discusses the impact of language metamodeling techniques on the consistency and completeness of a language specification. Sec. 4 summarizes places where the JSR-220 EJB3QL spec was found to be incomplete or imprecise. Sec. 5 is devoted mostly to tooling, explaining how to integrate in language processing tools the software artifacts generated from metamodels. Sec. 6 discusses related work, with Sec. 7 offering conclusions and possibilities for further work.

This paper assumes knowledge from the reader about object-oriented modeling and database query languages. The software artifacts developed as part of this case study are available for download from [16].

2   Reverse Engineering the EJB3QL Spec: How and Why

The EJB3QL spec includes an EBNF grammar which, as usual, cannot capture all the constraints for the static semantics (also called well-formedness rules, WFRs) of the language being defined. The lack of a machine-processable specification of all relevant WFRs leaves open the possibility of non-interoperable implementations of the semantic analysis component in language processing tools.

As a simple example of one such check, JSR-220 requires *"Entity names are scoped within the persistence unit and must be unique within the persistence unit."* (Sec. 4.3.1). The OCL formulation is as follows:

```
context PersistenceUnit
   inv WFR_4_3_1 :  self.entities ->isUnique(name)
```

Beyond the productivity gain (once expressed in OCL, Java code to evaluate it can be generated automatically), the fact that this check is specified declaratively instead of implemented procedurally makes the resulting artifacts amenable to formal verification.

The argument can be made that even if abstract syntax is expressed as a UML+OCL metamodel, an EBNF grammar is still required to specify a concrete textual syntax. Proposals exist [4,5] to decorate an object-oriented language description with annotations to specify concrete syntax by choosing among a fixed palette of alternatives (e.g. to indicate whether an operator is prefix or infix). A further use for such information is the generation of an unparser. Additionally, if a representation of the metamodel is available at runtime, the implementation of syntax-sensitive features (e.g. content assist) is made simpler.

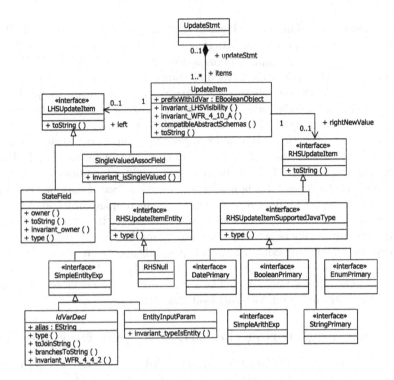

Fig. 1. Metamodel fragment for the UPDATE statement

3   Consistency and Completeness Enforced by Language Metamodeling

Expressing the structure and WFRs of a language as a UML+OCL metamodel forces the specification authors to consider corner cases that may be easily overlooked otherwise. While encoding in OCL the WFRs around type compatibility for comparison and for assignment expressions, we noticed that the spec is not clear about which combinations of (LHS type, RHS type) are valid in assignments (as part of the UPDATE statement), in case persistent entity types are involved. The spec is silent about whether assigning a B-typed value to a field with declared type A (where B is a subtype of A) is standard across implementations, implementation-dependent, or disallowed. Portability warnings for such cases are encoded in our metamodel as OCL invariants. The names of the invariants have been chosen to allow for easy cross-referencing with the spec, each such name starts with "WFR_" followed by the section number where the spec introduces the constraint. For example, *"State-fields that are mapped in serialized form or as LOBs may not be portably used in conditional expressions"* (Sec. 4.6 of the spec) can be found by searching for PORTABILITY_4_6. This section discusses in more detail our observations around the UPDATE statement.

Following the grammar in the spec, our metamodel allows an UPDATE statement to own one or more UpdateItem, each representing a LHS := RHS. All constructs that are allowed on the LHS support the UML interface LHSUpdateItem, similarly for those on the right hand side (Figure 1). For comparison, the EBNF counterpart is reproduced in Table 1.

Notice that all shared properties of alternatives in a production rule can be factored out into the interface that covers them. In the UPDATE example, all constructs (and only those) on the RHS that may evaluate to a primitive type conform to the interface RHSUpdateItemSupportedJavaType. In general, interfaces allow an OCL expression to abstract away from sub-cases.

Table 1. EBNF fragment for the UPDATE statement

```
update_statement ::= update_clause [where_clause]
update_clause ::=
  UPDATE abstract_schema_name [[AS] identification_variable]
  SET update_item {, update_item}*
update_item ::=
  [identification_variable.]
  {state_field | single_valued_association_field } = new_value
new_value ::=
  simple_arithmetic_expression |
  string_primary |
  datetime_primary |
  boolean_primary |
  enum_primary
  simple_entity_expression  |
  NULL
```

Sec. 4 10 of the spec deals with assignments involving primitive types only: *"The new_value specified for an update operation must be compatible in type with the state-field to which it is assigned."* The WFR for type compatibility for comparison (not assignment) between entities establishes: *"Two entities of the same abstract schema type are equal if and only if they have the same primary key value."* (Sec. 4.12).

Making explicit the underspecified assignment case is forced upon us by OCL type checking. It all starts when we consider the two sub-cases for a LHS: interface LHSUpdateItem is realized by classes StateField and by SingleValuedAssocField only (our metamodel faithfully enforces the partition semantics: the sub-cases cover completely and are disjoint with each other).

Listing 1.1 reproduces the OCL if-statement that specifies the compatibility condition for the primitive-types case (the then-branch) as well as the entity-types case (the else-branch). The else-branch in turn has to consider again the two partitioning sub-cases of the RHS: primitive or entity. The first case prompts returning false (the types are not assignment-compatible). The second case embodies a conservative approach: only assignments of entities of exactly the same declared type are allowed, for lack of additional assurance from the specification. This can be revised as the spec is updated.

Listing 1.1. OCL encoding of type compatibility for assignments in an UpdateItem

```
--  "The  new_value  specified  for  an  update  operation  must  be
--  compatible  in  type  with  the  state-field  to  which
--  it  is  assigned"
context UpdateItem
inv WFR_4_10_A :
if left.oclIsKindOf(ejb3qlmm::pathExp::StateField)
  then
      -- LHS is typed with SupportedJavaType
      if not rightNewValue.oclIsKindOf(
        ejb3qlmm::stmts::RHSUpdateItemSupportedJavaType)
      then false
      else let
      t1 : ejb3qlmm::schema::SupportedJavaType
        = left.oclAsType(ejb3qlmm::pathExp::StateField)
          .type(),
    -- RHS is either SimpleArithExp, StringPrimary,
    -- BooleanPrimary, DatePrimary, or EnumPrimary
      t2 : ejb3qlmm::schema::SupportedJavaType
        = rightNewValue.oclAsType(
          ejb3qlmm::stmts::RHSUpdateItemSupportedJavaType)
          .type()
      in ejb3qlmm::schema::SupportedJavaType::
            areTypeCompatible(t1, t2)
    endif
  else
      -- LHS is typed with AbstractSchema
      if not rightNewValue.oclIsKindOf(
            ejb3qlmm::stmts::RHSUpdateItemEntity)
      then false
      else let
        t1 : AbstractSchema = left.oclAsType(
            ejb3qlmm::schema::SingleValuedAssocField).type,
    -- RHS is either RHSNull, IdVarDecl, or EntityInputParam
        t2 : AbstractSchema = rightNewValue.oclAsType(
          ejb3qlmm::stmts::RHSUpdateItemEntity).type()
      in t1 = t2 -- TODO spec incomplete.
              -- What about inheritance?
    endif
endif
```

The metamodeling approach allows expressing "details" which are taken for granted as unstated assumptions in most language specs. Continuing with the example of UpdateItem, it can be made explicit that the fields being assigned are actually visible (declared or inherited) at the type of the entity being updated:

```
context UpdateItem
  inv LHSVisibility :
    self.updateStmt.fromClause.type().isVisible(self.left)
```

4   Selected Examples of Additional Corner Cases

Just like in SQL, queries and subqueries may declare one or more identification variables in a FROM clause. The SELECT, WHERE, GROUP BY, and HAVING clauses may then refer to these variables. In case subqueries are present, the spec is not clear about how to interpret a nested variable declaration with the same name as a declaration in the outer scope. Is it disallowed or does it hide the outer declaration? For example:

```
SELECT c
FROM Customer c
WHERE c.balanceOwed
      < ( SELECT avg(c.balanceOwed)
          FROM Customer c )
```

Our interpretation of the scope rules (Sec. 4.4.2 and 4.6.2 of the spec) can be summarized as follows: A FROM clause (and other constructs) introduces a new scope for identification variables. Scopes may be nested forming a tree hierarchy, with (new) variables declared in an inner scope hiding those with the same name in surrounding scopes. To confirm whether ORM (Object-Relational Mapping) engines conforming to the JSR-220 spec follow this interpretion, EJB3QL queries involving variable hiding were translated to SQL with two different engines. The resulting SQL exhibits variable hiding by explicitly renaming the declaration and usages of the inner variables.

In terms of our metamodel, we check in each query (including subqueries) whether all usages of variables refer to variables which are visible:

Listing 1.2. Declarations-before-usages for a SelectStmt

```
context SelectStmt
  inv WFR_4_6_2_A :
    ( not self.whereClause->isEmpty()
      implies
      self.whereClause.areAllReferredVarsVisible (
        self.locallyDeclaredIdVars() )
    ) and (
      not self.havingClause->isEmpty()
      implies
      self.havingClause.areAllReferredVarsVisible (
        self.locallyDeclaredIdVars() )
    )
```

The argument received by function areAllReferredVarsVisible() is a set containing the declarations of visible variables. The recursive nature of the check performed by areAllReferredVarsVisible() can be seen at work for a subquery. The overriding OCL defintion is shown in Listing 1.3. Before checking whether its WHERE and HAVING clauses (if any) fulfill the declares-before-usages constraint, the scope is augmented with the locally declared variables by using the OCL union() operator:

Listing 1.3. Declarations-before-usages for a subquery

```
context Subquery :: areAllReferredVarsVisible ( varsInScope :
    Set(ejb3qlmm :: idVarDecl :: IdVarDecl) )  :  Boolean
 body  :
  (    not  self . whereClause ->isEmpty ()
    implies
      self . whereClause . areAllReferredVarsVisible (
        varsInScope ->union ( self . locallyDeclaredIdVars ()))
  ) and (
      not  self . havingClause ->isEmpty ()
    implies
      self . havingClause . areAllReferredVarsVisible (
        varsInScope ->union ( self . locallyDeclaredIdVars ()))
  )
```

5   Integrating the Artifacts Generated from the Language Metamodel in a Software Project

After the EJB3QL metamodel passed the validation checks enforced by Octopus [6], artifacts were generated for use as building blocks in a larger toolset. These artifacts are available for download from [16]:

1. An in-house developed extension to Octopus was used to generate an AST library in Java. Our extension generates Java 5 code (using generics, enums) by building upon Octopus' approach to compiling OCL expressions into Java statements.
2. In another project, an Eclipse plugin was developed to translate a valid UML+OCL specification from Octopus into its EMF counterpart, by generating a human-readable Emfatic document [7] with annotations containing OCL expressions for interpretation at runtime [8]. In anticipation of this step, our metamodel was prepared using only those constructs of UML 1.4 amenable for translation into EMF.
3. The evaluation of OCL invariants takes place for individual ASTs which are built either programmatically or by means of a GUI. The GUI was generated by EMF and consists of a tree editor with property sheets. A console allows typing ad-hoc OCL queries for direct evaluation on selected elements. This prototype provided early feedback on visual AST construction.

6   Related Work

The (automatic) conversion of an EBNF-based language description into a meta-model based one (e.g. MOF-based) has been addressed before [9]. The resulting metamodel lacks WFRs which were not present in the grammar in the first place. These constraints can be added manually, with OO generalization and namespace mechanisms allowing for compact expressions.

Language metamodels based on UML+OCL ease the task of integrating different kinds of software artifacts in a single software repository, offering advantages over manipulating a subset of the artifacts that should remain inter-consistent (language schemas [10] have been used for this before). For example, a repository may warn about EJB3QL queries requiring full table scans, resulting from Cartesian products where the fields involved in the selection condition are not indexed. Finding such queries involves access to both a representation of the database physical schema and to the ASTs of the EJB3QL queries. Software repositories allowing querying with OCL have been reported [11].

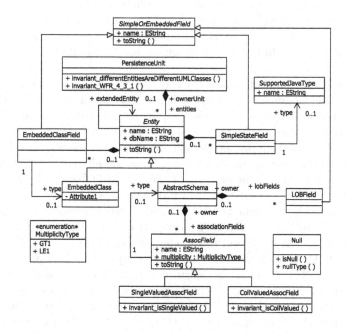

Fig. 2. Logical database schemas for EJB3QL are instantiations of this metamodel

An interesting issue around translating OCL queries into their EJB3QL realization is the adjustment to a similar but not identical type system (that for EJB3QL is depicted in Figure 2). This transformation surfaces in the context of the refinement of a Platform Independent Model (PIM) to a Platform Specific Model (PSM), in our case to Java Enterprise Edition, including EJB3QL.

One such adjustment has to do with the data modeling capabilities of PIM and PSM. For example, a UML+OCL (platform-independent) model abstracts the realization mechanism for {ordered} association ends. A particular PIM to PSM refinement will choose one of several mapping patterns to realize the {ordered} feature (involving at least an additional column, possibly additional tables). As a result, the automatic translation to EJB3QL of OCL queries relying on ordered collections must take the chosen pattern into account, making explicit use of it in the platform-specific representation. Patterns for mapping OCL constructs to SQL'92 (with stored procedures) have been reported [13].

7   Conclusions and Future Work

Improving the quality of enterprise-class software systems requires at some point advanced decision procedures, which in turn build upon precise language definitions. Reverse engineering and other activities in the software development process can cope with the increasing complexity of software architectures only by adopting precise language definitions as a foundation, while simultaneously addressing "productivity" and "correctness" as defined in Sec. 1. Our case study shows by construction how to achieve better language definitions by applying metamodeling techniques to a language used in building enterprise-class systems.

Language-processing algorithms can rely on tree walkers and visitor skeletons generated from language metamodels. For EJB3QL, an obvious example is a visitor for translating to SQL'92. More sophisticated visitors can also be implemented once the infrastructure reported in this paper is in place: predicting execution time, or displaying the access paths of a query (to visualize the depends-on relationships between materialized views). A metamodel for the syntax of SQL 99/2003 (without well-formedness as of now) is available for EMF [12], thus allowing AST-to-AST translation from EJB3QL to SQL.

As we have seen, different levels of formality are sufficient for different purposes. We plan to leverage the OCL formulation of WFRs by translating them into a logical formalism for which a model checker (TLA$^+$ [14], $^+$CAL [15]) is available. $^+$CAL is an imperative language meant to replace pseudo-code for writing high-level descriptions of algorithms, for which a translator to TLA$^+$ is available. Once the data structures and typing conditions specified in a language metamodel are expressed in $^+$CAL, assertions made for the algorithms can be model-checked. As mentioned in the $^+$CAL and TLA$^+$ literature, the expressive power of their underlying formalism precludes decidability (i.e. not all valid theorems can be proved by a tool), but experience has shown that the tools can cope with most specifications that engineers write.

An area we plan to explore is the suitability of an UML+OCL metamodel as a "formalism-independent" way to jumpstart a formal language specification. Once translated into the formalism of choice, we expect to give additional detail (e.g. behavioral semantics, security, quality-of-service) to be used in the formal verification of properties of interest.

Acknowledgement. Liu Yao proficiently contributed to the implementation of this case study as part of his master thesis on Eclipse-based support for Domain-Specific Languages.

References

1. Klint, P., Lämmel, R., and Verhoef. C., Towards an Engineering Discipline for Grammarware, *ACM Transactions on Software Engineering and Methodology*, Vol. 14, No. 3, July 2005, pp. 331-380.
2. Huang, S. S., Zook, D., Smaragdakis, Y.: Statically Safe Program Generation with SafeGen, In R. Glück and M. Lowry, editors, *4th Intnl. Conf. on Generative Programming and Component Engineering (GPCE'05)*, Tallin, Estonia. September 2005. LNCS, vol. 3676, pp. 309-326. Springer-Verlag, 2005.
3. Wang, J., Kim, S-K., Carrington, D.: Verifying Metamodel Coverage of Model Transformations. *aswec*, pp. 270-282, Australian Software Engineering Conference (ASWEC'06), Sydney, Australia. April 2006.
4. Jouault, F., Bézivin, J., and Kurtev, I.: TCS: a DSL for the Specification of Textual Concrete Syntaxes in Model Engineering. To appear in *Proc. of the 5th Intnl. Conf. on Generative programming and Component Engineering*, Portland, Oregon. October 2006.
5. Muller, P-A., et. al.. Model-Driven Analysis and Synthesis of Concrete Syntax. To appear in *Proc. of the MoDELS/UML 2006*, Genoa, Italy. October 2006.
6. Klasse Objecten, Octopus: OCL Tool for Precise Uml Specifications. http://octopus.sourceforge.net/
7. Emfatic Language for EMF, http://www.alphaworks.ibm.com/tech/emfatic
8. Damus, C. W.: Implementing Model Integrity in EMF with EMFT OCL. IBM developerWorks, August 2006. http://www.eclipse.org/articles/Article-EMF-Codegen-with-OCL/article.html
9. Alanen, M., Porres, I.: A Relation Between Context-Free Grammars and Meta Object Facility Metamodels. Tech. Rep. No. 606, Turku Centre for Computer Science, March 2003.
10. Jin. D., Cordy, J.R., Dean, T. R.: Where's the Schema? A Taxonomy of Patterns for Software Exchange, *10th International Workshop on Program Comprehension (IWPC'02)*, pp. 65-74, 2002.
11. Antoniol, G. Di Penta, M. Merlo, E.: YAAB (Yet another AST browser): using OCL to navigate ASTs. *11th IEEE International Workshop on Program Comprehension (IWPC '03)*, pp. 13- 22. Washington, DC, USA. May 2003.
12. SQL 99/2003 Metamodel. http://www.eclipse.org/datatools/project_modelbase/
13. Demuth, B., Hussmann, H.: Using OCL Constraints for Relational Database Design. *Proc. 2nd International Conference UML'99*, Springer LNCS 1723, pp. 598-613, 1999.
14. Specifying Systems: The TLA$^+$ Language and Tools for Hardware and Software Engineers. Leslie Lamport, Addison-Wesley (2002). ISBN 032114306X.
15. Lamport, L.: The $^+$CAL Algorithm Language. 2006. Submitted for publication, http://research.microsoft.com/users/lamport/pubs/pluscal.pdf
16. EJB3QL Metamodel and accompanying software artifacts. http://www.sts.tu-harburg.de/~mi.garcia/pubs/atem06

The 1st Workshop on Quality in Modeling

Ludwik Kuzniarz[1], Jean Louis Sourouille[2], and Miroslaw Staron[3]

[1] Department of Software Engineering and Computer Science,
Blekinge University of Technology, Ronneby, Sweden
Ludwik.Kuzniarz@bt.se
[2] INSA, Lyon, France
Ludwik.Kuzniarz@bth.se
[3] IT University, Goteborg, Sweden
Miroslaw.Staron@ituniv.se

Overview

Quality assessment and assurance constitute an important part of software engineering. The issues of software quality management are widely researched and approached from multiple perspectives and viewpoints. The introduction of a new paradigm in software development – namely Model Driven Development (MDD) and its variations (e.g., MDA [Model Driven Architecture], MDE [Model Driven Engineering], MBD [Model Based Development], MIC [Model Integrated Computing]) – raises new challenges in software quality management, and as such should be given special attention. In particular, the issues of early quality assessment, based on models at a high abstraction level, and building (or customizing the existing) prediction models for software quality based on model metrics are of central importance for the software engineering community.

The workshop is a continuation of a series of workshops on consistency that have taken place during the subsequent annual UML conferences and recently MDA-FA. The idea behind this workshop was to extend the scope of interests and to address a wide spectrum of problems related to MDD. It is also in line with the overall initiative of the shift from UML to MoDELS.

The goal of this workshop was to gather researchers and practitioners interested in the emerging issues of quality in the context of MDD. The workshop was intended to provide a premier forum for discussions related to software quality and MDD. And the aims of the workshop were:

- to present ongoing research related to quality in modeling in the context of MDD,
- to define and organize issues related to quality in the MDD.

The workshop was structured to contain two parts: presentation and discussion. The presentation part was aimed at reporting research results related to different aspects of quality in modeling. Seven papers were selected for the presentation out of 16 submissions. The discussion part included topics related to the notions of quality in modeling, the perspectives of quality, and the understanding of these perspectives.

T. Kühne (Ed.): MoDELS 2006 Workshops, LNCS 4364, pp. 76–79, 2007.
© Springer-Verlag Berlin Heidelberg 2007

Presentations

In general the submissions and presentations addressed specific issues, which were more closely related to consistency than to quality. In particular the papers considered such issues as:

- checking satisfiability of a given class diagram,
- checking consistency between two types of models,
- measuring semantic quality of a given model,
- using graph theory to assist in resolving inconsistencies,
- verification and validation of quality of models w.r.t. government standards,
- empirical evaluation of how modeling conventions influence the quality,
- measuring the quality of OCL expressions.

The trend in the presentations reflected to overall trend of the conference – introducing modeling methods and languages other than UML, although the majority of the papers were written in the context of UML. The presentations on the above topics raised discussions related to the understanding of UML, or more specifically, to the problems with the definition of the consistency.

Discussions

The second, especially important, part of the workshop was devoted to discussions related to the notion of quality in modeling.

Firstly, a general understanding of the notion of quality in modeling was discussed. The participants were involved in the discussions on the taxonomy of quality-related issues: the organization of these issues in perspectives. The pairs of perspectives could be the following:

- concepts and pragmatics,
- process and language,
- system and model,
- internal and external,
- maintenance and development.

Secondly, a detailed discussion on two of the identified perspectives took place. The discussion considered two orthogonal perspectives of quality:

- the concept of quality in modeling, and
- the pragmatics of quality management in modeling.

The combination of participants from industry and academia provided a unique opportunity to discuss both pragmatics and theory behind the notion of quality in modeling.

The discussion related to the first perspective, the concept of quality in modeling, led to a number of issues that need further research:

- understanding of the notion of quality in general,
- amount of model quality which is needed in software projects,

- measurements of quality – metrics and methods to work with these metrics,
- influence of the quality of models on certain product characteristics – quality of products, development effort, or project costs.

The second discussed perspective was the pragmatics of quality management. The discussions within this topic were focused on:

- cost of quality, with as sub-topics:
- costs of removing or working with low quality models
- benefits and costs of maintaining high quality of models
- scalability of quality maintenance methods

The final outcome of the workshop was a set of potential research areas which are of joint interest between industry and academia.

Important Future Research Directions

The main focus of the discussion was industrial applicability and relevance of the methods for improving, maintaining, and defining the quality of models. One of issues important for the audience was the visibility and evidence of a clear benefit for industry in the area of quality in modeling. The outcomes of this discussion can be summarized in the following points:

1. Industry expects the researchers to develop methods which will be directly usable in specific companies providing the researchers with the data.
2. There is a need for more empirical evidence and evaluation of the methods for quality assessment and management in modeling – e.g. to evaluate that the methods indeed bring improvements to the development processes and to given product characteristics.
3. Methods for improving quality in modeling require a large degree of scalability to increase their chances of being accepted by industry.
4. There is a need for empirical studies into applicability of general software quality methods to software models and which potential improvements are needed.
5. There is a need for methods for benchmarking the models w.r.t. various aspects of quality.

The above research directions formed an important outcome of the workshop and indicated the trend in the future shaping of this workshop, as a need for this kind of forum was sustained.

Summary

The workshop presentations were rather narrowly focused. They mostly concerned one specific aspect of quality, namely consistency. The discussion was broader and resulted in identifying perspectives from which quality should be addressed, as well as, foreseen areas and topics for the follow up activities.

The following two papers were chosen as the best papers of the workshop:

- Consistency of Business Process Models and Object Life Cycles, by Ksenia Ryndina1, Jochen M. Kuster, and Harald Gall,
- A Qualitative Investigation of UML Modeling Conventions, by Bart Du Bois, Christian F.J. Lange, Serge Demeyer and Michel R.V.Chaudron.

Consistency of Business Process Models and Object Life Cycles

Ksenia Ryndina[1,2], Jochen M. Küster[1], and Harald Gall[2]

[1] IBM Zurich Research Laboratory, Säumerstr. 4
8803 Rüschlikon, Switzerland
{ryn,jku}@zurich.ibm.com
[2] Department of Informatics, University of Zurich, Binzmühlestr. 14
8050 Zurich, Switzerland
gall@ifi.unizh.ch

Abstract. Business process models and object life cycles can provide two different views on behavior of the same system, requiring that these models are consistent with each other. However, it is difficult to reason about consistency of these two types of models since their relation is not well-understood. We clarify this relation and propose an approach to establishing the required consistency. Object state changes are first made explicit in a business process model and then the process model is used to generate life cycles for each object type used in the process. We define two consistency notions for a process model and an object life cycle and express these in terms of conditions that must hold between a given life cycle and a life cycle generated from the process model.

Keywords: consistency, business process model, object life cycle, activity diagram, state machine, UML.

1 Introduction

Business process models are nowadays a well-established means for representing business processes in terms of tasks that need to be performed to achieve a certain business goal. In addition to tasks, business process models also show the flow of *business objects* in a process. Complete behavior of business objects is usually modeled using a variant of a state machine called an *object life cycle* (see e.g. [5]). Object life cycle modeling is valuable at the business level to explicitly represent how business objects go through different states during their existence.

There are situations where it is beneficial or even required to use both process models and object life cycles. Consider an insurance company that uses business process models for execution and also maintains explicit business object life cycles. Life cycles may serve as a reference to employees for tracking progress of business objects. For instance, in response to an enquiry about the state of a submitted claim, an employee can explain the current claim state to the customer in the context of the entire claim life cycle that shows all the possible states and transitions for claims. Another example is encountered in compliance checking, where existing business process models are benchmarked against best practice models (e.g. ACORD [2] and IFW [4]) given as object life cycles. Given a best

T. Kühne (Ed.): MoDELS 2006 Workshops, LNCS 4364, pp. 80–90, 2007.

practice object life cycle, it is required to ensure that an existing business process model is compliant with it.

When both business process models and object life cycles are used, it is required that these models are *consistent* with each other. Inconsistencies can lead to unsatisfied customers or compliance violations. For example, a customer may be discontent if he/she is incorrectly informed about the processing that still needs to be done before his/her claim is settled. On the other hand, inconsistencies between an existing process model and a best practice object life cycle lead to compliance violations that can cause legal problems for a company.

Consistency of object-oriented behavioral models, such as scenarios and state machines, has already been extensively studied [9,10,16,18]. However, the relation between business process models and object life cycles is not yet well-understood, which makes it difficult to reason about their consistency.

In this paper, we present our approach to establishing consistency of a business process model and an object life cycle. In Section 2, we introduce subsets of *UML2.0 Activity Diagrams (UML AD)* and *State Machines (UML SM)* [3] chosen for business process and object life cycle modeling, respectively. In Sections 3 and 4, we describe our proposed solution that comprises a technique for object life cycle generation from a process model and two consistency notions that can be checked using the generated life cycles. Finally, we discuss related work in Section 5, and conclusions and future work in Section 6.

2   Business Process Models and Object Life Cycles

UML AD is one of the most widely used languages for business process modeling. We consider process models in a subset of UML AD that includes *action nodes* and *control nodes* (decision, merge, fork, join, start[1], flow final and activity final nodes). All these nodes can be connected with *control* and *object flows*. *Input* and *output pins* are used to model connection points that allow object flows to be attached to nodes, with the exception of start nodes that may not have outgoing object flows. Each object pin has an *inState* attribute that allows one to specify the possible states of objects passed through this pin. Data inputs and outputs of processes are modeled using *input* and *output parameters*. Our experience with case studies has shown that in practice most process models are created using this subset of UML AD. Therefore, currently we do not consider more advanced elements such as loop nodes and parameter sets, and further assume that hierarchy in process models can be flattened. The reader is referred to the UML AD specification [3] for further information about the language.

Figure 1 shows an example business process model for a *Claims handling* process from the insurance industry that is represented in the chosen subset of UML AD. In this diagram, we can see that the *Claims handling* process starts when a *Settlement* in state *Requested* is received by the process. Next, a new *Claim* object is created in state *Registered* by the *Register new claim* action.

---

[1] These are called *initial nodes* in UML AD, but renamed here to avoid confusion with initial states of object life cycles introduced later.

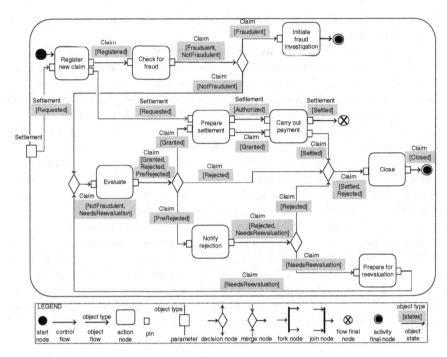

Fig. 1. *Claims handling* business process model

The *Claim* further goes through a number of processing steps that change its state and at the end of the process it is either found to be fraudulent, or it is rejected or settled and subsequently closed.

In Figure 1 we use a slightly tailored graphical representation of the chosen UML AD subset. We indicate object type above an object flow and not above each pin, because we make a simplifying assumption that an object flow can only connect two pins of the same type. We also assume that given two connected object pins (output pin and input pin), the states associated with the output pin are accepted by the input pin, i.e. the set of states of the output pin is a subset of the set of states of the input pin. In Figure 1 we indicate the states associated with the output pin on the connecting object flow.

Associating states with object pins is optional in UML AD, but required in our approach, as this explicit information about object states allows us to establish a relation between a business process model and object life cycles.

For modeling object life cycles, we use a subset of the UML SM language. This subset comprises *states*, with one *initial state* and one or more *final states*, and *transitions* connecting the states. Transitions that are initiated by a particular triggering event can be labeled with a *trigger label*. As our main application is in a business environment, we choose a simple notation for object life cycles, without considering composite and concurrent states of state machines.

Figure 2 shows two example life cycles for *Claim* and *Settlement* object types. In (a), it can be seen that all objects of type *Claim* go through state *Registered* directly after the initial state and pass through either *Fraudulent* or *Closed* states before they reach a final state. In (b), it is shown that after a *Settlement* is *Authorized*, the payment for the *Settlement* can either be made in full or in a number of installments.

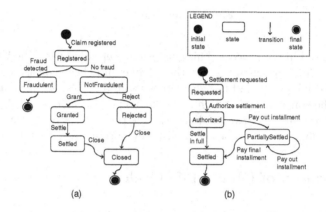

(a)   (b)

Fig. 2. Object life cycles: (a) *Claim* (b) *Settlement*

In this paper we use the following definition for an object life cycle, adapted from the definition of a UML State Machine in [14]:

Definition 1 (Object life cycle). *Given an object type o, its object life cycle $OLC_o = (S, s_\alpha, S_\Omega, L, T)$ consists of a finite set of states S, where $s_\alpha \in S$ is the initial state and $S_\Omega \subseteq S$ is the set of final states; a finite set of trigger labels L; a set of labeled transitions $T \subseteq S \times L \cup \bot \times S$, where for each transition $t = (s_1, l, s_2)$, s_1 is the source state and s_2 is the target state.*

We assume that an object life cycle is well-formed when the initial state has no incoming transitions, a final state has no outgoing transitions, and all other states have at least one incoming and at least one outgoing transition.

The *Claims handling* process model in Figure 1 and the life cycles in Figure 2 are concerned with behavior of the same object types: *Claim* and *Settlement*. We need to define what it means for these models to be consistent and how to check their consistency. According to an existing methodology for managing consistency of behavioral models [6,8], the consistency problem must first be identified by determining the *overlap* between the given models. Then, model aspects that contribute to the consistency problem must be mapped into a suitable *semantic domain*, where *consistency conditions* can be defined and checked.

An overview of our proposed solution is shown in Figure 3. In Step 1, we make the overlap between a business process model and object life cycles explicit by adding object state information to the process model using the *inState* attribute of object pins (as in Figure 1). Next in Step 2, we generate a life cycle for each

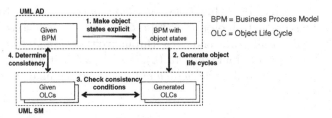

Fig. 3. Solution overview

object type used in the process. This generation step takes us to the UML SM as the semantic domain, where we can then define and check consistency between the generated life cycles and the given ones (Step 3), which in turn allows us to determine the consistency between the business process model and the given life cycles (Step 4). The next two sections describe the generation of life cycles from a process model and the proposed consistency notions, respectively.

3   Generation of Object Life Cycles

An object life cycle generated from a given business process model for a particular object type should capture all possible state changes that can occur for objects of this type in the given process. Initial and final states also need to be identified for each generated life cycle.

Given a business process model P where each object pin is associated with a non-empty set of states, we generate an object life cycle for each object type used in P. For an object type o, we first create an object life cycle OLC_{oP} that contains only the initial state. Then, for each unique state associated with object pins of type o, a state is added to OLC_{oP}. Transitions and final states are added to OLC_{oP} according to the generation rules shown in Figure 4.

Each row in Figure 4 represents a high-level generation rule, where the left-hand side shows patterns that are matched in the process model P and the right-hand side shows what is created in the generated object life cycle OLC_{oP}. Consider for example **Rule 2 (stateChange)**, which is applicable when some action A has input and output object pins of type o. When states of the output object pin are not the same as those of the input object pin, we deduce that action A changes the state of objects of type o. In OLC_{oP}, a transition from each incoming state to each possible outgoing state for objects of type o is added, for all cases where the outgoing state is different from the incoming state. These transitions are labeled A to indicate that they are triggered during the execution of this action. In **Rules 5** and **6**, the generated transitions are given special labels ($START_P$ and END_P) to indicate that these transitions are triggered as the process begins and ends execution, respectively. The rules ensure that the generated object life cycles are well-formed, provided that all object pins in the given process model are associated with non-empty state sets. All the generation rules are explained in detail in a longer version of this paper [13].

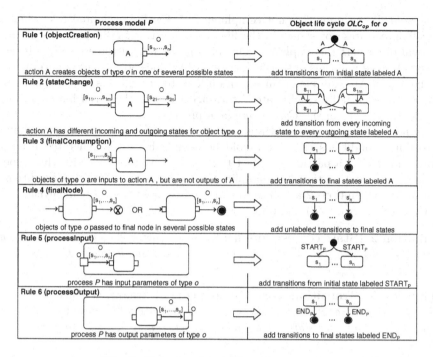

Fig. 4. Rules for object life cycle generation

Figure 5 shows life cycles for *Claim* and *Settlement* object types (right-hand sides of (a) and (b), respectively) generated from the *Claims handling* process model in Figure 1 according to the generation rules presented in this section.

In the next section we show how generated object life cycles are used for defining consistency conditions to establish whether a given process model is consistent with a given life cycle for a particular object type.

4   Consistency of Object Life Cycles

We identify two consistency notions for a given business process model and an object life cycle: *life cycle compliance* and *coverage*. A given process model is *compliant* with a given life cycle for a particular object type, if the process initiates only those state transitions for objects of this type that are defined in the given life cycle. Compliance allows objects of the given type to traverse only a part of their given life cycle in the process. On the other hand, *coverage* requires that objects traverse the entire given life cycle in the process, but additional transitions not defined in the given life cycle may also be incurred in the process.

Depending on the circumstances, one or both of these consistency notions may be required to hold. For example, if the *Claims handling* process (Figure 1) is used for execution and the *Claim* life cycle (Figure 2 (a)) is referenced by employees for interpreting the state of *Claim* objects, both compliance and coverage must hold. If the process is not compliant with the life cycle and takes *Claim* objects into states not shown in the life cycle or performs different transitions, this will disconcert the employees. On the other hand, customers will be incorrectly informed and thus unsatisfied if the process does not provide a coverage of the life cycle. An example of this occurs if a customer expects a *Claim* in state *Granted* to eventually reach state *Settled* according to the given life cycle, but this never happens in the *Claims handling* process.

We next give more precise definitions of compliance and coverage, providing consistency conditions that must hold between a life cycle generated from a process model for a particular object type and a given life cycle for that type. We first give two definitions that simplify the expression of consistency conditions that follow. Definitions 2 and 3 can be applied to any two object life cycles: $OLC_o = (S, s_\alpha, S_\Omega, L, T)$ and $OLC_o' = (S', s_\alpha', S_\Omega', L', T')$.

Definition 2 (State correspondence). *A state correspondence exists between a state $s \in S$ and a state $s' \in S'$, if and only if one of the following holds: $s = s'$, $s = s_\alpha$ and $s' = s_\alpha'$, or $s \in S_\Omega$ and $s' \in S_\Omega'$.*

Definition 3 (Transition correspondence). *A transition correspondence exists between a transition $t = (s_1, s_2) \in T$ and a transition $t' = (s_3, s_4) \in T'$ if and only if there are state correspondences between s_1 and s_3, and between s_2 and s_4.*

In Definition 2, we define a *state correspondence* between two states in different object life cycles if the states are equal (i.e. have the same name), if they are both initial states or they are both final states. In Definition 3, we define a *transition correspondence* between two transitions if there are state correspondences between their sources states and between their target states.

In Definitions 4 and 5, P is a given process model, $OLC_o = (S, s_\alpha, S_\Omega, L, T)$ is a given life cycle for object type o and $OLC_{oP} = (S_P, s_{\alpha P}, S_{\Omega P}, L_P, T_P)$ is the life cycle generated from P for o.

Definition 4 (Life cycle compliance). *A business process model P is compliant with an object life cycle OLC_o if and only if for each transition $t_P \in T_P$ that is not labeled START_P or END_P, there exists a transition $t \in T$ such that there is a correspondence between t_P and t.*

According to Definition 4, life cycle compliance requires that each transition in the generated object life cycle has a transition correspondence to some transition in the given life cycle. However, there are two exceptions to this consistency condition: transitions labeled START_P and END_P in the generated object life cycle. These transitions are generated when the given process model P has input or output parameters of object type o. We do not place restrictions on these transitions, thus allowing objects of type o to be received by and passed from the given process in any state and not necessarily a state following the initial state or preceding a final state.

Definition 5 (Life cycle coverage). *A business process model P provides a coverage of an object life cycle OLC_o if and only if all of the following conditions hold between OLC_o and OLC_{oP}: (a) For each transition $t \in T$ there exists a transition $t_P \in T_P$ such that there is a correspondence between t and t_P, (b) There are no transitions labeled $START_P$ or END_P in T_P.*

Condition (a) in Definition 5 requires every transition in the given object life cycle to have a transition correspondence to some transition in the generated life cycle. Furthermore, condition (b) requires that the given process does not have input or output parameters of the given type, hence objects of this type must be created and reach their final states within the process boundaries.

We next illustrate the notions of life cycle compliance and coverage using examples. Figure 5 shows the given object life cycles for the *Claim* and *Settlement* object types on the left and the object life cycles generated from the *Claims handling* process on the right. Transitions that have a correspondence between them are marked with the same number, while transitions without a correspondence are marked with a cross.

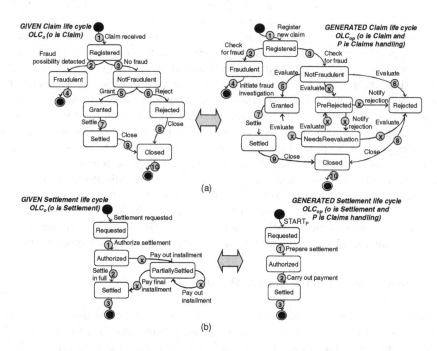

Fig. 5. Consistency of *Claim* and *Settlement* object life cycles

The *Claim* life cycles in Figure 5 (a) satisfy all the consistency conditions for life cycle coverage. Condition (a) from Definition 5 is satisfied since all the transitions in the given *Claim* life cycle have a correspondence to transitions in the generated *Claim* life cycle, and condition (b) is satisfied since the generated *Claim* life cycle does not contain transitions labeled $START_P$ or END_P.

Therefore, the *Claims handling* process provides a coverage of the given *Claim* life cycle. However, the *Claims handling* process is not compliant with this life cycle, due to transitions in the generated life cycle without transition correspondences to transitions in the given life cycle. Figure 5 (b) shows that the *Claims handling* process is compliant with the given *Settlement* life cycle, but does not provide a coverage for it.

5   Related Work

A related research area is *object life cycle inheritance*, where consistent specialization of behavior is required (see e.g. [5,11,14]). Currently, our main goal is to establish a link between business process models and object life cycles, and life cycle inheritance is not in focus. However, sometimes it may be required that the relation between a given process model and an object life cycle is a certain type of specialization. Thus, it would be beneficial for our approach to make use of the consistency notions already defined for life cycle inheritance.

Another related area is *synthesis of state machines from scenarios* [18,16], where scenario specifications are used to generate state machines for the objects that participate in these scenarios. There are several significant differences between process models and scenarios however, e.g. process models do not generally describe alternative scenarios and show the flow of objects between tasks rather than interaction between objects via messages modeled in scenarios. In state machine synthesis, it is possible that a synthesized state machine contains so-called *implied scenarios* [15,12], i.e. behaviors that are not valid with respect to the original scenario specifications. A similar phenomenon can occur in our life cycle generation step, which we plan to investigate further as future work.

Our consistency notions are related to the concepts of *equivalence* and *refinement* of formal process specifications [7]. However, as discussed in [17], it is challenging to apply the existing definitions to languages such as UML AD and SM, as they do not have an agreed formal semantics. As future work we intend to establish a relation of our consistency notions to the existing equivalence and refinement definitions and investigate which are most appropriate in practice.

6   Conclusion and Future Work

Consistency of business process models and object life cycles needs to be ensured in situations where process models manipulate business objects with an explicitly modeled life cycle. In this paper we have presented our approach to establishing this consistency. Our main contributions include a precise definition of two consistency notions, namely life cycle compliance and coverage, and a supporting technique for the generation of object life cycles from process models that enables consistency checking. With regards to tool support, we have developed a prototype as an extension to the IBM WebSphere Business Modeler [1] that allows us to capture object states in business process models, generate life cycles from process models and check the consistency conditions.

As future work, we intend to validate the proposed approach using a larger case study. We also plan to extend the approach to enable compliance and coverage checking for *several* process models that use objects of the same type and a life cycle for this type. Further future work includes an investigation of implied scenarios in the context of our life cycle generation and establishing a clear relation between our proposed consistency notions and the existing equivalence and refinement definitions.

References

1. IBM WebSphere Business Modeler. http://www-306.ibm.com/software/integration/wbimodeler/.
2. ACORD Life & Annuity Standard. ACORD Global Insurance Standards, Final Version 2.13.00, September 2005.
3. UML2.0 Superstructure, formal/05-07-04. OMG Document, 2005.
4. IBM Industry Models for Financial Services, The Information Framework (IFW) Process Models. IBM General Information Manual, 2006.
5. J. Ebert and G. Engels. Specialization of Object Life Cycle Definitions. Fachberichte Informatik 19/95, University of Koblenz-Landau, 1997.
6. G. Engels, J. M. Küster, L. Groenewegen, and R. Heckel. A Methodology for Specifying and Analyzing Consistency of Object-Oriented Behavioral Models. In *Proceedings of the 8th European Software Engineering Conference - ESEC'01*, pages 186–195. ACM Press, 2001.
7. A.-W. Fayez. Comparative Analysis of the Notions of Equivalence for Process Specifications. In *Proceedings of the 3rd IEEE Symposium on Computers & Communications - ISCC'98*, page 711, Washington, DC, USA, 1998. IEEE Computer Society.
8. J. M. Küster. *Consistency Management of Object-Oriented Behavioral Models.* PhD thesis, University of Paderborn, March 2004.
9. J. M. Küster and J. Stehr. Towards Explicit Behavioral Consistency Concepts in the UML. In *Proceedings of the 2nd International Workshop on Scenarios and State Machines: Models, Algorithms and Tools - ICSE'03*, 2003.
10. B. Litvak, S. Tyszberowicz, and A. Yehudai. Behavioral Consistency Validation of UML Diagrams. *1st International Conference on Software Engineering and Formal Methods - SEFM'03*, page 118, 2003.
11. M. Schrefl and M. Stumptner. Behavior-Consistent Specialization of Object Life Cycles. *ACM Transactions on Software Engineering and Methodology*, 11(1):92–148, 2002.
12. H. Muccini. An Approach for Detecting Implied Scenarios. In *Proceedings of the Workshop on Scenarios and State Machines: Models, Algorithms, and Tools - ICSE'02*, 2002.
13. K. Ryndina, J. M. Küster, and H. Gall. Consistency of Business Process Models and Object Life Cycles. In *Proceedings of the 1st Workshop on Quality in Modeling co-located with MoDELS 2006, Technical report 0627, Technische Universiteit Eindhoven*, 2006.
14. M. Stumptner and M. Schrefl. Behavior Consistent Inheritance in UML. In *Proceedings of Conceptual Modeling - ER 2000*, volume 1920 of *LNCS*, pages 527–542. Springer-Verlag, 2000.
15. S. Uchitel, J. Kramer, and J. Magee. Detecting Implied Scenarios in Message Sequence Chart Specifications. In *Proceedings of European Software Engineering Conference - ESEC/FSE'01*, 2001.

16. S. Uchitel, J. Kramer, and J. Magee. Synthesis of Behavioral Models from Scenarios. *IEEE Transactions on Software Engineering*, 29(2):99–115, 2003.
17. M. von der Beeck. Behaviour Specifications: Equivalence and Refinement Notions. In *Visuelle Verhaltensmodellierung verteilter und nebenläufiger Software-Systeme, 8. Workshop des Arbeitskreises GROOM der GI Fachgruppe 2.1.9 Objektorientierte Software-Entwicklung, Universität Münster*, 2000. Technical report 24/00-I.
18. J. Whittle and J. Schumann. Generating Statechart Designs from Scenarios. In *Proceedings of the 22nd International Conference on Software Engineering - ICSE'00*, pages 314–323, New York, NY, USA, 2000. ACM Press.

A Qualitative Investigation of
UML Modeling Conventions

Bart Du Bois[1], Christian F.J. Lange[2],
Serge Demeyer[1], and Michel R.V. Chaudron[2]

[1] Lab On REengineering, University of Antwerp, Belgium
{Bart.DuBois,Serge.Demeyer}@ua.ac.be
[2] Dept. of Mathematics and Computer Science, Technische Universiteit Eindhoven
{C.F.J.Lange,M.R.V.Chaudron}@tue.nl

Abstract. Analogue to the more familiar notion of coding conventions, modeling conventions attempt to ensure uniformity and prevent common modeling defects. While it has been shown that modeling conventions can decrease defect density, it is currently unclear whether this decreased defect density results in higher model quality, i.e., whether models created with modeling conventions exhibit higher fitness for purpose.

In a controlled experiment[1] with 27 master-level computer science students, we evaluated quality differences between UML analysis and design models created with and without modeling conventions. We were unable to discern significant differences w.r.t. the clarity, completeness and validity of the information the model is meant to represent.

We interpret our findings as an indication that modeling conventions should guide the analyst in identifying what information to model, as well as how to model it, lest their effectiveness be limited to optimizing merely syntactic quality.

1 Introduction

In [1], a classification of common defects in UML analysis and design models is discussed. These defects often remain undetected and cause misinterpretations by the reader. To prevent these defects, *modeling conventions* have been composed that, similar to the concept of code conventions, ensure a uniform manner of modeling [2]. We designed a pair of experiments to validate the effectiveness of using such modeling conventions, focusing on their effectiveness w.r.t. respectively (i) defect prevention; and (ii) model quality. We reported on the prevention of defects in [3]. Our study of the effect of modeling conventions on model quality forms the subject of this paper.

In the first experiment, we evaluated how the use of modeling conventions for preventing modeling defects affected defect density and modeling effort [3]. These modeling conventions are enlisted in Appendix A, and have been discussed previously in [1]. This set of 23 conventions has been composed through a literature

---

[1] A replication package is provided at http://www.lore.ua.ac.be/Research/Artefacts

T. Kühne (Ed.): MoDELS 2006 Workshops, LNCS 4364, pp. 91–100, 2007.

review and through observations from industrial case studies, and concern abstraction, balance, completeness, consistency, design, layout and naming. These conventions are *formative*, in that they focus on specifying *how* information should be modeled, rather than specifying *what* should be modeled.

Our observations on 35 three person modeling teams demonstrated that, while the use of these modeling conventions required more modeling effort, the defect density of resulting UML models was reduced. However, this defect density reduction was not statistically significant, meaning that there is a (small) possibility, albeit small, that the observed differences might be due to chance.

This paper reports on the second experiment, observing differences in representational quality between the models created in the first experiment. We define *representational quality* of a model as the clarity, completeness and validity of the information the model is meant to represent. Typical flaws in representational quality are information loss, misinformation, and ambiguity or susceptibility to misinterpretation. This study investigates whether models created using common modeling conventions exhibit higher representational quality.

The paper is structured as follows. The selected quality framework is elaborated in section 2. The set-up of the experiment is explained in section 3, and the analysis of the resulting data is discussed and interpreted in section 4. We analyze the threats to validity in section 5. Finally, we conclude in section 6.

For space considerations, the description of the experiment has been reduced to its essence. A more elaborate discussion of the experiment is provided in [4].

2   Evaluating Model Quality

Through a literature review of quality models for conceptual models, we selected Lindland's framework for its focus on clarity, completeness and validity. Lindland's framework relates different aspects of modeling to three linguistic concepts: syntax, semantics and pragmatics [5]. These concepts are described as follows (citing from [5]):

Syntax *relates the model to the modeling language by describing relations among language constructs without considering their meaning.*

Semantics *relates the model to the domain by considering not only syntax, but also relations among statements and their meaning.*

Pragmatics *relates the model to the audience's interpretation by considering not only syntax and semantics, but also how the audience (anyone involved in modeling) will interpret them.*

These descriptions of the concepts of syntax, semantics and pragmatics refer to relationships. The evaluation of these relationships gives rise to the notion of syntactic, semantic and pragmatic quality. We note that the effect of UML modeling conventions on syntactic quality has been the target of our previous experiment [3], and is therefore not included in this study.

In [6], Lindland's quality framework is extended to express one additional quality attribute. *Social quality* evaluates the relationship among the audience interpretation, i.e. to which extent the audience agrees or disagrees on the statements within the model.

With regard to representational quality, we are less interested in the relationship between the model and the audience's interpretation – indicated by pragmatic quality – than in the relationship between the domain and the audience's interpretation, as the former is unrelated to the information the model is meant to represent. Accordingly, we will not observe pragmatic quality, but instead introduce an additional quality attribute, *communicative quality*, that targets the evaluation of the audience's interpretation of the domain.

2.1 Measuring Model Quality

Lindland's quality framework evaluates the relationships between model, modeling domain and interpretation using the elementary notion of a statement. A *statement* is a *sentence representing one property of a certain phenomenon* [6]. Statements are extracted from a canonical form representation of the language, which in UML, is specific to each diagram type. An example of a statement in a use case diagram is the capability of an actor to employ a feature.

The set of statements that are relevant and valid in the domain are noted as D, the set of statements that are explicit in the model as M_E, and the set of statements in the interpretation of an interpreter i are symbolized with I_i. We say that a statement is *explicit* in case it can be confirmed from that sentence without the use of inference. Using these three sets, indicators for semantic quality (and also pragmatic quality, that we do not include in this study) have been defined that are similar to the concepts of recall and precision:

Semantic Completeness (SC) is the ratio of the number of modeled domain statements $|M_E \cap D|$ and the total number of domain statements $|D|$.

Semantic Validity (SV) is the ratio of the number of modeled domain statements $|M_E \cap D|$ and the total number of model statements $|M_E|$.

Krogstie extended Lindland's quality framework through the definition of *social quality* [6]. The single proposed metric of social quality is:

Relative Agreement among Interpreters (RAI) is calculated as the number of statements in the intersection between the statements in the interpretations of all n interpreters $|\bigcap_{\forall i,j \in [1,n]} I_i \cap I_j|$.

Similar to semantic quality, we introduce the following metrics for communicative quality:

Communicative Completeness (CC) is the ratio of the number of recognized modeled domain statements $|I_i \cap M_E \cap D|$ and the total number of modeled domain statements $|M_E \cap D|$.

Communicative Validity (CV) is the ratio of the number of recognized modeled domain statements $|I_i \cap M_E \cap D|$ and the total number of statements in the interpretation of interpreter i $|I_i|$.

Communicative completeness and validity respectively quantify the extent to which information has been lost or added during modeling.

The difficulty in applying the metrics for semantic, social and communicative quality mentioned above lies in the identification of the set of model statements (M_E), and interpretation statements (I_i). In contrast, the set of domain statements (D) is uniquely defined and can reasonably be expected to have a considerable intersection with the set of model and interpretation statements. Accordingly, we choose to estimate the sets of domain statements, model statements and interpretation statements, by verifying their intersection with a *selected* set of domain statements (D_s).

Semantic validity cannot be approximated in this manner, as it requires an estimate of the set of statements that lie outside the set of domain statements ($|M_E \setminus D|$). Nonetheless, the resulting set of estimates for semantic, social and communicative quality allows to assess typical representational quality flaws as information loss (semantic and communicative completeness estimates), misinformation (communicative validity estimate) and misinterpretation (social quality estimate).

3   Experimental Set-Up

Using the classical Goal-Question-Metric template, we describe the purpose of this study as follows: **Analyze** UML models **for the purpose of** evaluation of modeling conventions effectiveness **with respect to** the representational quality of the resulting model **from the perspective of** the analyst/designer **in the context of** master-level computer science student.

Using our refinement of representational model quality presented in the previous section, we define the following null hypotheses:

$H_{0,SeQ}$ − UML analysis and design models composed with or without modeling conventions do not differ w.r.t. *semantic quality.*

$H_{0,SoQ}$ − UML analysis and design models composed with or without modeling conventions do not differ w.r.t. *social quality.*

$H_{0,CoQ}$ − UML analysis and design models composed with or without modeling conventions do not differ w.r.t. *communicative quality.*

3.1   Experimental Design

In this study, we use a three-group posttest-only randomized experiment, consisting of a single control group and two treatment groups:

noMC − no modeling conventions. This group of subjects, referred to as the *control group* were given UML analysis and design models that were composed *without* modeling conventions.

MC − modeling conventions. The subjects in this treatment group received UML analysis and design models that were composed using the list of modeling conventions enlisted in Appendix A.

MC+T – tool-supported modeling conventions. Subjects in this treatment group received UML analysis and design models that were composed using both a list of modeling conventions and a tool to support the detection of their violation.

3.2 Experimental Subjects, Tasks and Objects

The experiment was performed using pen and paper only. Each student was provided with (i) a hardcopy of all diagrams of a single model; (ii) a questionnaire; and (iii) a vocabulary.

A total of 27 MSc computer-science students participated in the controlled experiment. This experiment was performed in the end of 2005 at the University of Mons-Hainaut and at the University of Antwerp (both in Belgium). We evaluated the subjects' experience with the different types of UML diagrams using a questionnaire. All subjects had practical (although merely academic) experience with the diagrams required to answer the questions.

The questionnaire contained a single introduction page that described the task. Another explanatory page displayed one example question and its solution, elaborating on the steps to be applied. The example question, illustrated in Table 1, asks the participant to verify whether a given UML analysis and design model confirms a given statement. As an argument for the confirmation of a statement, the participant should be able to indicate a diagram fragment dictating that the statement should hold. In case such a fragment can be found, the participant annotates the fragment with the question number.

Table 1. Example question and supporting diagram fragment

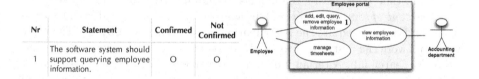

Nr	Statement	Confirmed	Not Confirmed
1	The software system should support querying employee information.	O	O

The main part of the questionnaire asked subjects to evaluate whether a given statement was explicitly confirmed by the given model. Only two options were possible, being either "confirmed", or "not confirmed". The questions[2] asked allow to estimate semantic, social and communicative quality. We have identified over 60 statements that are relevant and valid in the domain, derived from the informal requirement specification for which the subjects of the first experiment composed the UML models. From this set of 60 statements, a selection of 22 statements was made, comprising the set of selected domain statements D_s.

For each experimental group ($noMC$, MC, $MC+T$), a representative set of three UML analysis and design models was selected from the set of output models

---

[2] An elaborate discussion on the different categories of questions is provided in [4].

of the first experiment. The selected models serve as experimental objects, and were representative w.r.t. syntactic quality, defined as the density of modeling defects present in the model. These UML models – modeling a typical application in the insurance domain – consisted of six different types of UML diagrams used for analysis and design. The frequency of each of the diagram types in each model is provided in Table 2.

Table 2. Frequency of the diagram types in each model

	noMC			MC			MC+T		
type	no_2	no_4	no_8	MC_2	MC_4	MC_5	$MC+T_4$	$MC+T_6$	$MC+T_{10}$
Class Diagram	6	1	6	8	1	1	11	1	5
Package Diagram	1	0	0	0	0	0	0	0	1
Collaboration Diagram	0	0	0	0	0	0	0	1	0
Deployment Diagram	0	0	0	0	0	0	1	1	1
Use Case Diagram	7	1	5	0	3	5	6	5	1
Sequence Diagram	6	26	10	3	39	14	8	56	15
total	20	28	16	11	43	20	26	23	64

As the different models used synonyms for some concepts, a glossary was provided indicating which names or verbs are synonyms.

3.3   Experimental Procedure

The procedure for this experiment consisted of two major phases. First, in preparation of the experiment, the semantic quality of each selected model was assessed. Second, two executions of the experimental procedure (runs) were held to observe subjects performing the experimental task described in the previous subsection, thereby assessing the models' communicative and social quality.

Assessment of semantic quality. This assessment was performed by three evaluators, and did not require the participation of experimental subjects. The three evaluators were the first two authors of this paper, and a colleague from the first authors' research lab. After an individual assessment, conflicts were resolved resulting in agreement on the recognition of each selected domain statement in each model.

This evaluation procedure provided the data to calculate the semantic completeness and semantic validity of each of the nine selected models.

Assessment of social and communicative quality. Each experimental run was held in a classroom, and adhered to the following procedure. Subjects were first randomized into experimental groups, and then provided with the experimental material. Subjects were asked to write their name on the material, to take the time to read the instructions written on an introduction page, and finally to complete the three parts of the questionnaire.

No time restrictions were placed on the completion of the assignment.

3.4   Experimental Variables

The independent variable subject to experimental control is entitled *modeling convention usage*, indicating whether the model was composed without modeling conventions (*noMC*), with modeling conventions (*MC*) or with modeling conventions and a tool to detect their violations (*MC+T*). The observed dependent variables are the estimators for semantic completeness (SC), communicative completeness (CC), communicative validity (CV) and relative agreement among interpreters (RAI), as defined in section 2.1. As these variables are all calculated as ratios, we express them in percentage.

4   Data Analysis

Table 3 characterizes the experimental variables across the experimental groups.

Table 3. Statistics of the experimental variables

Hyp.	DV	Overall mean	MCU[1]	Mean	StdDev	Min	Max	$H(2)$	p-value
$H_{0,SeQ}$	SC	62.6%	noMC	66.7%	13.9%	54.5%	81.8%	0.4786	.7872
			MC	59.1%	9.1%	50.0%	68.2%		
			MC+T	62.1%	6.9%	54.5%	68.2%		
$H_{0,SoQ}$	RAI	59.6%	noMC	66.7%	15.6%	50.0%	81.8%	1.1556	.5611
			MC	59.1%	20.8%	36.4%	77.3%		
			MC+T	53.0%	17.2%	40.1%	72.7%		
$H_{0,CoQ}$	CC	76.9%	noMC	82.7%	14.1%	61.0%	100.0%	2.7298	.2554
			MC	74.5%	16.0%	36.0%	93.0%		
			MC+T	72.5%	13.1%	53.0%	92.0%		
	CV	85.0%	noMC	87.0%	7.9%	75.0%	100.0%	1.5235	.4668
			MC	85.9%	10.6%	60.0%	100.0%		
			MC+T	81.5%	8.9%	69.0%	92.0%		

[1]Modeling Convention Usage.

Semantic Completeness (SC) – The semantic completeness of models composed without modeling conventions was somewhat higher, within a margin of 10% (see top left figure in Table 4). I.e., the models from group *noMC* described slightly more modeling domain statements. However, the *noMC* group also exhibits a larger standard deviation.

Relative Agreement among Interpreters (RAI) – There was considerable higher (about 14%) agreement among interpreters of the models composed without modeling conventions (see top right figure in Table 4). However, we also observed considerable standard deviations in Table 3 in all treatment groups.

Communicative Completeness (CC) – The communicative completeness of models composed without modeling conventions was somewhat higher (around 10%) than that of models composed with modeling conventions.

Communicative Validity (CV) – The communicative validity is approximately equal between models composed with and without modeling conventions, as illustrated in in the bottom right figure in Table 4).

Table 4. Variation of SC, RAI, CC and CV across experimental groups

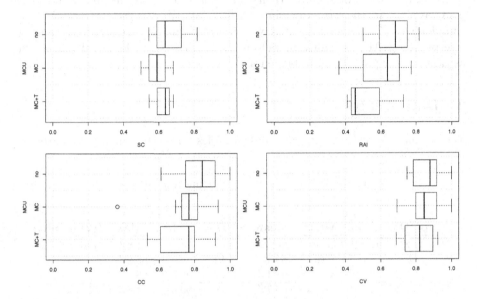

To verify whether the differences among experimental groups are statistically significant, Kruskal-Wallis test results are appended to Table 3. This test is a non-parametric variant of the typical Analysis of Variance (ANOVA), and is more robust with regard to assumptions about the distribution of the data, as well as unequal sample sizes ($\#noMC=10,\#MC=9,\#MC+T=8$). Moreover, the assumptions of at least an ordinal measurement level, independent groups and random sampling were also satisfied.

Table 3 indicates that the group differences concerning semantic, social and communicative quality are not statistically significant at the 90% level. Accordingly, we must accept the hypotheses stating that the UML analysis and design models composed with or without modeling conventions do not differ w.r.t. semantic, social and communicative quality.

5   Threats to Validity

Construct Validity is the degree to which the variables used measure the concepts they are to measure. We have decomposed representational quality, the main concept to be measured, into semantic, social and communicative quality, and have argued their proposed approximations.

Internal Validity is the degree to which the experimental setup allows to accurately attribute an observation to specific cause rather than alternative causes.

Particular threats are due to selection bias. The selection of statements from the domain D_s could not have introduced systematic differences, and the selection of model was performed as to be representative w.r.t. syntactic quality.

External Validity is the degree to which research results can be generalized outside the experimental setting or to the population under study. The set of modeling conventions was composed after a literature review of modeling conventions for UML, revealing design, syntax and diagram conventions. Our set of modeling conventions contains instances of these three categories.

6   Conclusion

Based on the results of this experiment, we conclude that UML modeling conventions focusing on the prevention of common UML modeling defects (as reported in [1]) are unlikely to affect representational quality.

We interpret our findings as an invitation to study the application of modeling conventions of a different nature. Conventions are needed that clarify which types of information are relevant to particular future model usages. Such modeling conventions might suggest the modeling of a type of information (e.g., features, concepts, interactions, scenarios) consistently in a particular (set of) diagram type(s). We hypothesize that this uniform manner of modeling different types of information is more likely to optimize semantic and communicative quality, as these types of information are the subject of their evaluation.

References

[1] C.F.J. Lange and M.R.V. Chaudron. Effects of defects in UML models - an experimental investigation. In *ICSE '06: Proceedings of the 28th International Conference on Software Engineering*, pages 401–411, 2006.

[2] C.F.J. Lange, M.R.V. Chaudron, and Johan Muskens. In practice: UML software architecture and design description. *IEEE Softw.*, 23(2):40–46, 2006.

[3] C.F.J. Lange, Bart Du Bois, M.R.V. Chaudron, and Serge Demeyer. Experimentally investigating the effectiveness and effort of modeling conventions for the UML. In *O. Nierstrasz et al. (Eds.): MoDELS 2006, LNCS 4199*, pages 27–41, 2006.

[4] Bart Du Bois, C.F.J. Lange, Serge Demeyer and M.R.V. Chaudron. A Qualitative Investigation of UML Modeling Conventions *First International Workshop on Quality in Modeling* at MoDELS 2006

[5] Odd Ivar Lindland, Guttorm Sindre, and Arne Solvberg. Understanding quality in conceptual modeling. *IEEE Softw.*, 11(2):42–49, 1994.

[6] John Krogstie. *Conceptual Modeling for Computerized Information Systems Support in Organizations*. PhD thesis, University of Trondheim, Norway, 1995.

[7] Friday, November 10, 2006 at 5:06 pmWilliam R. Shadish, Thomas D. Cook, and Donald T. Campbell. *Experimental and Quasi-Experimental Designs for Generalized Causal Inference*. Houghton Mifflin, 2002.

A   Modeling Conventions

Table 5 enlists the modeling conventions employed in a previous experiment. These conventions were used by two of the experimental groups (*MC* and

$MC + T$) while composing UML analysis and design models. As the resulting models were used in this experiment, it is relevant to recapitulate these conventions.

Table 5. Modeling Conventions

Category	ID	Convention
Abstraction	1	Classes in the same package must be of the same abstraction level.
	2	Classes, packages and use cases must have unique names.
	3	All use cases should cover a similar amount of functionality.
Balance	4	When you specify getters/setters/constructors for a class, specify them for all classes.
	5	When you specify visibility somewhere, specify it everywhere.
	6	Specify methods for the classes that have methods! Don't make a difference in whether you specify or don't specify methods as long as there is not a strong difference between the classes.
	7	Idem as 6 but for attributes.
Completeness	8	For classes with a complex internal behavior, specify the internal behavior using a state diagram.
	9	All classes that interact with other classes should be described in a sequence diagram.
	10	Each use case must be described by at least one sequence diagram.
	11	The type of ClassifierRoles (Objects) must be specified.
	12	A method that is relevant for interaction between classes should be called in a sequence diagram to describe how it is used for interaction.
	13	ClassifierRoles (Objects) should have a role name.
Consistency	14	Each message must correspond to a method (operation).
Design	15	Abstract classes should not be leafs.
	16	Inheritance trees should not have no more than 7 levels.
	17	Abstract classes should not have concrete superclasses.
	18	Classes should have high cohesion. Don't overload classes with unrelated functionality.
	19	Your classes should have low coupling.
Layout	20	Diagrams should not contain crossed lines (relations).
	21	Don't overload diagrams. Each diagram should focus on a specific concept/problem/functionality/...
Naming	22	Classes, use cases, operations, attributes, packages, etc. must have a name.
	23	Naming should use commonly accepted terminology, be non-ambiguous and precisely express the function/role/characteristic of an element.

Model Driven Development of Advanced User Interfaces (MDDAUI) – MDDAUI'06 Workshop Report

Andreas Pleuß[1], Jan van den Bergh[2], Stefan Sauer[3], Heinrich Hußmann[1], and Alexander Bödcher[4]

[1] University of Munich, Germany
{Andreas.Pleuss, Heinrich.Hussmann}@ifi.lmu.de
[2] Hasselt University, Belgium
Jan.VandenBergh@uhasselt.be
[3] University of Paderborn, Germany
sauer@upb.de
[4] University of Kaiserslautern, Germany
boedcher@mv.uni-kl.de

Abstract. This paper reports on the *2nd Workshop on Model Driven Development of Advanced User Interfaces (MDDAUI'06)* held on October 2nd, 2006 at the *MoDELS'06* conference in Genova, Italy. It briefly describes the workshop topic and provides a short overview on the workshop structure. In the main part it introduces the four topics discussed in the workshop's afternoon sessions and summarizes the discussion results.

1 Workshop Topic

The user interface of an application is often one of the core factors determining its success. While model-based user interface development is an important line of research in the human-computer-interaction (respectively human-machine-interaction) community, model-driven application development is an important area in the software engineering community. This workshop aims at integrating the knowledge from both domains, leading to a model-driven development of user interfaces. Thereby, the focus of the workshop lies on advanced user interfaces corresponding to the current state-of-the-art in human-computer-interaction, such as multimedia or context-sensitive user interfaces or multimodal interaction techniques.

The workshop builds up on the results of the previous edition [1, 2], which provided an overview on existing work and the challenges in the area of MDDAUI. On that base, the current workshop aims to go more into specific details and specific challenges on the field. This includes e.g. more specific models for advanced UIs, a stricter compliance to the concepts from model-driven engineering, explicit transformations between UI models which in particular provide concepts to ensure the usability of resulting UIs, and additional integration of informal techniques to achieve a better integration of usability and artistic design into the model-driven development process.

T. Kühne (Ed.): MoDELS 2006 Workshops, LNCS 4364, pp. 101–105, 2007.
© Springer-Verlag Berlin Heidelberg 2007

2   Submissions, Participants, and Program

Interested participants were asked to submit a short paper of four pages length
in double-column format. We received 18 submission from which 12 have been
accepted. The resulting spectrum of participants included people from different
areas in human-computer-interaction and software engineering. Besides people
from academia, there were also participants working in industrial context.

The workshop took one day during the MoDELS'06 conference. In the morning
sessions all accepted papers were presented either at short or as long presentations. The afternoon was mainly reserved for discussions. The detailed program
and the preliminary proceedings including all accepted papers can be found on
the workshop webpage [3]. Official proceedings will be available at [4].

3   Workshop Discussions

After the paper presentations four discussion groups were formed around the
following topics:

- Co-development of Models and Visualizations
- Runtime Interpretation of UI Models
- MDDAUI and Usability
- An Integrated Metamodel for MDDAUI

In the following we summarize the discussion results of these discussion groups,
which were also presented at the end of the workshop.

3.1   Co-development of Models and Visualizations

In the context of the discussion, visualization means the concrete visual appearance of the user interface. The user interface development process involves different developer groups, like graphic designer or usability experts. Some of them
usually work on concrete visualizations like sketches, hi-fi and low-fi prototypes.
Thus, their results have to be synchronized with the models which provides the
central information in an abstract way for all parties involved in the development
process.

As a consequence, there is a need for tools and transformations which allow
a bottom-up process, where the abstract information for the models is derived
from the various visualizations. Currently, most model-driven approaches focus
on the top-down process. Furthermore, it must be possible to update the visualizations when changes on the model occur. This leads to the need of a round-trip
engineering between models and different kinds of visualizations even in an early
stage of the development process.

Finally, the discussion addressed the issue that the relative importance of the
models versus visualizations changes for different kinds of applications. Visual
appearance of the user interface is especially important in applications for consumer products or in multimedia applications like in the automotive sector. On

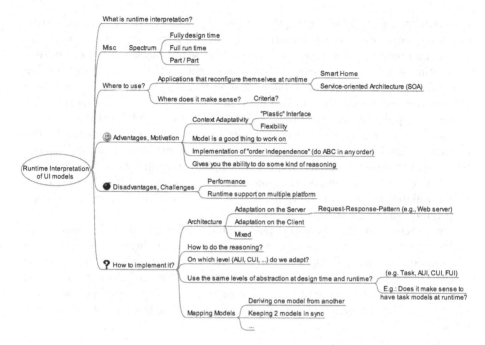

Fig. 1. Overview on the different aspects of runtime interpretation of user interface models

the other hand e.g. for a corporate intranet the flexible adaptation to the continuously changing information seems more important than the concrete visual appearance of the user interface.

3.2   Runtime Interpretation of UI Models

In the context of our discussion, runtime interpretation means that the abstract information from the model is kept during the execution of the modelled application and is interpreted by a specific runtime environment. This is necessary e.g. in ubiquitous computing scenarios where the user interface must be adapted at runtime to the context of the application, e.g. the currently available target devices. In the discussion we aimed for an overview on the current state-of-the art and the challenges in this area. As a result, we created the mind map shown in figure 1.

3.3   MDDAUI and Usability

A large part of the discussion in this group focused on identification of challenges to create usable interactive applications within industrial settings. A first challenge is the fact that the people involved with the design of these interactive applications are faced with some design decisions that are made without their involvement, especially regarding the hardware platform. For example, decisions regarding hardware in the automotive industry are largely driven by artistic designers and management decisions based on perceived market needs or desires.

Another important challenge is that the target platform can change during the design process, for example due to market changes. These changes can have a enormous impact on the design of the interactive application, especially for embedded applications where only a limited number of physical controls can be used and strong ergonomic rules apply to the usage of these controls. For example, a decision to replace a rotation knop for navigating through menus by a touch screen in a car can require a complete redesign of the user interface structure caused by the ergonomic rules that are associated with these controls. Using a higher level of abstraction through models may make it easier to cope with these changing hardware platforms.

The usage of models, however, poses some challenges since the teams that design interactive applications are very heterogenous. It therefore is a challenge to communicate designs, especially in abstract models, to all that are involved in the design of interactive applications. One possible path to cope with the problem that was considered to be worth further investigation is the usage of a domain-specific language with a specialized concrete syntax for the (abstract) models.

3.4   An Integrated Metamodel for UI Development

The discussion started with the idea, that most of the different approaches for different kinds of (advanced) user interfaces partially base on the same or very similar modeling concepts (for the core properties of a user interface) and partially very different concepts (e.g. for a specific property of the UI like context-sensitiveness, multimedia context, 3D, or a specific modality). Concepts from model-driven engineering – like explicit metamodels, operations on metamodels and explicit transformations – could perhaps help to define an overall framework to capture these commonalities and variabilities. This could result e.g. in an overall metamodel or a family of languages, which then allows the flexible combination of different concepts (metamodels) according to the properties of the user interface to be built. For example, one can then select the required models to develop a user interface which is context-sensitive but also includes 3D-animations.

To get a feeling about how this could look like, we first collected the most common models for UI development known from the literature. Then we discussed on alternatives how to integrate these different models. Two approaches were considered: The first is the creation of a core metamodel which is common to all MDDAUI approaches, complemented with extensions to cope with specific concerns. However, it seems difficult to agree on such a core metamodel. The second approach is creating metamodels for all MDDAUI approaches complemented with various operations on these metamodels. Examples of such operations are the transformations from one metamodel into another one or merging two metamodels. This allows a flexible and modular specification of models and transformations and even the co-existence of an arbitrary number of alternative approaches.

For the further discussion we decided for the second approach. A collection of metamodels and transformations can be realized by metamodel repositories or 'metamodel zoos' as proposed by several initiatives on the MoDELS'06 conference. In the last part of the discussion we structured the collected models into packages, which could be for example: A package *Domain* which contains models for the application logic, a package *Context* which contains models for the context of the user interface, a package *Behavior* which contains models for the behavior of the user interface and a package *Appearance* which contains models for the structure and the concrete layout of the user interface.

4   Conclusion

The growing number of workshop participants from different communities indicates the high relevance of model-driven user interface development. The workshop's results show that the involved research areas, software engineering and human-computer-interaction, can both strongly benefit from the integration of their knowledge. In the context of the workshop topic, the workshop contributions show on the one hand that applying concepts and standards from model-driven engineering – like explicit metamodels and transformations or round-trip-engineering techniques – can seriously contribute to the solution of current challenges in user interface development. On the other hand, the area of model-driven engineering benefits not only through the consideration of knowledge from human-computer-interaction itself, but also through new insights and challenges arising from the complex application domain of user interface development.

Acknowledgements. We would like to thank the workshop participants for their high quality contributions as well as the program committee members for their help and the valuable reviews.

References

[1] Pleuß, A., Van den Bergh, J., Hußmann, H., Sauer, S.: Workshop Report: Model Driven Development of Advanced User Interfaces (MDDAUI). In: Jean-Michel Bruel (Ed.): Satellite Events at the MoDELS 2005 Conference, LNCS 3844, Springer 2006
[2] Pleuß, A., Van den Bergh, J., Hußmann, H., Sauer, S.: Proceedings of Model Driven Development of Advanced User Interfaces. CEUR Workshop Proceedings, Vol. 159, 2005, http://ceur-ws.org/Vol-159
[3] Second International Workshop on Model Driven Development of Advanced User Interfaces (MDDAUI 2006), Workshop Webpage, 2006 http://planetmde.org/mddaui2006/
[4] Pleuß, A., Van den Bergh, J., Hußmann, H., Sauer, S., Bödcher, A.: Proceedings of Model Driven Development of Advanced User Interfaces 2006. CEUR Workshop Proceedings (to appear), http://ceur-ws.org/

A Model-Driven Approach to the Engineering of Multiple User Interfaces

Goetz Botterweck

Institute for IS Research, University of Koblenz-Landau, Germany
`botterweck@uni-koblenz.de`

Abstract. In this paper, we describe MANTRA[1], a model-driven approach to the development of multiple consistent user interfaces for one application. The common essence of these user interfaces is captured in an abstract UI model (AUI) which is annotated with constraints to the dialogue flow. We consider in particular how the user interface can be adapted on the AUI level by deriving and tailoring dialogue structures which take into account constraints imposed by front-end platforms or inexperienced users. With this input we use model transformations described in ATL (Atlas Transformation Language) to derive concrete, platform-specific UI models (CUI). These can be used to generate implementation code for several UI platforms including GUI applications, dynamic web sites and mobile applications. The generated user interfaces are integrated with a multi tier application by referencing WSDL-based interface descriptions and communicating with the application core over web service protocols.

Keywords: Model-driven, multiple user interfaces, multiple front-ends, user interface engineering, user interface modelling, model transformation, ATL, Atlas Transformation Language.

1 Introduction

An elementary problem in user interface engineering is the complexity imposed by the diversity of platforms and devices which can be used as foundations. The complications increase when we develop multiple user interfaces (based on different platforms) which offer access to the same functionality. In that case we have to find a way to resolve the inherent contradiction between redundancy (the user interfaces of one application have something in common) and variance (each user interface should be optimized for its platform and context of use). Model-driven approaches appear to be a promising solution to this research problem, since we can use models to capture the common features of all user interfaces and model transformations to produce multiple variations from that. The resulting implementations can be specialized (because we can embed platform-specific implementation knowledge into the transformations) as well as consistent (as they are all derived from the same common model and hence share the same logical structure).

---

[1] Model-based engineering of multiple interfaces with transformations.

T. Kühne (Ed.): MoDELS 2006 Workshops, LNCS 4364, pp. 106–115, 2007.

2   Related Work

The *mapping problem* [1], a fundamental challenge in model-based approaches, can occur in various forms and can be dealt with by various types of approaches [2]. One instance of this is the question of how we can identify concrete interaction *elements* that match a given abstract element and other constraints [3]. A similar challenge is the derivation of *structures* in a new model based on information given in another existing model. Many task-oriented approaches use requirements given by the task model to determine UI structures; for example, temporal constraints similar to the ones in our approach have been used to derive the structure of an AUI [4] or dialogue model [5].

Florins et al. [6] take an interesting perspective on a similar problem by discussing rules for splitting existing presentations into smaller ones. That approach combines information from the AUI and the underlying task model - similar to our approach using an AUI annotated with temporal constraints which are also derived from a task model.

Many model-driven approaches to UI engineering have proposed a hierarchical organization of interaction elements grouped together into logical units [7]. A number of approaches to multiple user interfaces has been collected in [8].

3   Abstract Description of User Interfaces

The MANTRA model flow (cf. Fig. 1) is structured vertically by abstraction levels similar to the CAMELEON framework [9]. The goal of our process (in Fig. 1 going from top to bottom) is to create several user interfaces (front-ends) for the functionality provided by the core of that application.

Further steps are illustrated by a simple time table application. Fig. 2 shows the corresponding AUI model. The user can search for train and bus connections by specifying several search criteria like departure and destination locations, time of travel or the preferred means of transportation (lower part of Fig. 2). The matching connections are retrieved by a web service operation and displayed as a list (upper right part of Fig. 2). At first, the AUI model only contains UI elements (☐) and UI composites (◯) organized in a simple composition hierarchy (indicated by ◆——— relations) and the web service operation necessary to retrieve the results. This model is the starting point of our approach (cf. result of ❶ in Fig. 1) and captures the common essence of the multiple user interfaces of the application in one abstract UI. This AUI contains platform-independent interaction concepts like "Select one element from a list" or "Enter a date".

The AUI is then further annotated by dialogue flow constraints based on the temporal relationships of the ConcurTaskTree approach [10]. For instance we can describe that two interaction elements have to be processed sequentially (>>) or can be processed in any order (|=|).

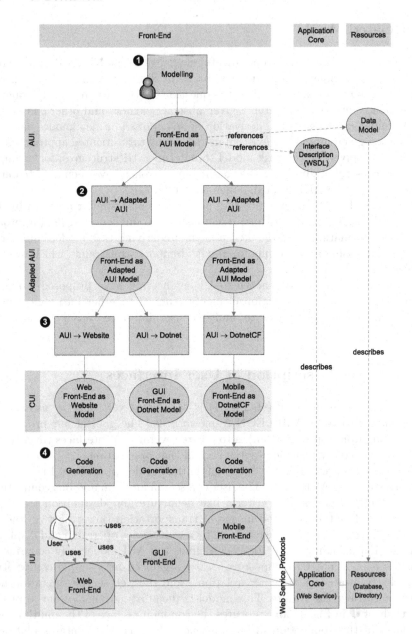

Fig. 1. Model flow in the MANTRA approach

4   Adapting on the AUI Level

As a next step (❷ in Fig. 1) we augment the AUI by deriving dialogue and pre-sentation structures. These structures are still platform-independent. However, they can be adapted and tailored to take into account constraints imposed, for

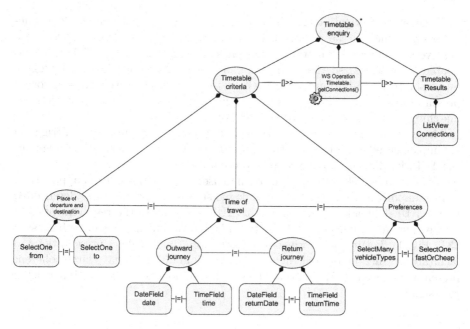

Fig. 2. AUI model of the sample application annotated with temporal constraints (horizontal lines)

instance, by platforms with limited display size or by inexperienced users. The result of this process step, the adapted AUI model, is shown in Fig. 3.

4.1 Clustering Interaction Elements to Generate Presentation Units

To derive this adapted AUI model we cluster UI elements by identifying suitable UI composites. The subtrees starting at these nodes will become presentations in the user interface (⌂). For instance we decided that "Time of Travel" and all UI elements below it will be presented coherently. This first automatic clustering is done by heuristics based on metrics like the number of UI elements in each presentation or the nesting level of grouping elements. To further optimize the results the clustering can be refined by the human designer.

4.2 Inserting Control-Oriented Interaction Elements

Secondly, we generate the navigation elements necessary to traverse between the presentations identified in the preceding step. For this we create triggers (■). These are abstract interaction elements which can start an operation (OperationTrigger) or the transition to a different presentation (NavigationTrigger). In graphical interfaces these can be represented as buttons, in other front-ends they could also be implemented as speech commands.

To generate NavigationTriggers in a presentation p we calculate dialogueSuccessors(p) which is the set of all presentations which can "come next" if we observe the temporal constraints. We can then create NavigationTriggers (and related Transitions) so that the user can reach all presentations in dialogueSuccessors(p). In addition to this we have to generate OperationTriggers for all presentations which will trigger a web service operation, e.g. "Search" to retrieve matching train connections (lower right corner of Fig. 3).

These two adaptation steps (derivation of presentations, insertion of triggers) are implemented as ATL model transformations. These transformations augment the AUI with dialogue structures (e.g. presentations ⬭ and transitions ⟶) between them) which determine the paths a user can take through our application.

It is important to note that the dialogue structures are *not* fully determined by the AUI. Instead, we can adapt the AUI according to the requirements and create different variants of it (cf. the two adapted AUI models resulting from step ❷ in Fig. 1). For instance, we could create more (but smaller) presentations to facilitate viewing on a mobile device – or we could decide to have large coherent presentations, taking the risk that the user has to do lots of scrolling if restricted to a small screen.

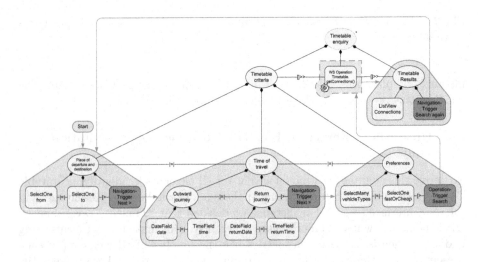

Fig. 3. Adopted AUI model with generated presentations and triggers

4.3 Selecting Content

As an additional adaptation step we can filter content retrieved from the web service based on priorities. For instance, if a user has a choice, higher priority is given to knowing when the train is leaving and where it is going before discovering whether it has a restaurant. This optional information can be factored out to separate "more details" presentations.

A similar concept are substitution rules which provide alternative representations for reoccurring content. A train, for example, might be designated as InterCityExpress, ICE, or by a graphical symbol based on the train category (for instance, ✯✯ to indicate a luxury train) depending on how much display space is available. These priorities and substitution rules are domain knowledge which cannot be inferred from other models. The necessary information can therefore be stored as annotations to the underlying data model.

5   Generating Concrete and Implemented User Interfaces

Subsequently we transform the adapted AUI models into several CUIs using a specialized model transformation (❸ in Fig. 1) for each target platform. These transformations encapsulate the knowledge of how the abstract interaction elements are best transformed into platform-specific concepts. Hence, they can be reused for other applications over and over again.

As a result we get platform-specific CUI models. These artefacts are still represented and handled as models, but use platform-specific concepts like "HTML-Submit-Button" or ".NET GroupBox". This makes it easier to use them as a basis for the code generation (❹ in Fig. 1) which produces the implementations of the desired user interfaces in platform-typical programming or markup languages.

6   AUI Metamodel

6.1   User Interface Structure

The core structure of a user interface is given by the composition hierarchy of the various user interface components. In the AUI metamodel this is modeled by a "Composite" design pattern [11] consisting of the classes UIComponent, UIElement and UIComposite (cf. ❶ in the simplified excerpt from the AUI metamodel in Fig. 4).

There are two types of UIComponents: The first subtype are UIElements (cf. ❷ in the metamodel in Fig. 4) which cannot contain further UIComponents. Hence, they become the "leaves" of the hierarchy tree (cf. the ☐ symbols in the Timetable sample in Fig. 2). Subclasses of UIElement can be used to describe various abstract interaction tasks, such as the editing of a simple string value (InputField) or the selection of one value from a list (SelectOne). A special case of UIElements are Triggers which can start the transition to another presentation (NavigationTrigger) or start a (potential data modifying) transaction (TransactionTrigger). Please note that the AUI modelling language contains many more UIElement subclasses, but they have been omitted here to simplify the illustration.

The second subtype of UIComponents are UIComposites (cf. ❸ in Fig. 4). UIComposites can contain other UIComponents via the association "uiComponents" and hence build up the "branches" of the hierarchy tree (cf. the ◯ symbols in the Timetable sample in Fig. 2). A UIComposite can be connected to

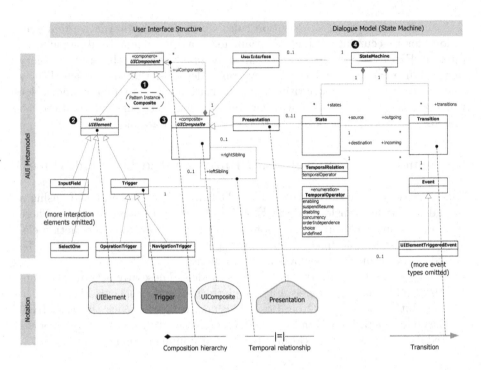

Fig. 4. Simplified excerpt from the AUI metamodel and the related notation symbols

its left and right sibling by temporal relations (cf. the horizontal lines ——|=|—— in Fig. 2). In the metamodel this is described by an instance of the association class TemporalRelation which connects two UIComposites "leftSibling" and "rightSibling". There are several kinds of temporal operators, such as "enabling", "suspendResume" or "choice" (cf. the enumeration "TemporalOperator").

There are two special cases of UIComposites: A UserInterface represents the whole user interface and is therefore the root of the hierarchy. In the Timetable sample this is the node "Timetable enquiry" (cf. Fig. 2).

Another special case of an UIComposite is a Presentation. A Presentation is a hierarchy node that was selected during the adaptation process, because all UIElements contained in the subtree below it should be presented coherently. For instance see the node "Time of travel" in the Timetable sample (Fig. 3): This node and the subtree below it are surrounded by a marked area to indicate that all UIComponents within that area will be presented in one coherent Presentation. Hence, this UIComposite will be converted into a Presentation in further transformation steps.

6.2 Dialogue Model

The dialogue model of an abstract user interface is described by a StateMachine (cf. ❹ in Fig. 4) which is based on UML Statecharts [12]. It consists of States, which are linked to Presentations generated in the adaptation process. As long as the UserInterface is one particular state the related Presentation is displayed (or presented in different ways on non-visual interfaces). When the UserInterface performs a Transition to a different State the next Presentation is displayed. Transitions can be started by Events, for instance by a UIElementTriggeredEvent, which fires as soon as the related UIElement, such as a Trigger, is triggered. There are many other event types, which have been omitted here to simplify the metamodel illustration.

7 Applied Technologies

We described the metamodels used in MANTRA (including platform-specific concepts) in UML and then converted these to Ecore, since we use the Eclipse Modeling Framework (EMF) [13] to handle models and metamodels.

The various model transformations (e.g. for steps ❷ and ❸ in Fig. 1) are described in ATL [14]. On the one hand, the integration of ATL with Eclipse and EMF was helpful as it supported the development in an integrated environment which was well-known to us. On the other hand, the work with ATL model transformations turned out to be time consuming; for instance, ATL was sensitive even to small mistakes and then often did not provide helpful error messages.

We use a combination of Java Emitter Templates and XSLT to generate (❹ in Fig. 1) arbitrary text-oriented or XML-based implementation languages (e.g. C-Sharp or XHTML with embedded PHP).

The coordination of several steps in the model flow is automated by mechanisms provided by the Eclipse IDE and related tools, e.g. we use the software management tool Apache Ant [15] (which is integrated in Eclipse) and custom-developed "Ant Tasks" to manage the chain of transformations and code generation.

We use web services as an interface between the UIs and the application core. Hence, the UI models reference a WSDL based description of operations in the application core. The generated UIs then use web service operations, e.g. to retrieve results for a query specified by the user.

8 Conclusion

We have shown how our MANTRA approach can be used to generate several consistent user interfaces for a multi tier application (cf. Fig. 5).

At the moment, the *automated* model flow (cf. Fig. 1) starts at the AUI level. But nothing prevents us from starting with a task model (e.g. in CTT) and then either manually transferring the task structures into an AUI model, or extending the automated model flow to support task models from which the annotated AUI model can be derived.

We discussed how the user interface can be adapted on the AUI level by tailoring dialogue and logical presentation structures which take into account requirements imposed by front-end platforms or inexperienced users. For this we used the hierarchical structure of interaction elements and constraints on the dialogue flow which can be derived from a task model.

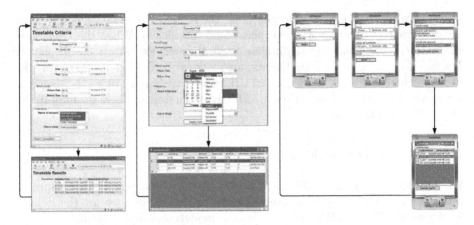

Fig. 5. The generated front-ends (Web, GUI, mobile)

The approach generates fully working prototypes of user-interfaces on three target platforms (GUI, dynamic website, mobile device) which can serve as front-ends to arbitrary web services.

Acknowledgements

We would like to thank the anonymous reviewers for their constructive and valuable feedback.

References

1. Puerta, A.R., Eisenstein, J.: Interactively mapping task models to interfaces in MOBI-D. In: DSV-IS 1998 (Design, Specication and Verication of Interactive Systems), June 3-5, Abingdon, UK (1998) 261–273
2. Clerckx, T., Luyten, K., Coninx, K.: The mapping problem back and forth: customizing dynamic models while preserving consistency. In: TAMODIA '04 (Third annual conference on Task models and diagrams), November 15-16, Prague, Czech Republic, ACM Press (2004) 33–42
3. Vanderdonckt, J.: Advice-giving systems for selecting interaction objects. In: UIDIS'99 (User Interfaces to Data Intensive Systems), September 5-6, Edinburgh, Scotland (1999) 152–157
4. Paternò, F.: One model, many interfaces. In: CADUI'02 (Fourth International Conference on Computer-Aided Design of User Interfaces), May 15-17, Valenciennes, France (2002)
5. Forbrig, P., Dittmar, A., Reichart, D., Sinnig, D.: From models to interactive systems – tool support and XIML. In: IUI/CADUI 2004 workshop "Making model-based user interface design practical: usable and open methods and tools", Island of Madeira, Portugal (2004)
6. Florins, M., Simarro, F.M., Vanderdonckt, J., Michotte, B.: Splitting rules for graceful degradation of user interfaces. In: IUI'06 (Intelligent User Interfaces 2006), January 29 - February 1, Sydney, Australia (2006) 264–266

7. Eisenstein, J., Vanderdonckt, J., Puerta, A.R.: Applying model-based techniques to the development of UIs for mobile computers. In: IUI '01 (6th international conference on Intelligent user interfaces), January 14-17, Santa Fe, NM, USA (2001) 69–76
8. Seffah, A., Javahery, H.: Multiple user interfaces : cross-platform applications and context-aware interfaces. John Wiley & Sons, New York, NY, USA (2004)
9. Calvary, G., Coutaz, J., Thevenin, D., Limbourg, Q., Bouillon, L., Vanderdonckt, J.: A unifying reference framework for multi-target user interfaces. Interacting with Computers **15**(3) (2003) 289–308
10. Paternò, F., Mancini, C., Meniconi, S.: ConcurTaskTrees: A diagrammatic notation for specifying task models. In Howard, S., Hammond, J., Lindgaard, G., eds.: Interact'97 (Sixth IFIP International Conference on Human-Computer Interaction), July 14-16, Sydney, Australia, Chapman and Hall (1997) 362–369
11. Gamma, E., Helm, R., Johnson, R., Vlissides, J.: Design patterns: Elements of reusable object-oriented software. Addison-Wesley, Reading, MA, USA (1995)
12. OMG: Uml 2.0 superstructure specification (formal/05-07-04). Object Management Group (2005)
13. Budinsky, F., Steinberg, D., Merks, E., Ellersick, R., Grose, T.J.: Eclipse modeling framework : a developer's guide. The eclipse series. Addison-Wesley, Boston, MA, USA (2003)
14. Jouault, F., Kurtev, I.: Transforming models with ATL. In: Model Transformations in Practice (Workshop at MoDELS 2005), October 3, Montego Bay, Jamaica (2005)
15. Holzner, S., Tilly, J.: Ant : the definitive guide. 2nd edn. O'Reilly, Sebastopol, CA, USA (2005)

Model-Driven Dynamic Generation of Context-Adaptive Web User Interfaces

Steffen Lohmann, J. Wolfgang Kaltz, and Jürgen Ziegler

University of Duisburg-Essen,
Lotharstrasse 65, 47057 Duisburg, Germany
{lohmann, kaltz, ziegler}@interactivesystems.info

Abstract. The systematic development of user interfaces that enhance interaction quality by adapting to the context of use is a desirable, but also highly challenging task. This paper examines to which extent contextual knowledge can be systematically incorporated in the model-driven dynamic generation of Web user interfaces that provide interaction for operational features. Three parts of the generation process are distinguished: selection, parameterization, and presentation. A semantically enriched service-oriented approach is presented that is based on the CATWALK framework for model interpretation and generation of adaptive, context-aware Web applications. Automation possibilities are addressed and an exemplary case study is presented.

Keywords: Context-aware Web User Interfaces, Web Service Integration, Ontology-based Modeling, Model Interpretation, Model-Driven User Interface Generation, Parameterization, Semantically Enriched SOA.

1 Introduction

The systematic development of complex applications requires a significant effort in modeling throughout the whole life cycle. A promising approach is to use these models not only as design basis for subsequent manual implementation or for semiautomatic generation of application code, but rather consider these models as an inherent part of the system. Changes in the models are then directly visible in the application (or in a prototype used for testing). We developed CATWALK, a Web application framework that follows this design paradigm by interpreting ontology-based models at run-time for dynamic generation of adaptive, context-aware Web applications (cp. [6]).

Building upon this framework, we investigate in this paper how Web user interfaces for operational features can be dynamically selected, generated, and adapted according to the context of use with the motivation to enhance user interaction and reach better usability. By operational features, we mean interactive application functionality that goes beyond hypertext navigation (cp. [1]). By context, we understand the generic meaning of the term, including various aspects such as the user's profile, current task and goal, the location, time, and device used. In [7], we give a formal definition of context for Web scenarios.

T. Kühne (Ed.): MoDELS 2006 Workshops, LNCS 4364, pp. 116–125, 2007.

First, we provide some background information by discussing work related to the modeling and generation of adaptive Web applications and by giving an overview of the CATWALK architecture and the underlying ontology-based modeling method.

2   Related Work

Several existing approaches that address the systematic development of Web applications (Web Engineering) use conceptual models to describe the application's domain. Further aspects such as the application's navigational structure or presentation issues are defined on the basis of these conceptual models. Additional modeling is required for the definition of adaptive system behavior.

The *UML-based Web Engineering* (UWE) approach [9] explicitly addresses adaptivity issues in Web Engineering by providing extra user and adaptation models. UML is used for modeling; the models are stored in XMI. The development framework *Apache Cocoon* has been extended for the generation of application code from the UWE models [10]. However, user and adaptation models are not considered thus far by the code generation framework and the generated Java classes and XSLT stylesheets cannot be executed directly, but need to be manually completed first. Furthermore, UWE addresses primarily the modeling and adaptation of content, navigation and presentation; the integration of operational features and the generation of corresponding user interfaces are not covered by UWE.

The *XML-based Web Modeling Language* (WebML) [4] supports the integration of operational features via Web Services in modeling and application generation [11], but it is not discussed in detail how user interfaces for these features are generated. Further, possibilities for the consideration of context in WebML have been proposed [3], but not in conjunction with the modeling and generation of user interfaces for operational features.

The model-driven generation of user interfaces is also a major research topic in the Human-Computer Interaction (HCI) community. The development of so-called *Multiple* or *Plastic User Interfaces* gains growing interest in the last couple of years (for an overview see e.g. [13]). The focus is on the transformation from abstract platform independent descriptions to concrete user interfaces for various platforms. However, further contextual influences on the different levels of the generation process are rarely addressed in these approaches.

Generally speaking, existing user interface engineering approaches do not consider contextual influences in their modeling and application generation processes to a full degree. They typically consider either information about user preferences or about the location (see [8] for a survey) or address the model-driven generation of multiple-platform user interfaces. Web Engineering approaches that address adaptivity are primarily concerned with issues of how the application's navigation or contents can be adapted. The generation of adaptive, context-aware Web user interfaces for the interaction with operational features is not covered by existing approaches.

3   Ontology-Based Web Application and Context Modeling

Our approach is rooted within the WISE research project [14], where ontologies are used for conceptual Web application modeling. Ontology-based software engineering allows for advanced semantic expressive power in modeling and model exchange compared to other modeling techniques (cp. [5]). Especially for the interoperable integration of contextual knowledge, ontology-based modeling appears promising. The model base of our approach is a repository consisting of the following models (see also Figure 1):

- A *domain ontology*, defining concepts, instances, and relations of the application's domain as well as referencing resources used by the application.
- Several *context ontologies*, defining concepts, instances, and relations of the context of use which are relevant for adaptive system behavior.
- A *context relations model*, defining contextual influences, e.g. by means of weighted relations between entries of the domain ontology and entries of the context ontologies.
- A *navigation*, a *view*, and a *presentation model*, each containing *adaptation specifications* that define rules for adaptive system behavior based on the ontology entries and the defined context relations.

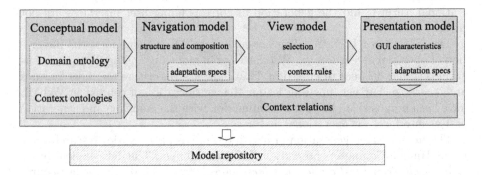

Fig. 1. Application and context modeling in the WISE methodology

4   The CATWALK Framework

CATWALK [6] is a component-oriented framework that interprets the models at run-time to generate an adaptive, context-aware Web application. It is based on Apache Cocoon; Figure 2 gives an architectural overview. The components of CATWALK can be assigned to one of two categories. The first category consists of components that provide core functionality for context-awareness and reasoning. The second category consists of components that are responsible for adaptive Web application generation. White arrows indicate the process flow: each client request is matched in the *Cocoon pipeline* and processed through a series of components responsible for application generation, ultimately resulting in a response to the client (e.g. a Web page). Arrows with dotted lines indicate calls between components. Each component implements a specific concern, in the sense of the *separation of concerns* architectural design principle. A component is implemented by one or more Java classes and may use additional artefacts (such as XSLT stylesheets for XML transformation). The model repository is accessed via a Cocoon pseudo-protocol in each generation step and the corresponding model parts are interpreted at run-time. A central component (the *Adaptation Engine*) coordinates adaptive system behavior by interpreting context relations and adaptation specifications and considering the respective contextual state (provided by the *Context Manager* component).

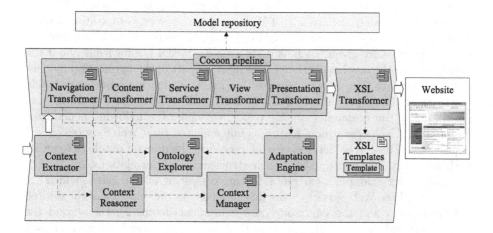

Fig. 2. Component architecture of the CATWALK framework

5 Generation of Adaptive, Context-Aware User Interfaces

Contextual knowledge affects different levels of the user interface generation process. The following questions can be addressed: In what situations should a user interface (or a part of it) be generated (selection)? Which values can be preselected (parameterization)? What should the user interface look like (presentation)?

With these questions in mind, we now take a closer look at our approach to incorporate contextual knowledge in the different steps of the user interface generation process. This is accompanied by an example scenario for better illustration: a Web portal for automobile services that provides a car rental functionality. Beforehand, we shortly address the representation of operational features in our approach.

5.1 Representation

CATWALK follows a service-oriented approach – operational features that are offered by the Web application are encapsulated in Web Services. Representing operational features is therefore primarily a Web Service composition and coordination problem. Two dimensions can be distinguished: one, defining how to combine discrete Web Services to more complex functionalities, and another, defining the order in which Web Services are executed. The main challenge is the definition of mappings and transformations between the different Web Services' input and output values and the consideration of preconditions and effects. The required modeling effort depends on the degree of semantic description that is provided by the Web Services' interfaces. The aim of the *Semantic Web Services* approach is to provide best possible semantic descriptions of Web Services to support the (partial) automation of Web Service discovery, composition, execution, and interoperation (see e.g. OWL-S [12]). If solely syntactic descriptions of Web Services are given (such as is the case for WSDL), knowledge about the capabilities of the involved Web Services must be part of the application models.

Context-aware Web Service composition and coordination models are not in the focus of this paper and shall not be further discussed here (for details, see e.g. [2]). For the remainder of this paper, we make the following generalized assumption: Each operational feature is implemented by n Web Services ($n = 1$ is possible). These Web Services are referenced in the domain ontology together with necessary information about their structure and interrelations.

Consider for example a car rental feature consisting of four parts, which are realized by three Web Services – the first implements the selection of the desired vehicle type(1) and the car model and equipment details(2), the second the booking(3) and the third the payment(4). An ontology entry is created for each part of the operational feature referencing the corresponding WSDL description. The user shall interact with these Web Services in sequence – the ontology entries are interconnected by appropriate relations and assigned to a master concept that represents the whole feature. Additionally, parameters of the Web Services are mapped (see section 5.3).

Alternatively, to briefly mention automation and extension possibilities for Semantic Web Service scenarios, solely a formal semantic description of the desired operational feature would be defined instead of explicit references to Web Services. Then, the challenge is the automated discovery and composition of Web Services that realize the desired operational feature.

5.2 Selection

The first step in the user interface generation process consists in the dynamic selection of those operational features for which user interfaces should be presented in the current Web page.

The navigation model defines the navigational structure of the Web application by means of relations between entries of the domain ontology. The navigational structure is mapped onto the user's current navigational position to identify application items, including operational features, that should potentially be offered in the current Web page. Furthermore, context relations between operational features and concepts of the context ontologies are defined. Adaptation specifications in the navigation model determine the current relevance of operational features in dependence of the context relations and the degree of activation of context concepts (cp. [6]). According to these specifications and the relations defined in the context relations model, none, one or several appropriate operational features are selected for which user interfaces have to be presented in the current Web page. This selection mechanism is independent of the exact representation of the operational features in the domain ontology. It is merely concerned with the selection of operational features that fit into the contextual situation and the user's navigational position.

Let us consider the car rental example scenario and suppose that the user has accessed the homepage of the Web portal for automobile services. A relation between the ontology entry of the homepage and the ontology entry of the reservation feature has been defined in the navigation model. Furthermore, a context relation has been modeled between the reservation feature and the 'owns car' concept of the user context ontology; this concept is activated if the user owns a car. At last, an adaptation specification has been defined, stating that a user interface for the reservation feature should be presented if the related context concept ('owns car') is deactivated. As a result of this modeling, the reservation feature will be presented directly on the homepage to users who do not own a car whereas car owners reach it only via navigation. The context-dependent selection of user interfaces should be considered as supporting rather than withholding. Clearly, all essential functionality should always be alternatively accessible by the user (e.g. via navigation).

5.3 Parameterization

In the next step, the user interface is pre-parameterized according to the contextual situation to provide initial support for user interaction. To achieve this, context relations are defined between parameter entries of the operational features and concepts of the context ontologies. The arrows linking the two windows in Figure 3 illustrate these relations. The activated concepts of the context ontologies (window on the right hand side) determine the parameter value selection in the Web page (window on the left hand side). In the example given, the parameter 'Model' is mapped with the user's favorite car model. Likewise, the parameter 'Color' with the user's favorite car color. The parameter 'Convertible' is mapped with the season and the 'Pick-up' point with the user's current location. If a mapped context concept is activated, the corresponding value is handled as the default value and is preselected in the user interface. The way a value is preselected depends on the type of user interface element, which is determined in the subsequent generation step in accordance to the contextual conditions.

Again, automation possibilities depend on the degree of semantic description and shared understanding of the concepts. The automatic retrieval of context concepts that match the required parameter values (e.g. the favorite car model) is conceivable in a semantically rich scenario. Ultimately, if for every parameter value a matching context concept is found or modeled, no user interaction at all is required. However, user interaction (and control) might be necessary and useful in many cases.

Generally, the danger of erroneous mapping or incorrectly retrieved context exists that confuses instead of support the user. Suppose another city than Duisburg would be preselected as pick-up location in the example scenario that is further away from the user's current location. Then, the user would possibly assume that there exists no pick-up location in Duisburg and would accept the preselection without verifying his (false) assumption.

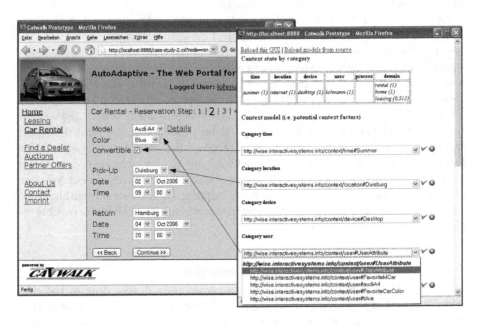

Fig. 3. Contextually adapted user interface of a car rental feature

5.4   Presentation

In the last step, the user interface elements' look and feel is built. Alternative presentation forms come into question, depending on the situational relevance of an operational feature and the contextual conditions. CATWALK is designed to support the definition of various UI patterns for this purpose. Each pattern consists of an XSLT-template (and optionally an additional CSS-stylesheet) and is referenced in the domain ontology. Similar to the modeling of the naviga- tional structure, relations between pattern entries and entries of operational features are defined – this time in the presentation model. These relations de- termine for each operational feature or a set of features which patterns are suit- able. Furthermore, relations between pattern entries and concepts of the context ontologies are modeled in the context relations model. Adaptation specifications define which pattern should be selected for an operational feature in accordance to the context relations and activated concepts.

The left window in Figure 3 shows a possible implementation of a user interface for a part of the car rental example scenario. Suppose the user chose the vehicle type in the first step and now has to select the desired car model, some equipment details, as well as dates, times, pick-up, and return locations. The user accesses the Web portal via a desktop PC in the example scenario – the corresponding concept of the device context ontology is activated. Due to the modeled context relations and the adaptation specifications of the presentation model, a pattern is selected that is suitable for desktop PCs. Alternative patterns and respective context relations and adaptation specifications can be defined for other client devices such as PDAs or cellular phones. Varying patterns can also be used in dependence of a feature's relevance or for different user types (e.g. for visually handicapped people, a CSS-stylesheet defining larger GUI-elements might be selected).

Information required for the generation of suitable user interface elements is either stored in the domain ontology or have to be retrieved from the Web Service. Two ways of retrieval have to be distinguished: using the Web Service's WSDL description, in particular the XML Schema definitions, or using Web Service calls. The first allows the creation of a suitable (X)HTML form element for every XML Schema element by the pattern's XSLT-stylesheet, depending on the type of Schema element and (possibly) the number of provided value options. In the example scenario, the Web Service's WSDL description defines the complex type 'Model' that includes a list of car models that are all permitted parameter values. The XSLT-stylesheet transforms these values in an HTML dropdown listbox. Likewise, it transforms the complex type 'Color' that defines a list of car colors. The Boolean type 'Convertible' is transformed in an HTML checkbox. Corresponding data types are assigned to the parameters 'Date' and 'Time' in the WSDL description - common date and time picker elements are created. Again, semantically richer Web Service descriptions and a shared understanding of interface parameters would help to enhance the transformation of interface parameters to HTML form elements.

In the simplest way, the Web Service is invoked after submission of the whole HTML-form for the first time. Then, the selected values and their interdependencies are validated by the Web Service and possibly a message informing about conflicting values is send back. In such a case, the user might have to select different parameter values again and again until all value conflicts are resolved (e.g., the desired car might not be available for a specific location, date, and time). A more comfortable way is to trigger Web Service calls after certain user interactions to update the list of parameter values that can be selected by the user taking interdependencies into account. *Ajax*-based techniques are appropriate for such an implementation. Ultimately, the Web Services determine how sophisticated the user interface can be by providing or not providing such functionality. In the simplest case, the XML Schema element name is used for caption and text boxes are created allowing the input of parameter values (with preselected recommendations, see section 5.3).

6   Conclusion and Future Work

The homogenous integration of user interfaces for interaction with operational features is an emerging issue in the course of the evolution of Web applications from simple information systems to complex interactive applications. In the presented service-oriented approach, contextual influences have been considered in the modeling process right from the start for different parts of the generation process: selection, parameterization, and presentation. The approach builds upon an ontology-based modeling method and upon the CATWALK framework that provides run-time generation of adaptive, context-aware Web applications from these models.

We have shown how the incorporation of contextual knowledge can support user interaction and may lead to better usability that could make the additional modeling effort worthwhile in certain cases. We have also discussed some automation possibilities, especially in conjunction with Semantic Web Services. Likewise, it has become apparent that incorrect adaptation can confuse the user and reduce interaction quality. Thus, automation possibilities are restricted to some degree and careful modeling is demanded. The empirical investigation of adaptation effects is a difficult task; however, heuristic methods should provide a good basis for design decisions in many cases.

The presented approach is independent of specific context sensing mechanisms. However, possibilities for the exchange and the evaluation of externally sensed context information would be useful extensions. Other topics for future work include the definition of various context-specific UI patterns as well as a better support for the modeling of interaction processes. The empirical investigation of different adaptation strategies and their effects on usability issues are further topics of interest.

Acknowledgements

This work was partially supported by the German Federal Ministry of Education and Research (BMBF) under grant no. 01ISC30F.

References

1. Baresi, L., Garzotto, L., Paolini, P.: From Web Sites to Web Applications: New Issues for Conceptual Modeling. In Proceedings of the Workshops on Conceptual Modeling Approaches for E-Business and The World Wide Web and Conceptual Modeling: Conceptual Modeling for E-Business and the Web, London, UK. Springer LNCS 1921 (2000) 89–100

2. Ben Mokhtar, S., Fournier, D., Georgantas, N., Issarny, V.: Context-aware Service Composition in Pervasive Computing Environments. In Proceedings of the 2nd International Workshop on Rapid Integration of Software Engineering techniques (RISE'05), Heraklion Crete, Greece. Springer LNCS 3943 (2006) 129–144
3. Ceri, S., Daniel, F., Matera, M., Facca, F.: Model-driven Development of Context-Aware Web Applications. ACM Trans. Inter. Tech. (TOIT) 7(2) (2007), to appear
4. Ceri, S. et al.: Designing Data-Intensive Web Applications. Morgan Kaufmann (2002).
5. Hesse, W.: Ontologies in the Software Engineering Process. In Proceedings of the 2nd Workshop on Enterprise Application Integration (EAI'05), Marburg, Germany. CEUR 141 (2005)
6. Kaltz, J.W.: An Engineering Method for Adaptive, Context-aware Web Applications. PhD thesis, University of Duisburg-Essen. Utz (2006). Also published online at http://purl.oclc.org/NET/duett-07202006-093134
7. Kaltz, J.W., Ziegler, J., and Lohmann, S.: Context-Aware Web Engineering: Modeling and Applications. RIA - Revue d'Intelligence Artificielle, Special Issue on Applying Context Management 19(3) (2005) 439–458
8. Kappel, G., Pröll, B., Retschitzegger, W., and Schwinger, W.: Customisation for Ubiquitous Web Applications - A Comparison of Approaches. Int. J. Web Eng. and Technol. (IJWET) 1(1) (2003) 79–111
9. Koch, N.: Software Engineering for Adaptive Hypermedia Systems: Reference Model, Modeling Techniques and Development Process. PhD thesis, Ludwig-Maximilians-University Munich (2001)
10. Kraus, A., Koch, N.: Generation of Web Applications from UML Models using an XML Publishing Framework. In Proceedings of the 6th World Conference on Integrated Design and Process Technology (IDPT'02), Pasadena, USA (2002)
11. Manolescu, I. et al.: Model-Driven Design and Deployment of Service-Enabled Web Applications. ACM Trans. Inter. Tech. 5(3) (2005) 439–479.
12. Martin, D. et al.: Bringing Semantics to Web Services: The OWL-S Approach. In Proceedings of the 1st International Workshop on Semantic Web Services and Web Process Composition (SWSWPC'04), San Diego, USA. Springer LNCS 3387 (2003) 26–42.
13. Seffah, A., Javahery, H.: Multiple User Interfaces: Crossplatform Applications and Context-Aware Interfaces. J.Wiley (2003)
14. WISE - Web Information and Service Engineering http://www.wise-projekt.de (2006/Oct/28)

Modelling and Analysis of Real Time and Embedded Systems – Using UML

Susanne Graf[1], Sébastien Gérard[2], Øystein Haugen[3], Iulian Ober[4], and Bran Selic[5]

[1] VERIMAG, Grenoble, France
Susanne.Graf@imag.fr
[2] CEA-List, Sacley, France
Sebastien.Gerard@cea.fr
[3] University of Oslo, Norway
Oystein.Haugen@ifi.uio.no
[4] IRIT, Toulouse, France
ober@iut-blagnac.fr
[5] IBM, Canada
bselic@ca.ibm.com

Abstract. This paper presents an overview on the outcomes of the workshop MARTES on Modelling and Analysis of Real Time and Embedded Systems that has taken place for the second time in association with the MoDELS/UML 2006 conference. Important themes discussed at this workshop concerned (1) tools for analysis and model transformation and (2) concepts for modelling quantitative aspects with the perspective of analysis.

Keywords: Modelling, Analysis, Real Time, Embedded Systems.

1 Introduction

The motivation for holding this workshop is rooted in the increasing request to use UML and related modelling formalisms also for the development of real-time and embedded systems and by their particular needs with respect to modelling concepts and analysis.

Even more than in other domains, in the context of real-time and embedded systems, the idea of model-based development, where models representing specifications of software and system level aspects are compiled into code for particular platforms, is highly attractive. In such systems, the inherent complexity due to the presence of concurrency makes a posteriori analysis difficult. Moreover, for safety critical systems the need for certification requires a rigorous design process. Replacing – at least partly – code-based analysis by model-based analysis and coding by an a priori valid code generation method, is extremely attractive then: it allows both to achieve higher quality and speed up the development process.

In particular application domains, tools supporting such an approach have been developed already in the past. Good examples are the Esterel and the SCADE tools [Est] for the development of real-time controllers with guaranteed properties for specific, and relatively simple platforms. These tools come with a set of theories

T. Kühne (Ed.): MoDELS 2006 Workshops, LNCS 4364, pp. 126–130, 2007.

which allow establishing the correctness of the implemented methodology and code generation technique as well as with a set of analysis and verification tools supporting the methodology.

In order make this attractive approach available for a wider range of applications and for a less restricted set of modelling paradigms and platforms, the above mentioned modelling languages need to be enriched – in particular for distributed and performance oriented systems, as well as for modelling relevant aspects of the target platform architecture. Tool support needs to be provided for such richer frameworks. The targeted systems are intrinsically more difficult to analyse, and finding new compromises between flexibility, performance and analysability remains a great challenge. UML provide a rich syntactic framework that can be used for this purpose, but tool supported frameworks have still to be defined.

The main topics of the MARTES workshop were:

1. **UML profiles** or other **modelling languages** which both attack this challenge and come with a semantic underpinning.
2. **Analysis methods and tools** that are useful for such modelling languages and are or could be integrated in the development process. Tool support concerns model-based analysis and validation, compilation and model-transformation, as well as analysis of such transformation methods.
3. Finally, demonstrating the practical **applicability** of such modelling languages and tools for real time and embedded applications on hand of **case studies**.

An additional goal was to bring together researchers from academia and industry to discuss and progress on these issues, as well as other issues in the context of time, scheduling and architecture in UML and UML-related notations..

2   The Issues Discussed at the Workshop

Nine quality contributions were presented at the workshop, backed by a full paper or by a shorter position paper. All the papers together are available on the workshop webpage[1]. 50 participants from academia and from industry underline the importance of the topics discussed.

We give an overview on the topics addressed by the different papers and discuss how they are related. All main topics were addressed and approached even from quite different angles. We note some general tendency to work on modelling concepts and methodologies by relegating the issues related to analysis to a later point of time. We believe that it is of uttermost importance to conceive the concepts jointly with appropriate methods supporting analysis and code derivation. From the discussion at the workshop, it becomes quite obvious that no modelling language or UML profile will suffice in a development process if there is no appropriate tool support, going well beyond graphical editing tools.

Two papers appear in these proceedings; they have been selected by considering their intrinsic quality but also the particular interest with respect to the aims of this workshop.

---

[1] See http://www.martes.org/ provides access also to the proceedings [GGH*06].

2.1   Profiles and Modelling Languages

A first step to the inclusion of extra-functional characteristics into the modelling framework has been achieved by the "UML profile for Schedulability, Performance and Time" [OMG03]. More recently, several efforts have been and are being undertaken to improve this initial proposal in several aspects, e.g. to integrate the profile with UML 2.0 rather than UML 1.4.

- A "UML Profile for Modelling Quality of Service and Fault Tolerance Characteristics and Mechanisms (QoS)" [OMG04].
- The IST project Omega aimed also at the definition of a UML profile for real-time and embedded systems with a semantic foundation [GOO05] and with tool support for validation [OGO05]. The resulting profile defines a set of modelling elements, expressive enough to define a precise semantics for all the time constraints introduced in SPT as tag values or stereotypes by means of constraints between well defined occurrences of *events*.
- The MARTE profile has a larger scope. It addresses all concepts important for real time embedded systems.

In last year's workshop [GGH+05], some aspects of it have been discussed, in particular the domain model for analysis relevant quantitative annotations [EGP+05]. This year an almost achieved version of this aspect of the MARTE profile has been presented in [EMD+06].

[ACS+06] refers also to MARTE. It introduces "logical clocks" as a means for characterizing semantically all the time constraints expressed by the above mentioned annotations in terms of constraints on clocks, where *clocks* correspond to *events* of the Omega profile [GOO05], but the way of expressing constraints is different, and in fact not fully defined yet for [ACS+06].

[HKH06] introduces extensions to UML2 sequence diagrams which offer support for more complete and precise behaviour specifications. The mechanism of *exceptions* proposed in [HKH06] is very expressive for capturing behaviours triggered by violated constraints, and shows good qualities concerning refining and composability. The immediate applicability and the level of user interest in these results explains why the paper is included in these proceedings.

2.2   Techniques and Tools

Several contributions presented tools that performed some analysis based on descriptions in their targeted profile of UML. They represent some step towards frameworks for tool supported UML-based development, but much more is still needed.

[NWW+06] was chosen to appear in this volume since it presents promising new ideas to cope with growing complexity of embedded systems. Backed by an impressive prototype tool they showed how traditional graphical modelling can be supplemented by rule-based specification in a domain specific language. The rules for model configuration are then fed to a constraint solver that may also guide the developer through the configuration.

[SG06] gives a way to describe performance characteristics of a product line in a UML profile and how to analyze performance systematically from such descriptions.

Similarly, [RGD⁺06] presents an improved profile targeting software radio and a corresponding tool for rapid prototyping and investigating performance of such systems. Finally, [GHH06] applies the author's previously presented approach, Mechatronic UML, to hard real-time modelling problems such as issues of individually drifting clocks.

2.3 Applications

On the side of applications, this year we focussed on system-oriented specifications including real-time and safety critical requirements. The [CBL⁺06] contribution discussed the modelling in SysML of a known benchmark system specification, and provided insight on the application of this emerging standard as well as comparisons to a general language like UML 2.

2.4 Discussion and Conclusions

The outcome of the discussions and requests from the audience -- in particular those responsible for designing and developing software for real-time and embedded systems – underlines the importance of tool support for the entire development process, from high level models to running code. This tool support must also include those new concepts and paradigms that appeared more recently in the context of real-time and embedded systems in order to cope with always more complex systems in which concurrent and distributed software, including local and wide area distribution, are of steadily increasing importance.

References

[ACS⁺06]   Ch. André, A. Cuccuru, R. de Simone, Th. Gautier, F. Mallet, and JP. Talpin *"Modelling with logical time in UML for real-time embedded system design"* in [GGH⁺06]

[CBL⁺06]   Pietro Colombo, Vieri Del Bianco, Luigi Lavazza, Alberto Coen-Porisini *"An Experience in modelling real-time systems with SysML"* in [GGH⁺06].

[EGP⁺05]   Huáscar Espinoza, Hubert Dubois, Sébastien Gérard, Julio Medina, Dorina C. Petriu, Murray Woodside. Annotating UML Models with Non-Functional Properties for Quantitative Analysis. In [GGH⁺05].

[EMD⁺06]   H. Espinoza, J. Medina, H. Dubois, S. Gerard, F. Terrier, *"Towards a UML-based Modelling Standard for Schedulability Analysis of Real-time systems"* in [GGH⁺06].

[Est]   Esterel Technologies *"The Scade and Esterel development environments"*, see also http://www.esterel-technologies.com/.

[GGH⁺05]   S. Gérard, S. Graf, O. Haugen, I. Ober and B. Selic, editors. MARTES 2005, Workshop on Modelling and Analysis of Real Time and Embedded Systems, with MODELS 2005. LNCS.

[GGH⁺06]   S. Gérard, S. Graf, O. Haugen, I. Ober and B. Selic, editors. MARTES 2006, Workshop on Modelling and Analysis of Real Time and Embedded Systems. Research Report 343, Univ. of Oslo, Department of Informatics, ISBN 82–7368–299–4 October 2006.

[GHH06]   Holger Giese, Stefan Henkler, and Martin Hirsch *"Analysis and Modelling of Real-Time Systems with Mechatronic UML taking Clock Drift into Account"* in [GGH⁺06].

[GOO05]   S. Graf, I. Ober, and I. Ober. Timed annotations in UML. STTT, Int. Journal on Software Tools for Technology Transfer, April 2006.

[HKH06]   Oddleif Halvorsen, Ragnhild Kobro Runde, Øystein Haugen *"Time Exceptions in Sequence Diagrams"* in this volume.

[NWW⁺06]   Andrey Nechypurenko, Egon Wuchner, Jules White, Douglas C. Schmidt *"Applying Model Intelligence Frameworks for Deployment Problem in Real Time and Embedded Systems"* in this volume.

[OGO05]   I. Ober, S. Graf, and I. Ober. Validating timed UML models by simulation and verification. Int. Journal on Software Tools for Technology Transfer, April 2006.

[PSB⁺06]   Steffen Prochnow, Gunnar Schäfer, Ken Bell, and Reinhard von Hanxleden *"Analyzing Robustness of UML State Machines"* in [GGH⁺06].

[RGD⁺06]   S. Rouxel, G. Gogniat, J-P. Diguet, J-L. Philippe, C. Moy *"A3S method and tools for analysis of real time embedded systems"* in [GGH⁺06].

[SG06]   Julie A. Street and Hassan Gomaa *"An Approach to Performance Modelling of Software Product Lines"* in [GGH⁺06].

Time Exceptions in Sequence Diagrams

Oddleif Halvorsen[1], Ragnhild Kobro Runde[2], and Øystein Haugen[2]

[1] Software Innovation
[2] Department of Informatics, University of Oslo
{oddleif|ragnhilk|oysteinh}@ifi.uio.no

Abstract. UML sequence diagrams partially describe a system. We show how the description may be augmented with exceptions triggered by the violation of timing constraints and compare our approach to those of the UML 2.1 simple time model, the UML Testing Profile and the UML profile for Schedulability, Performance and Time. We give a formal definition of time exceptions in sequence diagrams and show that the concepts are compositional. An ATM example is used to explain and motivate the concepts.

Keywords: specification, time constraints, exception handling, formal semantics, refinement.

1 Introduction

UML sequence diagrams [9] are a useful vehicle for specifying communication between different parts of the system. A sequence diagram specifies a set of positive traces and a set of negative traces. A trace is a sequence of events, representing a system run. The positive traces represent legal behaviors that the system may exhibit, while the negative traces represent illegal behaviors that the system should not exhibit.

Timing information may be included in the diagram as constraints. These constraints may refer to either absolute time points (e.g. the timing of single events) or durations (e.g. the time between two events). The described behavior is negative if one or more time constraints are violated.

In practice, it may often be impossible to ensure that a time constraint is never violated, for instance when the constrained behavior involves communication with the environment. Usually, a sequence diagram does not describe what should happen in these exceptional cases. In this paper we demonstrate how the specification may be made more complete by augmenting the sequence diagram with exceptions that handle the violation of time constraints. The ideas behind our approach originate from [2], which treats exceptions triggered by wrong or missing data values in the messages.

Modeling violation of time constraints as exceptions rather than using the alt-operator for specifying alternative behaviors, has the advantage that

- specifying the exceptional behavior separately from ordinary/expected behavior makes the diagrams simpler and more readable,

T. Kühne (Ed.): MoDELS 2006 Workshops, LNCS 4364, pp. 131–142, 2007.

- exceptional behavior can easily be added to normal behavior in separate exception diagrams.

A single event may violate a time constraint by occurring too early, too late or never at all. All three situations will result in an exception, but the exact exception handling to be performed will typically be very different depending on the nature of the violation. Here we focus on the last case, where an event has not occurred within the given time limit and we therefore assume that it will not occur at all. If the event for some reason occurs at some later point it should be treated as another exception.

2 Background

Both the UML 2.1 simple time model (Sect. 2.1) and the UML profile for Schedulability, Performance and Time (Sect. 2.2) introduce concepts and notations for defining time constraints, but do not consider what should happen in case of violations. TimedSTAIRS (Sect. 2.3) distinguishes between the reception and the consumption of a message, but being based on UML 2.1 simple time model, TimedSTAIRS does not consider violations either. The default concept of UML Testing Profile (Sect. 2.4) and our previous work on exception handling (Sect. 2.5) consider violation of constraints, but mainly regarding wrong or missing data values, and not time constraint violations.

2.1   The UML 2.1 Simple Time Model

UML 2.1 [9] includes a simple time model intended to define a number of concepts relating to timing constraints. In general the semantics of the timing constraints follow the general interpretation of constraints in UML: "A Constraint represents additional semantic information attached to the constrained elements. A constraint is an assertion that indicates a restriction that must be satisfied by a correct design of the system." Furthermore the timing constraints always refer to a range of values, an interval. "All traces where the constraints are violated are negative traces (i.e., if they occur in practice the system has failed)." Some notation is introduced to define such interval time constraints and we apply this notation in this paper. UML 2.1 only states that when the constraints are violated the system is in error. Exceptions triggered by time constraint violations are not considered.

2.2   UML Profile for Schedulability, Performance and Time

The UML profile for Schedulability, Performance and Time Specification [7] is a profile based on UML 1.4 [6] describing in great detail concepts relating to timely matters. The profile, hereafter referred to as SPT, will have to be updated to UML 2.1. There is now ongoing work to upgrade the real time profile under the name MARTE.

SPT introduces a large number of concepts. They represent most often properties of behavioral units needed for their scheduling and for performance analysis. Exceptions are not mentioned at all. By introducing concepts that allow to define "timing marks", it is possible to describe constraints on these timing marks, and in principle express time and duration constraints similar to what is the case with UML 2.1 simple time model. SPT allows constraints to be expressed on a large number of properties having been declared on behavioral units, but it never considers what happens if the constraint is not met. Implicitly this means that if the constraint is not met, the system is in complete failure.

2.3 TimedSTAIRS

TimedSTAIRS [4] is an approach to the compositional development of timed sequence diagrams. With time constraints, we argue that it is important to know whether a given constraint applies to the reception or the consumption of the message. Hence, in [4] we introduce a three-event semantics for timed sequence diagrams. In some cases, the time constraint should apply to the receiving of the message, while it in other situations should apply to the consumption.

In order to make a graphical distinction between reception and consumption, [4] uses a double arrow for reception and the standard single arrow for consumption. We will follow this convention in our examples. If only the consumption event is present in the diagram, the reception event is taken implicitly, while if only the reception event is present, the implicit consumption event may or may not take place.

In TimedSTAIRS, the semantics of a sequence diagram is a set of positive (i.e. legal) behaviors and a set of negative (i.e. illegal) behaviors. All traces that are not described in the diagram are said to be inconclusive. These may later supplemented either the positive or the negative traces to refine the specification. Please see Sect. 4 for a more precise semantics.

2.4 UML Testing Profile — Default Concept

The U2TP (UML Testing Profile) [8] introduces the notion of Defaults that aims to define additional behavior when a constraint is broken. The notion of Defaults come from TTCN (Testing and Test Control Notation) [1] where it is used in a more imperative sense than sequence diagrams. In the UML Testing Profile the semantics is given by an elaborate transformation algorithm that in principle produces the traces of the main description combined with the Defaults on several levels.

However, U2TP says little about the semantics of defaults triggered by the violation of time constraints. The idea behind the defaults on different levels is that even the notoriously partial interactions are made complete and actually describing all behaviors. But the U2TP definition is not adequately precise in this matter and there are no convincing examples given to explain what happens when a time constraint is violated.

2.5   Proposed Notation for Exceptions in Sequence Diagrams

In [2] we introduce notation for exceptions in sequence diagrams. The constraints
that are violated are always on data values at the event associated with the
exception. Violation of time constraints is not considered. The semantics of the
behavior including the exceptions are given by a transformation procedure quite
similar to that of U2TP. The idea is that supplementing traces are defined in
the exception starting from the prefix of traces leading up to a triggering event.

The other novelty of our approach in [2] is that it suggests a scheme of dynamic
gate matching that makes it possible to define exceptions independently. That
idea is orthogonal to what we try to convey in this paper.

3   Time Exceptions in the ATM Example

An example with an Automatic Teller Machine (ATM) shows how time exceptions supplement the description and make the specification more complete and
comprehensive without losing sight of the normal scenarios. The ATM example
is based on the case from [2].

3.1   The Normal Flow

The normal flow refers to a happy day scenario when everything goes right. We
show the use of an ATM to withdraw money. The user communicates with an
ATM, which in turn communicates with the Bank.

Withdrawal in Fig. 1 specifies that the user is expected to insert a card and
enter a four digit pin, whereas the ATM is to send the pin to the bank for
validation. While the bank is validating the pin, the ATM asks the user for the
amount to withdraw. If a valid pin is given, the bank will return OK. Then the

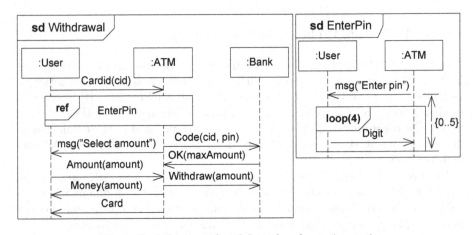

Fig. 1. Specification of withdrawal and entering a pin

ATM orders the Bank to withdraw the money from the account and gives the cash and the card to the user.

EnterPin in Fig. 1 specifies how the user gives the ATM the four digit pin. The loop(n) construct may be viewed as a syntactical shorthand for duplicating the contents of the loop n times. An interaction use (here: referring EnterPin) means the same as an inclusion of a fragment equal to the referred sequence diagram.

This specification is not very robust, and cannot serve as a sufficient specification for implementation. What if the user enters a wrong pin, the ATM is out of money, the user's account is empty or the ATM loses contact with the bank? We argue for the need to handle exceptions, even though sequence diagrams will always be partial description that are not supposed to cover every possible trace. Still, we aim at making the diagrams more complete, focusing on the important functionality of the system. Another goal is to make a clearer separation of normal and exceptional behavior and thus increase readability.

3.2   Applying Time Exceptions to the ATM

Sequence diagrams are often filled with various constraints, but they seldom say much about what to do if a constraint breaks. Hence the system has completely failed if a constraint is broken. This is less expressive than desired. In order to make the specification more robust, we will add time exceptions to the ATM case. A time exception may be that the user for some reason leaves before completing the transaction, or that the bank spends too long time to validate the given pin.

As mentioned, time violations are of three kinds, either the event arrives too early, too late or never. Here we assume that if an event has not occurred within the specified constraint, it will never happen. If the event for some reason occurs after the constraint was violated it should be treated as another exception.

The semantics of time constraints builds on timestamps. We assume that the running system performs some kind of surveillance of the system, to evaluate the constraints. Intuitively, this means that we consider time constraints conceptually to behave like alarm clocks. If the associated event is too late the alarm goes off and the exception handler is triggered.

3.3   Time Exceptions in EnterPin

We present the notation by applying a time exception to the EnterPin diagram. An exception occurs when the user enters less than four digits or that the digits for some reason is not received by the ATM. If we do not handle this, the ATM will not be ready when the next user arrives. We need a way to decide whether the user has left, and then take the card from the card reader and store it some place safe before canceling the user's session.

In EnterPin in Fig. 2 we have added a time constraint stating that if the ATM has not received all the digits within the specified time, the exception UserLeftCard will fire. The time constraint itself is initialized on the send event on msg, and attached to the bottom of the loop fragment. Attaching it to the bottom of the loop fragment indicates that the time constraint must hold for the last event, and hence all the preceding ones as well.

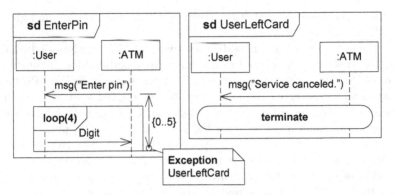

Fig. 2. EnterPin with time exception

UserLeftCard in Fig. 2 shows how the UserLeftCard exception is handled. In the case that the user leaves the ATM before proper completion of the service, the ATM sends a message stating that the service was canceled. By stating terminate we mean that the service, withdrawal of money, is to terminate — not the whole ATM. This will be explained in more detail below.

3.4 Time Exceptions in Withdrawal

In Fig. 3 we apply time exceptions to a more complex example to highlight some challenging situations.

Notice that the ATMPinValidation exception uses three-event semantics as described in TimedSTAIRS (see Sect. 2.3). This states that the message only needs to be received in the message buffer within the specified time constraint

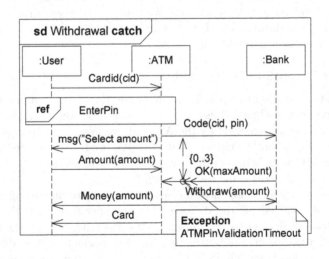

Fig. 3. Withdrawal with time exception

and not consumed. The reason for this time constraint is mainly to make sure that we do not lose contact with the bank during the request.

Fig. 4 specifies how an ATMPinValidationTimeout exception is handled by the ATM and the Bank. The exception is triggered if the ATM does not receive the result of the pin validation within the specified time. Our first exceptional reaction is to repeat the request to the Bank. If the response from the bank again fails to appear within the given time, the ATMCancel exception is triggered.

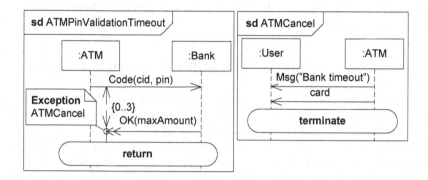

Fig. 4. Handling of pin validation timeout on the ATM

Fig. 4 illustrates that an exception may end with return or with terminate. While return means a perfect recovery back to the original flow of events, terminate means that the service should be terminated gracefully. Termination concludes the closest invoker declaring catch as shown in Fig. 3. If neither return nor terminate is given, return is assumed. If no catch is found, the system will not continue.

The events of a sequence diagram may in relation to an exception trigger be divided in three groups. First there are the events that have occurred before the trigger. Second we have events that must occur after the exception, and third the events enabled but not executed at the trigger. Such enabled events may happen in parallel with the exception handling.

If we apply this to Withdrawal, Fig. 3, we notice that the ATM must at least send a code for validation to the bank before the timeout event may occur. Actually the exception may only occur more than three time units after the sending of the validation request. That is, before the ATMPinValidationTimeout may occur the user must have given a card, entered the pin, the ATM must have sent the pin for validation and three time units must have elapsed. After a possible recovery from the ATMPinValidationTimeout exception we can continue with sending the withdrawal message and returning the card and money.

The challenging part is how to handle the selection of amount if an exception occurs. Since these events are enabled they may happen in parallel with the exception. That is because the user is outside the ATMs sphere of control. We have three separate lifelines (User, ATM and Bank) that each communicates with the others through messages. Each lifeline in this distributed environment is considered autonomous meaning that they are independent processes. We may therefore run the exception handling in parallel with other enabled events.

By enabled events we mean events that may happen regardless of whether the exception occurs or not. In the ATM example, an enabled event is the consumption of msg("Select amount"), and events only depending on that (here: user sending Amount). These events are outside the control of the exception handling, and must be allowed to continue. An example of a non-enabled event is the sending of Money from the ATM. This event can never be sent before the OK message is received.

4   The Formal Semantic Domain of Sequence Diagrams

In this section we briefly recount the main parts of the semantics of timed sequence diagrams as defined in [4]. In Sect. 5 we give our proposal for how this semantics may be extended to handle time exceptions.

Formally, we use denotational trace semantics in order to capture the meaning of sequence diagrams. A trace is a sequence of events, representing one run of the system. As explained in Sect. 2.3, we have three kinds of events: the sending, reception and consumption of a message, denoted by !, $\sim$ and ?, respectively. A message is a triple (s, tr, re) consisting of a signal s (the content of the message), a transmitter tr and a receiver re. The transmitter and receiver are lifelines, or possibly gates. (For a formal treatment of gates, see [5].)

Each event in the sequence diagram has a unique timestamp tag to which real timestamps will be assigned. Time constraints are expressed as logical formulas with these timestamp tags as free variables. Formally, an event is a triple (k, m, t) of a kind k (sending, reception or consumption), a message m and a timestamp tag t. As an example, EnterPin in Fig. 2 consists of six events: $(!, m, t_1)$, $(\sim, m, t_2)$, $(?, m, t_3)$, $(!, d, t_4)$, $(\sim, d, t_5)$ and $(?, d, t_6)$ where $m = (msg(Enterpin), ATM, User)$ and $d = (Digit, User, ATM)$. Notice that in Fig 2 the reception events are implicit, meaning that they may happen at any time between the corresponding send and receive events. The given time constraint may be written as $t_6 \leq t_1 + 5$.

$\mathcal{H}$ denotes the set of all well-formed traces. For a trace to be well-formed, it is required that

- for each message, the send event occurs before the receive event if both events are present in the trace.
- for each message, the receive event occurs before the consumption event if both events are present in the trace.
- the events in the trace are ordered by time.

$\mathcal{E}$ denotes the set of all syntactic events, and $[\![\, \mathcal{E} \,]\!]$ is the set of all corresponding semantical events with real timestamps assigned to the tags:

$$[\![\, \mathcal{E} \,]\!] \stackrel{\text{def}}{=} \{(k, m, t \mapsto r) \mid (k, m, t) \in \mathcal{E} \wedge r \in \mathbb{R}\} \qquad (1)$$

Parallel composition $s_1 \parallel s_2$ of two trace-sets is the set of all traces such that all events from one trace in s_1 and one trace in s_2 are included (and no other events), and the ordering of events from each of the traces is preserved. Formally:

$$s_1 \parallel s_2 \stackrel{\text{def}}{=} \{h \in \mathcal{H} \mid \exists p \in \{1,2\}^{\infty} : \tag{2}$$
$$\pi_2((\{1\} \times [\![\, \mathcal{E} \,]\!]) \textcircled{T} (p, h)) \in s_1 \ \wedge\ \pi_2((\{2\} \times [\![\, \mathcal{E} \,]\!]) \textcircled{T} (p, h)) \in s_2\}$$

The definition makes use of an oracle, the infinite sequence p, to determine the order in which the events from each trace are sequenced. π_2 is a projection operator returning the second element of a pair, and $\textcircled{T}$ is an operator filtering pairs of sequences with respect to pairs of elements.

Weak sequencing, $s_1 \succsim s_2$, is the set of all traces obtained by selecting one trace h_1 from s_1 and one trace h_2 from s_2 such that on each lifeline, the events from h_1 are ordered before the events from h_2:

$$s_1 \succsim s_2 \stackrel{\text{def}}{=} \{h \in \mathcal{H} \mid \exists h_1 \in s_1, h_2 \in s_2 : \forall l \in \mathcal{L} : h \lceil l = h_1 \lceil l \frown h_2 \lceil l\} \tag{3}$$

where $\mathcal{L}$ is the set of all lifelines, $\frown$ is the concatenation operator on sequences, and $h \lceil l$ is the trace h with all events not taking place on the lifeline l removed.

Time constraint keeps only traces that are in accordance with the constraint:

$$s \wr C \stackrel{\text{def}}{=} \{h \in s \mid h \models C\} \tag{4}$$

where $h \models C$ holds if the timestamps in h does not violate C.

The semantics $[\![\, d \,]\!]$ of a sequence diagram d is given as a pair (p, n), where p is the set of positive and n the set of negative traces. Parallel composition, weak sequencing and time constraint and inner union ($\uplus$) of such pairs are defined as follows:

$$(p_1, n_1) \parallel (p_2, n_2) \stackrel{\text{def}}{=} (p_1 \parallel p_2, (n_1 \parallel (p_2 \cup n_2)) \cup (n_2 \parallel p_1)) \tag{5}$$

$$(p_1, n_1) \succsim (p_2, n_2) \stackrel{\text{def}}{=} (p_1 \succsim p_2, (n_1 \succsim (n_2 \cup p_2)) \cup (p_1 \succsim n_2)) \tag{6}$$

$$(p, n) \wr C \stackrel{\text{def}}{=} (p \wr C, n \cup (p \wr \neg C)) \tag{7}$$

$$(p_1, n_1) \uplus (p_2, n_2) \stackrel{\text{def}}{=} (p_1 \cup p_2, n_1 \cup n_2) \tag{8}$$

Finally, the semantics of the sequence diagram operators of interest in this paper are defined by:

$$[\![\, d_1 \text{ alt } d_2 \,]\!] \stackrel{\text{def}}{=} [\![\, d_1 \,]\!] \uplus [\![\, d_2 \,]\!] \tag{9}$$

$$[\![\, d_1 \text{ par } d_2 \,]\!] \stackrel{\text{def}}{=} [\![\, d_1 \,]\!] \parallel [\![\, d_2 \,]\!] \tag{10}$$

$$[\![\, d_1 \text{ seq } d_2 \,]\!] \stackrel{\text{def}}{=} [\![\, d_1 \,]\!] \succsim [\![\, d_2 \,]\!] \tag{11}$$

$$[\![\, d \text{ tc } C \,]\!] \stackrel{\text{def}}{=} [\![\, d \,]\!] \wr C \tag{12}$$

$$[\![\, \text{skip} \,]\!] \stackrel{\text{def}}{=} (\{\langle\rangle\}, \emptyset) \tag{13}$$

where tc is the operator used for time constraints and skip is the empty diagram (i.e. doing nothing). Definitions of other operators may be found in e.g. [5].

5   The Formal Semantics of Time Exceptions

In Sect. 3 we informally explained the semantics of time exceptions. In this section we define the semantics formally, based on the formalism introduced in Sect. 4. Furthermore we give theorems stating some desirable properties related to time exceptions and refinement. Due to lack of space, we have omitted the proofs from this paper. However, proofs may be found in [3].

5.1   Definitions

An exception diagram is mainly specified using the same operators as ordinary sequence diagrams, and its semantics may be calculated using the definitions given in Sect. 4. As explained in Sect. 3, the additional constructs used in exception diagrams is that the exception handling always ends with either return or terminate. Formally, the semantics of an exception (sub-)diagram marked with either return or terminate is defined by:

$$[\![\, d \text{ return} \,]\!] \stackrel{\text{def}}{=} [\![\, d \,]\!] \tag{14}$$

$$[\![\, d \text{ terminate} \,]\!] \stackrel{\text{def}}{=} appendTT([\![\, d \,]\!]) \tag{15}$$

where $appendTT$ is a function appending a special termination event TT to every trace in its operand (i.e. all the positive and negative traces in $[\![\, d \,]\!]$).

With this new termination event, weak sequencing of trace sets must be redefined so that traces that end with termination are not continued:

$$s_1 \succsim s_2 \stackrel{\text{def}}{=} \{h \in \mathcal{H} \mid \exists h_1 \in s_1, h_2 \in s_2 : \tag{16}$$
$$(term(h_1) \wedge h = h_1) \vee (\neg term(h_1) \wedge \forall l \in \mathcal{L} : h \lceil l = h_1 \lceil l \frown h_2 \lceil l)\}$$

where $term(h_1)$ is true if the trace h_1 ends with TT, and false otherwise.

For parallel composition of trace sets, the traces may be calculated as before and then removing all events that occur after TT from the trace:

$$s_1 \parallel s_2 \stackrel{\text{def}}{=} \{h \in \mathcal{H} \mid \exists h' \in s_1 \parallel' s_2 : h = chopTT(h')\} \tag{17}$$

where $\parallel'$ is parallel composition as defined by definition 2 and $chopTT$ is a function removing all events occurring after a potential TT in the trace.

A sequence diagram d marked as catching termination events then has the semantic effect that the termination mark is removed from the trace, meaning that the trace continues as specified by the diagram that is enclosing d:

$$[\![\, d \text{ catch} \,]\!] \stackrel{\text{def}}{=} removeTT([\![\, d \,]\!]) \tag{18}$$

where $removeTT$ is a function removing TT from all traces in its operand.

Finally, we need to define the semantics of a sequence diagram which contains exceptions. The kind of exceptions considered in this paper is always connected to a time constraint on an event. Syntactically, we write d tc $(C$ exception $e)$

to specify that d is a sequence diagram with time constraint C, and that the sequence diagram e specifies the exception handling in case C is violated. We use $q(C)$ to denote the event constrained by C, and $ll(C)$ to denote the lifeline on which this event occurs.

Obviously, a trace should be negative if the exception handling starts before the time constraint is actually violated. As an example, consider the specification of EnterPin in Fig. 2. Here, we have the constraint $t_6 \leq t_1 + 5$ as explained in Sect. 4. Letting t_7 be the timestamp of the sending of the message in User-LeftCard, we then intuitively have the corresponding constraint $t_7 > t_1 + 5$. Formally, we let e_C be the exception diagram where the time constraint C has been transformed into the corresponding time constraint for the first event in e (or several such constraints if there is a choice of first event for e).

The semantics of a sequence diagram with an exception is then defined by:

$$[\![\, d \text{ tc } (C \text{ exception } e)\,]\!] \overset{\text{def}}{=} [\![\, d \text{ tc } C\,]\!] \uplus \qquad (19)$$
$$\{h \in \mathcal{H} \mid h \upharpoonright ll(C) \in [\![\, d[e_C/q(C)]\,]\!] \upharpoonright ll(C)\} \circledS [\![\, d[\text{skip}/q(C)] \text{ par } e_C \,]\!]$$

where $d[d_{new}/d_{old}]$ is the sequence diagram d with the sub-diagram d_{new} substituted for d_{old}, $\circledS$ is a filtering operator such that $S \circledS (p,n)$ is the pair (p,n) where all traces that are not in the set S are removed, $h \in (p,n)$ is a short-hand for $h \in p \lor h \in n$, and $\upharpoonright$ is overloaded from traces to pairs of sets of traces in standard pointwise manner.

In definition 19, the first part corresponds to the semantics without the exception. The second part is all traces where the event $q(C)$ has not occurred, and the exception handling is performed instead. $[\![\, d[\text{skip}/q(C)]\,]\!]$ gives the diagram d without the triggering event $q(C)$, executed in parallel with the exception e. However, this set is too comprehensive as we require that the lifeline of the triggering event, the lifeline $ll(C)$, must perform all of the exception handling before continuing with the original diagram. This is expressed by the set preceding the filtering operator.

5.2   Refinement

TimedSTAIRS [4] defines supplementing and narrowing as two special cases of refinement. Supplementing means adding more positive or negative traces to the sequence diagram, while narrowing means redefining earlier inconclusive traces as negative. Formally, a diagram d' with semantics (p', n') is said to be a refinement of another diagram d with semantics (p, n), written $d \rightsquigarrow d'$, iff

$$n \subseteq n' \land p \subseteq p' \cup n' \qquad (20)$$

It should be clear from our explanations in Sect. 3 that adding exception handling to a sequence diagram constitutes a refinement. Adding a time constraint is an example of narrowing, as traces with invalid timestamps are moved from positive to negative when introducing the time constraint. More generally, we have the following theorem:

Theorem 1. *Assuming that the exception diagram e is not equivalent to the triggering event* $q(C)$, *i.e.* $[\![e]\!] \neq (\{\langle q(C)\rangle\}, \emptyset)$, *we have that*

1. $d \rightsquigarrow d$ tc C
2. d tc $C \rightsquigarrow d$ tc $(C$ exception $e)$
3. $d \rightsquigarrow d$ tc $(C$ exception $e)$

Finally, the following theorem demonstrates that for a diagram containing exceptions, the normal and exceptional behavior may be refined separately:

Theorem 2. *Refinement is monotonic with respect to exceptions as defined by definition 19, i.e.:*

$$d \rightsquigarrow d \wedge e \rightsquigarrow e' \Rightarrow d \text{ tc } (C \text{ exception } e) \rightsquigarrow d' \text{ tc } (C \text{ exception } e')$$

6   Conclusions

We have shown that introducing time exceptions improve the completeness of sequence diagram descriptions while keeping the readability of the main specification. We have defined concrete notation for exceptions built on existing symbols of UML 2.1 and the simple time notation. Finally, we have given a precise formal definition of time exceptions and shown that our concepts are compositional since refinement is monotonic with respect to exceptions.

References

1. ETSI. *The Testing and Test Control Notation version 3 (TTCN-3); Part 1: TTCN-3 Core Language*, document: European Standard (ES) 201 873-1 version 2.2.1 (2003-02). Also published as ITU-T Recommendation Z.140 edition, 2003.
2. Oddleif Halvorsen and Øystein Haugen. Proposed notation for exception handling in UML 2 sequence diagrams. In *Australian Software Engineering Conference (ASWEC)*, pages 29–40. IEEE Computer Society, 2006.
3. Oddleif Halvorsen, Ragnhild Kobro Runde, and Øystein Haugen. Time exceptions in sequence diagrams. Technical Report 344, Department of Informatics, University of Oslo, 2006.
4. Øystein Haugen, Knut Eilif Husa, Ragnhild Kobro Runde, and Ketil Stølen. Why timed sequence diagrams require three-event semantics. In *Scenarios: Models, Transformations and Tools*, volume 3466 of *LNCS*, pages 1–25. Springer, 2005.
5. Øystein Haugen, Knut Eilif Husa, Ragnhild Kobro Runde, and Ketil Stølen. Why timed sequence diagrams require three-event semantics. Technical Report 309, Department of Informatics, University of Oslo, 2005.
6. Object Management Group. *OMG Unified Modeling Language 1.4*, 2000.
7. Object Management Group. *UML profile for Schedulability, Performance and Time Specification*, document: ptc/05-01-02 edition, 2005.
8. Object Management Group. *UML Testing Profile*, document: ptc/05-07-07 edition, 2005.
9. Object Management Group. *UML 2.1 Superstructure Specification*, document: ptc/06-04-02 edition, 2006.

Applying Model Intelligence Frameworks for Deployment Problem in Real-Time and Embedded Systems

Andrey Nechypurenko[1], Egon Wuchner[1], Jules White[2],
and Douglas C. Schmidt[2]

[1] Siemens AG, Corporate Technology (SE 2), Otto-Hahn-Ring 6,
81739 Munich, Germany
{andrey.nechypurenko, egon.wuchner}@siemens.com
[2] Vanderbilt University, Department of Electrical Engineering and Computer Science,
Box 1679 Station B, Nashville, TN, 37235, USA
{jules, schmidt}@dre.vanderbilt.edu

Abstract. There are many application domains, such as distributed
real-time and embedded (DRE) systems, where the domain constraints
are so restrictive and the solution spaces so large that it is infeasible
for modelers to produce correct solution manually using a conventional
graphical model-based approach. In DRE systems the available resources,
such as memory, CPU, and bandwidth, must be managed carefully to
ensure a certain level of quality of service. This paper provides three
contributions to simplify modeling of complex application domains: (1)
we present our approach of combining model intelligence and domain-
specific solvers with model-driven engineering (MDE) environments, (2)
we show techniques for automatically guiding modelers to correct solutions and how to support the specification of large and complex systems
using intelligent mechanisms to complete partially specified models, and
(3) we present the results of applying an MDE tool that maps software
components to Electronic Control Units (ECUs) using the typical automotive modeling and middleware infrastructure.

Keywords: modeling, Prolog, constraint solver, model completion,
model checking, automotive.

1 Introduction

Graphical modeling languages, such as UML, can help to visualise certain aspects
of the system and automate particular development steps via code-generation.
Model-driven engineering (MDE) tools and domain-specific modeling languages
(DSMLs) [3] are graphical modeling technologies that combine high-level visual
abstractions that are specific to a domain with constraint checking and code-
generation to simplify the development of certain types of systems. In many
application domains, however, the domain constraints are so restrictive and the
solution spaces so large that it is infeasible for modelers to produce correct solutions manually. In these domains, MDE tools that simply provide solution

T. Kühne (Ed.): MoDELS 2006 Workshops, LNCS 4364, pp. 143–151, 2007.

correctness checking via constraints provide few benefits over conventional approaches that use third-generation languages.

Regardless of the modeling language and notation used, the inherent complexity in many application domains is the combinatorial nature of the constraints, and not the code construction per se. For example, specifying the deployment of software components to hardware units in a car in the face of configuration and resource constraints can easily generate solution spaces with millions or more possible deployments and few correct ones, even when only scores of model entities are present. For these combinatorially complex modeling problems, it is impractical, if not impossible, to create a complete and valid model manually. Even connecting hundreds of components to scores of nodes by pointing and clicking via a GUI is tedious and error-prone. As the number of modeling elements increases into the thousands, manual approaches become infeasible.

To address the challenges of modeling combinatorially complex domains, therefore, we need techniques to reduce the cost of integrating a graphical modeling environment with *Model Intelligence Guides (MIGs)*, which are automated MDE tools that help guide users from partially specified models, such as a model that specifies components and the nodes they need to be deployed to but not how they are deployed, to complete and correct ones, such as a model that not only specifies the components to be deployed but what node hosts each one. This paper describes techniques for creating and maintaining a *Domain Intelligence Generator* (DIG), which is an MDE that helps modelers solve combinatorially challenging modeling problems, such as resource assignment, configuration matching, and path finding.

The rest of the paper is organised as follows: Section 2 discusses challenges of creating deployment models in the context of the EAST-EEA Embedded Electronic Architecture [1] which is the European Union research project and is the predecessor of the AUTOSAR [2] middleware and modeling standard. We use EAST-EEA architecture as a motivating example; Section 3 describes key concepts used to create and customize MIGs; Section 4 shows the results of applying MIGs to component deployments; and Section 5 presents concluding remarks and outlines future work.

2   Motivating Example

EAST-EEA defines the embedded electronic architecture, structure of the automotive middleware. The goal of EAST-EEA is to standardize solutions to many problems that arise when developing large-scale, distributed real-time and embedded (DRE) systems for the automotive domain. For instance, concert efforts is required to relocate components between Electronic Control Units (ECUs), *i.e.*, computers and micro-controllers running software components within a car. Key complexities of relocation include: (1) components often have a many constraints that need to be met by the target ECU and (2) there are many possible deployments of components to ECUs in a car and it is hard to find the optimal one.

For example, it is hard to manually find a set of interconnected nodes able to run a group of components that communicate via a bus. Modelers must determine whether the available communication channels between the target ECUs meet the bandwidth, latency, and framing constraints of the components that communicate through them. In the automotive domain—as with other embedded systems domains— it is also important to reduce the overall cost of the solution, which necessitates optimizations, such as finding deployments that use as few ECUs as possible or minimize bandwidth to allow cheaper buses. It is infeasible to find these solutions manually for a production systems.

To illustrate the practical benefits of generating and integrating MIGs with a DSML, we describe an MDE tool we developed to solve EAST-EEA constraints for validly deploying software components to ECUs. There are two architectural views in EAST-EEA based systems:

- The *logical collaboration structure* that specifies which components that should communicate with each other via which interfaces, and
- The *physical deployment structure* that captures the capabilities of each ECU, their interconnecting buses, and their available resources.

Historically, automotive developers have manually specified the mapping from components in the logical view to ECUs in the physical view via MDE deployment tools, as shown in Figure 1. This approach worked relatively well when there were a small number of components and ECU. Modern cars, however, can be equipped with 80 or more ECUs and several hundred or more software components. Simply drawing arrows from 160 components to 80 ECUs is tedious. Moreover, many requirements constrain which ECUs that can host certain components, including the amount of memory required to run, CPU power, programming language, operating system type and version, etc. These constraints must be considered carefully when deciding where to deploy a particular component. The problem is further exacerbated when developers consider the physical communication paths and aspects, such as available bandwidth in conjunction with periodical real-time messaging.

The remainder of this paper shows how the EAST-EEA MDE tool we developed helps automate the mapping of software components to ECUs in EAST-EEA models without violating the known constraints. The following sections describe our approach and show how MIGs can significantly reduce the complexity of creating EAST-EEA deployment models.

3   Domain-Specific Model Intelligence

Based on the challenges related to the EAST-EEA example presented in Section 2, the goals of our work on MIGs are to (1) specify an approach for guiding modelers from partially specified models to complete and coorrect ones and (2) automate the completion of partially specified models using information extracted from domain constraints.

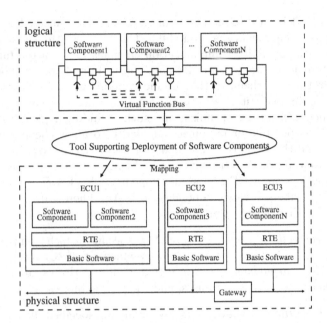

Fig. 1. Mapping from the logical collaboration to the physical deployment structure

In previous work [5,4], we showed how MDE tools and DSMLs can improve the modeling experience and bridge the gap between the problem and solution domain by introducing domain-specific abstractions. At the heart of these efforts is the *Generic Eclipse Modeling System* (GEMS), which provides a convenient way to define the metamodel, *i.e.*, the visual syntax of the DSML. Given a metamodel, GEMS automatically generates a graphical editor that enforces the grammar specified in the DSML. GEMS provides convenient infrastructure (such as built-in support for the Visitor pattern) to simplify model traversal and code generation. We used GEMS as the basis for our MIGs EAST-EEA deployment modeling tool and our work on domain-specific model intelligence.

3.1   Domain Constraints as the Basis for Automatic Suggestions

A key research challenge was determining how to specify the set of model constraints so they could be used by MIGs *not only to check the correctness of the model, but also to guide users through a series of model modifications to bring it to a state that satisfies the domain constraints.* We considered various approaches for constraint specification language, including Java, the Object Constraint Language (OCL), and Prolog. To evaluate the pros and cons of each approach, we implemented our EAST-EEA deployment constraints in each of the three languages.

As a result of this evaluation, we selected Prolog since it provided both constraint checking and model suggestions. In particular, Prolog can return the set of possible facts from a knowledge base that indicate why a rule evaluated to "true." The declarative nature of Prolog significantly reduced the number of lines of code written to transform an instance of a DSML into a knowledge base and to create constraints (its roughly comparable to OCL for writing constraints). Moreover, Prolog enables MIGs to derive sequences of modeling actions that converts the model from an incomplete or invalid state to a valid one. As shown in Section 1, this capability is crucial for domains, such as deployment in complex DRE systems, where manual model specification is infeasible or extremely tedious and error-prone.

The remainder of this section describes how Domain Intelligence Generation (DIG) uses Prolog and GEMS to support the creation of customizable and extensible domain-specific constraint solver and optimization frameworks for MIGs. Our research focuses on providing modeling guidance and automatic model completion, as described below.

3.2 Modeling Guidance On-the-Fly

To provide domain-specific model intelligence, an MDE tool must capture the current state of a model and reason about how to assist and guide modelers. To support this functionality, MIGs use a Prolog knowledge base format that can be parameterized by a metamodel to create a domain-specific knowledge base. GEMS metamodels represent a set of model entities and the role-based relationships between them. For each model, DIG populates a Prolog knowledge base using these metamodel-specified entities and roles. For each entity, DIG generates a unique id and a predicate statement specifying the type associated with it.

In the context of our EAST-EEA example, a model is transformed into the predicate statement *component(id)*, where id is the unique id for the component. For each instance of a role-based relationship in the model, a predicate statement is generated that takes the id of the entity it is relating and the value it is relating it to. For example, if a component with id 23 has a *TargetHost* relationship to a node with id 25 the predicate statement *targethost(23,25)* is generated. This predicate statement specifies that the entity with id 25 is a *TargetHost* of the entity with id 23. Each knowledge base generated by DIG provides a domain-specific set of predicate statements.

The domain-specific interface to the knowledge base provides several advantages over a generic format, such as the format used by a general-purpose constraint solver like CLIPS. First, the knowledge base maintains the domain-specific notations from the DSML, making the format more intuitive and readable to domain experts. Second, maintaining the domain-specific notations allows the specification of constraints using domain notations, thereby enabling developers to understand how requirements map to constraints. Third, in experiments that we conducted, writing constraints using the domain-specific predicates produced rules that had fewer levels of indirection and thus outperformed rules written using a generic format. In general, the size of the performance advantage depended on the generality of the knowledge base format. To access properties of the model entities, the predicate syntax presents the most specific knowledge base format. Given an entity id and role name, the value can be accessed with the statement *role(id, Value)*, which has exactly zero or one facts that match it.

Based on this domain-specific knowledge base, modelers can specify user-defined constraints in form of Prolog rules for each type of metamodel relationship. These constraints semantically enrich the model to indicate the requirements of a correct model. They are also used to automatically deduce the sets of valid model changes to create a correct model.

For example, consider the following constraint to check whether a node (ECU) is a valid host of a component:

is_a_valid_component_targethost(Comp,Node). It can be used to both check a Component to Node combination (*e.g.*,
is_a_valid_component_targethost(23,[25]).) and to find valid *Nodes* that can play the *TargetHost* role for a particular component (*e.g.*,
is_a_valid_component_targethost(23,Nodes).). This latter example uses Prolog's ability to deduce the correct solution, *i.e.*, the *Nodes* variable will be assigned the list of all constraint-valid nodes for the *TargetHost* role of the specified component. This example illustrates how constraints can be used to check *and* to generate the solution, if one exists.

Figure 2 shows how dynamic suggestions from Prolog are presented to modelers. The upper part of the figure shows the fragment of the metamodel that

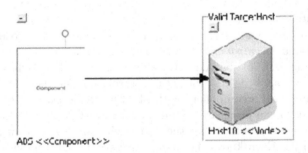

Fig. 2. Highlighting valid target host

describes the "Deployment" relationship between "Component" and "Node" model entities. The lower part of the picture shows how the generated editor displays the corresponding entity instances. This screenshot was made at the moment a modeler had begun dragging a connection begining from the "ABS" component. The rectangle around "Host10" labelled "Valid TargetHost" is drawn automatically as a result of triggering the corresponding solver rule and receiving a valid solution as feeback. GEMS also can also trigger arbitrary Prolog rules from the modeling tool and incorporate their results back into a model. This mechanism can be used to solve for complete component to ECU deployments and automatically add deployment relationships based on a (partially) complete model.

To enable modeling assistance, different subsystems must collaborate within the modeling environment. It is the responsibility of the modeler (or MDE tool creator) to provide the set of constraints and supply solvers for new constraint types. The GEMS metamodel editor updates the knowledge base and incorporates the new rules into the generated MIG. User-defined solver(s) can be based on existing Prolog algorithms, the reusable rules generated by GEMS, or a hybrid of both. Solvers form the core of the basic MIG generated by GEMS. Below we describe the solver we developed for completing partially specified models in our EAST-EEA deployment tool.

3.3   Model Completion Solvers

Using a global deployment (completion) solver, it is possible to ask for the completion of partially specified models constrained by user-defined rules. For example, in the EAST-EEA modeling tool, the user can specify the components, their requirements, the nodes (ECUs), and their resources and ask the tool to find a valid deployment of components to nodes. After deploying the most critical components to some nodes by using MIGs step-wise guidance, modelers can trigger a MIG global deployment solver to complete the deployment. This solver attempts to calculate an allocation of components to nodes that observes the deployment constraints and update the connections between components and nodes accordingly. This global solver can aim for an optimal deployment structure by using constraint-based Prolog programs or it could integrate some domain-specific heuristics, such as attempting to find a placement for the components that use the most resources first.

In some cases, however, the modeled constraints cannot be satisfied by the available resources. For example, in a large EAST-EEA model, a valid bin-packing of the CPU requirements for the components into EPUs may not exist. In these cases the complexity of the rules and entity relationships could make it extremely hard to deduce *why* there is no solution and *how* to change the model to overcome the problem. For such situations, we developed a solver that can identify failing constraints and provide suggestions on how to change the model to make the deployment possible.

4   Case Study: Solving EAST-EEA Deployment Problem

To validate our DIG MDE tool, we created a DSML for modeling EAST-EEA deployment problems. This DSML enables developers to specify partial solutions as sets of components, requirements, nodes (ECUs), and resources. A further requirement was that the MIGs should produce both valid assignments for a single component's *TargetHost* role and global assignments for the *TargetHost* role of all components. In the automotive domain certain software components often cannot be moved between ECUs from one model car to the next due to manufacturing costs, quality assurance, or other safety concerns. In these situations, developers must fix the *TargetHost* role of certain components and allow MIGs to solve for valid assignments of the remaining unassigned component *TargetHost* roles.

For the first step, we created a deployment DSML metamodel that allows users to model components with arbitrary configuration and resource requirements andnodes (ECUs) with arbitrary sets of provided resources. Each component configuration requirement is specified as an assertion on the value of a resource of the assigned *TargetHost*. For example, *OSVersion > 3.2* would be a valid configuration constraint. Resource constraints were created by specifying a resource name and the amount of that resource consumed by the component. Each Node could only have as many components deployed to it as its resources could support. Typical resource requirements were the RAM usage and CPU usage.

Each host can provide an arbitrary number of resources. Constraints comparisons on resources were specified using the $<$, $>$, -, and $=$ relational operators to denote that the value of the resource with the same name and type (*e.g.*, OS version) must be less, greater, or equal to the value specified in requirement. The "-" relationship indicates a summation constraint, *i.e.*, the total value of the demands on a resource by the components deployed to the providing node must not exceed the amount present on the node. After defining the metamodel and generating the graphical editor for the deployment DSML using GEMS, we added a set of Prolog constraints to enforce the configuration and resource constraint semantics of our models.

4.1   Defining Constraints and Solvers

Our constraint rules specified that for each child requirement element of a component, a corresponding resource child of the TargetHost must satisfy the requirement. The core part of the configuration constraint rule is as following.

```
is_a_valid_component_targethost(Owner, Value) :-
( self_targethost(Owner, [Value]), ! %deployed
  ;
  (is_a(Value,node),
   self_requires(Owner, Requirements),
   forall( member(Req,Requirements),
     (requirement_to_resource(Req, Value, Res),
     requirement_resource_constraint(Req, Res))
) ) ).
```

These lines of code are providing not only configuration constraint checking for an arbitrary set of requirements and resources but also enabling domain-specific GEMS editors to provide valid suggestions for deploying a component. Moreover, this solution was intended as a proof-of-concept to validate the approach and thus could be implemented with even fewer lines of code. The rest of the required predicates to implement the solver were generated by GEMS.

In our experiments with global solvers, Prolog solved a valid global deployment of 900 components to 300 nodes in approximately 0.08 seconds. This solution met all configuration constraints.

The rules required for solving for valid assignments using resource constraints were significantly more complicated since resource constraints are a form of bin-packing (an NP-Hard problem). We were able to devise heuristic rules in Prolog, however, that could solve a 160 component and 80 ECU model deployment in approximately 1.5 seconds and an entire 300 component and 80 ECU deployment, a typical EAST-EEA sized problem, in about 3.5 seconds. These solution times are directly tied to the difficulty of the problem instance. For certain instances, times could be much higher, which would make the suggestive solver from Section 3 discussed in the previous section applicable. In cases where the solver ran too long, the suggestive solver could be used to suggest ways of expanding the underlying resources and making the problem more tractable.

5   Concluding Remarks

The work presented in this paper addresses scalability problems of conventional manual modeling approaches. These scalability issues are particularly problematic for domains that have large solutions spaces and few correct solutions. In such domains, it is often infeasible to create correct models manually, so constraint solvers are therefore needed.

Turning a DSML instance into a format that can be used by a constraint solver is a time-consuming task. Our DIG MDE tool generates a domain-specific constraint solver that leverages a semantically rich knowledge base in Prolog format. It also allows users to specify constraints in declarative format that can be used to derive modeling suggestions.

GEMS and the MIGs generation framework is an open-source project available from: www.eclipse.org/gmt/gems or www.sf.net/projects/gems.

References

1. East-eea embedded electronic architecture web site - http://www.east-eea.net. 2004.
2. Automotive open system architecture - http://www.autosar.org/find02_ns6.php. 2006.
3. J. Sztipanovits and G. Karsai. Model-integrated computing. *Computer*, 30(4):110–111, 1997.
4. J. White and D. C. Schmidt. Simplifying the development of product-line customization tools via mdd. In *Workshop: MDD for Software Product Lines, ACM/IEEE 8th International Conference on Model Driven Engineering Languages and Systems*, October 2005.
5. J. White and D. C. Schmidt. Reducing enterprise product line architecture deployment costs via model-driven deployment and configuration testing. In *13th Annual IEEE International Conference and Workshop on the Engineering of Computer Based Systems*, 2006.

OCL for (Meta-)Models in Multiple Application Domains

Dan Chiorean[1], Birgit Demuth[2], Martin Gogolla[3], and Jos Warmer[4]

[1] "Babeş-Bolyai" University of Cluj-Napoca, Romania
[2] Technische Universität Dresden, Germany
[3] University of Bremen, Germany
[4] Ordina, The Netherlands
`chiorean@cs.ubbcluj.ro`, `bd1@inf.tu-dresden.de`,
`gogolla@informatik.uni-bremen.de`, `jos.warmer@ordina.nl`

Abstract. The workshop OCLApps 2006 was organized as a part of MoDELS/UML Conference in Genova, Italy. It continues the series of five OCL (Object Constraint Language) workshops held at previous UML/MoDELS conferences between 2000 - 2005. Similar to its predecessors, the workshop addressed both people from academia and industry. The advent of the MDA (Model Driven Architecture) vision and the rapid acceptance of MDE (Model Driven Engineering) approaches emphasize new application domains (like Semantic Web or Domain Specific Languages) and call for new OCL functionalities. In this context, the OCLApps 2006 Workshop, was conceived as a forum enabling researchers and industry experts to present and debate how the OCL could support these new requirements.

1 Motivation and Goals

In recent years, MDE, MDA and associated methodologies, multiple approaches and languages emphasized the role that OCL has to play in MDE development. Beyond using OCL in querying models, in specifying assertions and operations, new approaches and visions revealed beneficial usage of OCL to model behavior description, compilation and evaluation of models, model transformation, and code generation. All these usages concern modeling languages in general, and UML in particular. As visual modeling languages evolve, complementary textual formalisms must evolve in accordance.

The workshop promoted contributions and experience reports related to the adequacy of OCL specifications, new and classical usages, OCL refactoring and extensions in order to support new usages of OCL specifications and new applications domains. Topics of interest included (but were not limited to):

- OCL as a textual formalism for specifying (meta-)models, irrespective of the abstraction level,
- Use of OCL in Domain Specific Languages (DSLs),
- Use of OCL in specifying model behavior, extensions required for this usage, examples of applications,

T. Kühne (Ed.): MoDELS 2006 Workshops, LNCS 4364, pp. 152–158, 2007.

- Using OCL expressions in specifying aspects,
- OCL usage for navigating and querying models and databases,
- OCL as a neutral standard for specifying multi-tier applications,
- Tools supporting model compilation and execution,
- OCL and Model Transformations, needed extensions, experience reports,
- Using OCL specifications in metamodeling, completeness and correctness of well-formedness rules,
- OCL and business process modeling,
- OCL and ontology modeling, experience reports on OCL usage in the Semantic Web application domain,
- Experience reports on OCL usage in profile specification and profile usage in application domains, OCL for the implementation of domain specification languages, and
- Aspects needing to be clarified in OCL specifications, for example the semantics of undefined values and the evaluation of expressions containing undefined values, or overriding OCL expressions.

2   Organization

The workshop continued the series of OCL workshops held at previous MODELS/UML conferences: York, 2000, Toronto, 2001, San Francisco, 2003, Lisbon, 2004, and Montego Bay, 2005. The workshop was organized by Dan Chiorean, Birgit Demuth, Martin Gogolla, and Jos Warmer. The organizers were at the same time co-chairs of the Program Committee. Each submission was reviewed by two to three members of the Program Committee. Based on the reviews, the decisions regarding papers acceptance were taken unanimously. Three papers were co-authored by one of the workshop PC members. The review process ensured that the authors had no influence on the acceptance/rejection decision for papers written by them.

The PC (in addition to the workshop organizers) consisted of:

- Thomas Baar (EPFL Lausanne, Switzerland)
- Jordi Cabot (Universitat Oberta de Catalunya, Spain)
- Tony Clark (Xactium, United Kingdom)
- Andy Evans (Xactium, United Kingdom)
- Robert France (Colorado State University, USA)
- Heinrich Hussmann (LMU Munich, Germany)
- Marcel Kyas (University of Oslo, Norway)
- Richard Mitchell (Inferdata, USA)
- Octavian Patrascoiu (LogicaCMG, United Kingdom)
- Mark Richters (EADS, Germany)
- Shane Sendall (Switzerland)
- Peter Schmitt (Universität Karlsruhe, Germany)
- Burkhart Wolff (ETH Zurich, Switzerland)

3   Topics and Approaches of Accepted Papers

The 18 accepted papers, [DCGW06] cover a large spectrum of OCL related topics. They reflect research contributions and experience reports about using OCL for models and metamodels in multiple application domains. In order to manage the paper presentations, the accepted papers were divided into four sections: new applications, model transformations, implementation of OCL support in tools and language issues.

In their paper *Customer Validation of Formal Contracts*, [HJ] Heldal and Johannisson present a modality of translating OCL assertions into natural language. In order to obtain good results, the formal specifications have to comply with some rules. Considering the natural sequence of activities realized in a specification process, from informal to formal, the proposal can be viewed as supporting a kind of round-trip engineering support, helping customers in understanding whether their informal requirements comply with the formal ones. As the authors mentioned, taking into account that the formalisms used by UML have different degrees of formality, the obtained results could be used in a broader framework for UML model transformation.

Kolovos, Paige and Polack describe in the paper *Towards Using OCL for Instance-Level Queries in Domain Specific Languages*, [KPP] an ongoing work towards defining a rigorous approach meant to align the OCL query and navigation facilities with DSLs. In their approach, the authors used a new language, very closed to OCL, defined by themselves and named EOL. The work presented confirmed again that OCL is well-suited for model querying in metamodeling, where navigating models from one abstraction level to another is a mandatory requirement.

In the paper *OCL-based Validation of a Railway Domain Profile*, [Ber] Kirsten Berkenkötter proves that using UML, tailored by means of dedicated profiles, represents an alternative to DSLs. Undoubtedly, each of these above mentioned approaches presents both advantages and drawbacks. Therefore, now, accumulating experiences related to these different ways represents a mandatory task. Berkenkoötter's paper, succeeds in proving that using OCL in specifying profiles for a real application represents a valuable approach. The quantity and quality of application code, automatically generated, is among the main benefits obtained by using profiles specified with OCL.

An experience showing that OCL 2.0 is expressive enough to be used as a query language for model analysis is presented by Joanna Chimiak-Opoka and Chris Lenz in *Use of OCL in a Model Assessment Framework: An experience report*, [COL]. The assessment framework was composed by three different components: a Modeling Environment, a Model Data Repository and an Analysis Tool. The considered metamodel was meant to support optimization of clinical processes in the framework of a real project named MedFlow. The paper proves that using OCL in real applications is profitable and that using different components (tools) represents a viable approach.

Tsukasa Takemura and Tetsuo Tamai state that using OCL in modeling business processes, their approach can bypass a well-known problem, named the

"Business-IT gap". Their position is presented in the paper *Rigorous Business Process Modeling with OCL*, [TT]. The approach uses activity diagrams enriched by OCL expressions. Also, in order to fully support the specific requirements, appropriate OCL extensions are proposed.

In model transformations, a crucial activity for MDE success, OCL usage is one preferred approach for researchers. In this context, a metamodel-driven model interchange was proposed by Dragan Gasevic and his colleagues in *On Interchanging between OWL/SWRL and UML/OCL*, [MGG+]. The paper aims to reuse the results obtained in MDA to Semantic Web Languages. Moreover, the described work represents a new step towards the reconciliation of Meta Object Facility (MOF) based languages and Semantic Web Languages. The authors go beyond the approach established by the OMG's ODM (Ontology Definition Metamodel) specification that only addresses mappings between OWL and UML, and extend this with mappings between SWRL and OCL. The proposals made by authors are grounded on practical experience.

In the paper *Realizing UML Model Transformations with USE*, [BB] - Fabian Büttner and Hanna Bauerdick enrich the specification language of USE with imperative elements in order to provide a flexible instrument meant to support experiments with different transformations and transformation formalisms.

A modality for specifying OCL constraints in an automated manner by using "constraints patterns" is described by Wahler, Koehler and Bruckner in the paper *Model-Driven Constraint Engineering*, [WKB]. Inspired by design patterns, the authors prove that the use of patterns could be useful for constraints also. Patterns support modelers to focus on relevant aspects enabling the use of verified specifications. The example used for introducing the problem is excellent from a pedagogical perspective. It proves that even very simple UML models need in some cases complex OCL specifications. An important conclusion is that OCL represents the appropriate tool supporting models in a complete and unambiguous manner.

The efficiency of OCL support in large scale modeling environments is analyzed by Altenhofen, Hettel and Kusterer in the paper entitled *OCL support in an industrial environment*, [AHK]. The described problem concerns the reduction of necessary evaluations for OCL constraints, when the underlying model changes. The experiences presented by authors were meant to realize an efficient OCL integration into the next generation modeling infrastructure of SAP, called MOIN.

Stölzel, Zschaler and Geiger discuss in the paper *Integrating OCL and Model Transformations in Fujaba*, [MSG] the integration of the Dresden OCL Toolkit into the Fujaba Tool Suite. This integration adds OCL support to class diagrams and makes OCL usable in Fujaba's model transformations. The Fujaba support for model transformations gets more powerful, platform independent and easier to read for developers familiar with OCL. The possibility of using OCL in Fujaba story diagrams in order to support code generation is also presented. Integrating different tools like Fujaba, the Dresden OCL Toolkit and Eclipse are among the most interesting topics approached in this paper.

An optimization algorithm for the evaluation of OCL constraints used in graph rewriting based model transformations is presented by Mezei, Levendovszky and Charaf in their paper *Restrictions for OCL constraint optimization algorithms*, [MLC]. This is an important topic because efficient constraint handling is essential in UML, in metamodeling, and also in model transformation.

Brucker, Doser and Wolff describe in the paper *An MDA Framework Supporting OCL*, [BDWa] a tool chain for processing UML/OCL specifications, including a proof environment and flexible code generation. In the presented framework, named SecureUML, OCL supports both model verification and transformation, including code generation. As the authors mention, using conjoint functionalities for checking, prooving and transforming offers opportunities for new and up to now unexpected applications.

Amelunxen and Schürr explain in the paper *On OCL as part of the metamodeling framework MOFLON*, [AS] the role of OCL in the metamodeling framework MOFLON, designed to support the definition of domain specific languages with MOF, OCL and graph transformations. Beyond this interesting problem, the authors present a set of constraints (well-formedness rules) which corrects, completes and improves MOF 2.0 for the application as graph schema language.

In the paper *Ambiguity issues in OCL postconditions*, [Cab] Cabot identifies common ambiguities appearing in OCL postconditions and proposes an approach to automatically disambiguate these situations by means of providing a default interpretation for each kind of ambiguous expression. The advantages of the proposed solutions are: a more rigorous specification and a better quality of the code generated for OCL postconditions.

Akehurst, Howells and McDonald-Maier discuss in the paper *UML/OCL - Detaching the Standard Library*, [AHMM] about an OCL Standard Library that is independent from different modeling languages. Considering the increasing use of OCL as a query language for models, the independence of the standard library is an important user requirement that has to be supported by OCL implementations in DSLs.

The results of a long-term project, intended to provide a formalized, machine-checkable semantic basis for a theorem proving environment for OCL is described by Brucker, Doser and Wolff in the paper entitled *Semantic Issues of OCL: Past, Present, and Future*, [BDWb]. The final objective of the above mentioned project, is to make OCL more fit for future extensions towards program verifications and specification refinement.

The paper *Improving the OCL Semantics Definition by Applying Dynamic Meta Modeling and Design Patterns*, [CP] by Chiaradía and Pons presents an alternative definition for the OCL semantics metamodel by applying the Visitor design pattern. The proposal claims to avoid circularity in the OCL definition, and to increase its extensibility, legibility and accuracy.

Süß proposes in the paper *Sugar for OCL*, [Süß] three shorthand notations for the layout of OCL in the Latex, HTML, and Unicode (a la ObjectZ) encoding systems, in order to obtain specifications which more readable.

4   Discussion and Conclusion

In the following, we summarize some of the topics that were discussed at the workshop:

- OCL offers support for model transformation, including automated code generation. In this last context, the OCL use is advantageous from two perspectives: firstly, for the support in querying models and secondly, for offering important additional information for code generation.
- The use of the constraint language in large scale models needs to consider the efficiency of evaluating specifications.
- As different language extensions are required for an efficient use of OCL in different domains (like Business Process Modeling or the Semantic Web), considering OCL as a family of languages becomes a more important requirement.
- Fixing different ambiguities concerning the OCL must be realized.
- As Eclipse tends to be a quasi unanimously tool in the modelers world, efficiently promoting OCL needs strong support within the Eclipse framework.

References

[AHK]   Michael Altenhofen, Thomas Hettel, and Stefan Kusterer. OCL support in an industrial environment. In *OCL for (Meta-)Models in Multiple Application Domains*, pages 126–139. TUD-FI06-04.

[AHMM]   D. H. Akehurst, W.G.J. Howells, and K.D. McDonald-Maier. UML/OCL - Detaching the Standard Library. In *OCL for (Meta-)Models in Multiple Application Domains*, pages 205–212. TUD-FI06-04.

[AS]   C. Amelunxen and A. Schürr. On OCL as part of the metamodeling framework MOFLON. In *OCL for (Meta-)Models in Multiple Application Domains*, pages 182–193. TUD-FI06-04.

[BB]   Fabian Büttner and Hanna Bauerdick. Realizing UML Model Transformations with USE. In *OCL for (Meta-)Models in Multiple Application Domains*, pages 96–110. TUD-FI06-04.

[BDWa]   Achim D. Brucker, Jürgen Doser, and Burkhart Wolff. An MDA Framework Supporting OCL. In *OCL for (Meta-)Models in Multiple Application Domains*, pages 166–181. TUD-FI06-04.

[BDWb]   Achim D. Brucker, Jürgen Doser, and Burkhart Wolff. Semantic Issues of OCL: Past, Present, and Future. In *OCL for (Meta-)Models in Multiple Application Domains*, pages 213–228. TUD-FI06-04.

[Ber]   Kirsten Berkenkötter. OCL-based Validation of a Railway Domain Profile. In *OCL for (Meta-)Models in Multiple Application Domains*, pages 38–52. TUD-FI06-04.

[Cab]   Jordi Cabot. Ambiguity issues in OCL postconditions. In *OCL for (Meta-)Models in Multiple Application Domains*, pages 194–204. TUD-FI06-04.

[COL]   Joanna Chimiak-Opoka and Chris Lenz. Use of OCL in a Model Assessment Framework: An experience report. In *OCL for (Meta-)Models in Multiple Application Domains*, pages 53–67. TUD-FI06-04.

[CP]   Juan Martín Chiaradía and Claudia Pons. Improving the OCL Semantics
            Definition by Applying Dynamic Meta Modeling and Design Patterns. In
            OCL for (Meta-)Models in Multiple Application Domains, pages 229–239.
            TUD-FI06-04.

[DCGW06]   Birgit Demuth, Dan Chiorean, Martin Gogolla, and Jos Warmer, editors.
            OCL for (Meta-)Models in Multiple Application Domains, TUD-FI06-
            04. Institut für Software- und Multimediatechnik, Technische Universität
            Dresden, 09 2006. ISSN 1430-211X.

[HJ]   Rogardt Heldal and Kristofer Johannisson. Customer Validation of For-
            mal Contracts. In *OCL for (Meta-)Models in Multiple Application Do-
            mains*, pages 13–25. TUD-FI06-04.

[KPP]   Dimitrios S. Kolovos, Richard F. Paige, and Fiona A. C. Polack. Towards
            Using OCL for Instance-Level Queries in Domain Specific Languages. In
            OCL for (Meta-)Models in Multiple Application Domains, pages 26–37.
            TUD-FI06-04.

[MGG$^+$]   Milan Milanovic, Dragan Gasevic, Adrian Giurca, Gerd Wagner, and
            Vladan Devedzic.   On Interchanging Between OWL/SWRL and
            UML/OCL. In *OCL for (Meta-)Models in Multiple Application Domains*,
            pages 81–95. TUD-FI06-04.

[MLC]   Gergely Mezei, Tihamer Levendovszki, and Hassan Charaf. Restrictions
            for OCL constraint optimization algorithms. In *OCL for (Meta-)Models
            in Multiple Application Domains*, pages 151–165. TUD-FI06-04.

[MSG]   Steffen Zschaler Mirko Stölzel and Leif Geiger. Integrating OCL and
            Model Transformations in Fujaba. In *OCL for (Meta-)Models in Multiple
            Application Domains*, pages 140–150. TUD-FI06-04.

[Süß]   Jörn Guy Süß. Sugar for OCL. In *OCL for (Meta-)Models in Multiple
            Application Domains*, pages 240–252. TUD-FI06-04.

[TT]   Tsukasa Takemura and Tetsuo Tamai. Rigorous Business Process Mod-
            eling with OCL. In *OCL for (Meta-)Models in Multiple Application Do-
            mains*, pages 68–80. TUD-FI06-04.

[WKB]   Michael Wahler, Jana Koehler, and Achim D. Brucker. Model-Driven
            Constraint Engineering. In *OCL for (Meta-)Models in Multiple Applica-
            tion Domains*, pages 111–125. TUD-FI06-04.

OCL-Based Validation of a Railway Domain Profile

Kirsten Berkenkötter

University of Bremen,
P.O. Box 330 440,
28334 Bremen, Germany
`kirsten@informatik.uni-bremen.de`

Abstract. Domain-specific languages become more and more important these days as they facilitate the close collaboration of domain experts and software developers. One effect of this general tendency is the increasing number of UML profiles. UML itself as a popular modeling language is capable of modeling all kinds of systems but it is often inefficient due to its wide-spectrum approach. Profiles tailor the UML to a specific domain and can hence be seen as domain-specific dialects of UML. At the moment, they mainly introduce new terminology, often in combination with OCL constraints which describe the new constructs more precisely. As most tools do not support validation of OCL expressions let alone supplementing profiles with OCL constraints, it is difficult to check if models based on a profile comply to this profile. A related problem is checking whether constraints in the profile contradict constraints in the UML specification. In this paper, it is shown how to complete these tasks with the tool USE. As an example, a profile from the railway control systems domain is taken which describes the use of its modeling elements strictly my means of OCL. Models based on this profile serve as a foundation for automated code generation and require unambiguous meaning.

1 Introduction

The current interest in model driven architecture (MDA) [OMG03] and its surrounding techniques like metamodeling and model driven development (MDD) has also increased the interest in domain-specific languages (DSL) and their development. In this context, several standards have been developed like the Meta Object Facility (MOF) [OMG06] for designing metamodels and the Unified Modeling Language (UML) [OMG05c, OMG05b] as a modeling language which has become the de-facto standard for modeling languages and is supported by various tools. Due to its wide-spectrum approach, UML can be used for modeling all kinds of systems. This is an advantage as one tool can be used to develop different kinds of systems. In contrast, it may also lead to inefficiency and inaccuracy as each domain has its own needs. Another problem are semantic variation points in UML that are necessary for the wide-spectrum approach but not useful if the model is used as basis of transformations or code generation. Here, unambiguous models are needed.

T. Kühne (Ed.): MoDELS 2006 Workshops, LNCS 4364, pp. 159–168, 2007.

A good example are railway control systems that are described in specific terminology and notation. The domain of control are track networks that consist of elements like segments, points, or signals. Routes are defined to describe how trains travel on the network. In addition, there are rules that specify in which way a network is constructed and how it is operated. Some rules apply to all kinds of railway systems and some are specific for each kind of railway system, e.g. tramway or railroads. In principle, UML is capable of modeling such systems. The problem is that we have to model each kind of railway system with all rules explicitly. The domain knowledge that covers the common parts of all railway control systems is not captured in such models. Neither is specific notation that is used in the domain like symbols for signals and sensors.

Domain-specific languages are a means to overcome these disadvantages [Eva06]. Designing a new modeling language from scratch is obviously time-consuming and costly, therefore UML profiles have become a popular mechanism to tailor the UML to specific domains. In this way, different UML dialects have been developed with considerably low effort. New terminology based on existing UML constructs is introduced and further supplied with OCL [OMG05a, WK04] constraints to specify its usage precisely. Semantics are often described in natural language just as for UML itself.

With respect to railways, the Railway Control Systems Domain (RCSD) profile has been developed [BH06] as domain-specific UML derivative with formal semantics. With the help of the profile, the system expert develops track networks for different kind of railway systems consisting of track segment, signal, points, etc. The software specialist works on the same information to develop controllers. In the end, controller code which satisfies safety-critical requirements shall be generated automatically. Railway control systems are especially interesting as the domain knowledge gathered in the long history of the domain has to be preserved while combining it with development techniques for safety-critical systems. Structural aspects are specified by class and object diagrams (see Fig. 4 and Fig. 5) whose compliance to the domain is ensured by OCL constraints. Semantics are based on a timed state transition system that serves as foundation for formal transformations towards code generation for controllers as well as for verification tasks. In this paper, the focus is on the validation of the structural aspects to ensure the correct and successful application of transformations and verification. Details about semantics can be found in [PBD+05, BH06].

A problem that has not been tackled until now is validating that the constraints of a profile comply to the ones of UML and that models using a profile comply to this profile. One reason for this is that CASE tools often support profiles as far as new terminology can be introduced but lack support of OCL [BCC+05]. One of the few tools that support OCL is USE (UML Specification Environment) [Ric02, GFB05]. It allows the definition of a metamodel supplied with OCL constraints and checks whether models based on this metamodel fulfill all constraints. Using (a part of) the UML metamodel in combination with a profile as the USE metamodel allows for fulfilling three goals: (a) Validating that this profile complies to the UML metamodel as each model has to fulfill the invariants of the UML metamodel and the profile. (b) Validating that class diagrams comply to the profile. (c) Validating that object diagrams comply to the profile if the profile describes instances as well as instantiable elements. This approach has been used to validate the RCSD profile and models based on it.

The paper is organized in the following way: the next section gives a short introduction to the railway domain, followed by a description of the RCSD profile and typical constraints in Sec. 3. After that, Sec. 4 describes the validation with USE on the different levels. At last, the results of this validation approach and future work are discussed in Sec. 5.

2   Short Introduction to the Railway Domain

Creating a domain specific profile requires identifying the elements of this domain and their properties. In the railway domain, track elements, sensors, signals, automatic train runnings, and routes have been proven essential modeling elements as e.g. described in [Pac02]. They are described shortly in the following, more details can be found in [BH06]:

Track Elements. The track network consists of segments, crossings, and points. Segments are rails with two ends, while crossings consist of either two crossing segments or two interlaced segments. Points allow a changeover from one segment to another one. Single points have a stem and a branch. Single slip points and double slip points are crossings with one, resp. two, changeover possibilities.

Sensors. Sensors are used to identify the position of trains on the track network, i.e. the current track element. To achieve this goal, track elements have entry and exit sensors located at each end. The number of sensors depends on the allowed driving directions, i.e. the uni- or bidirectional usage of the track element.

Signals. Signals come in various ways. In general, they indicate if a train may go or if it has to stop. The permission to go may be constrained, e.g. by speed limits or by obligatory directions in case of points. As it is significant to know if a train moves according to signaling, signals are always located at sensors.

Automatic Train Running. Automatic train running systems are used to enforce braking of trains, usually in safety-critical situations. Automatic train running systems are also located at sensors.

Route Definition. As sensors are used as connection between track elements, routes of a track network are defined by sequences of sensors. They can be entered if the required signal setting of the first signal of the route is set. This can only be done if all points are in the correct position needed for this route. Conflicting routes cannot be released at the same time.

3   RCSD Profile

Unfortunately, defining eight stereotypes as suggested by the domain analysis in Sec. 2 is not sufficient. New primitive datatypes, enumerations, and special kinds of association to model interrelationships between stereotypes are needed. Furthermore, UML supports two modeling layers, i.e. the model layer itself (class diagrams) and the instances layer (object diagrams). In the RCSD profile, both layers are needed: class diagrams are used to model specific parts of the railway domain, e.g. tramways or railroad models, while object diagrams show explicit track layouts for such models. Hence, stereotypes on the object level have to be defined. For these reasons, the RCSD profile is structured in five parts: the definition of primitive datatypes and literals, network elements on class level, associations between these elements, instances of network elements and associations, and route definitions. In the following, we focus on network elements, their instances, and routes as the domain knowledge is mostly gathered in these parts.

3.1   Network Elements

The next part of the profile defines track network elements, i.e. segments, crossing, points, signals, sensors, and automatic train runnings (see Fig. 1). *Segment*, *Crossing*, and *Point* have in common that they form the track network itself, therefore they are all subclasses of the abstract *TrackElement*. Similarly, *Single-Point* and *SlipPoint* are specializations of *Point*. Enumerations are defined to specify values of properties. All elements are equipped with a set of constraints that define which properties must be supported by each element and how it is related to other elements.

An instance of *TrackElement* on the model layer must provide several properties: *maximalNumberOfTrains* to restrict the number of trains on a track element at one point in time (mandatory) and *limit* to give a speed limit (optional). Both properties have to be integers. The first one has a fixed multiplicity 1, the second

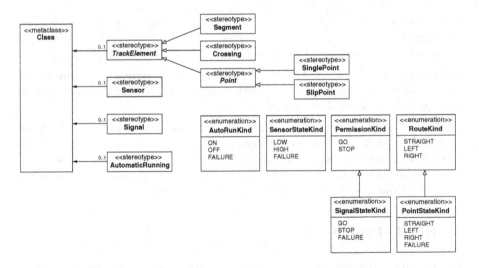

Fig. 1. Network elements of the RCSD profile

one may have multiplicities 0..1 or 1. Such requirements for *TrackElement* are defined in the following way:

```
ownedAttribute->one(a | a.name->includes('maxNumberOfTrains') and
                       a.type.name->includes('Integer') and
                       a.upperBound() = 1 and a.lowerBound() = 1 and
                       a.isReadOnly = true)
```

To understand the structure of these constraints, a look at the UML metamodel is helpful. As all network elements are stereotypes of *Class* from the UML 2.0 Kernel package, we can refer to all properties of *Class* in our constraints. Properties on the model level are instances of class *Property* on the metamodel level, which are associated to *Class* by *ownedAttribute*. As a *StructuralFeature*, *Property* is also a *NamedElement*, a *TypedElement*, and a *MultiplicityElement*, which allows to restrain name, type, and multiplicity as shown in the constraint above. Similar constraints are defined for all network elements.

3.2 Instances of Network Elements

For each non-abstract modeling element and each association, there exists a corresponding instance stereotype that also defines domain-specific notation. In Fig. 2, two unidirectional segments connected by a sensor *S1* are shown. For comparison, the same constellation in object notation is given in Fig. 3.

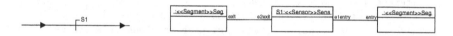

Fig. 2. RCSD notation   **Fig. 3.** UML notation

The instances are heavily restricted by OCL constraints as the instance level serves as the basis for automated code generation, e.g. the limit of track elements must have a value from ℕ if present. A more interesting constraint is that each *Point* has a *plus* and *minus* position. One of these has to be *STRAIGHT* and the other one *LEFT* or *RIGHT*:

```
slot->select(s1 | s1.definingFeature.name->includes('minus') or
                  s1.definingFeature.name->includes('plus'))->
  one(s2 | s2.value->size()= 1 and
           s2.value->first().oclIsTypeOf(InstanceValue) and
           s2.value->first().oclAsType(InstanceValue).instance.name->
             includes('STRAIGHT')) and
slot->select(s1 | s1.definingFeature.name->includes('minus') or
                  s1.definingFeature.name->includes('plus'))->
  one(s2 | s2.value->size()= 1 and
           s2.value->first().oclIsTypeOf(InstanceValue) and
           (s2.value->first().oclAsType(InstanceValue).instance.name->
             includes('LEFT') or
           s2.value->first()->oclAsType(InstanceValue).instance.name->
             includes('RIGHT')))
```

Another example are identification numbers of sensors that have to be unique: each *Sensor* must have a property *sensorId* whose value is unique with respect to all *SensorInstances*:

```
SensorInstance.allInstances->collect(slot)->asSet->flatten->
  select(s | s.definingFeature.name->includes('sensorId'))->
    iterate(s:Slot;
      result:Set(LiteralSensorId) = oclEmpty(Set(LiteralSensorId)) |
      result->including(s.value->first.oclAsType(LiteralSensorId)))->
        isUnique(value)
```

3.3   Route Definitions

Moreover, the profile defines routes and their instances. Each *Route* is defined by an ordered sequence of sensor ids. The signal setting for entering the route and sets of required point positions and of conflicts with other routes are further necessary information. A typical constraint demands that every sensor id in a route definition must refer to an existing sensor. Hence, the following constraint must hold for each *RouteInstance*:

```
let i:Set(Integer) =
  slot->select(s | s.definingFeature.name->includes('routeDefinition'))->
    asSequence->first().value->
      iterate(v:ValueSpecification;
              result:Set(Integer)=oclEmpty(Set(Integer)) |
              result->including(v.oclAsType(LiteralSensorId).value))
in
  i->forAll(id | SensorInstance.allInstances->exists(sens |
    sens.slot->select(s | s.definingFeature.name->includes('sensorId'))->
      asSequence->first().value->first().
        oclAsType(LiteralSensorId).value = id))
```

4   Validation of Wellformedness Rules with USE

The next step is adapting the profile and its various invariants to USE for the validation process. USE expects a model in textual notation as input. In our case, this is the metamodel consisting of (a part of) the UML metamodel and the profile. Instance models can be checked with respect to the invariants in the metamodel, both on class and object layer. A similar application of USE with respect to the four metamodeling layers of UML is shown in [GFB05].

This metamodel file includes both the necessary part of the UML 2.0 metamodel and the RCSD profile for two reasons: first, the profile cannot exist without its reference metamodel and second, one goal is to check the compliance of the profile to the metamodel. This task must be performed implicitly as USE does not check if the given constraints contradict. Instead, we assume the profile compliant to the metamodel as long as both the constraints in the metamodel and the constraints in the profile are all valid.

4.1   Modeling the UML Metamodel and the RCSD Profile for USE

In the metamodel file, a description of classes with attributes and operations, associations, and OCL expressions is expected. OCL expressions are either invariants as shown in Sec.3, or definitions of operations. For the validation of the profile, all invariants must be fulfilled by the instance model(s).

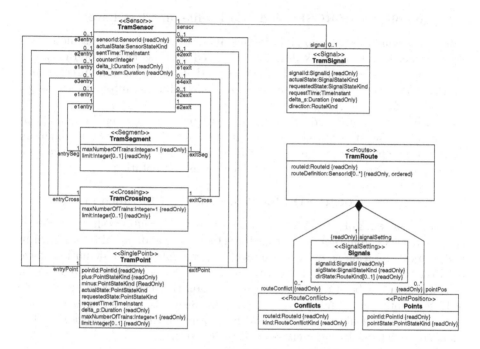

Fig. 4. Tram network definitions - class level

From the UML metamodel, the *Kernel* package has been modeled with some modifications: (a) Packages are not needed by the RCSD profile and therefore skipped in all diagrams, diagram *Packages* has been omitted completely. (b) Lower and upper bounds of multiplicities have been changed to *LiteralInteger* instead of *ValueSpecification* for easier handling. One reason is that the invariants in the context of *MultiplicityElement* are not specific enough to guarantee that the *ValueSpecification* really evaluates to *LiteralInteger* as necessary. Therefore, expressions cannot be used to specify multiplicities. The invariants of *MultiplicityElement* have been adapted to this. (c) Several invariants and operations had to be rewritten or omitted completely as they are erroneous in the UML specification. More information about this problem can be found in [BGG04]. (d) Some names in the UML specification had to be changed due to conflicts with USE keywords or multiple usage in the specification which also leads to conflicts. This problem is also described in [BGG04]. (e) USE does not support *UnlimitedNatural* as type. This problem has been overcome by using *Integer* and additional constraints that restrict corresponding values to N. All in all, 34 invariants have been specified here.

Profiles are not directly supported by USE. This problem has been overcome by modeling each RSCD stereotype as a subclass from its metaclass, i.e. a metamodel extension. All in all, 311 invariants have been specified for the RCSD profile.

4.2   Compliance of RCSD Model to Profile on Class Level

Evaluating constraints is possible for instances of the given (meta)model. As an example, a tram network description is used on class level. Tram networks consist of segments, crossing and single points that are all used unidirectionally. Furthermore, there are signals, sensors, and routes, but no automatic runnings. This constellation is shown in Fig. 4.

In USE, an instance model can be constructed step by step by adding instances of classes and associations of the metamodel to an instance diagram. More convenient is the usage of a *.cmd command file where instance creation and setting of property values are specified in textual notation.

4.3   Compliance of RCSD Model to Profile on Instance Level

A concrete network of a tram maintenance site with six routes is shown in Fig. 5. Note that this is diagram is given in RCSD notation and can also be shown in UML object notation as discussed in Sec. 3. The explicit route definitions have been omitted for the sake of brevity, but can be easily extracted from Fig. 5. This diagram has been used for the validation on the instance level. It consists of 12 segments, 3 crossing, 6 points, 25 sensors, 3 signals, and 6 routes, specified in a second *.cmd file. The two *.cmd files form a complete instance model of the metamodel consisting of classes and their instances.

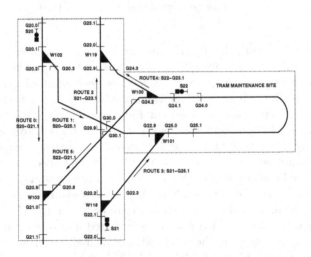

Fig. 5. Concrete track network - instance level

4.4 Results

In this example, all invariants have been fulfilled. The correctness of the OCL constraints could be easily checked by adding intentional errors like incorrect association ends or signals with the same id. USE facilitates tracing of such errors by (a) showing which instance of the metamodel has violated an invariant and by (b) decomposing the invariant in all sub-clauses and giving the respective evaluation.

For the validation process, some effort with respect to the USE metamodel is unavoidable. Fortunately, the metamodel and profile have to be modeled only once for each profile. The part of the UML metamodel that has to be included varies from profile to profile depending on the metaclasses references by stereotypes. The current version of the USE metamodel consists of approximately 4000 lines. With respect to the RCSD profile, the instance model on class level has to be modeled once per specific railway system, e.g. once for trams. With this part of the instance model, all kinds of concrete track layouts can be checked. The tram example consists of approximately 1500 lines of input data to USE. These can be generated from class diagrams by parsing the output of CASE tools and adapting them to USE. Concrete track layouts can also be generated, this time from object diagrams. In this way, all kinds of track layouts for one system can be checked. The example track layout consists of about 5000 lines.

5 Conclusion

The validation of models of the RCSD profile and the profile itself based on OCL constraints with USE has been proven useful in several ways. It has been shown that the profile complies to UML as it is required and that an example model for tramways is valid in the RCSD context. This makes object diagrams for such tramways applicable for transformation and verification purposes. Another effect of the validation with USE was the improvement of the OCL constraints themselves. As most case tools have no OCL support, it is hard to detect if constraints exhibit syntax errors or if complicated constraints really have the intended meaning.

An adaption of the validation process to other profiles can be performed straightforward. It is possible that the UML metamodel part has to be enhanced for other profiles as this depends on the metaclasses referenced by stereotypes. Validation is reasonable in each profile whose application relies on a solid and unambiguous model.

With respect to the RCSD profile, future work has to investigate the behavioral aspects of track layouts as described in [BH06]. At the moment, only statical aspects have been examined, but USE can also be applied to the validation and test of controllers that have been generated for a concrete track network. Passing trains have to be simulated by changes of sensor values just as route requests by trains to the controller. Signals and points have to be switched by the controller with respect to safety conditions like 'only one tram on a point at one point in time' or 'only one tram on conflicting routes'. Such safety requirements can also be expressed in OCL. As train movements just as signal and point switches can be modeled by changes of variable values, the outcome is always a new object diagram whose invariants can be checked.

Acknowledgments. Special thanks go to Fabian Büttner and Arne Lindow for their help with USE and to Ulrich Hannemann for his valuable feedback to the first versions of this paper and the related work.

References

[BCC⁺05]   Thomas Baar, Dan Chiorean, Alexandre Correa, Martin Gogolla, Heinrich Hußmann, Octavian Patrascoiu, Peter H. Schmitt, and Jos Warmer. Tool Support for OCL and Related Formalisms - Needs and Trends. In Jean-Michel Bruel, editor, *Satellite Events at the ModELS'2005 Conference*, volume 3844 of *LNCS*, pages 1–9. Springer-Verlag, 2005.

[BGG04]   Hanna Bauerdick, Martin Gogolla, and Fabian Gutsche. Detecting OCL Traps in the UML 2.0 Superstructure. In Thomas Baar, Alfred Strohmeier, Ana Moreira, and Stephen J. Mellor, editors, *Proceedings 7th International Conference Unified Modeling Language (UML'2004)*, volume 3273 of *LNCS*, pages 188–197. Springer-Verlag, 2004.

[BH06]   Kirsten Berkenkötter and Ulrich Hannemann. Modeling the railway control domain rigorously with a uml 2.0 profile. In J. Górski, editor, *Safecomp 2006*, volume 4166 of *LNCS*, pages 398–411. Springer, 2006. to appear.

[Eva06]   Andy   Evans.   Domain   Specific   Languages   and   MDA. http://www.xactium.com, 2006.

[GFB05]   Martin Gogolla, Jean-Marie Favre, and Fabian Büttner. On Squeezing M0, M1, M2, and M3 into a Single Object Diagram. Technical Report LGL-REPORT-2005-001, Ecole Polytechnique Fédérale de Lausanne, 2005.

[OMG03]   Object Management Group. MDA Guide Version 1.0.1, June 2003.

[OMG05a]   Object Management Group. OCL 2.0 Specification, version 2.0. http://www.omg.org/docs/ptc/05-06-06.pdf, June 2005.

[OMG05b]   Object Management Group. Unified Modeling Language: Superstructure, version 2.0. http://www.omg.org/docs/formal/05-07-04.pdf, July 2005.

[OMG05c]   Object Management Group. Unified Modeling Language (UML) Specification: Infrastructure, version 2.0. http://www.omg.org/docs/ptc/04-10-14.pdf, July 2005.

[OMG06]   Object Management Group. Meta Object Facility (MOF) 2.0 Core Specification. http://www.omg.org/docs/formal/06-01-01.pdf, January 2006.

[Pac02]   Joern Pachl. *Railway Operation and Control*. VTD Rail Publishing, Mountlake Terrace (USA), 2002. ISBN 0-9719915-1-0.

[PBD⁺05]   Jan Peleska, Kirsten Berkenkötter, Rolf Drechsler, Daniel Große, Ulrich Hannemann, Anne E. Haxthausen, and Sebastian Kinder. Domain-specific formalisms and model-driven development for railway control systems. In *TRain workshop at SEFM2005*, September 2005.

[Ric02]   Mark Richters. *A Precise Approach to Validating UML Models and OCL Constraints*, volume 14 of *BISS Monographs*. Logos Verlag, Berlin, 2002. Ph.D. thesis, Universität Bremen.

[WK04]   Jos Warmer and Anneke Kleppe. *Object Constraint Language 2.0*. MITP-Verlag, Bonn, 2004.

OCL Support in an Industrial Environment

Michael Altenhofen[1], Thomas Hettel[2], and Stefan Kusterer[3]

[1] SAP Research, CEC Karlsruhe,
76131 Karlsruhe, Germany
michael.altenhofen@sap.com
[2] SAP Research, CEC Brisbane,
Brisbane, Australia
thomas.hettel@sap.com
[3] SAP AG, 69190 Walldorf, Germany
stefan.kusterer@sap.com

Abstract. In this paper, we report on our experiences integrating OCL evaluation support in an industrial-strength (meta-)modeling infrastructure. We focus on the approach taken to improve efficiency through what we call *impact analysis* of model changes to decrease the number of necessary (re-)evaluations. We show how requirements derived from application scenarios have led to design decisions that depart from or resp. extend solutions found in (academic) literature.

1 Introduction

The MDA [1] vision describes a framework for designing software systems in a platform-neutral manner and builds on a number of standards developed by the OMG.

With its upcoming standard-compliant modeling infrastructure, SAP plans to support large-scale MDA scenarios with a multitude of meta-models that put additional requirements on the technical solution, that are normally considered out-of-scope in academic environments. This may lead to solutions that may be considered inferior at first sight, but actually result from a broader set of (sometimes non-functional) requirements.

This paper focuses on one particular aspect in SAP's modeling infrastructure, namely an efficient support for the OCL [3] constraint language. We will show how he have modified some of the existing approaches to better fit the requirements we're facing in our application scenarios.

The rest of the paper is organized as follows: In Section 2, we will give an overview of SAP's modeling infrastructure focusing on features that are considered critical in large-scale industrial environments. Then, in Section 3, we will summarize related work in the area of OCL impact analysis that has guided our work leading to a more detailed description of our approach in Section 4. In Section 5, we will report on first experimental experiences and conclude in Section 6 by summarizing our work.

T. Kühne (Ed.): MoDELS 2006 Workshops, LNCS 4364, pp. 169–178, 2007.

2   The SAP Modeling Infrastructure (MOIN)

Mid of 2005, SAP launched "Modeling Infrastructure" (MOIN), as development project within the NetWeaver[1] organization. The goal of the MOIN project is to implement the consolidated platform for SAP's next generation of modeling tools.

2.1   Overview on the Architecture and Services of MOIN

The requirements for MOIN resulted in an architecture, which consists of the components described in the following sections as major building blocks.

Repository. First and foremost, MOIN is a repository infrastructure for meta-models and models capable of storing any MOF compliant meta-model together with all the associated models. For accessing and manipulating this content, client applications can use JMI compliant interfaces, which are generated for the specific meta-model.

The MOF standard does not impose any concepts for physical structuring of model content onto the implementer, however, some notion of a meaningful group of model elements is required. For that, MOIN offers the concept of model-partitions, which allows users splitting up the graphs represented by model content into manageable buckets loaded and stored by the MOIN repository.

Query Mechanism. JMI is well suited for exploring models, by accessing attributes, following links etc. However, for many use-cases more powerful means of data retrieval are needed. The MOIN query API (including a query language) therefore provides flexible methods for retrieving model elements, based on their types, attribute values, relationships to other model elements etc.

Eventing Framework. Events can be used by MOIN clients to receive notifications for e.g. changes on models. This supports an architecture of loosely coupled components. The event types supported by the framework will be discussed in section 4.

Model Transformation Infrastructure (MTI). The model transformation infrastructure (MTI) is planned as basis for model-to-model and model-to-text transformations. MTI will provide a framework for defining and executing these transformations, where OCL is considered as an option for describing query parts of transformation rules.

MOIN Core. The MOIN core is the central component in the MOIN architecture, implementing and enforcing MOF semantics. It is independent from the deployment options and development infrastructure aspects and calls the other components for implementing all of MOIN's functionality.

By managing the object instances, representing model elements, the MOIN core can also be seen as in-memory cache for model content. However, it also

---

[1] SAP and SAP NetWeaver are trademarks or registered trademarks of SAP AG in Germany and in several other countries.

manages the complete life-cycle of objects, triggers events, and uses the repository layer to read or write data.

OCL Components. For dealing with OCL expressions, MOIN contains an OCL parser, OCL evaluator, and an OCL impact analysis component, managed by the MOIN core.

The impact analysis is essential for the efficient implementation of constraint checking, as it avoids the unnecessary evaluation of constraints in specific situations. The impact analysis is described in section 4 in more detail.

3   Related Work

To our knowledge, there is not much related work in the area of optimization of OCL expression evaluation at the moment. In [5] the authors describe an algorithm to reduce the set of OCL expressions that have to be evaluated if a model change occurs. We follow that approach, but had to relax it since we have to deal with any sort of OCL expression whereas [5] only deals with OCL constraints where further optimization are possible, based on the assumption that initially all constraints are valid. However, there are application scenarios in MOIN where this assumption does not hold at all. E.g., it may be desirable, or at least tolerable to temporarily leave meta-models in an inconsistent state, like situations where the architect or designer is not yet able to provide all mandatory information. In a second paper [6], the same authors describe a method to reduce the number of context instances for which relevant OCL constraints have to be evaluated as a further optimization on top of the approach in [5]. The idea of decomposing expressions into sub-expression and building paths through the model was taken from there. However, the approach taken in [6] violates one of our requirements that meta-models should stay intact avoiding modifications not intended by the user. Furthermore, we had to extend the algorithm to support all language features of OCL.

In [7], the authors go even one step further, and actively rewrite constraints for further optimizations. This may even lead to attaching a constraint to a new context. While this approach may definitely lead to a better performance than our approach, we did not consider optimizations in that direction, because this would introduce additional management overhead if we hid that transformation from the modeller and kept the two versions of constraints in sync.

In [8] a rule-based simplification of OCL constraints is introduced, including, e.g., constant folding, and removing tautologies. We intentionally abandoned that approach in our work, again because of the additional overhead introduced.

4   OCL Impact Analysis in the SAP Modeling Infrastructure

This section presents the architecture and functionality of the OCL impact analysis and how it fits into SAP's modeling infrastructure.

4.1   Architecture

To support a wide range of different usage scenarios we decided to implement the *impact analyzer* (IA) as a general optimization add-on to applications, which have to deal with OCL in some way.

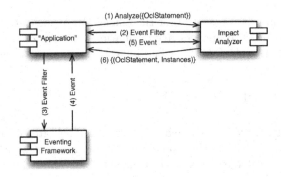

Fig. 1. Impact Analyzer Architecture

As indicated in Figure 1, interacting with the IA happens in two phases: Firstly, in the *analysis* phase (steps 1-3), a set of parsed OCL expressions is passed to the IA, whereupon a filter expression is returned. This filter can then be used to register with the eventing framework, so the application will only be notified about relevant model change events. Secondly, in the *filter* phase (steps 4-6), a received event can be forwarded to the IA to identify the OCL expressions affected by a change and the set of context instances per expression, for which the expression has to be evaluated.

In fact, IA does not actually return a set of context instances, but OCL expressions evaluating to that set. This allows for quick responses and leaves further optimizations to the evaluator. Furthermore, in contrast to [6], this approach does not rely on an extension of the meta-model.

During the analysis phase, internal data structures are built up, which are then used in the filter phase for quick look-ups. These data structures are based on so-called *internal events* which represent classes of *model change events* provided by MOIN's eventing framework. The relationship between internal events and model change events is shown in Table 1.

The analysis phase itself is split up into a *class scope analysis* and a subsequent (optional) *instance scope analysis*. Both methods are described in the following sections.

4.2   Class Scope Analysis

The goal of the class scope analysis is to find the set of internal events (i.e., all types of model change events) which affect a given expression, assumming that all affected expressions have to be evaluated for all its context instances[2].

---

[2] Hence the name *class scope* analysis.

Table 1. Mapping between InternalEvents and ModelChangeEvents

Internal Event	Model Change Event
CreateInstance(MofClass c)	ElementAddedEvent(RefObject o), c being the type of o
DeleteInstance(MofClass c)	ElementRemovedEvent(RefObject), c being the type of o
AddLink(AssociationEnd e)	LinkAddedEvent(Link l), e and l referring to the same association
RemoveLink(AssociationEnd e)	LinkRemovedEvent(Link l), e and l referring to the same association
UpdateAttribute(Attribute a)	AttributeValueEvent(RefObject o, Attribute b), a and b referring to the same attribute

As outlined in Section 3, we use a generalized approach from [5] and walk the abstract syntax tree (AST) representing the given OCL expression in a depth-first manner, tagging each node[3] with internal events that are relevant to it:

- Variable expressions referring to `self` → `CreateInstance(C)`, where C identifies the type of `self`
- `C.allInstances()` → `CreateInstance(C)`, `DeleteInstance(C)`
- Association end calls to `aE` → `AddLink(l)`, `RemoveLink(l)`, where l refers to the association to which the association end `aE` belongs
- Attribute call expressions to `a` → `UpdateAttribute(a)`

Given a concrete model change event during the filter phase, IA determines the corresponding internal event and simply looks up the OCL expressions affected by that event.

```
context Department inv maxJuniors:
self.employee->select(e|e.age<23)->size()<self.maxJuniors
```

Listing 1.1. OCL expression [5] for the running example

For the OCL expression in Listing 1.1 [4], the Class Scope Analysis returns the following internal events: `CreateInstance(Department)`, `AddLink(employee)`, `RemoveLink(employee)`, `UpdateAttribute(age)`, and `UpdateAttribute(maxJuniors)`.

---

[3] For user-defined attributes and operations, the analyzer recurses into their bodies. The evaluation of a user-defined attribute or operation changes if its body is affected by a change to the model, thus affecting the evaluation of any expression referring to that user-defined operation or attribute.

[4] Within a department only a certain number of junior employees are allowed.

4.3   Instance Scope Analysis

The goal of instance scope analysis is to reduce the number of context instances for which an expression needs to be evaluated. Following the approach in [6], this is done by identifying navigation paths[5]. Given an element affected by a change, the set of relevant context instances can be found by following the reverse of the navigation paths. Once identified, these reverse paths are turned into OCL expressions and stored in the internal data structure. By evaluating these expressions, the set of context instances can be computed from a given changed element.

The following sections describe in more detail how sub-expressions and subsequently navigation paths can be identified and how they are reversed and translated into OCL.

Identifying Sub-expressions. The first step is to find sub-expressions. Sub-expressions start with a variable, or `allInstances()` and end in a node being the source of an operation with a primitive return type or in a node being a parameter of an operation or the body of a loop expression. Sub-expressions can also contain child sub-expressions in the body of a loop expression.

Two types of sub-expressions can be distinguished: *class* and *instance*. *Class sub-expressions* start (directly or indirectly) with `allInstances()` and thus have to be evaluated for all instances of a class. *Instance sub-expressions* on the other hand start (directly or indirectly) with `self`. In this case, a subset of context instances can be identified for which the expression has to be evaluated. The following steps only apply to instance sub-expression.

Example: Given the OCL expression in Listing 1.1, the following sub-expressions can be identified: `self.employee->select()`, `e.age`, and `self.maxJuniors`.

Identifying Navigation Paths. As per definition, sub-expressions consist only of navigation operations, but do not necessarily start at the context. To get a sequence of navigation operations starting at the context, the navigation contained in a child sub-expression has to be concatenated with the navigation of the parent sub-expression[6].

Example: For the example in Listing 1.1 the context-relative navigation paths are: `<employee>`, `<employee, age>` [7], and `<maxJuniors>`.

For loop expressions with a different return type than their source (e.g. collect, iterate), the loop body contains vital information which has to be included; otherwise, the navigation path would contain a gap.

---

[5] I.e. the sequences of attributes and association ends, in an expression starting at the context. If an object is changed, an OCL expression has to be evaluated for those context instances from where the changed object can be reached by navigating along these paths.

[6] This approach only works for loop expressions calculating a subset of their source (e.g. select, reject).

[7] As the second sub-expression does not start at the context, its navigation path has to be concatenated with the navigation path of its parent, i.e., the first sub-expression.

Example: Considering the OCL expression in Listing 1.2, the following two navigation paths can be identified: <employer, employee, ... > (for the parent subexpression), and < employer, employee > (for the child sub-expression).

```
context Employee inv :
  self . employer –> collect ( d : Department | d . employee ) – >...
```

Listing 1.2. An OCL expression including a `collect` subexpression

In this case, the `collect` operation takes a set of Departments and returns a set of Employees. Only by examining the body it can be said how to get from Department to Employee: by following the employee association end.

Reversing Navigation Paths. For each tagged node in the AST, the way back to the context (variable) of the expression has to be identified. This is done by reversing the path from the variable subexpression to the AST node.

Example: Continuing the running example in Listing 1.1, we get the reverse navigation paths for each relevant internal event identified by class scope analysis as shown in Table 2.

Table 2. Internal events and corresponding navigation paths

Internal Event	Reverse Navigation Path
CreateInstance(Department)	<>
AddLink(employee), RemoveLink(employee)	<>
UpdateAttribute(age)	< employer >
UpdateAttribute(maxJuniors)	<>

If a new Department is created, the expression obviously has to be evaluated for that Department, therefore, the reverse navigation path is empty. If an employee is added to, or removed from, a department, the reverse navigation path is empty as well. More interesting is the case when the age of an employee is changed. In this case, navigating along the *employer* association end (opposite of employee) reveals the department, for which the expression has to be evaluated.

Translating into OCL. Reverse navigation paths are translated into OCL and stored in the internal data structure which relates each internal event with a number of relevant expressions. For each such pair of internal event and expression a set of OCL expressions is maintained, which, when evaluated for a changed model element, results in the set of affected context instances.

For navigating along association ends, translation is straight forward: An association call expression is created referring to the opposite association end. Reversing object-valued attributes, however, is not that easy. Unfortunately, OCL does not offer a construct to find the owner of an attribute value. However, a legal

OCL expression can be constructed which finds the attribute value's owner. The construct simply iterates through all instances of a type T and checks whether it's attribute a points to the given value v: `T.allInstances()->select(a=v)` [8].

Example: Continuing the running example from Listing 1.1, in case of an `UpdateAttribute(age)` event, the relevant Department instances are computed from the OCL expression `self.employer`.

5   Preliminary Results

To show the efficiency of our approach we present empirical results from a test scenario using the MOF constraints defined in [2] with the UML meta-model as an instance of MOF.

5.1   UML-meta-model + MOF-constraints

To have a more realistic assessment of the performance benefits achieved by IA, we used a subset of the MOF-constraints and the UML-meta-model, an instance of MOF, as a test scenario. We ran the tests with three types of applications: a *naive application (1)* that evaluates all constraints on any model change, a *class scope application (2)* that only uses the Class Scope Analysis part of the IA, and an *instance scope application (3)* that uses the IA to its fullest extend.

Reduction of Expressions. We consider the number of expressions which have to be evaluated after an event has been reported. In Figure 2 we compare the results from *(2)* to those from *(1)*[9]. The performance gains are due to the fact that the *CSA* does not have to evaluate expressions which cannot have changed due to the reported event.

For about 1/4 of the events, the number of relevant expressions could be reduced to one by applying class scope analysis. This is a reduction by 97%. For about 1/8 of the events, the number of relevant expressions could only be reduced to 12 and 11 respectively. Still, this is a reduction by 68% (71%). In average, the number of expressions to evaluate was reduced by 88%, with a Median of 92%.

Reduction of Context Instances. Here we consider the number of *evaluator calls* (the evaluation of one expression for one context instance) necessary to evaluate all affected expressions. The numbers in Figure 3 also include calls necessary to compute the set of affected context instances. As the number of expressions to evaluate is reduced in (2), the number of evaluator calls is reduced as well. Therefore, the number of evaluator calls experiences about the same reduction as the number of expressions. After an already substantial reduction in

---

[8] For performance reasons, an optimized evaluator could simply replace such a construct by a `v.immediateComposite()` call on the JMI object to determine the value's owner.

[9] As instance scope analysis does not further reduce the number of expressions, it is not included in the chart.

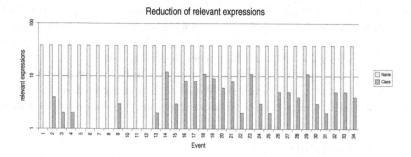

Fig. 2. Reduction of relevant expressions

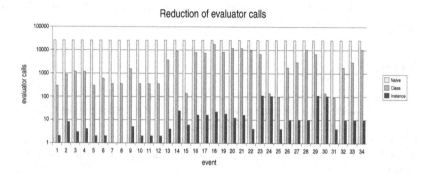

Fig. 3. Reduction of evaluator calls (including calls for computing context instances)

(2), (3) achieves another enormous reduction: From several thousands to twenty or less for about 77% of the events (compare Figure 3). In total, the number of evaluator calls was reduced by three to four orders of magnitude, which is an enormous benefit in performance compared to some 26000 calls per event in (1).

6   Conclusion

While efficient support for OCL is considered crucial in large-scale modeling environments, surprisingly little work has been published on optimizing OCL expression evaluation in case of arbitrary model changes. In this paper, we have reported on our experiences with integrating OCL into SAP's next generation modeling infrastructure MOIN.

Although some of the basic approaches from literature could be reused [5,6], the actual implementation had to divert from these methods to cope with the (non-)functional requirements pertinent to MOIN. Most notably, we currently refused to implement any techniques that would result in silent or user-invisible changes to either the meta-models or the related OCL expressions. We know that this may lead to sub-optimal results in terms of performance, but preliminary experimental results show that the implemented techniques can still lead to a significant and hopefully sufficient performance gain. Further optimization techniques may be considered in the future, but they will have to be evaluated carefully on their trade-offs regarding other desired features.

Another path of optimization that we have not fully explored yet is the way how context instances are computed. We plan to investigate how the usage of the internal MOIN Query Language could speed up this computational step.

Acknowledgements

We would like to thank our colleagues Kristian Domagala, Harald Fuchs, Hans Hofmann, Simon Helsen, Diego Rapela, Murray Spork, and Axel Uhl for fruitful discussions during the design and the implementation of the OCL Impact Analyzer.

References

1. Object Management Group: MDA Guide. June 2003.
2. Object Management Group: Meta Object Facility (MOF) Specification. April 2002. http://www.omg.org/docs/formal/02-04-03.pdf.
3. Object Management Group: OCL 2.0 Specification (ptc/2005-06-06). June 2005.
4. Object Management Group: UML 2.0 Superstructure Specification (pct/03-08-02). August 2003.
5. Cabot, J., Teniente, E.: Determining the Structural Events that May Violate an Integrity Constraint. In: Proc. 7th Int. Conf. on the Unified Modeling Language (UML'04), LNCS, 3273 (2004) 173-187
6. Cabot, J., Teniente, E.: Computing the Relevant Instances that May Violate an OCL constraint. In: Proc. 17th Int. Conf. on Advanced Information Systems Engineering (CAiSE'05), LNCS, 3520 (2005) 48-62
7. Cabot, J., Teniente, E.: Incremental Evaluation of OCL Constraints. In: Proc. 17th Int. Conf. on Advanced Information Systems Engineering (CAiSE'06), June 2006.
8. Giese M., Hähnle R., Larsson, D.: Rule-based simplification of OCL constraints. In: Workshop on OCL and Model Driven Engineering at UML2004, pages 84-89, 2004.

Report on the 3rd MoDeVa Workshop – Model Design and Validation

Benoît Baudry[1], David Hearnden[2], Nicolas Rapin[3], and Jörn Guy Süß[2]

INRIA, France
University of Queensland, Australia
CEA/LIST, France

Abstract. Software systems are becoming increasingly large and complex, and run the risk of serious failures from unforeseen behaviour. Model driven development (MDD) is emerging as a solution with strong potential for dealing with these difficulties using models and model transformations. However, effective validiation and verification techniques are required to take full advantage of the expected benefits of MDD.

The MoDeVa (Model Design and Validation) series of workshop aims at bringing together researchers and practitioners to discuss links between MDD and model-based validation. This document summarizes the results of MoDeVa'06 that was the third edition of the workshop. Reviewing the workshop, the organisers feel that a community is forming which aims for practical integration of model-driven development and V&V and that specific research topics are being identified and addressed. As an illustration of this, it is important to notice that three papers this year were dedicated to V&V for model transformations. This trend may be due to increasing maturity and scale of use of MDD and thus to a better understanding of hard points and research challenges in this new approach for software development. There is recognition that specific solutions in this area are needed.

Workshop Formation

This year's edition of the MoDeVa series of workshops resulted from a merge of three separate workshop proposals. In addition to the continuation of the MoDeVa workshop, there was a proposal more focused on the Model-Driven Architecture and one other dedicated to model-based testing. 32 participants attended the workshop, despite competition posed by several other scientific gatherings with a similar topic (e.g. the MARTES workshop). The workshop included eight papers organized into three sessions dealing with V&V of models, V&V of transformations and advances in model-based testing. The session topics were used to structure the discussions. The workshop included an organised lunch with ensuing coffee in a bar that gave further opportunity for interaction.

V&V for Models

The session on V&V for models underscored the need to assign a mathematical semantics to UML, in order to apply traditional V&V methods. Works presented

T. Kühne (Ed.): MoDELS 2006 Workshops, LNCS 4364, pp. 179–181, 2007.

in this session underlined the need to identify a portion of the UML amenable to the application of formal semantics. The approaches presented carefully examine possibilities to manage state space growth, recognising it as the major property that can limit the adoption of those methods in practice. The ease of use of these approaches in an industrial context was also discussed. Indeed, adding formal contracts to models or transforming models to feed them into a model-checker are techniques that have been available for some years now but are still not widely adopted. Beyond the challenge of state space explosion, approach usability, i.e. the skill set required of developers in order to manipulate and build formal models, was perceived as a major issue.

V&V for Transformations

The session on V&V of transformations showed that the different approaches to the definition of transformations have significant impact on the preferred style of V&V. Declarative transformation languages, represented in the session by an approach based on triple graph grammars, enable the use of theorem provers. This provides great confidence in the correctness of the solution as crucial properties of the transformation are implicitly proven correct for all cases. Hence, this may be a good V&V approach for code generators that build critical code for embedded systems. However, two issues arise when using this approach. First, if the prover can not prove the property correct, it does not provide support to locate the fault in the transformation. Second, the transformation's specification has to be transformed into the target formalism of the prover, which may be non-trivial. Imperative transformations, exemplified by a business language transformation framework by IBM research, fare better with an intent-guided method of test-case generation, that provides clear counter-examples in the case of errors, but whose coverage is necessarily partial.

Testing

The session on model-based testing showed maturing approaches in this area that took into account the usability of these approaches by proposing lightweight solutions (based on contracts) for model-based test generation and the integration in the development process. The exact nature of a test model in the different approaches arose as a major point of discussion. Even if there seemed to be agreement on the need for a test model that is different from the design or implementation model, the content of this model or moment of its creation in the development cycle differed: a test model might be a refinement of the analysis model, a variant of the design model, or a completely independent model.

Debate

Following the three topic-based sessions, the final part of the workshop was dedicated to a structured debate on the thesis that: "MDA does not need V&V

or Testing". Participants were divided into three groups: one to attack the thesis, one to defend it and a third to judge the quality of the arguments.

An interesting observation in this session was that while participants generally recognised models as the basis of development, the term MDA appeared to be weakly delineated. In preparation for the debate, some immediately generalized MDA to the notion of model-driven development. Those that discussed MDA found it hard to agree on a common definition.

Evaluation

The workshop's format called for the presenters of each session to conclude by forming a common panel for general discussion. Questions on general aspects of the papers were to be delayed for this panel discussion. The panel discussions viability depended on the closeness of the subjects treated in the presentations, however the discussion managed to address general concerns in each domain. The panel discussions may have been even more constructive with more panel members. Both the panel discussions that took place (the Testing panel discussion was cancelled on the day due to time constraints) only had two panel members, however we were expecting the Transformation V&V and Testing V&V panels to have three members. Participants found the final debating exercise interesting and enjoyable.

The two best papers were awarded based on preferential votes cast by the participants, and these votes correlated very well with the scores from the paper reviews. The participant vote had the benefit of being a cheap and transparent form of measurement from a medium-sized population, however it meant that the votes were cast on the presentation rather than the paper. An alternative voting system incorporating the program committee may result in a more objective selection, however it would necessarily introduce a much greater burden on the program committee.

Summarily, the MoDeVa workshop has become a point of reference for the community around MDD and V&V. It is seeing steady growth in the community and helps to promote verification and testing techniques in the MDD domain and to ready them for use in large software development. The organisers feel that the investments into structure and the provision of a high quality environment has paid of through recognition by the participants.

To carry the workshop forward, a dedicated website at the University of Queensland has been established as an information point of reference for past and future MoDeVa editions. A poll of this years participants will be carried out to seek their opinion on this years edition and on recommendations for improvement. Their input will help to improve proposals for the next issue of MoDeVa, at MoDELS 2007 in Nashville, Tennessee.

Towards Model-Driven Unit Testing

Gregor Engels[1,2], Baris Güldali[1], and Marc Lohmann[2]

[1] Software Quality Lab
[2] Department of Computer Science
University of Paderborn, Warburgerstr. 100, 33098 Paderborn, Germany
engels@upb.de, bguldali@s-lab.upb.de, mlohmann@upb.de

Abstract. The Model-Driven Architecture (MDA) approach for constructing software systems advocates a stepwise refinement and transformation process starting from high-level models to concrete program code. In contrast to numerous research efforts that try to generate executable function code from models, we propose a novel approach termed *model-driven monitoring*. On the model level the behavior of an operation is specified with a pair of UML composite structure diagrams (visual contract), a visual notation for pre- and post-conditions. The specified behavior is implemented by a programmer manually. An automatic translation from our visual contracts to JML assertions allows for monitoring the hand-coded programs during their execution.

In this paper[1] we present how we extend our approach to allow for *model-driven unit testing*, where we utilize the generated JML assertions as test oracles. Further, we present an idea how to generate sufficient test cases from our visual contracts with the help of model-checking techniques.

Keywords: Design by Contract, visual contracts, test case generation, model checking.

1 Introduction

Everyone who develops or uses software systems knows about the importance of software qualities, e.g. correctness and robustness. However, the growing size of applications and the demand for shorter time-to-market hampers the development of high-quality software systems. To get a better handle on the complexity, the paradigm of model-driven development (MDD) has been introduced. In particular, the Object Management Group (OMG) pushed its Model-Driven Architecture (MDA) [1] initiative based on the Unified Modeling Language (UML) that provides the foundation for MDA. However, the MDA is still in its infancy compared to its ambitious goals of having a (semi-)automatic, tool-supported stepwise refinement process from vague requirements specifications to a fully-fledged running program. A lot of unresolved questions exist for modeling tasks as well as for automated model transformations.

---

[1] This paper is an abbreviated version of our same-titled contribution to MoDeV²a 2006. For related work, refer to the longer version in the MoDeV²a 2006 workshop proceedings or to our web page at http://www.upb.de/cs/ag-engels.

T. Kühne (Ed.): MoDELS 2006 Workshops, LNCS 4364, pp. 182–192, 2007.

Nevertheless, in today's software development processes models are an established part for describing the specification of software systems. In principle, models provide an abstraction from the detailed problems of implementation technologies. They allow software designers to focus on the conceptual task of modeling static as well as behavioral aspects of the envisaged software system. Unfortunately, abstraction naturally conflicts with the desired automatic code generation from models. To enable the latter, fairly complete and low-level models are needed. Today, a complete understanding of the appropriate level of detail and abstraction of models is still missing. Thus, in today's software development processes developers are normally building an application manually with respect to its abstract specification with models.

In our work, we introduced a new modeling approach. We do not follow the usual approach that models should operate as source for an automatic code generation step that produces the executable function code of the program. Rather, we restrict the modeling task to providing structural information and minimal requirements towards behavior for the subsequent implementation. We expect that only structural parts of an implementation are automatically generated, while the behavior is manually added by a programmer.

As a consequence it can not be guaranteed that the hand-coded implementation is correct with respect to the modeled requirements. Therefore, we have shown in previous publications [2,3,4] how models can be used to generate assertions which monitor the execution of the hand-coded implementation. Herewith, violations of the modeled requirements will be detected at runtime and reported to the environment. We call this novel approach *model-driven monitoring*. It is based on the idea of Design by Contract (DbC) [5], where so-called contracts are used to specify the desired behavior of an operation. Contracts consist of pre- and post-conditions. Before an operation is executed, the pre-condition must hold, and in return, after the execution of an operation, the post-condition must be satisfied.

The DbC approach has been introduced at the level of programming languages. For instance, the Java Modeling Language (JML) extends Java with DbC concepts [6] which are annotated to the source code. During the execution of such an annotated Java program, the assertions are monitored. An exception is raised as soon as a violation of the assertions is detected. With the concepts of *visual contracts* [2] we have lifted the idea of contracts to the level of models. A visual contract allows for specifying a contract by pairs of UML composite structure diagrams for the pre- and post-conditions. A transformation of our visual contracts into JML allows for monitoring a system that is implemented manually.

Now we want to extend our approach to allow for *model-driven unit testing*. The visual contracts respectively the generated JML assertions are viewed as test oracles to decide whether the results calculated by a hand-coded implementation are correct. Additionally, we want to generate test cases from our models with the help of model-checking techniques.

2   Overview of the Approach

Test-driven development [7] is an important part of agile processes. E.g. Extreme Programming (XP) [8] emphasizes the test-first approach. When handling a programming task, programmers always begin writing unit tests. This tests formalizes the requirements. If all tests run successfully then the coding is complete. To accent the agile part of our model-driven monitoring approach we want to support the test-driven development by enabling model-driven unit testing. Therefore, beside the generation of runtime assertions we want to automatically generate test cases from our models. Figure 1 shows our development process enabling model-driven monitoring and model-driven unit testing.

On the design level, a software designer has to specify a model of the system under development. This model consists of class diagrams and visual contracts. The class diagrams describe the static aspects of the system. Each visual contract specifies the behavior of an operation. The behavior of the operation is given in terms of data state changes by pre- and post-conditions, which are modeled by a pair of UML composite structure diagrams as explained in Sect. 3.

In the next step, we generate code fragments from the design model. This generation process consists of two parts. First, we generate Java class skeletons from the design class diagrams. Second, we generate JML assertions from every visual contract and annotate each of the corresponding operations with the generated JML contract. The JML assertions allow us to check the consistency of models with manually derived code at runtime. The execution of such checks is transparent in that, unless an assertion is violated, the behavior of the original program remains unchanged.

Then, a programmer uses the generated Java fragments to fill in the missing behavioral code in order to build a complete and functional application. His programming task will emanate from the design model of the system. Particularly, he will use the visual contracts as reference for implementing the behavior of operations. He has to code the method bodies, and may add new operations to existing classes or even completely new classes, but he is not allowed to change the JML contracts. If new requirements for the system demand new functionality then the functionality has to be specified with visual contracts before the programmer can start programming. Using our visual contracts this way in a software development process resembles agile development approaches.

When a programmer has implemented the behavioral code, he uses the JML compiler to build executable binary code. This binary code consists of the programmer's behavioral code and additional executable runtime checks which are generated by the JML compiler from the JML assertions. The manual implementation of a programmer leads to system state changes. The generated runtime checks monitor the pre- and post-conditions during the execution of the system.

To further integrate agile approaches in our process we additionally want to integrate *model-driven unit testing* in our development process. Therefore, we have to address the following three problems of model-driven testing [9]:

1. the generation of test cases from models,
2. the generation of a test oracle to determine the expected results of a test,
3. the execution of tests in test environments.

The basic idea of our testing approach is that the specification of an operation by a pre- and post-conditions (visual contract) can be viewed as a test oracle [10] and runtime assertion checking can be used as a decision procedure. Thus, our visual contacts

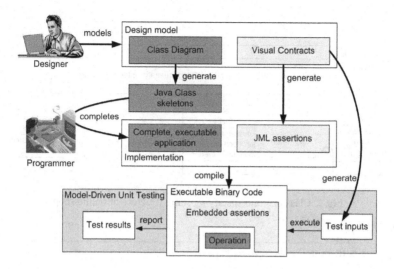

Fig. 1. Overview of the testing approach

can be viewed as test oracles since the JML assertions are generated from our visual contracts. Still, we need to answer the problem of how to generate test cases from models. Therefore, we want to combine well-known testing techniques for the generation of test input parameters and model checking to be able to create concrete system states. The idea how to create test cases is described in detail in Sect. 5.1.

3   Modeling with Visual Contracts

We show how to specify a system with visual contracts by the example of an online shop. We distinguish between a static and a functional view. UML class diagrams are used to represent the *static view* of a system specification. Figure 2 shows the class diagram of the sample online shop. We use the stereotypes control and entity expressing a different role of a class in the implementation. Instances of control classes encapsulate the control related to a specific use case and coordinate other objects. Entity classes model long-lived or persistent information. The control class OnlineShop is connected to the entity classes of the system via qualified associations. A rectangle at an association end with a qualifier (e.g. productNo) designates an attribute of the referenced class. The qualifier allows us to get direct access to specific objects.

Class diagrams are complemented by visual contracts that introduce a *functional view* integrating static and dynamic aspects. Visual contracts allow us to describe the effects of an operation on the system state of the system. Thus, for our visual contracts we take an operation-wise view on the internal behavior.

In the following, we want to explain our visual contracts by two examples. The operation cartCreate of the control class OnlineShop creates a new cart. Figure 3 shows a visual contract that describes the behavior of the operation. The visual contract is enclosed in a frame, containing a heading and a context area. The keyword vc in

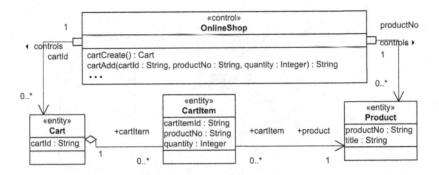

Fig. 2. Class diagram specifying static structure of online shop

Fig. 3. Visual contract for operation *cartCreate*

the heading refers to the type of diagram, visual contract in this case. The keyword is followed by the name of the operation that is specified by the visual contract. The operation name is followed by a parameter-list and a return-result if they are specified in the class diagram. The parameter-list is an ordered set of variables and the return-result is also a variable. The variables of the parameter-list and the return-result are used in the visual contract.

The visual contract is placed in the context area and consists of two UML composite structure diagrams [11], representing the pre- and the post-condition of an operation. Each of them is typed over the design class diagram. The semantics of our visual contracts is defined by the loose semantics of open graph transformation systems [12]. The basic intuition for the interpretation of a visual contract is that every model element, which is only present on the right-hand side of the contract, is newly created, and every model element that is present only on the left-hand side of the contract, is being deleted. Elements that are present on both sides are unaffected by the contract. Additionally, we may extend the pre- or post-condition of a visual contract by negative pre-conditions (i.e., negative application conditions [13]) or respectively by negative post-conditions. A negative condition is represented by a dark rectangle in the frame. If the dark rectangle is on the left of the pre-condition, it specifies object structures that are not allowed to be present before the operation is executed (see Fig. 4). If the dark rectangle is on the right of the post-condition, it specifies object structures that are not allowed to be present after the execution of the operation.

The contract as described in Fig. 3 expresses that the operation cartCreate can always be executed, because the pre-condition only contains the model element self, i.e. the object executing the operation. As an effect, the operation creates a new object

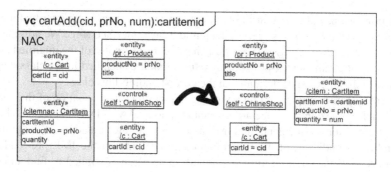

Fig. 4. Visual contract for operation *cartAdd*

of type `Cart` and a link between the object `self` and the new object. Additionally, the object `c:Cart` is the return value of the operation `cartCreate` as indicated by the variable `c` used in the heading.

Figure 4 shows a more complex contract specifying the operation `cartAdd`. This operation adds a new `CartItem`, which references an existing `Product`, to an existing `Cart`. In contrast to the visual contract of Fig. 3, the variables of the parameter-list and the return-value are now used to specify values of attributes of the objects. For a successful execution of the operation, the object `self` must know two different objects with the following characteristics: an object of type `Cart` that has an attribute `cartId` with the value `cid`, and an object of type `Product` that has an attribute `productNo` with the value `prNo`. The concrete argument values are bound when the client calls the operation. The same `Cart` object is reused in the negative pre-condition. The negative pre-condition extends the pre-condition by the requirement that the `Cart` object is not linked to any object of type `CartItem` that has an attribute `productNo` with the value `prNo`. This means, it is not permitted that the product is already contained in the cart. As a result, the operation creates a new object of type `CartItem` with additional links to previously identified objects. The return value of the operation is the content of the attribute `cartItemId` of the newly created object.

4   Translation to JML

After describing the modeling of a software system with visual contracts, we now present how the model-driven software development process continues from the design model. A transformation of visual contracts to JML constructs provides for model-driven monitoring of the contracts. The contracts can be automatically evaluated for a given state of a system, where the state is given by object configurations. The generation process as well as the kind of code that is generated from a class diagram and the structure of a JML assertion that is generated from a visual contract are described in detail in [2,4]. Here we only describe the transformation more generally and from a methodical perspective.

Each UML class is translated to a corresponding Java class. For attributes and associations, the corresponding access methods (e.g., `get`, `set`) are added. For multi-valued associations we use classes that implement the Java interface `Set`. Qualified associations are provided by classes that implement the Java interface `Map`. We add methods like `getProduct(int productNo)` that use the attributes of the qualified associations as input parameters. Operation signatures that are specified in the class diagram are translated to method declarations in the corresponding Java class.

For each operation specified by a visual contract, the transformation of the contract to JML yields a Java method declaration that is annotated with JML assertions. The pre- and post-conditions of the generated JML assertions are interpretations of the graphical pre- and post-conditions of the visual contract. When any of the JML pre- and post-conditions is evaluated, an optimized breadth-first search is applied to find an occurrence of the pattern that is specified by the pre- or post-condition in the current system state. The search starts from the object `self` which is executing the specified behavior. If the JML pre- or post-condition finds a correct pattern, it returns true, otherwise it returns false.

5   Test Case Generation and Test Execution

In the previous sections we explained how a software designer develops a design model and how Java class skeletons and JML assertions can be generated from them. We also explained how a programmer can complete the generated code fragments to build a complete executable application. After these steps we want to test our application. In Sect. 2 we explained the three tasks of model-driven testing.

In this section we will explain how we handle the first and the third task, i.e. the generation of test cases and the execution of a test. The second task (the generation of a test oracle) is described in Sect. 4 since we can interpret the JML assertions as test oracles.

Similar to classical unit-testing, our test items are operations. The behavior of an operation is dependent of the input parameters and the system state. Thus, a test case has to consider the parameter values of an operation and a concrete system state.

5.1   Test Case Generation

A test case for an operation consists of concrete parameter values and a concrete system state. We can generate a test case for an operation from our model in three successive steps. In the following, we explain how to generate a sample test case for the operation `cartAdd` (Fig. 4). Figure 5 illustrates the three steps.

In the first step, we generate values for the input parameters of an operation as specified in the class diagram. In Fig. 5 we generated the parameter values for the operation `cartAdd` randomly. For the parameter `cid` the value "abc" is generated. The parameter `prNo` gets the value "def" and the variable `num` gets the value "1". Beside a the random generation of input parameters, we could also use other techniques for test data generation, e.g. equivalence-class partitioning or boundary value analysis (see e.g. [14]).

To generate a sufficient system state for testing, we have to execute two further steps. Since the visual contracts specify system state requirements, we use them as source

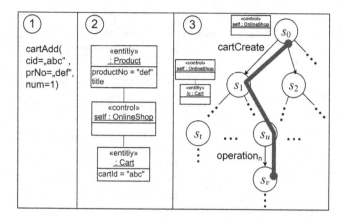

Fig. 5. Three steps of test case generation

for generating the system state. Therefore, we initialize the pre-condition of a visual contract with the parameter values generated in step one. The variables in the parameter-list are used to restrict the attribute values of objects in the pre-condition as explained in Sect. 3. Thus, the initialization gives an object structure. In this object structure some of the attributes have concrete values. Figure 5 shows how the attributes productNo and cartId of the classes Product and Cart are initialized with the parameter values of step one according to the pre-condition in Fig. 4. It is important to notice that this object structure describes a system state only partially.

In the last step of our test case generation, we have to find out how to generate a system state which contains the object structure found in step two. Due to the fact that the object structure in the previous step defines a system state only partially, we cannot just build a system state by creating the known objects and attribute values. Such a system state would be incomplete and it would be artificial in a sense that the application would never create such a system state at runtime. Additional objects or attribute values can be created during the execution of the systems at runtime and these may have side-effects on the execution of an operation. Thus, tests should work on realistic system states.

To avoid these artificial system states it would be useful to build a system state by using the control operations of the system itself. We assume that each operation call leads to a state change of the system. Thus, we have to find a sequence of operation calls that starting from the initial system state lead to a sufficient system state which contains this object structure. As a visual contract describes the system state change of an operation, we can use these contracts to compute all possible states of the system. Therefore, we consider a system state as a *graph* and the visual contracts constitute *production rules* of a *graph transition system*.

Figure 5 illustrates how we want to generate a transition system. Initially the system state comprises just an instance (self) of the controller class OnlineShop. Executing, e.g., the operation cartCreate makes the in Fig. 3 specified changes on the system state. Thus, a new object of type Cart is generated and linked to the control object self. Executing further operations brings the system to a state s_v which contains the object structure generated in step two. Knowing all visual contracts and an

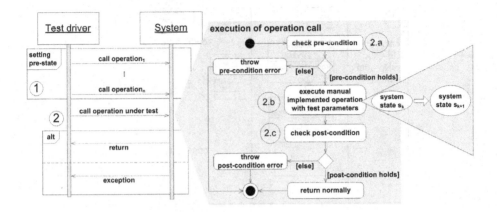

Fig. 6. Run-time behavior of test execution

initial state, we can compute the graph transition system and search for a production sequence that creates a system state which contains the object structure found in step two. These computations can be done automatically with *model checking* techniques [15]. The computed production sequence directly refers to an operation sequence which brings the system state to some desired state containing the object structure computed in step two. If no sufficient production sequence is found in the graph transition system (the searched object structure cannot be constructed using the existing operations), our test case generation approach has to backtrack to step one and generate other test data.

5.2 Test Execution with Embedded Oracles

After test cases are generated, the test execution can start. Test execution comprises two main steps as shown in Fig. 6. First, the operation sequence determined by the test case generation must be executed in order to set the system state. Second, the operation under test is called with the test input parameters also generated by the test case generation.

The embedded assertions lead to a run-time behavior of an operation call as shown in Fig. 6. When the operation under test is called, a pre-condition check method evaluates the method's pre-condition and throws a pre-condition violation exception if it does not hold. If the pre-condition holds, then the original, manually implemented operation is invoked. After the execution of the original operation, a post-condition check method evaluates the post-condition and throws a post-condition violation exception if it does not hold. If the embedded assertions throw an exception then the implementation does not behave according to its specification. Thus, we have found an error.

6 Tool Support

Most of the steps of our approach can be supported by tools. In former publications we have reported on our Visual Contract Workbench, an integrated development environment for using visual contracts in a software development process [16]. This development environment allows software designers to model class diagrams and specify the behavior of operations by visual contracts. It further supports automatic code generation as described in Sect. 4.

The most challenging task of our test generation approach is finding an operation sequence for setting a system state as explained in Sect. 5.1. This task can be automatically solved by *model checking* tools. A candidate for our purposes is GROOVE [17], a model checker for attributed graph transition systems. The test execution can be implemented by a test driver as shown in Fig. 6. In the context of JML, we can use the JMLUnit tool [18] for this purpose.

7 Conclusion

We have developed an approach that lifts the Design by Contract (DbC) idea, which is usually used at the code level, to the model level. Visual contracts are used as a specification technique. They are used to specify system state transformations with pre- and post-conditions which are modeled by UML (composite) structure diagrams. Further, we presented how to use the visual contracts in a software development process. A translation of the visual contracts into the Java Modeling Language, a DbC extension for Java, enables the model-driven monitoring. To support model-driven monitoring, we provide a visual contract workbench that allows developers to model class diagrams and visual contracts. Further the workbench supports automated code generation.

In this paper, we have shown how we want to extend our approach with model-driven unit testing. In our testing approach, a test case consists of parameter values and a concrete system state. The visual contracts – respectively the generated JML assertions – serve as test oracles to decide whether a manual implementation is correct according to its specification. In future work we will concretize our testing approach and extend our workbench with testing facilities.

References

1. Meservy, T.O., Fenstermacher, K.D.: Transforming software development: An MDA road map. IEEE Computer **38** (2005) 52–58
2. Lohmann, M., Sauer, S., Engels, G.: Executable visual contracts. In Erwig, M., Schürr, A., eds.: 2005 IEEE Symposium on Visual Languages and Human-Centric Computing (VL/HCC'05). (2005) 63–70
3. Engels, G., Lohmann, M., Sauer, S., Heckel, R.: Model-driven monitoring: An application of graph transformation for design by contract. In: International Conference on Graph Transformation (ICGT) 2006. (2006) 336–350
4. Heckel, R., Lohmann, M.: Model-driven development of reactive informations systems: From graph transformation rules to JML contracts. International Journal on Software Tools for Technology Transfer (STTT) (2006)
5. Meyer, B.: Applying "Design by Contract". IEEE Computer **25** (1992) 40–51
6. Leavens, G., Cheon, Y.: Design by Contract with JML (2003)
7. Beck, K.: Test Driven Development: By Example. Addison-Wesley Professional (2002)

8. Beck, K.: Extreme Programming Explained. Embrace Change. The XP Series. Addison-Wesley Professional (1999)
9. Heckel, R., Lohmann, M.: Towards model-driven testing. Electr. Notes Theor. Comput. Sci. **82** (2003)
10. Antoy, S., Hamlet, D.: Automatically checking an implementation against its formal specification. IEEE Transactions on Software Engineering **26** (2000) 55–69
11. OMG (Object Management Group): UML 2.0 superstructure specification - revised final adopted specification (2004)
12. Heckel, R., Ehrig, H., Wolter, U., Corradini, A.: Double-pullback transitions and coalgebraic loose semantics for graph transformation systems. APCS (Applied Categorical Structures) **9** (2001) 83–110
13. Habel, A., Heckel, R., Taentzer, G.: Graph grammars with negative application conditions. Fundamenta Informaticae **26** (1996) 287–313
14. Binder, R.V.: Testing Object-Oriented Systems. Addison-Wesley (2000)
15. Rensink, A., Schmidt, Á., Varró, D.: Model checking graph transformations: A comparison of two approaches. In: International Conference on Graph Transformation (ICGT) 2004. (2004) 226–241
16. Lohmann, M., Engels, G., Sauer, S.: Model-driven monitoring: Generating assertions from visual contracts. In: 21st IEEE/ACM International Conference on Automated Software Engineering (ASE) 2006 Demonstration Session. (2006) 355–356
17. Rensink, A.: The GROOVE simulator: A tool for state space generation. In: Applications of Graph Transformations with Industrial Relevance (AGTIVE) 2003. (2003) 479–485
18. Cheon, Y., Leavens, G.T.: A simple and practical approach to unit testing: The JML and JUnit way. In: European Conference on Object-Oriented Programming (ECOOP) 2002. (2002) 231–255

Validation of Model Transformations – First Experiences Using a White Box Approach

Jochen M. Küster[1] and Mohamed Abd-El-Razik[2,3,*]

[1] IBM Zurich Research Laboratory, Säumerstr. 4, 8803 Rüschlikon, Switzerland
jku@zurich.ibm.com
[2] IBM Cairo Technology Development Center, El-Ahram, Giza, Egypt
[3] Department of Computer Science, American University in Cairo, Egypt
mohrazik@aucegypt.edu

Abstract. Validation of model transformations is important for ensuring their quality. Successful validation must take into account the characteristics of model transformations and develop a suitable fault model on which test case generation can be based. In this paper, we report our experiences in validating a number of model transformations and propose three techniques that can be used for constructing test cases.

Keywords: Model transformations, Testing.

1 Introduction

The success of model-driven engineering generates a strong need for techniques and methodologies for developing model transformations. How to express model transformations and build appropriate tool support is a widely discussed research topic and has led to a number of model transformation languages and tool environments.

For practical use in model-driven engineering, the quality of model transformations is a key issue. If models are supposed to be semi-automatically derived using model transformations, then the quality of these models will depend on the quality of model transformations. Proving correctness of model transformations formally is difficult and requires formal verification techniques. An alternative approach widely applied in the industry is validation by testing. Today, it is common practice to apply large-scale testing for object-oriented programs using tools such as JUnit.

Model transformations can either be implemented as programs (e.g. in Java) or using one of the available transformation languages (e.g. [1,2,3]). In both cases, they require a special treatment within testing. One of the key challenges for testing model transformations is the construction of 'interesting' test cases, i.e. those test cases that show the presence of errors. For black box testing of model transformations, the meta model of the input language of the transformation can be used to systematically generate a large set of test cases [4,5]. If the result

---

* Part of this research was conducted while at the IBM Zurich Research Lab.

T. Kühne (Ed.): MoDELS 2006 Workshops, LNCS 4364, pp. 193–204, 2007.

of the model transformation is supposed to be executable, a possible testing approach is to take the output of a model transformation and to test whether it is executable [6]. By contrast, a white box approach to testing takes into account design and implementation of the model transformation for constructing test cases. Compared with the extensive work on model-based testing of reactive systems (see Utting et al. [7] for a taxonomy and tool overview), testing of model transformations can still be considered to be in its early stages. A recent overview of model transformation testing techniques has been published by Baudry et al. [8]. For a detailed discussion of related work, the reader is referred to the long version of this paper [9].

In this paper, we present our first experiences with a white box model-based approach to testing of model transformations. Our techniques have been developed while implementing a set of five model transformations for business-driven development [10,11] which are used in a model-driven engineering approach for business process modeling. We propose three techniques for constructing test cases and show how we have used them to find errors in our model transformations.

The paper is structured as follows: We first introduce the motivation for our model transformations as well as how we design and implement them in Section 2. In Section 3, we introduce three techniques for constructing test cases and explain how we apply them to validate our transformations. We finally discuss several conclusions drawn from our experience.

2   Model Transformations for Business Process Models

The field of business process modeling has a long standing tradition. Business-driven development is a methodology for developing IT solutions that directly satisfy business requirements. The idea includes that business process models are iteratively refined and transformed using model transformations, to move semi-automatically from a higher to a lower abstraction level.

We present business process models in the notation of the IBM WebSphere Business Modeler [12], which is based on UML 2.0 activity diagrams [13]. The language supported by the WebSphere Business Modeler makes some extensions to UML and can be considered as a domain-specific language for business process modeling. In these models, we distinguish *task* and *subprocess* elements. While tasks capture the atomic, not further dividable activities in the business process models, subprocesses can be further refined into more subprocesses and tasks. *Control and data flow* edges connect tasks and subprocesses. The control and data flow can be split or merged using *control actions* such as *decision, fork, merge*, and *join*. Process start and end points are depicted by *start* and *end nodes*. In addition, the language also contains a number of specific actions such as *broadcast* for broadcasting signals and *accept signal* for receiving signals or *maps* for mapping input data to output data.

In the language supported by the WebSphere Business Modeler, pin sets (based on parameter sets in UML2) are used for expressing implicit forks and joins as well as decisions and merges. Although these constructs leave a lot of freedom to the developer, they are problematic for complex transformations. As a consequence, we distinguish between models that only use control actions and those that only use pin sets. A model in the Control Action Normal Form (CANF) requires that an action has at most one pin set with exactly one pin in it [14]. A model in the Pinset Normal Form (PNF) requires that all forks, joins, decisions and merges are expressed implicitly using pin sets [14].

To support the idea of business-driven development, we have designed and implemented a number of model transformations for business process models (see Koehler et al. [11] for a detailed overview). One of these transformations is the *Control Action to Pinset* (CAToPinset) transformation [14] which transforms a business process model into the Pinset Normal Form. Figure 1 shows an example of a process model in the Control Action Normal Form (upper model) and the Pinset Normal Form (lower model) and the transformation.

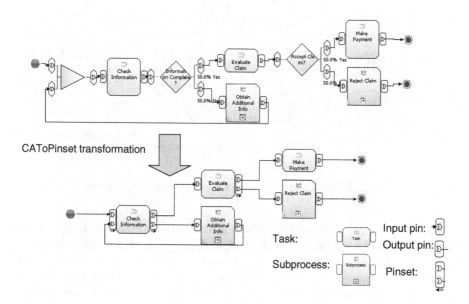

Fig. 1. Example of a process model in both normal forms

For design and implementation of the model transformations, we apply an iterative approach [15] that consists of producing a high-level design which is then used as a basis for the implementation. The high-level design of a model transformation aims at producing a semi-formal description of a transformation, abstracting from its details such as all possible cases to be supported. The main objective of this activity is to capture the fundamentals of the transformation graphically to produce a description that can then be used for discussions among the developers.

A model transformation within high-level design is specified with a set of *conceptual transformation rules* $r : L \rightarrow R$, each consisting of a left and right side. The left side L and right side R show subsets of the source and target models for the transformation respectively. Concrete syntax of the underlying modeling languages is used, depicting how a part of the source model resembling the left side L is replaced by the part of the model described by R. In addition, those elements that are considered to be abstract are represented using additional abstract elements. These elements will typically be refined in later design phases or during implementation.

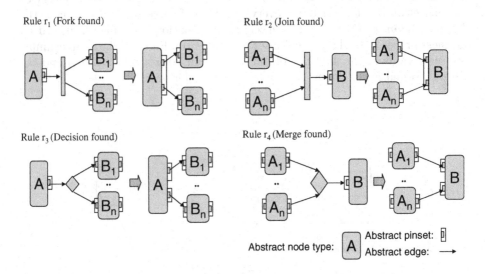

Fig. 2. Rules of the Control Action to Pinset transformation

In Figure 2, rules of the CAToPinset transformation are shown. In addition to concrete syntax elements such as the *fork*, abstract elements are used, such as an abstraction for the node type. Overall, the rules abstract from the details such as the number of pins in a pin set, the number of outgoing or incoming edges, the type of the nodes and the type of the edge (control or data flow). Nevertheless, the main idea of each transformation rule is captured. For example, rule r_1 removes a fork, creates a new pin within the pin set of A, and connects the edges outgoing from the fork directly to the pins of A.

In general, different ways of implementing a model transformation exist. A pure model-driven approach consists of using one of the existing transformation engines, e.g. supporting the standard QVT [16]. In our case, we decided to implement the transformations directly in Java. This target implementation was then packaged as an Eclipse plugin and executed in the WebSphere Business Modeler.

In both cases, the conceptual rules of the transformation have to be refined by identifying the different cases they have abstracted from and defining how to handle them. For example, rule r_1 in Figure 2 has to be specified in more detail to take into account the possibility of data flow along the edges, the possibility of having multiple edges and special cases where parts of the fork are unconnected. In addition, the rule has to be refined with regards to the different possible node types for A and B_1 to B_n. In our case, possible node types include *start* and *end nodes, task, subprocess*, loop nodes such as a *while* loop, all control action nodes, and a number of specific action nodes such as the *broadcast* node. It is because of this number of model elements together with attached constraints that the transformation requires some effort during implementation as well as thorough testing.

3   Systematic Testing of Transformations

Along the line of general principles of software engineering [17], we can distinguish between testing in the small and in the large. Testing in the small applied to model transformations can be considered as testing each transformation rule whereas testing in the large requires testing of each transformation. For both types of testing, challenges of testing specialized to model transformations can be expressed as follows (adapted from [18]):

- the generation of test cases from model transformation specifications according to a given coverage criterion,
- the generation of test oracles to determine the expected result of a test, and
- the execution of tests in suitable test environments.

In our approach to model transformation development, the third challenge is easy to overcome because we can execute tests directly in our development environment. The main challenges are the first and second ones because the model transformation specification in our case is based on the informal conceptual rules introduced above. In the following, we will show how we can partially overcome these challenges. First, we will discuss common types of errors that we have encountered when implementing the transformations. Then we discuss three techniques for test case generation and discuss cases where the test oracle problem is easy to overcome.

3.1   Fault Model for Model Transformations

A fault model describes the assumptions where errors are likely to be found [19]. Given our approach to model transformation development, we can apply a model-based testing approach that takes into account the conceptual transformation rules as models. Based on our experience, the following errors can occur when coding a conceptual transformation rule:

1. *Meta model coverage*: the conceptual transformation rule has been coded without complete coverage of the meta model elements, leading to the problem that some input models cannot be transformed (e.g. the rule only works for certain node types, only for control flow edges, or only for one edge between two tasks but not for two edges).

2. *Creation of syntactically incorrect models*: the updating part of the transformation rule has not been implemented correctly. This can lead to models that do not conform to the meta model or that violate constraints specified in the meta model of the modeling language.
3. *Creation of semantically incorrect models*: the transformation rule has been applied to a source model for which it is not suitable, i.e. the result model is syntactically correct but it is not a semantically correct transformation of the source model.
4. *Confluence*: The transformation produces different outputs on the same model because the transformation is not confluent. This also includes the possibility that the transformation leads to intermediate models that cannot be transformed any further because non-confluence of the transformation has not been detected and treated.
5. *Correctness of transformation semantics*: the transformation does not preserve a desired property that has been specified for the transformation. Possible properties include syntactic and semantic correctness (see above) but also refinement or behavioral properties such as deadlock freedom.
6. *Errors due to incorrect coding*: there are also errors possible that cannot be directly related to one of the other categories. These errors can be classical coding errors.

Often, there is an interplay between meta model coverage and syntactic correctness. A meta model coverage error can lead to a syntactically incorrect model. The challenge in all cases is how to systematically generate test cases and how to create the appropriate test oracles. Errors due to incorrect coding are indirectly found when testing for the first four types of errors. In addition, further techniques such as code walk-throughs can be applied. In the following, we introduce three techniques and discuss how they can be applied to find different types of errors. The last two types of errors are not explicitly dealt with in this paper and are left to future work.

3.2   Meta Model Coverage Testing

In our approach to model transformation development, a given conceptual rule can be transformed into a *meta model template*. The idea of a meta model template is to be able to create automatically template instances that represent suitable test cases.

In the transition from a conceptual rule to a meta model template, abstract elements must either be made concrete or must be resolved by parameters together with a parameter set. To identify for each parameter in the conceptual rule the possible parameter values, the meta model of the underlying modeling language must be taken into account.

Figure 3 b) shows a meta model template derived from rule r_1 shown in Figure 3 a). We make concrete the number of available nodes $B_1, .. ,B_n$ and fix it to be $n = 2$. Further, we also fix the pin set structure of the nodes. The remaining abstraction of the nodes is parameterized by the possible meta model

a) Conceptual rule:

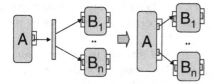

b) Template(X,Y,Z):

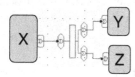

X={StartNode, Fork, Join, Decision, Merge, Task, Subprocess,
        LoopNode, Broadcast, AcceptSignal}

Y={FinalNode, Fork, Join, Decision, Merge, Task, Subprocess,
        LoopNode, Broadcast, AcceptSignal, Map}

Z={FinalNode, Fork, Join, Decision, Merge, Task, Subprocess,
        LoopNode, Broadcast, AcceptSignal, Map}

c) Template instances:

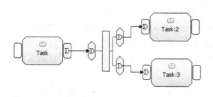

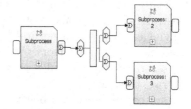

Fig. 3. Conceptual rule, meta model template and possible instances

classes. These can be identified when looking at the meta model and must be captured for each parameter in the meta model template. Figure 3 c) shows two template instances derived from the template.

Due to the abstraction process, one conceptual transformation rule can give rise to a number of different meta model templates. Note that when specifying the parameters for X, Y, Z one has to take into account well-formedness constraints of the language.

It is important to realize that meta model coverage testing is a classical case where white box testing is very powerful. This is because from each rule a number of templates can be derived that together can ensure a high degree of meta model coverage (per rule). If we obtain meta model coverage for each rule, we can deduce meta model coverage for the entire transformation.

After meta model templates have been defined, automatic generation of template instances yields a set of test cases for the transformation rule for which the template has been defined. Both the systematic instantiation of the templates and the testing can be automated. In the context of our work, a straightforward generation of templates has been implemented [14] that requires specification of the template and the suitable parameters. Based on this, a number of test cases is then generated automatically.

Beyond finding meta model coverage errors, meta model coverage testing can also be applied to find both syntactic and semantic correctness errors as well as errors due to incorrect coding. For syntactic correctness, the test oracle is the tool environment which in our case can detect whether the transformation result is syntactically correct. With regards to semantic correctness, each result must be manually compared and evaluated.

As test cases for meta model coverage are derived directly from a transformation rule, this technique has its limitations for those cases in which *constraints* are formulated for a number of model elements: If these model elements are not part of a certain rule, no test case generated using meta model coverage testing will be a suitable test case. This is why in the next section we present a technique that, given a constraint, aims at construction of test cases for this particular constraint.

3.3   Using Constraints for Construction of Test Cases

Typically, the meta model of a language also specifies well-formedness constraints. These constraints can be expressed using the Object Constraint Language (OCL) or in natural language. Violations of constraints give rise to syntactic correctness errors. As constraints can be violated by the interplay of several transformation rules, they cannot be completely detected by meta model coverage testing.

As a consequence, we believe that existing constraints specified in the language specification should be used to construct interesting test cases that aim at discovering errors due to the violation of constraints. As a transformation changes model elements, it needs to be tested that all constraints that may be violated due to the change hold after applying a transformation. We can test constraints both on the rule and transformation level.

After identification of the changed model elements, we take those constraints into consideration that are dependent on the model elements changed. A constraint is independent of a model element if the existence or value of the model element instance does not influence the value of the constraint, otherwise it is dependent.

The idea to construct test cases to ensure constraints after application of the transformation is then as follows:

- Identify model elements changed by the transformation.
- Identify constraints that are dependent on these model elements.
- For each constraint, construct a test case that checks validity of the constraint under the transformation.

The test oracle for these tests is again the execution environment which in our case checks the constraints after application of the transformation.

An important issue is how we can detect which model elements are changed by the transformation, in the absence of a complete specification of the transformation rules. Partially, these elements can be detected when regarding the conceptual rule. At the same time, one can also obtain this information directly from the programmer.

With regards to the CAToPinset transformation, the model elements changed by r_1 are the pin set of A, because r_1 extends the pin set by adding an additional pin. Furthermore, edges are affected because r_1 changes their source or target nodes. In a similar way, we can find model elements changed by the other rules.

In our example of business process models, some of the constraints that are dependent on the changed model elements are:

- C1: A final node has one incoming edge.
- C2: An initial node has one outgoing edge of type control flow.

All constraints are concerned with edges or with pin sets and are thus dependent on the changed model elements.

Given a constraint, we construct a test case for it as follows: Constraints can be divided into positive constraints requiring the existence of model elements and negative ones requiring the non-existence of model elements. In both cases, we try to create test cases that, after the transformation has been applied, can result into a violation of the constraint.

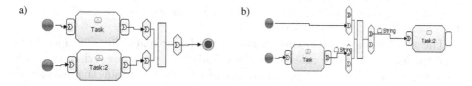

Fig. 4. Test cases for constraints

For example, with regards to constraint C_1, which requires that a final node has one incoming edge, we try to create a test case that after transformation results in the situation that the final node has two incoming edges. Figure 4 a) shows such a test case. An incorrect implementation will simply remove the *join* node and try to reconnect the incoming edges to the final node, which of course results into a syntactically incorrect model. Figure 4 b) shows a test case for C_2 (removal of the *join* node can lead to the creation of a *String* data flow edge from the start node, if incorrectly coded). All of these test cases have revealed errors in the implementation of the model transformation CAToPinset.

3.4   Using Rule Pairs for Testing

Another source of errors arises from the interplay of rules: The application of one rule at some model element in the model might inhibit the application of another rule at the same model element. The property of confluence requires that the application of transformation rules on the same or an equivalent model yields the same result. As stated in [20], confluence of transformations need not always be ensured. However, it is important to detect whether the overall transformation is confluent because this can cause very subtle errors that are difficult to detect and reproduce. Confluence errors can give rise to syntactic as well as semantic errors.

In theory, the concept of parallel independence [21] of two rules has been developed which requires that all possible applications of the two rules do not inhibit each other i.e. it is always the case that if one rule r_1 was applicable before applying r_2 it is also applicable afterwards. If two rules are not parallel independent, they might give rise to confluence errors. In [20], we have discussed a set of criteria for detection of confluence errors which are based on the construction of critical pairs. The idea of a critical pair is to capture the conflicting transformation steps in a minimal context and analyze whether a common successor model can be derived. For exact calculation of critical pairs, a complete specification of the rules is required, e.g. in one of the model transformation languages.

In testing, the challenge is to construct test cases systematically that lead to the detection of confluence errors. In our approach, a complete specification of the transformation rules is not available. However, we can still use the conceptual rules for construction of test cases: Based on the idea of critical pairs, we argue that it is useful to construct all possible overlapping models of two rules. These overlapping models can represent a critical pair and can thus be used to *test* for the existence of a confluence error.

The overlapping models can be constructed systematically. The idea is to take the left sides of two rules and then calculate all possible overlaps of model elements. Based on an overlap, a model is constructed which joins the two models at the overlapping model elements. If the overlapping model is syntactically incorrect, it is discarded. Otherwise, it is taken as a test case.

For example, for rules r_1 and r_3 in Figure 2 one possible overlap is to identify the node B_1 of r_1 with node A of rule r_3. The result is shown in Figure 5 a), assuming $n = 2$, a *task* node type for all nodes and a simple edge structure. Figure 5 b) shows another test case which gave rise to a confluence error because removing the *fork* leads to the construction of a pin set with two pins at the *decision*, which is forbidden in the language. This leads to an execution error because in our environment the construction of invalid intermediate models is not possible. If the fork is removed first, then no invalid model is constructed. Note that in a different execution environment supporting invalid intermediate models, the test case would not lead to an execution error.

4   Conclusions

Validation of model transformations is a key issue to ensure their quality and thereby enables the vision of model-driven engineering become reality. In the context of business-driven development, model transformations are used for transforming more abstract models into more concrete ones and to move between different representations of models. In this paper, we have reported our first experiences with testing a set of model transformations for business process models systematically.

a)   b)

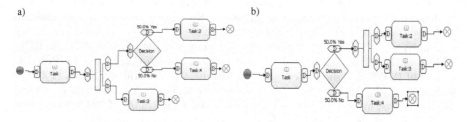

Fig. 5. Test cases for confluence

We have proposed three techniques which follow a white box testing approach. Using this approach, we have been able to significantly improve the quality of the model transformations under development. Both the meta model coverage technique as well as the construction of test cases driven by constraints has shown the existence of a number of errors. Rule pairs have indicated fewer errors, possibly due to the low number of rules.

There remain further challenges that we have not been able to address yet, for example, the automation of constructing test cases from OCL constraints. Here we see two possible improvements, firstly the automatic detection of constraints that could be violated by providing an algorithm that, given a meta model element, finds all relevant constraints. Secondly, the automatic conversion of such a constraint into a possible test case. Future work also includes the elaboration of tool support in order to fully automate testing of transformations.

Acknowledgements. We thank Ksenia Ryndina, Michael Wahler, Olaf Zimmermann and Hoda Hosny for their valuable comments on drafts of this paper.

References

1. Csertán, G., Huszerl, G., Majzik, I., Pap, Z., Pataricza, A., Varró, D.: VIATRA: Visual Automated Transformations for Formal Verification and Validation of UML Models . In: Proceedings 17th IEEE International Conference on Automated Software Engineering (ASE 2002), Edinburgh, UK (2002) 267–270
2. Jouault, F., Kurtev, I.: Transforming Models with ATL. In Bruel, J.M., ed.: Satellite Events at the MoDELS 2005 Conference, Revised Selected Papers. Volume 3844 of LNCS. (2005) 128–138
3. Karsai, G., Agrawal, A., Shi, F., Sprinkle, J.: On the Use of Graph Transformation in the Formal Specification of Model Interpreters. Journal of Universal Computer Science **9** (2003) 1296–1321
4. Fleurey, F., Steel, J., Baudry, B.: Model-Driven Engineering and Validation: Testing model transformations. In: Proceedings SIVOES-MoDeVa Workshop. (2004)
5. Ehrig, K., Küster, J.M., Taentzer, G., Winkelmann, J.: Generating Instance Models from Meta Models. Volume 4037 of LNCS, Springer (2006) 156–170
6. Dinh-Trong, T., Kawane, N., Ghosh, S., France, R., Andrews, A.: A Tool-Supported Approach to Testing UML Design Models. In: Proceedings of ICECCS'05, Shanghai, China. (2005)

7. Utting, M., Pretschner, A., Legeard, B.: A taxonomy of model-based testing. Technical report, Department of Computer Science, The University of Waikato (New Zealand), Technical Report 04/2006 (2006)
8. Baudry, B., Dinh-Trong, T., Mottu, J.M., Simmonds, D., France, R., Ghosh, S., Fleurey, F., Traon, Y.L.: Model Transformation Testing Challenges. In: Proceedings of IMDT workshop in conjunction with ECMDA'06, Bilbao, Spain. (2006)
9. Küster, J.M., Abd-El-Razik, M.: Validation of Model Transformations - First Experiences using a White Box Approach. In: Proceedings of 3rd International Workshop Modeva: Model Development, Validation and Verification. (2006) 62–77
10. Mitra, T.: Business-driven development. IBM developerWorks article, http://www.ibm.com/developerworks/webservices/library/ws-bdd, IBM (2005)
11. Koehler, J., Hauser, R., Küster, J., Ryndina, K., Vanhatalo, J., Wahler, M.: The Role of Visual Modeleling and Model Transformations in Business-Driven Development. In: Proceedings of the 5th International Workshop on Graph Transformations and Visual Modeling Techniques. (2006) 1–12
12. IBM WebSphere Business Modeler. (http:///www-306.ibm.com/software/integration/wbimodeler/)
13. Object Management Group (OMG): UML 2.0 Superstructure Final Adopted Specification. OMG document pts/03-08-02. (2003)
14. Abd-El-Razik, M.: Business Process Normalization using Model Transformation. Master thesis, The American University in Cairo, in collaboration with IBM (2006) In preparation.
15. Küster, J.M., Ryndina, K., Hauser, R.: A Systematic Approach to Designing Model Transformations. Technical report, IBM Research, Research Report RZ 3621 (2005)
16. Object Management Group (OMG): Meta Object Facility (MOF) 2.0 Query/View/Transformation. Final Adopted Specification. OMG document ad/2005-11-01. (2005)
17. Ghezzi, C., Jazayeri, M., Mandrioli, D.: Fundamentals of Software Engineering. Prentice-Hall (1991)
18. Heckel, R., Lohmann, M.: Towards Model-Driven Testing. ENTCS **82** (2003)
19. Binder, R.: Testing Object-Oriented Systems: Models, Patterns and Tools. Addison Wesley (1999)
20. Küster, J.M.: Definition and validation of model transformations. Software and Systems Modeling Volume **5**, Number 3, (2006) 233–259
21. Corradini, A., Montanari, U., Rossi, F., Ehrig, H., Heckel, R., Löwe, M.: Algebraic Approaches to Graph Transformation Part I: Basic Concepts and Double Pushout Approach. In Rozenberg, G., ed.: Handbook of Graph Grammars and Computing by Graph Transformation, Volume 1: Foundations. World Scientific (1997) 163–245

Summary of the 2006 Model Size Metrics Workshop

Frank Weil and Andrij Neczwid

Motorola, Schaumburg, IL 60196, USA
{Frank.Weil,A.Neczwid}@motorola.com

Abstract. A standardized and consistent means of determining the size of an artifact is fundamental to the ability to collect metrics such as defect density and productivity about the artifact. For example, source lines of code is often used as the size metric for C code. However, the concept of lines of code does not readily apply to modeling languages such as UML and SDL. This report summarizes the presentations and discussions on this topic from the 2006 Model Size Metrics workshop.

Keywords: Model Size Metrics, Model-Driven Engineering, UML, SDL.

1 Overview

There were two main goals of the Model Size Metrics workshop: Share practical experience, current work, and research directions related to techniques for calculating the size of a model; and form an industrial and academic consortium related to model size metrics. A standardized method of determining model size that allows for the effective baselining and comparison of model concepts is a crucial need within the MoDELS community. Such metrics enable the effective estimation and quality management of model-driven development.

As part of the workshop, plans were also discussed on how to fit this work into a broader umbrella covering model-driven engineering, such as the Re-MoDD (Repository for Model Driven Development) effort. The goal of the Re-MoDD project is to create a community resource of model-driven engineering artifacts that will provide an infrastructure to improve the use of model-based development.

The attendees of the workshop were practitioners and researchers interested in the process, estimation, and quality aspects of modeling languages. The workshop consisted of individual presentations based on submitted position papers, followed by open discussions of the presented material as well as plans for future work.

The position papers presented many complementary views of the concept of model size and how it can be measured. While some work exists on specific facets of the topic, the workshop raised more questions than answers—a good indication that this is a nascent field rich with opportunities for research and empirical studies.

T. Kühne (Ed.): MoDELS 2006 Workshops, LNCS 4364, pp. 205–210, 2007.

2   Workshop Presentations

As part of the discussions throughout the workshop, many questions and points to consider were raised. In order to give more structure to this summary, we have collected these separately in Section 4.

One point that was generally agreed upon was that the relevance of a given model element varies depending on what metric its size is being counted for. For example, a Use Case may have a low direct impact on code size, but it may have a high impact on cost to fix defects discovered in the code. This implies that a simple count of number of elements in a model is only part of the equation. In order to determine size for a given metric, relative weights must be applied to the counts. Essentially, what constitutes a model of a system has expanded to include requirements, test cases, design artifacts, etc.

The idea of the size of change, or "delta," between two versions of a model was also raised. For line-based languages, one can count additions, deletions, and changes based on standard "diff" techniques. While these same ideas can be used for textual portions of models, such as OCL, there are other changes which are inherent to graphical languages. For example, there are presentational changes such as moving an element on a diagram, resizing an element, or re-orienting an element. There are also organizational changes such as moving an element between diagrams or reorganizing the diagrams within a model, and more fundamental changes such as renaming an element.

Christian Lange discussed abstraction levels and how they may affect the metrics, but pointed out that it is not clear how one would measure objectively the abstraction level of a model or what factors it depends on. An interesting observation was also made about whether the completeness of the model makes a difference. Also presented was work on modifying the Fenton and Pfleeger [3] categorization measures for software as an approach to measuring models. In particular, the concept of relative size was introduced, which is a ratio of two absolute sizes and measures how well something is covered.

Harald Störrle discussed the use of metrics for comparison, defect density, complexity, etc. He presented the concept of having length, width, and breadth of population measures, from which one could then derive density and strength of the model. Also discussed was the quantification of the "method of creation" to describe slots to be filled, and then identifying default values which are deemed the characteristics of the slots, and whether they are changed or unchanged with respect to modifying the size of the model. This idea has been applied with some success to SDL models.

Miroslaw Staron discussed measuring the size of stereotypes, Profiles, and stereotyped designs in UML based on work with industrial modeling projects and their stereotype usage. The idea of Profile cohesion was presented, including what goes into this measure, such as the model library, metamodel, extensions, and a combination of stereotypes, classes, and data types. In their case studies, size did *not* correlate well to defects or quality of Profiles using the framework from Briand et al. [2] for effective metrics. It was also noted that one cannot compare a model with one Profile applied against the same model with a different Profile applied—they are essentially two different models.

Jacqueline McQuillan presented some observations on the application of software metrics to UML models. She discussed how to apply metrics to artifacts at early stages of development, again raising the issue of abstraction level. The observation was made that metrics can be measured from the viewpoints of the model and the implementation, and that the differences of measurements themselves are metrics. This suggests the approach of defining a metamodel of the elements to be measured and then measuring the model based on this metamodel. It is difficult, though, to correlate these metrics with external attributes.

Betty Cheng presented on the initial work on the ReMoDD model repository project with Robert France. A fruitful discussion ensued, covering how to administer such a repository, how to make it most useful, what the requirements for its contents should be, and how groups with conflicting constraints (e.g., the proprietary nature of industry models versus the need for open access for academic research projects) can collaborate.

Jean Bézivin discussed measuring model repositories themselves and brought up the idea of model "zoos". This work was done in the context of the Eclipse Modeling Project. Some work was also presented that defined a "measure" metamodel.

Horst Kargl discussed measuring the explicitness of modeling concepts in metamodels, introducing the relationship between metamodel elements and notational elements. It is possible to identify both the hidden concepts in a metamodel (unused meta-model elements) and the overspecified concepts (those for which multiple notational elements exist).

Jordi Cabot presented a metric for measuring the complexity of OCL expressions embedded in a model based on the number of objects involved in the evaluation of the expression. While in some ways the issue of complexity is similar to that of other languages, OCL must be understood in the context of the model in which it is embedded.

Vieri Del Bianco discussed experience with and a proposal for object-oriented model size measurement. He presented Function Point Analysis [1] as applied to models and proposed the translation of a model to some intermediate form (such as Java) which can then be measured directly.

3   Group Discussions

Following the discussions based on the position papers, an open discussion was held on what the most pressing questions were and how some progress could be made on them. The key question selected for detailed discussion was: What are the types of metrics that can be collected?

Based on the Goal/Question/Metric (GQM) method, it is important to ask what the goals of model metrics are. It is clear that an overall strategy is needed, perhaps based around common goals. A high-level and non-exhaustive list of metrics goals as related to modeling was collected:

- Project estimation and tracking
  - Effort, including what effort is being spent on different parts of the model
  - Productivity
  - Efficiency
- Quality determination
  - Defects
  - Defect density
  - Defect slip-through
- Method and tool comparison
  - Expressiveness
  - Scalability
  - Verifiability
  - Understandability
  - Maintainability
  - Complexity of description
- Metric dynamics

The appropriateness of "size" for each of these measures was discussed at length. In particular, the relationship of model size to project tracking was highlighted. If there is an estimation of what the final size of a model will be, and one can measure the size of the partial model during development, one can determine what percentage has been completed and the growth trend.

This lead to an interesting discussion of what the growth curve should look like for a "healthy" modeling project. There are three factors that impact model characteristics (and possibly growth): complexity, quality, and effort. It was argued that complexity is an important consideration, but in general most people disagreed, the opinion being that complexity was not necessarily the most important factor when trying to measure a model. It was pointed out that models now, as opposed to with previous programming languages, contain so many more artifacts related to product information. It is not just "code" anymore, which only captures a representation of the behavior. Even though each of the three characteristics of a model may be growing at different rates (various diagrams will grow faster during some stages and slower during other stages), the size of the entire model should follow a rather linear upward trend overall.

This expectation applies to any "reasonably sized" model, so that an averaging effect comes into play. There may be dips and plateaus as time progresses, but a trend line should establish itself. The opinion was that the slope (or shape) of the trend was what was most important.

An interesting thought was proposed about the visualization of metrics data, and how the data could be presented to users to help recognize pattern and trends beyond simple linear ones.

An issue was raised on whether or not it was appropriate to use the size-measure approach of collecting everything possible and then sorting out the relevant information at the end. Given that this approach would lead to large redundancy in the data collected, perhaps one should apply Principal Component Analysis to the data to identify multiple correlations.

Overall, it was a very productive set of discussions, with many interesting and diverse viewpoints being represented.

4   Open Questions

The following is a representative sampling of the questions and issues that were raised during the workshop. They represent interesting areas for future work.

1. To what extent should language semantics be taken into account? For example, is the size of an asterisk state in SDL the same as the size of a simple state?
2. Sufficiently powerful code generators for any modeling language can produce code that is approximately equal in object size, so what are the underlying semantic concepts that allow this to be true? Does "semantic size" matter in practice? The overall question of how to compute the semantic size is potentially intractable. Is it good enough to compute an approximation of the semantic size from the syntactic size?
3. How should UML Profiles be accounted for?
4. What are the units of the size metrics? They need to have some reference to known units in order to compare to traditional metrics. There is a need to account for "internal" versus "external" measures. For example, an enormous baseline of data based on source lines exists, and that cannot be discarded.
5. How does one accurately measure reuse of model elements?
6. How does the size of a model grow over time? What are the typical curves for healthy and unhealthy projects?
7. Should the way one calculates size change over the life cycle? Should it change with the development paradigm (agile, waterfall, etc.)?
8. How should delta size be computed? This is often more important for industrial projects than raw size. Does moving a graphical element matter? The move was presumably done for a reason, and some effort went into it, so it should count somehow. How does one count a fundamental operation such as renaming an element? It is really just one change even if it shown up on several diagrams. Is renaming a class inherently different than renaming a `struct` in C?

5   Plans and Summary

Research into and use of model size metrics are of general interest, and that requires the definitions to be universal and standardized. Not only will this leverage the efforts of others and provide a large pool of data, but it will help drive common tool support. A close association with model-repository projects such as ReMoDD is planned.

To facilitate this collaboration and to continue the discussions, an as-yet-to-be-named consortium of interested parties is being formed, and a mailing list will be created. More information is available at the Model-Driven Engineering TWiki site at `http://modeldrivenengineering.org`.

One of the tasks of the consortium will be to respond to the Request For Proposal (RFP) by the Object management Group Architecture-Driven Modernization (OMG ADM) Task Force for a *Software Metrics Metamodel* [4]. The consortium plans to submit not as a proposal submitter, but instead to present the recommendations, issues, and questions from this workshop to the committee selected to review responders to the RFP. This can help provide a means of evaluating submissions against real-world criteria. This would help ensure that any accepted proposals at least do not prevent particular directions of work as viewed by members of this consortium. A longer-term goal related to the OMG would be to issue a separate RFP if the one from the ADM does not address specific needs such as how to actually measure the size of models.

For further information, please contact the authors or visit the web site named above. The full workshop proceedings are also available on that site.

References

1. Albrecht, A.: Measuring Application Development Productivity. In: Proc. Joint SHARE/GUIDE/IBM Application Development Symp. (1979) 83–92
2. Briand, L., Morasca, S., Basili, V.: Property-Based Software Engineering Measurement. IEEE Trans. on Software Eng., Vol. 22 (1996) 68–87
3. Fenton, N., Pfleeger, S.: Software Metrics, A Rigorous and Practical Approach. 2nd edn. Thomson Computer Press (1996)
4. Object Management Group: Request For Proposal: Software Metrics Metamodel. OMG Document: admtf/2006-09-01 (2006)

Model Size Matters

Christian F.J. Lange

Department of Mathematics and Computer Science
Technische Universiteit Eindhoven, The Netherlands
C.F.J.Lange@tue.nl

Abstract. Size is an important attribute of software artefacts; for most artefact types exists a body of measurement knowledge. As software engineering is becoming more and more model-centric, it is surprising that there exists only little work on model size metrics (MoSMe). In this position paper we identify the goals justifying the need for MoSMe, such as prediction, description and progress measurement. Additionally, we identify challenges that make it difficult to measure the size of UML models and that MoSMe have to deal with. Finally, we propose a classification of MoSMe and concrete examples of metrics for the size of UML models.

Keywords: Models, UML, Size, Metrics, Measurement, Prediction, GQM.

1   Introduction

Measurement is a popular and well-established instrument in software development and maintenance. Metrics are used to evaluate, predict, measure and understand software products, processes, and resources. A large body of measurement knowledge exists for source code. The earliest and still popular metrics for source code include size metrics. Nowadays software engineering is shifting to models instead of source code as the central software artefact. Simultaneously, the measurement activities shift to measure properties of models. Surprisingly, quality metrics draw a large amount of attention, whereas metrics for the model size have not been actively addressed. This is surprising, because the notion of size seems to be much more simple than the notion of quality, and furthermore size seems to play an important role in the discussion of quality.

The purpose of this position paper is to provide a discussion about model size metrics (in the remainder of this paper referred to as *MoSMe*). In particular we will discuss the need for MoSMe, challenges in defining MoSMe, and we will propose and evaluate approaches to measure the size of models.

The mostly used language for modeling is the UML [13]. Therefore we limit the scope of our discussion to MoSMe for UML models, however, we expect most parts will be generalizable to a broader scope of models with similar characteristics (e.g. MOF-based models [14]).

This paper is structured as follows: in Section 2 we present the goals of measuring model size, in Section 3 we discuss challenges that have to be dealt with,

T. Kühne (Ed.): MoDELS 2006 Workshops, LNCS 4364, pp. 211–216, 2007.
© Springer-Verlag Berlin Heidelberg 2007

in Section 4 we present ideas for approaches and a classification, and in Section 5 we will draw conclusions and discuss opportunities for future work.

2   Why Do We Need Model Size Metrics?

UML models contain a large number of model elements of various types such as classes, associations, messages, actions, methods, states and so on. For UML models exist various representations, such as diagrams, XMI representations, or mappings to other data models. This huge amount of information of a model allows to define an even larger amount of different metrics, all measuring some concept of size. However, to enable selecting metrics, that measure the concept we are interested in from a particular point of view, it is necessary to define the goal of the measurement. The Goal Question Metric Paradigm by Basili et al. (GQM [2]) provides a framework to derive metrics that serve specific goals. According to the GQM paradigm we define goals for measuring the size of models. These goals are a basis for the discussion of MoSMe. Here we present possible goals for measuring model size. As the purpose of this paper is to provoke a discussion about MoSME, the list is not exhaustive and should be extended to include additional goals.

- **Comparing Models.** Enabling to compare the size of models, e.g. different versions of the same model, different models for the same system, models for different systems ....
- **Measuring Progress.** Answering questions like 'How fast is our model growing?'.
- **Effort Prediction.** Predicting for example the effort needed for a project (note that size is the main driver in the COCOMO model [3]), or the size of the implementation of the system.
- **Quality Evaluation.** To measure defect density, it is necessary to measure size. There is some anecdotal evidence, that size is a predictor for fault-proneness of software modules, but in literature there is only limited support for this claim [6].
- **Description.** Describing the characteristics of a model, e.g. in a repository such as ReMoDD [4] and in empirical studies it is necessary to describe carefully characteristics of the model under study [8].

3   What Are the Challenges?

In the discussion of MoSMe we have to deal with a number of challenges inherent to the UML. In this section we present a non-exhaustive list of challenges for the definition of MoSMe.

- **Multi-View Language.** The UML consists of 13 diagram types to describe systems from multiple views. Each of the diagram types may require specific MoSMe. Two challenges are related to the multi-view nature of the language: first, MoSMe have to be robust to overlapping information in diagrams, and second, we have to address the challenge, that a model can be large with respect to a certain diagram type and another model can be large with respect to a different diagram type.

- **Abstraction Level.** UML models can describe a system at different abstraction levels. This involves that we have to distinguish between the size of the model and the size of the modeled system. In previous work on a quality model [10] for UML we described that it is necessary to distinguish between properties of the model (the description) and the modeled (the described). Two models that describe the same system at different abstraction levels will differ in the number of model elements. Usually at a higher abstraction level fewer model elements are used. It is assumed that the abstraction level of a model influences its external quality attributes. Verelst [15] showed, that a higher abstraction level can increase the evolvability of a model. A possible indication for a model's level of abstraction is the level of detail applied to the model (e.g. are methods, attributes, multiplicities,... modeled?). An additional challenge is that within one single model different levels of abstraction can exist (by purpose or accidentally).
- **Level of Detail.** Examples of detailed modeling are the use of explicit information about multiplicity, about types of attributes, and method parameters. A higher level of detail leads to an increased number of model elements. When defining MoSMe, we have to be aware of this and we have to decide whether the level of details accounts for model size.
- **Completeness of Modeling.** There are two notions of completeness. The first notion of model completeness is concerned with how well the requirements are addressed by the model. The second notion of completeness is concerned with partial information. It deals with the question whether model elements have corresponding counterparts in other diagrams (e.g. does an object in a sequence diagram correspond to a class in the class diagram?). Empirical investigations have shown [9][11] that in practice models contain a large amount of completeness issues. Both notions of completeness affect measuring the model size.
- **Scope of Modeling.** When modeling a system, there are several possible choices of the scope of modeling, that affect the size of the model. Examples are: the model describes only the source code that must be written, or the model can additionally describe test code, libraries, external components, or hardware devices.
- **Tools.** The choice of modeling tool may affect the model size or the size of its representation.
- **Distinction between Model and System.** A model is a description of a system. Several of the above mentioned challenges are related to the distinction between the *size of the model as a description* and the *system described by the model*. The measurement goal affects which notion of size we are interested in. Effort prediction for example, requires measuring the size of the system to be implemented. For describing a model used in an empirical study about model inspection it might be sufficient to describe the size of the model as a description of the system.

In future research questions must be formulated to achieve the described goals using the MoSMe.

4   Possible Approaches

4.1   What Is Model Size?

Size is a property of an entity. In the 'real-world' entities are usually physical objects like humans or cars. Their size is generally captured by the dimensions height, width and depth. This already indicates that one single size measure is not sufficient to describe an entity. In the software world, entities are artefacts like requirements, models and source code (or their elements). Most existing literature discussing size of software is concerned with source code. Fenton and Pfleeger [7] define four dimensions of size for source code: length, complexity, functionality, and reuse.

4.2   Proposed Approaches

We use the four dimensions proposed by Fenton and Pfleeger as a starting point for categorizing our proposed approaches for MoSMe. We will replace 'length' by what we call 'absolute size' and we will extend the set of dimensions with 'relative size'.

Absolute Size. 'Length' can be measured of source code, because it is organized as a sequence of characters and lines. However, UML models are not sequences and there exists no meaningful notion of length. Therefore we replace 'length' by 'absolut size'. Metrics that measure a model's absolute size are the numbers of elements. Example MoSMe are the number of classes, the number of use cases, the number of sequence diagrams, or the number of classes in a diagram. These examples of MoSMe take the multi-diagram structure of the UML into account.

Other possible MoSMe would be related to the representation; examples are the size of the model file or the XMI file of the model. The drawback of these approaches is that the multi-diagram structure of the UML is not taken into account and that model representations strongly depend on the modeling tool and the XMI version.

Relative Size. We introduce the dimension of 'relative size' to address the UML's multi-diagram structure more accurately and to deal with completeness issues mentioned in Section 3. For this dimension we propose ratios between absolute size metrics, such as $\frac{Number of Sequence Diagrams}{Number of Use Cases}$, $\frac{Number of Objects}{Number of Classes}$, or $\frac{Number of State Charts}{Number of Classes}$. These metrics enable to compare the relative size (or *proportions*) of different models with each other and they give an indication about the completeness of models.

Complexity. We distinguish complexity of the (describing) model and complexity of the (described) system. We propose to measure the complexity of the model by a subset of the absolute and relative size metrics. Additionally properties of the diagrams (such as the *Number of Crossing lines*) relate to model complexity. The system complexity should be measured by commonly accepted complexity metrics such as the metrics suite by Chidamber and Kemerer [5].

Functionality. Established metrics for the functionality are Function Points [1] and Object Points [3]. We expect that there exist relations between functionality metrics and MoSMe that enable to assess a model's completeness (by mapping function metrics to model elements) or the model's level of abstraction (by comparing function metrics to absolute and relative size metrics).

Reuse. The amount of reuse in a software project affects the required effort and the amount of new software that must be created. Hence, to fulfill their goals, MoSMe must take reuse into account. We propose that a measure for reuse should be included in the collection of MoSMe. A simple metric would be the *percentage of reuse*. A reuse metric can only be applied to a UML model that makes use of a profile to denote reuse (such as OMG's Reusable Asset Specification [12]).

5   Conclusions and Future Directions

In this paper we provide a basis for a discussion about establishing Model Size Metrics (MoSMe). According to the Goal-Question-Metric paradigm we discuss goals justifying the need for MoSMe. Additionally we discuss challenges inherent to the UML that have to be dealt with when developing MoSMe. Based on the discussion of goals and challenges we propose approaches including some concrete MoSMe metrics. We conclude that model size cannot be measured with a single metric, but a set of metrics is required to answer different questions about the size of a model.

During the discussion at the workshop we would like to extend and refine the goals, challenges and the MoSMe approaches. Future work should lead to a more detailed description of these concepts. In particular the proposed MoSMe must be related to the measurement goals and to the challenges in measuring the size of UML models. Finally the proposed MoSMe must be validated to ensure that they measure the desired attribute of the model.

References

1. Allan J. Albrecht. Measuring application development productivity. In *Tutorial – Programming Productivity: Issues for the Eighties*, pages 35–44. IEEE Computer Society, 1986.
2. Victor R. Basili, G. Caldiera, and H. Dieter Rombach. The goal question metric paradigm. In *Encyclopedia of Software Engineering*, volume 2, pages 528–532. John Wiley and Sons, Inc., 1994.

3. Barry W. Boehm, Ellis Horowitz, Ray Madachy, Donald Reifer, Bradford K. Clark, Bert Steece, A. Winsor Brown, Sunita Chulani, and Chris Abts. *Software Cost Estimation with Cocomo II*. Prentice Hall, April 2000.
4. Betty Cheng, Robert France, and James Bieman. ReMoDD: A repository for model driven development.
5. S. R. Chidamber and C. F. Kemerer. A metrics suite for object-oriented design. *IEEE Transactions on Software Engineering*, 20(6):476–493, 1994.
6. Norman E. Fenton and Niclas Ohlsson. Quantitative analysis of faults and failures in a complex softwaresystem. *IEEE Transactions on Software Engineering*, 26(8):797–814, August 2000.
7. Norman E. Fenton and Shari Lawrence Pfleeger. *Software Metrics, A Rigorous and Practical Approach*. Thomson Computer Press, second edition, 1996.
8. Barbara A. Kitchenham, Shari Lawrence Pfleeger ans Lesley M. Pickard, Peter W. Jones, Davic C. Hoaglin, Khaled El-Emam, and Jarrett Rosenberg. Preliminary guidelines for empirical research in software engineering. Technical Report NRC 44158 ERB-1082, National Research Council Canada, 2001.
9. Christian F. J. Lange and Michel R. V. Chaudron. An empirical assessment of completeness in UML designs. In *Proceedings of the 8th International Conference on Empirical Assessment in Software Engineering (EASE'04)*, pages 111–121, May 2004.
10. Christian F. J. Lange and Michel R. V. Chaudron. Managing model quality in UML-based software development. In *Proceedings of 13th IEEE International Workshop on Software Engineering and Practice (STEP '05)*, 2005.
11. Christian F. J. Lange, Michel R. V. Chaudron, and Johan Muskens. In practice: UML software architecture and design description. *IEEE Software*, 23(2):40–46, March 2006.
12. Object Management Group. *Reusable Asset Specification, version 2.2*, formal 05-11-02 edition, November 2005.
13. Object Management Group. *Unified Modeling Language, UML 2.0 Superstructure Specification*, formal/05-07-04 edition, July 2005.
14. Object Management Group. *Meta Object Facility (MOF) Core, v2.0*, formal/06-01-01 edition, January 2006.
15. Jan Verelst. The influence of the level of abstraction on the evolvability of conceptual models of information systems. *Empirical Software Engineering*, 10(4):467–494, 2005.

On the Application of Software Metrics
to UML Models

Jacqueline A. McQuillan and James F. Power

Department of Computer Science, National University of Ireland, Maynooth,
Co. Kildare, Ireland
{jmcq,jpower}@cs.nuim.ie
http://www.cs.nuim.ie/research/pop/

Abstract. In this position paper we discuss a number of issues relating
to model metrics, with particular emphasis on metrics for UML models.
Our discussion is presented as a series of nine observations where we
examine some of the existing work on applying metrics to UML models,
present some of our own work in this area, and specify some topics for
future research that we regard as important. Furthermore, we identify
three categories of challeges for model metrics and describe how our nine
observations can be partitioned into these categories.

Keywords: software metrics, object-oriented systems, UML,
metamodels.

1   Introduction

Many object-oriented metrics have been proposed specifically for the purpose
of assessing the design of a software system. However, most of the existing approaches to measuring these metrics involve the analysis of source code. As a
result, it is not always clear how to apply existing metrics at the early stages of
the software development process. With the increasing use of the Unified Modelling Language (UML) to model object-oriented systems at the early stages of
the software development process, research is required to investigate how the
metrics can be measured from UML models and prior to the implementation of
the system.

Being able to measure the metrics accurately from both UML models and
source code is important for several reasons:

- The quality of the system can be assessed in the early stages of the software
  life-cycle when it is still cost effective to make changes to the system.
- The implementation can be assessed to determine where it deviates from its
  design. This can be achieved by applying metrics to both the UML and source
  code and comparing the results. Variations in the metric values may help to
  identify parts of the implementation that do not conform to its design.
- Evaluation of the correctness of round trip engineering tools can be performed. Again, applying the same metrics to both the UML and source code

T. Kühne (Ed.): MoDELS 2006 Workshops, LNCS 4364, pp. 217–226, 2007.

may help in identifying parts of the system that have been incorrectly forward or reverse engineered.

In this position paper we review some of the existing work on applying metrics to UML models, present some of our own work in this area, and outline some topics for future research that we regard as important. However, in order to serve as a basis for discussion, we have chosen to present this position paper as a series of nine observations.

2   General Observations

In this section we present three basic observations regarding the nature of metric definitions and calculation at the model level. The observations themselves are hardly contentious, but they serve as a framework for discussing related work in the area.

Observation 1. Defining model metrics is a metamodelling activity.

Many metrics for object-oriented software have been proposed in the literature [1,2]. However, one of the difficulties with comparing and evaluating these metrics is in interpreting and understanding their exact definition. For example, when counting methods in a class, should constructors, finalisers/destructors and accessor methods count as ordinary methods? Should methods that are inherited but not defined in a class be included? Should abstract methods count as empty methods, or not at all? In order to answer these questions, it is necessary to model the entities being measured, and to then define the metrics in terms of this model. In standard terminology, metrics are defined on the metamodel of the entities being measured.

Several attempts have been made to address the problem of ambiguous metric definitions. Briand *et al.* propose an integrated measurement framework, based on a model of object-oriented systems, for the definition, evaluation and comparison of object-oriented coupling and cohesion metrics [3,4]. Harmer and Wilkie have developed an extensible metrics analyser tool for object-oriented programming languages based on a general object-oriented programming language metamodel in the form of a relational database schema [5]. Reißing defines metrics over a formal model called ODEM (Object-oriented DEsign Model) which consists of an abstraction layer built upon the UML metamodel [6].

Our own work uses a middle level model to define metrics over Java programs [7]. By defining metrics on this metamodel i.e. at the meta-level, we were able to quickly specify and implement a number of different versions of *cohesion* within a class, and evaluate the metrics over a number of large software systems.

Observation 2. Implementing metrics that are defined at the meta-level is (almost) free.

Using a clearly defined metamodel is important for facilitating unambiguous definitions of metrics, but it also has clear advantages in terms of implementation.

Many metamodelling frameworks facilitate the implementation of corresponding APIs that allow for the representation and traversal of model instances. The canonical example is the XML Metadata Interchange (XMI) for OMG's MetaObject Facility (MOF) [8], but closely related frameworks include the Eclipse Modelling Framework (EMF)[1] and the NetBeans Metadata Repository project (MDR)[2].

Previous research has exploited the implementation aspect of metamodels by defining metrics as queries. El-Wakil *et al.* propose the use of XQuery as a metric definition language to extract metric data from XMI design documents, specifically UML designs [9]. Harmer and Wilkie, working from a relational schema, express metric definitions as SQL queries over this schema [5]. Baroni *et al.* have built a library called FLAME (Formal Library for Aiding Metrics Extraction) that uses the Object Constraint Language (OCL) and the UML metamodel as a mechanism for defining UML-based metrics [10]. Goulão *et al.* have utilised this approach for defining component based metrics and used the UML 2.0 metamodel as a basis for their definitions [11].

In our own work, we have specified outline metrics on UML class diagrams, using OCL queries over the UML 2.0 metamodel [12]. The scope of such metrics is somewhat limited, since many of the features they measure relate to method internals, which are not available in class diagrams. Nonetheless, a prototype tool, *dMML*, was developed as an Eclipse plug-in to implement and measure these metrics [13].

However, some issues still exist. Assumptions have to be made when specifying how to instantiate the metamodels, such assumptions will have an effect on the metric definitions. In addition, the process of creating instances of the metamodels must be verified. Errors or omissions in this process would have a fundamental impact on the correctness of the calculated metrics.

Observation 3. Defining new metrics is (almost regrettably) easy.

One of the problems with software metrics is that they can be easy to define, but difficult to justify or correlate with external quality attributes. For example, Halstead's metrics [14] are often cited, but almost equally often criticised. Working at the model level provides a whole new layer of elements and relationships that can be grouped and counted. However, it is important to avoid the trap of proposing metrics that count these elements without offering evidence that such counts are really useful in evaluating the model. Much of the literature on the proposal of metrics for UML models has concentrated on only one or a small number of the different diagrams and views available in an overall UML specification of a software system. Furthermore, the majority of the UML metrics proposed are primarily simple counting metrics (e.g. number of use-cases in a model).

One of the earliest sets of metrics proposed for UML models are those described by Marchesi who propose metrics that can be applied to class and use

---

[1] http://www.eclipse.org/emf/

[2] http://mdr.netbeans.org/

case diagrams [15]. Genero *et al.* have proposed a set of metrics for assessing the structural complexity of class diagrams and have performed several experiments to empirically validate these metrics [16,17]. Various other metrics have been proposed for class diagrams and a comparison of these metrics can be found in [18]. Genero *et al.* have also developed a set of metrics for measuring the size and structural complexity of state-chart diagrams [19]. Kim and Boldyreff have defined a set of 27 metrics to measure various characteristics of a UML model [20]. However, the metrics are described informally and for some of these measures it is unclear which UML diagrams should be used to calculate the measures.

There has been relatively little work on measuring existing design metrics from *all* of the available views and diagrams of a UML model and there is as yet no convergence of opinion on the usefulness, or indeed the use, of these model level metrics.

3   Relationship with Code

The area of software metrics is reasonably well developed, and a discussion of model level metrics would be incomplete without considering what we can learn from existing lower level metrics. In particular, the relationship between models of a software system and the corresponding code can be explored through evaluation of similar metrics at each level of abstraction.

Observation 4. We can "lift" code metrics to the model level.

One of the most well known suites of object-oriented metrics is the one proposed by Chidamber and Kemerer (CK) [1]. These metrics were proposed to capture different aspects of an object-oriented design including complexity, coupling and cohesion. Several studies have been conducted to validate these metrics and have shown that they are useful quality indicators [21]. Baroni *et al.* have formalised the CK metrics using the OCL and the UML 1.3 metamodel [22]. We have also formalised the CK metrics using the OCL but have based our definitions on the UML 2.0 metamodel [12,13]. These definitions specify how to obtain the CK metrics from class diagrams but do not take any of the other UML diagrams into consideration. Tang and Chen have also attempted to specify how the CK metrics can be measured from UML diagrams [23]. They have developed an algorithm for computing the metrics from UML class, activity and communication diagrams.

The CK metrics suite consists of six metrics: Weighted Methods Per Class (WMC), Depth of Inheritance Tree (DIT), Number of Children (NOC), Coupling between Object Classes (CBO), Response For a Class (RFC), and Lack of Cohesion in Methods (LCOM). Each of the metrics refer to the individual class in the software system and not to the whole system. Figure 1 reviews each of these metrics and briefly discusses which UML diagrams need to be examined in order to gain accurate measures of the metrics.

In addition, it may be possible to obtain further information for the calculation of these metrics, e.g. method invocations and variable usages of methods and classes, by inspecting OCL constraints of the system. Interpreting such information requires further research.

Weighted methods per class (WMC): This metric is concerned with the complexity of the methods within a given class. It is equal to the sum of the complexities of each method defined in a class. If we consider the complexity of each method to be unity then the WMC metric for a class is equal to the number of methods defined within that class, we refer to this as WMC_1. The WMC_1 metric for a class can be obtained from the class diagrams of a UML model by identifying the class and counting the number of methods in that class. Alternatively, we can consider the complexity of each method to be McCabe's Cyclomatic complexity [2], which we refer to as WMC_{cc}. The activity, sequence and communication diagrams clearly contain information relevant to WMC_{cc}, but it is equally plausible that the state machine diagram could be used to compute this value for the class as a whole.

Number of children (NOC): This is the number of immediate descendants of a given class, that is the number of classes which directly inherit from the class. Again, this metric can be measured for a class by taking the union of all the class diagrams in a UML model and examining the inheritance relationships of the class.

Response for a class (RFC): This is a measure of the number of methods that can potentially be invoked by an object of a given class. The number of methods for a class can be obtained from a class diagram, but the number of methods of other classes that are invoked by each of the methods in the class requires information about the behaviour of the class. This information can be derived by inspecting the various behavioural diagrams, such as sequence and collaboration in order to identify method invocations.

Coupling between object classes (CBO): Two classes are coupled to each other if a method of one class uses an instance variable or method of the other class. An estimate for this metric can be obtained from the class diagrams by counting all the classes to which the class has a relationship with and counting all the reference types of the attributes and parameters of the methods of the class. To obtain a more precise value, information from the behavioural diagrams can be taken into account in order to get information about the usage of instance variable and invocation of methods. For example, a sequence diagram gives direct information about the interactions between methods in different classes.

Depth of inheritance tree (DIT): This is a measure of the depth of a class in the inheritance tree. It is equal to the maximum length from the class to the root of the inheritance tree. This metric can be computed for a class by taking the union of all the class diagrams in a UML model and traversing the inheritance hierarchy of the class.

Lack of cohesion in methods (LCOM): Calcuating the LCOM for a given class involves working out, for each possible pair of methods, whether the sets of instance variables accessed by each method have a non-empty intersection. In order, to compute a value for this metric, information on the usage of instance variables by the methods of a class is required. This information cannot be obtained from a class diagram. However, an upper bound for this metric can be computed using the number of methods in the class. Diagrams that contain information about variable usages, e.g. sequence diagrams can be used to compute this metric.

Fig. 1. An overview of applying the CK metrics to UML models. In this figure we review the diagrams in a UML model that can contribute to calculating the CK metrics.

Observation 5. Models can represent partial and/or overlapping information.

In the latest version of UML (2.0), there are 13 different basic diagrams that can be used to specify a software system. Existing object-oriented metric suites, such as the CK suite, are mainly relevant to class diagrams, since they measure structural elements of the design. Source code provides this information in the same format at the same level of abstraction but UML models can represent many different kinds of information. For example

- A single class may appear in a number of different class diagrams, with different degrees of elaboration of its attributes, methods and associations in each. This information needs to be merged in a consistent way before metric calculation.
- Some UML diagrams represent a view of a system, rather than a single overview. For examples, sequence diagrams are typically used to provide details of a usage scenario. It is not obvious how we should calculate metrics across such diagrams, and how we should merge the information from different diagrams with the same elements.

Defining how to integrate these different sources of information is a significant issue in model level metrics.

Observation 6. Differences between metric values are themselves metrics.

Ideally, following a Model Driven Architecture (MDA) approach to software development, the design models and the implementation are synchronised, so that changes in one are reflected in the other [24]. In practice, UML models can represent a design stage of a project, used perhaps once to develop a prototype implementation, and then not updated as the software develops. In this context, differences between the values of similar metrics measured at the model and source code level will reflect properties of the evolution of the system, rather than its design.

Even when models and implementation are synchronised, there will be a difference between metric values. For example, internal complexity measures for method bodies may not be available in the model, but can be calculated from the code. In this context, the model could be used to specify boundary values for the implementation, or the difference between metric values at the model and implementation level can capture the level of additional complexity added by the implementation process. For example, one might expect a prototype implementation to preserve many of the model level metric values, whereas the ultimate "real" implementation might introduce significant changes in the metric values.

Identifying differences between the values of the same metric applied to the same system could also have potential use in reverse engineering. It has already been noted that a significant level of variation exists between existing tools that reverse engineer class diagrams [25]. Software metrics, measured at the model level and then compared, can be used to evaluate the correctness of reverse engineering tools, or to quantify their perspective on the abstraction of high-level concepts, such as aggregation and composition, from the source code.

4   Some Future Directions

In this section we outline some directions for future research in the area of model level metrics that we regard as important.

Observation 7. Metric definitions should be re-usable.

Standard concepts measured by metrics, such as DIT or NOC, apply equally to models and code. Ideally, it should be possible to define these concepts once, and then adapt them to each relevant metamodel in turn. This provides not only for economy of expression, but also assurance that the same concepts are being measured at each level. However, this is not as easy as it may appear. Even a relatively simple metric, such as DIT, involves traversing relationships that may be represented quite differently in different models.

The simplest approach might be to define a single model over which the metrics are defined, and then apply transformations to map other models into this canonical model. However, given the range of UML diagrams, and possible contributions from language metamodels, a single canonical model may not be realistic. Instead, we may need to examine the possibility of mapping the metric definitions across different models.

Observation 8. The relationship between behavioural models and coverage needs to be explored.

A number of the UML diagrams represent behavioural aspects of a system, for example, use case, sequence and communication diagrams. Calculating metrics for such diagrams involves measuring a particular usage of the system, rather than its design as a whole. We have previously mentioned the difficulty of merging such partial information, but there are also unexplored issues regarding how such information should be interpreted.

Previous work, including our own, has explored some of the issues relating to defining and evaluating metrics at run-time [26,27]. Such metrics can be shown to capture additional information about the program but are, of course, dependent on the context in which the program is run. Indeed it is arguable that metrics at this level represent *coverage* data, rather than metrics in the usual sense. The use of such information, or its integration into testing strategies, is still relatively undeveloped.

Observation 9. Standardisation is multi-faceted; interoperability is the key.

One of the benefits of metamodelling is that interoperability between models is facilitated; metamodel Zoos [3] represent an important contribution here. However, there are other aspects that can contribute to comparing and evaluating metric results; some of these include:

- Benchmark suites
  The importance of benchmarks in software engineering in general, and in evaluating fact extractors in particular, has been noted by Sim *et al.* [28].

---

[3] For example, `http://www.eclipse.org/gmt/am3/zoos/`

They note the importance of benchmark suites, such as the SPEC suite, in other areas of computer science, and argue for a similar approach to software engineering research. Similarly, a call for benchmarks for software visualisation was issued in 2003 [29], but it is not clear what level of acceptance this has gained. The selection of a number of common programs and models for use in metric studies would greatly facilitate comparison between metrics and evaluation of new metrics.

– Data sets

An interesting recent development towards standardisation and repeatability of results is the *Promise Software Engineering Repository* [30]. This is a collection of publicly available datasets "created to encourage repeatable, verifiable, refutable, and/or improvable predictive models of software engineering". At the moment the repository is still in the early stages of development and contains relatively specialised data sets, but it represents a promising trend in software engineering research.

– Non-code artifacts

One of the difficulties in evaluating metrics at the UML level is the relatively small supply of UML and other design level artifacts. Open source software provides a rich source of information at the code level; it would be highly desirable if design level documents could be made available in a similar fashion. One initiative is the *Repository for Model Driven Development (ReMoDD)* project [31]. The objective of this project is to develop a repository of artifacts for use by researchers and industry practioners in the area of Model Driven Engineering of software systems. Also as an approximation, UML diagrams can be reverse engineered from code, and the reverse engineering community has already provided for interoperability through formalisms such as GXL [32] and our own *g4re* artifact repository [33]. However, reverse engineering artifacts are fundamentally different from design artifacts, and can at best only serve as an approximation for the real thing.

5   Summary

In this position paper we have discussed a number of issues relating to model metrics, with particular emphasis on metrics for UML models. We have structured our discussion around nine observations, which we can also partition into three levels of challenges for model metrics:

– The *technical challenge* of defining, comparing and reusing metrics over different descriptions of the same software system (Observations 1, 6, 7)
– The *conceptual challenge* of defining how to measure metrics from partial descriptions of models, and of the change in metrics between different representations of the software (Observations 3, 5, 8)
– The *practical challenge* of gathering, comparing and interpreting new and existing metrics (Observations 2, 4, 9)

Our own work in this area, as cited above, is concentrated on addressing the technical challenges of defining reusable metrics at the meta-level.

References

1. Chidamber, S., Kemerer, C.: A metrics suite for object oriented design. IEEE Transactions on Software Engineering **20**(6) (1994) 476–493
2. Fenton, N., Lawrence Pfleeger, S.: Software Metrics: A Rigorous and Practical Approach. International Thompson Computer Press (1996)
3. Briand, L., Daly, J., Wuest, J.: A unified framework for coupling measurement in object-oriented systems. IEEE Transactions on Software Engineering **25**(1) (1999) 91–121
4. Briand, L., Daly, J., Wuest, J.: A unified framework for cohesion measurement in object-oriented systems. Empirical Software Engineering **3**(1) (1998) 65–117
5. Wilkie, F., Harmer, T.: Tool support for measuring complexity in heterogeneous object-oriented software. In: IEEE International Conference on Software Maintenance, Montréal, Canada (October 3-6 2002)
6. Reißing, R.: Towards a model for object-oriented design measurement. In: ECOOP Workshop on Quantative Approaches in Object-Oriented Software Engineering, Budapest, Hungary (June 18-19 2001)
7. McQuillan, J., Power, J.: Experiences of using the Dagstuhl Middle Metamodel for defining software metrics. In: Proceedings of International Conference on Principles and Practices of Programming in Java, Manheim, Germany (August 30 - September 1 2006) 194–198
8. The Object Management Group: UML 2.0 draft superstructure specification (2003)
9. El-Wakil, M., El-Bastawisi, A., Riad, M., Fahmy, A.: A novel approach to formalize object-oriented design metrics. In: Evaluation and Assessment in Software Engineering, Keele, UK (April 11-12 2005)
10. Baroni, A., Brito e Abreu, F.: A formal library for aiding metrics extraction. In: ECOOP Workshop on Object-Oriented Re-Engineering, Darmstadt, Germany (July 21 2003)
11. Goulão, M., Brito e Abreu, F.: Formalizing metrics for COTS. In: ICSE Workshop on Models and Processes for the Evaluation of COTS Components, Edinburgh, Scotland (May 25 2004)
12. McQuillan, J., Power, J.: A definition of the Chidamber and Kemerer metrics suite for the Unified Modeling Language. Technical Report NUIM-CS-TR-2006-03, Dept. of Computer Science, NUI Maynooth, Co. Kildare, Ireland (October 2006)
13. McQuillan, J., Power, J.: Towards re-usable metric definitions at the meta-level. In: PhD Workshop of the 20th European Conference on Object-Oriented Programming, Nantes, France (July 4 2006)
14. Halstead, M.: Elements of Software Science. First edn. Elsevier, North Holland (1977)
15. Marchesi, M.: OOA metrics for the Unified Modeling Language. In: Second Euromicro Conference on Software Maintenance and Reengineering, Florence, Italy (March 8-11 1998)
16. Genero, M., Piattini, M., Calero, C.: Early measures for UML class diagrams. L'Object **6**(4) (2000) 489–515
17. Genero, M., Jimnez, L., Piattini, M.: A controlled experiment for validating class diagram structural complexity metrics. In: International Conference on Object-Oriented Information Systems, Montpellier, France (September 2-5 2002)
18. Yi, T., Wu, F., Gan, C.: A comparison of metrics for UML class diagrams. ACM SIGSOFT Software Engineering Notes **29**(5) (2005) 1–6

19. Genero, M., Miranda, D., Piattini, M.: Defining and validating metrics for UML statechart diagrams. In: 6th ECOOP Workshop on Quantitative Approaches in Object-oriented engineering, Malaga, Spain (June 11 2002)

20. Kim, H., Boldyreff, C.: Developing software metrics applicaple to UML models. In: 6th ECOOP Workshop on Quantitative Approaches in Object-oriented engineering, Malaga, Spain (June 11 2002)

21. Basili, V., Briand, L., Melo, W.: A validation of object-oriented design metrics as quality indicators. IEEE Transactions on Software Engineering **22**(10) (1996) 751–761,

22. Baroni, A., Brito e Abreu, F.: An OCL-based formalization of the MOOSE metric suite. In: Proceedings of ECOOP Workshop on Quantative Approaches in Object-Oriented Software Engineering, Darmstadt, Germany (July 22 2003)

23. Tang, M.H., Chen, M.H.: Measuring OO design metrics from UML. In: International Conference on The Unified Modeling Language, Dresden, Germany (September 30 - October 4 2002)

24. Warmer, J., Kleppe, A.: The Object Constraint Language. Addison-Wesley (2003)

25. Guéhéneuc, Y., Albin-Amiot, H.: Recovering binary class relationships: putting icing on the UML cake. In: Object Oriented Programming Systems Languages and Applications, Vancouver, BC, Canada (October 24-28 2004) 301–314

26. Arisholm, E., Briand, L., Foyen, A.: Dynamic coupling measures for object-oriented software. IEEE Transactions on Software Engineering **30**(8) (2004) 491–506

27. Mitchell, A., Power, J.: A study of the influence of coverage on the relationship between static and dynamic coupling metrics. Science of Computer Programming **59**(1-2) (January 2006) 4–25

28. Sim, S., Easterbrook, S., Holt, R.: Using benchmarking to advance research: A challenge to software engineering. In: International Conference on Software Engineering, Portland, Oregon, USA (May 3-10 2003) 74–83

29. Maletic, J., Marcus, A.: CFB: A call for benchmarks - for software visualization. In: 2nd IEEE Workshop of Visualizing Software for Understanding and Analysis, Amsterdam, The Netherlands (September 22 2003) 108–113

30. Shirabad, J.S., Menzies, T.J.: The PROMISE Repository of Software Engineering Databases. School of Information Technology and Engineering, University of Ottawa, Canada (2005)

31. Cheng, B., France, R., Bieman, J.: ReMoDD: A repository for model driven development

32. Holt, R., Schrr, A., Sim, S., Winter, A.: GXL: A graph-based standard exchange format for reengineering. Science of Computer Programming **60**(2) (2006) 149–170

33. Kraft, N., Malloy, B., Power, J.: Toward an infrastructure to support interoperability in reverse engineering. In: Working Conference on Reverse Engineering, Pittsburgh, PA (November 8-11 2005) 196–205

Summary of the Workshop Models@run.time at MoDELS 2006

Nelly Bencomo[1], Gordon Blair[1], and Robert France[1,2]

[1] Lancaster University, Comp. Dep., InfoLab21,
Lancaster, UK, LA1 4WA,
Computer Science Department, Colorado State University
Fort Collins, CO, USA, 80523-1873
{nelly,gordon}@comp.lancs.ac.uk, france@cs.colostate.edu

Abstract. The first edition of the workshop Models@run.time was co-located with the ACM/IEEE 9th International Conference on Model Driven Engineering Languages and Systems (formerly the UML series of conferences). The workshop took place in the antique city of Genoa, Italy, on the 1st of October, 2006. The workshop was organised by Gordon Blair, Robert France, and Nelly Bencomo. This summary gives an overview an account of the presentations and lively discussions that took place during the workshop.

Keywords: model-driven engineering, reflection, run-time systems.

1 Introduction

We are witnessing the emergence of new classes of application that are highly complex, inevitably distributed, and operate in heterogeneous and rapidly changing environments. Examples of such applications include those from pervasive and Grid computing domains. These systems are required to be adaptable, flexible, reconfigurable and, increasingly, self-managing. Such characteristics make systems more prone to failure when executing and thus the development and study of appropriate mechanisms for run-time validation and monitoring is needed.

In the model-driven software development area, research effort has focused primarily on using models at design, implementation, and deployment stages of development. This work has been highly productive with several techniques now entering the commercialisation phase. The use of model-driven techniques for validating and monitoring run-time behaviour can also yield significant benefits. A key benefit is that models can be used to provide a richer semantic base for run-time decision-making related to system adaptation and other run-time concerns. For example, one can use models to help determine when a system should move from a consistent architecture to another consistent architecture. Model-based monitoring and management of executing systems can play a significant role as we move towards implementing the key self-* properties associated with autonomic computing.

T. Kühne (Ed.): MoDELS 2006 Workshops, LNCS 4364, pp. 227–231, 2007.

Goal

The goal of this workshop was to look at issues related to developing appropriate model-driven approaches to managing and monitoring the execution and operation of systems. This is the first MoDELS workshop to address this theme. The workshop brought together researchers from a variety of communities including researchers working on model-driven software engineering, software architectures, computational reflection, and autonomic and self healing systems. At least twenty-seven people attended from Austria, Brazil, France, Germany, Italy, Norway, the UK and the US.

The call for papers invited submissions on a number of focus topics including: Relevance and suitability of different model-driven approaches to monitoring and managing systems during run-time, Compatibility (or tension) between different model-driven approaches, Forms of run-time models, Relation with other phases of the software engineering lifecycle, Maintainability and validation of models, and The role of reflection in maintaining the causal connection between models and run-time systems.

In response to the call for papers, nine (9) papers were submitted, of which five (5) papers were accepted for long presentation and two (2) papers for short presentation. Each submitted paper was reviewed by 3 program committee members. After lengthy discussions two papers were chosen as the best papers; the decision took into account the quality of the papers and the relevance of the papers to the goals of the workshop. These papers were extended and improved. The extended versions of these two papers are published in this proceeding.

2   Workshop Format

The workshop was designed to facilitate focused discussion on the use of models during run time. It was structured into presentation and work (discussion) sessions. During the morning the guest speaker Prof. Betty Cheng from Michigan State University gave the talk "*Modeling and Analyzing Dynamically Adaptive Software*". This presentation was based on the article "Model-Based Development of Dynamically Adaptive Software" that received an ACM SIGSOFT Distinguished Paper Award in ICSE'06, [1]. Betty presented an approach to creating formal models of adaptive software behaviour. The approach separates the adaptation behaviour and non-adaptive behaviour specifications of adaptive programs, making the models easier to specify and more amenable to automated analysis and visual inspection. Betty presented a process to construct adaptation models, automatically generate adaptive programs from the models, and verify and validate the models. The content of her talk was strongly relevant to the workshop and provided a good kick off and inspiration for lively discussion during the rest of the day.

After Betty's talk, the paper sessions followed. There were two types of presentations, full presentations and short presentations. To ensure effectiveness of the format full presentations were limited to 10 minutes and short presentations were limited to 5 minutes. Both kinds of presentations were followed by 5 minutes of discussion and questions. Furthermore, to facilitate an informed and fruitful discussion, the full presentations were followed by presentations of paper analyses by assigned independent readers. Each independent reader was someone other than a paper author assigned to discuss the extent to which the paper had addressed the research questions posed in the Call for Papers. After the presentations of the accepted papers, invited speaker Veronique Normand from Thales Research and Technology gave a presentation about the project MODELPLEX.

The afternoon was dedicated to focused discussions on research challenges. Gordon Blair, who was a patient and watchful observer during the morning, took note of the raised questions and comments. Based on his comments and observations, he gave final remarks to shape the discussions of the rest of the afternoon.

The workshop was closed by a general discussion, including an evaluation of the event itself by the participants. Details of the various sessions and other events are provided in Sections 3 and 4 below. The proposed format worked very well, with all attendees contributing to the workshop through full, open, constructive and friendly discussion.

3 Session Summaries

Nelly Bencomo welcomed the participants and explained the motivation and format of the workshop.

Session 1
The session chair of the session was Robert France who introduced and chaired the discussions of the presentation of the papers:

"*Experiments in Run-Time Model Extraction*", presented by Jean Bézivin.

"*Applying OMG D&C Specification and ECA Rules for Autonomous Distributed Component-based Systems*", presented by Jérémy Dubus. Fabio Costa was the second reader.

"*Models at Run-time for sustaining User Interface Plasticity*", presented by Jean-Sébastien Sottet. Arnor Solberg was the second reader.

Session 2
After the coffee break, the second session started. The chair of the session was Nelly Bencomo, who introduced and managed the discussions about the papers:

"*A Run-time Model for Multi-Dimensional Separation of Concerns*", presented by Ruzanna Chitchyan. Jon Oldevik was the second reader.

"*Towards a More Effective Coupling of Reflection and Run-time Metamodels for Middleware*", presented by Fabio Costa. Jean-Marc Jezequel was the second reader.

"*Model-driven development of self-managing software*", presented by Marko Boskovic. Steffen Zschaler was the second reader.

After lunch an invited presentation on the MODELPLEX project was given by Veronique Normand. Several related topics were covered by her presentation. During her talk she discussed how important it is that humans are treated as key parts when making decisions and when defining models. In addition, several perspectives have to be handled, for example design-time system configuration and operation time system reconfiguration or design-time vs. operation time verification. This last statement was repeated by other presenters during the workshop.

Gordon Blair then provided a summary of the morning. He started off by commenting that we had seen an interesting jigsaw of pieces and it was up to us to put all the pieces together in the afternoon. He followed this by stating that this problem area is probably impossible to solve in the general case and most of the successful work we heard about in the morning narrowed the problem either by focusing on a given application domain and/or by focusing on a particular design methodology (e.g. components, AOSD). He also commented that when addressing the problems it is important to appreciate the reality of distributed systems and solutions must be scalable, must perform well, and must be extensible.

He then highlighted the important role of the software engineering process in identifying complete methodologies for adaptive and autonomic systems (see for example the invited talk by Betty Cheng). It is the premise of the workshop that models have a role throughout such a methodology from early requirements through to run-time.

He commented that many of the contributions in the morning concerned models for run-time, i.e. examples of models that had a role to play during the run-time of the system, whereas what we really need is to step forward and have models at run-time, i.e. models that are an intrinsic part of the systems architecture. This requires a clear understanding of appropriate models, of the running system and of the relationship between them. This leads to the inevitable conclusion that we are concerned with reflection, where the models represent a causally connected self-representation of the system at run-time.

The summary concluded by highlighting some key questions to shape the rest of the discussions:

1. What should a run-time model look like?
2. How can the models be maintained at run-time?
3. What is their role in system validation?
4. What are the best overall model-driven approaches for adaptive and autonomous systems?

In addition, it is important to reflect on the following key meta-level questions:

1. What do we know (useful building blocks)?
2. What do we not know (towards a roadmap)?
3. .... And of course, what should we do next!

4 Discussions

The rest of the afternoon saw the group divided in two discussion subgroups. Both groups shared the same interests and discussed the same set of questions. Summary reports were produced by the leader discussant of each breakout session (Ruzanna Chitchyan and Steffen Zschaler). As the two breakout groups reassembled to summarize their work it was interesting to see how different groups reached very similar conclusions.

When defining what a run-time model looks like both groups coincide in saying that it is related with reflection as it is necessary to have a self representation of the system in operation. A run-time model is no different from any other model where a model is defined as a simpler representation of "reality" that serves a given purpose. The model in this case should be an ongoing representation of the system that is running. There should be a causal connection between the run-time model and the system on execution. The defined model will depend on the problem that is being tackled. Run-time models can offer support to simplify decision making and manipulation, can drive the execution of the application or simply can support for debugging, validation, monitoring, and maintainability.

Each of the questions posed by Gordon cannot be answered without more research. There is need to promote research that explores diverse ways of adapting software during run-time. Furthermore, presentations and discussions make us consider that model-driven approaches offer valuable potential to support run-time adaptability. Model-driven software development would help providing the infrastructure to reconfigure and adapt a run-time system based on input QoS and context based values. The perspective of models at run-time consists in bringing this model-based capability forward to the run-time.

In the end, the workshop itself was evaluated. The organizers asked the participants to provide feedback about the workshop and attendants declared to be very satisfied with the presentations and discussions. It was concluded that the research community should be encouraged to study the issues raised during this workshop.

Acknowledgments. We would also like to thank the members of the program committee who acted as anonymous reviewers and provided valuable feedback to the authors: Jan Aagedal, Walter Cazzola, Wolfgang Emmerich, Gang Huang, Jean-Marc Jezequel, Rui Silva Moreira, Marten van Sinderen, Arnor Solberg, and Thaís Vasconcelos Batista. Last but not least, the authors of all submitted papers are thanked for helping us making this workshop possible.

Reference

1. J. Zhang and B. H. C. Cheng:Model-Based Development of Dynamically Adaptive Software. in *International Conference on Software Engineering (ICSE'06)*, (China, 2006).

Using Runtime Models to Unify and Structure the Handling of Meta-information in Reflective Middleware⋆

Fábio Moreira Costa, Lucas Luiz Provensi, and Frederico Forzani Vaz

Institute of Computing, Federal University of Goiás
Campus Samambaia, UFG, 74690-815, Goiânia-GO, Brazil
{fmc,lucas,frederico}@inf.ufg.br
http://www.inf.ufg.br/~fmc

Abstract. Reflection plays an important role in the flexibilisation of middleware platforms. Through dynamic inspection, middleware interfaces can be discovered and invoked at runtime, and through adaptation the structure and behaviour of the platform can be modified on-the-fly to meet new user or environment demands. Metamodeling, on the other hand, has shown its value for the static configuration of middleware and other types of system as well. Both techniques have in common the pervasive use of meta-information as the means to provide the system's self-representation. However similar they are, these two techniques usually fall on different sides of a gap, namely development time and runtime, with little interplay between them. In this paper, we review our approach for the combination of reflection and metamodeling, presenting some concrete applications of the concept in the context of distributed systems middleware, as well as proposing further potential applications.

Keywords: Runtime metamodels, Structural reflection, Reflective middleware.

1 Introduction

Meta-information is at the core of both reflection [1] and metamodeling [2] techniques. It is the means through which the reified features of a base-level system (such as a middleware platform) are represented in reflective architectures. It is also the reason for metamodeling techniques to exist, that is, to represent meta-information in a consistent way. Although metamodeling usually deals with meta-information in a well-structured way, reflection typically handles it in an ad hoc fashion. On the other hand, while metamodeling is traditionally limited to the static (*cf.* design time) representation of meta-information, reflection enables its dynamic use and evolution. It thus seems natural to combine the two techniques, enabling the dynamic use of well-structured meta-information.

⋆ This work was funded by CNPq-Brazil (the Brazilian Government's agency for the promotion of scientific and technological development), grants 478620/2004-7 and 506689/2004-2.

T. Kühne (Ed.): MoDELS 2006 Workshops, LNCS 4364, pp. 232–241, 2007.

In the approach advocated in this paper, the structures of meta-information represented in a metamodel are kept accessible at runtime. As such, they can be used both at static configuration time, before the system is put to run, and at runtime, as the basis for the reflective meta-objects to construct the representation of the reified base-level system. While other approaches can be found in the literature for the combination of metamodeling and reflection, such as in [3] and [4], we believe that the approach discussed here is a more natural fit, besides its potential to be applied in conjunction with those other approaches.

This paper discusses the basic ideas of our approach and presents some of its concrete applications in the context of middleware platforms. The paper is structured as follows. Section 2 discusses the fundamental concepts of reflection and metamodeling as they are used in our work. Section 3 discusses the relationship between reflection and metamodeling and presents our approach for the combination of the two techniques. The use of the approach for middleware configuration and runtime adaptation in diverse and dynamic deployment environments is also illustrated in this section. Further extensions and applications of the approach are considered in Section 4, while Section 5 discusses and compares related work. Finally, Section 6 presents some concluding remarks.

2 Foundations

2.1 Reflection

The adopted approach to reflective middleware is based on the Lancaster Open ORB project [5]. The architecture is clearly divided into a *base-level*, which contains the usual middleware functionality (such as remote binding, remote method execution, and object references), and a *meta-level*, which provides the reification of the base-level features. Both the base- and meta-level are defined in terms of a uniform component model, which facilitates the identification, at runtime, of the several functional elements of the platform. The meta-level is accessed through meta-interfaces that expose a well-defined meta-object protocol for both inspection and modification (a.k.a. adaptation) of the base-level. Furthermore, in order to cope with complexity, the meta-level is further divided into four meta-space models: *interface* (for the discovery of an interface's methods and attributes, as well as for dynamic invocation); *interception* (for interposing extra behaviour in the pre/post-processing of interactions); *architecture* (for the manipulation of the component configuration of the platform); and *resources* (which allow the underlying resources, such as memory and processor, to be inspected and reconfigured). Critically, these meta-space models are concerned with particular kinds of meta-information about the features of the base-level system, although not necessarily in a structured or unified way. In this paper, we address this limitation.

2.2 Metamodeling

Metamodeling is achieved through the four-level approach of the Meta-Object Facility (MOF) [6]. The first level (level 0) represents the actual system entities, while, level 1 contains the model from which those entities were instantiated. Level 2 then consists of the meta-model, which defines a language for describing models, while Level 3 is the core language for describing meta-models. In the context of metamodeling for middleware, we are particularly interested in levels 2 and 1, which represent, respectively, the platform's type system, and the actual definitions of the (types and templates of the) entities that comprise particular middleware configurations. Using a metamodeling tool such as the MOF or, more recently, the Eclipse Modeling Framework (EMF) [7], a middleware metamodel can be defined and customised, allowing the automatic generation of tools (such as a repository) that facilitate the definition and storage of types and templates. Finally, from the type and template meta-information items that are kept in the repository, generic factories can be used to instantiate concrete platform configurations (level 0).

The implementation of this meta-information management tool in EMF is currently under work. When using EMF, it is worth noting that this technology is mainly meant for model-driven engineering, where a model of a system is defined and tools are used to automatically generate code for the system. That is, metamodeling is not a main intent of EMF. However, the distinction between a model and a metamodel is only a matter of reference point, that is, a model can be taken as the (meta-)model of a another model, instead of directly modeling a level 0 system. In our case, thus, the metamodel of a middleware platform is defined as a usual core model in EMF. Then, the code that is generated from this model (extended with a few customisations) is actually the implementation of a meta-information repository to store definitions of custom middleware components. This repository contains facilities for creating, accessing, deleting and evolving (see below) such meta-information. The interpretation and use of this meta-information is outside the scope of EMF and is performed, as described above, by external component factories, which are provided in the form of middleware services. In addition, although EMF is mainly meant to be used within Eclipse, with the exception of the UI editor, the generated implementation can be used by standalone applications. Indeed, the generated EMF.edit plug-in can be customised with extensions and used as a true repository of model-related meta-information, which can be accessed by standalone Java applications (such as by the factories mentioned above) through a programmatic interface.

3   Combining Reflection and Metamodeling

The reflection and meta-information approaches described above have been combined in a reflective middleware architecture called Meta-ORB [8]. This architecture was first prototyped in Python [9] as a reference implementation. It was later reimplemented in Java, using both J2SE and J2ME, aiming at its deployment in portable devices. This latter implementation is called MetaORB4Java [10]. Although a complete description of this platform is outside the scope of this position paper, in the following we describe its main features in what concerns the combination of reflection and metamodeling.

3.1   The Meta-ORB Metamodel

The Meta-ORB architecture is actually a meta-architecture for middleware. Its core consists of a type system defining the constructs that can be used to define special-purpose entities used to build custom middleware configurations. The main constructs are components (which encapsulate functionality) and binding objects (which encapsulate interaction behaviour). A particular middleware configuration can be built in terms of a composition of components interconnected by binding objects (which are, themselves, recursively defined in terms of component and binding compositions).

This type system is represented as a metamodel according to the EMF core modeling constructs and the EMF Eclipse plug-in was used to generate a basic repository implementation. This basic repository consists of the implementation of model elements, with the standard EMF accessor methods, plus editting functions (both programmatic and UI-based). This repository is currently being extended with more elaborate accessor methods, in a way that resembles the CORBA Interface Repository [11]. For instance, the *lookup_name* and *lookup_id* methods were introduced to enable the search for type definitions in the repository hierarchy based on their short names or fully qualified names, respectively.

Figure 1 presents the main parts of the platform's metamodel. It is organised in terms of four packages. The BaseIDL package is based on the core constructs of the CORBA type system, with features that describe the primitive and constructed data types used in the definition of models. The Component_and_Bindings package defines the constructs used to define component and binding objects, which are the central structural concepts when building platform configurations. The Interfaces package defines the language to define the interfaces of components and binding objects, while the Media_QoS package defines the primitives used to associate media types and QoS annotations to interface definitions.

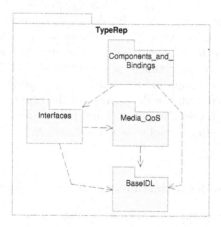

Fig. 1. High-level view of the Meta-ORB metamodel

3.2   Using the Model to Instantiate Platform Configurations

As a representative example of the use of the repository, component and binding definitions are expressed as instances of their corresponding metamodel elements and stored in the repository. For instance, the definition of a binding
type/template consists of the (names of the) types of the interfaces that the
binding is used to connect at its several endpoints, together with a graph of
internal components and bindings (which are refered to by the names of their
respective types) that comprise the internal configuration of the binding. The
creation of such type definitions can be easily done using the generated UI-based
editor plug-in. Two generic factories were implemented, respectively for the creation of components and binding objects. These factories obtain the necessary
meta-information elements from the repository (using the *lookup*-like methods
described above) and use them as the blueprint to create concrete, customised,
middleware configurations composed of components interconnected by binding
objects. Note that a single type definition can be used to define the whole platform configuration. This can be the definition of a distributed binding object
composed of internal components and other, lower-level, bindings. Although this
recursive structure is mirrored in the repository (in terms of separate type definitions that contain or reference other type definitions), the factories (the binding
factory in this case) only needs to be given the name (or *id*) of the outermost
type definition; the type definitions for the internal components and bindings are
implicitly obtained by the factories without the intervention of the middleware
developer.

Figure 2 illustrates the process of instantiating a new binding object in terms
of meta-information obtained from the Type Repository. From the binding type
and the types of the interfaces to be bound, the factory works out the number and
types of binding endpoints that need to be created. The factory then retrieves
the endpoint definitions (EndPDefA and EndPDefB) from the repository. As
each endpoint is to be created in a different location, the factory delegates their
creation to local factories at each host. Although not shown in the figure, it is the
job of the local factories to retrieve detailed meta-information (e.g., component
types) from the repository to guide the instantiation of the components that
make up each of the binding endpoints. Interestingly, the local factories can
distinguish the kind of environment where the endpoint is being deployed, in
order to instantiate an appropriate version of its configuration. In particular,
we have experimented with the deployment of distributed binding objects in a
heterogeneous environment composed of desktop computers and PDAs, where a
minimal version of endpoint configuration is chosen for deployment on the latter
kind of machine.

3.3   Using the Model to Instantiate Reflective Meta-objects

From the moment particular middleware configurations have been instantiated
and put to run, they can also be subject to the reflection mechanisms of the
platform (see Section 2.1). This means that the components and binding objects

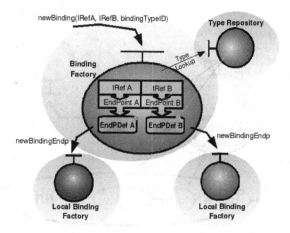

Fig. 2. Using the Type Repository to build platform configurations – an example show-ing the instantiation of a distributed binding object

that make up a configuration can be inspected and adapted at run time. In order to enable this, the meta-objects that perform the reflection mechanisms need precise meta-information about such components and bindings in order to reify them. The meta-objects obtain this meta-information from the respective component and binding definitions stored in the repository. For instance, as illustrated in Figure 3, in order to reify the internal configuration of a binding object, the architecture meta-object needs to obtain the part of that binding's definition that describes the component graph (where the nodes are component types and the edges are either local or distributed bindings) used to instantiate the binding. From that point on, the meta-object can be used to manipulate the binding's self-representation in a causally-connected way, i.e., with all changes in the representation being reflected in the actual structure of the binding object. Notice that this self-representation is an exact copy of the corresponding meta-information defined in the configuration's model.

The above subsections illustrate one side of the combination of reflection and metamodeling proposed in this work. The other side is related to the use of reflection to build new component and binding types that are persisted in the repository, and is described next.

3.4   Creating New Model Elements Using Reflection

This side of the combined approach refers to the evolution of a model's elements as a result of reflection. More specifically, architectural reflection can be used to dynamically change a component or binding object so that it becomes more suitable to varying operating conditions or user requirements. Often, this process leads to new component and binding definitions that might be useful in other contexts. Therefore, there is a case for making such evolved definitions persistent

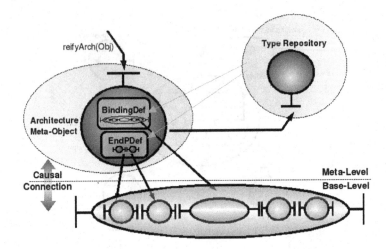

Fig. 3. Using the Type Repository to get the necessary meta-information to initialise an architecture meta-object

so they can be reused later. In our approach, these evolved definitions take the form of *versions* of the original component or binding definitions (so as to avoid potential conflicts with other existing definitions) and are stored in the repository alike. Later, they can be retrieved by factories in order to generate new instances of components and bindings that incorporate, from the begining, the results of the adaptations that were made through reflection.

4   Further Applications of the Approach

As can be seen from the above, the integrated management of middleware configuration and dynamic adaptation is a direct benefit of the uniform treatment given to meta-information. More precisely, the same constructs used to statically configure a middleware platform also constitute the primitives through which dynamic adaptation is achieved.

More recently, we are investigating the use of this technique to model other aspects of middleware platforms, in particular: resource management in grid computing middleware, and context-awareness in middleware for mobile computing. In the former, an extension of the metamodel is being defined to model the several kinds of resources available in the machines of a grid, such as processing power, memory capacity and network bandwidth. This meta-information will be used to flexibly (re-)configure the scheduling and allocation of tasks to processors. In the latter, a metamodel is being defined to allow the representation of context meta-information associated with the entities in a mobile computing environment, such as users, devices and applications. This will enable well-informed, i.e., context-aware, architectural adaptation of the Meta-ORB platform. As a consequence of this extension, the metamodel now has constructs to also represent the entities of the platform's deployment environment. In both cases, the advantage of using a runtime explicit metamodel is the intrinsic extensibility, which allows new kinds of resource or context meta-information to be seamlessly integrated into the system in a dynamic way. Such dynamic extensions of the meta-model can be matched by corresponding architectural adaptations on the parts of the middleware that are responsible for the manipulation of context and resource meta-information. In general, we believe that any kind of meta-information present in a system (such as a middleware platform) can be leveraged by the ability to represent it as part of a runtime metamodel integrated with reflective capabilities.

5 Related Work

A number of research efforts have approached the theme of using runtime models for configuration and dynamic adaptation. The Adaptive Object Model approach [3] is among the first ones. It uses a runtime model of a system in order to facilitate dynamic changes to the business rules of the system. Instead of coding the changes, the user can modify the system's model and those changes are reflected into the actual system. This work is similar to ours in the sense the the runtime model is causally connected to the system. However, it mainly deals with application-level structural adaptation, whereas we are interested in adaptation at the underlying middleware level. In addition, the AOM approach is not explicitly based on a metamodelling technique, which means that the metamodel governing the runtime models is essentially fixed.

The reflective middleware families approach [12,13] is another current effort towards merging reflection and runtime modelling. The approach is based on visual domain-specific modelling techniques to model component frameworks for middleware. The model is used to generate particular middleware configurations that conform to a family/framework, as well as to consistently adapt such configurations at runtime. This work is similar to ours in that the runtime model is effectively used as a basis for reflective adaptation. However, it does not make an explicit definition of the meta-model that governs the definition of domain-specific models – there is a fixed meta-model, namely the OpenCOMv2 component model [14], without explicit provisions for its extension. In addition, the issue of evolving the model as a result of dynamic adaptations, as proposed in our work, is not considered.

In a more general context, we can compare our work with the trend towards model-driven architecture [15] and, more generally, model-driven engineering [16,17]. In common with our approach, modelling is used to describe the architecture of a system and to generate particular configurations conforming to the architecture. However, the use of models in MDE is mostly restricted to static (i.e., configuration) time, without an option to use the model to guide dynamic adaptations at runtime. In addition, the work on MDE has been mainly focused on application development, whereas our work focuses on middleware platform configuration and reconfiguration. On the other hand, the MDA emphasis on the mapping from platform-independent models to platform-specific models, so as to model distributed applications on a middleware-neutral basis, is not addressed in our work.

Finally, considering other kinds of meta-information and their association with reflection, the CARISMA middleware [18] provides an environment where reflection and metadata (more specifically, context-related metadata) are integrated to provide the basis for runtime adaptation. Both structural and behavioural adaptation are carried out as a result of changes in the application's context, which in turn are detected by changes in the corresponding metadata. Similarly to our work, metadata is used as part of the systems self-representation. Differing their work from ours is the fact that there is not an emphasis on the definition of an explicit metamodel with clearly defined and common constructs and tools that are used to model context and architectural metadata, as well as to perform runtime adaptation.

6 Concluding Remarks

This paper has reviewed the main ideas and applications of our approach for the combination of runtime metamodels with reflection in the context of distributed systems middleware. The approach focuses on the integration of the design-time and runtime uses of an explicit metamodel for middleware (with all the related meta-information) with reflective introspection and adaptation techniques. The main benefit is the uniform treatment given to static configuration and dynamic reconfiguration of the platform, which are based on the common constructs and abstractions defined in the metamodel. While other approaches have been proposed in the literature to integrate reflection-like techniques and modeling, as described in section 5, we believe that an effective integration can only be achieved when such uniformity is present. In this way, it is possible to aply the same knowledge and tools at configuration time and at runtime.

Although the core ideas of our approach have been around for a while [8,19], its potential contribution is still underexploited. We believe that the exploitation of the proposed ideas in mainstream middleware platforms, in conjunction with more ellaborate techniques for architectural reflection and separation of concerns, can be of great benefit for the advancement of flexible and adaptive middleware technologies. It is our goal to contribute to raise this discussion in both the middleware and the modeling communities, aiming to identify new research opportunities in the area of reflective middleware and runtime metamodels.

References

1. Maes, P.: Concepts and experiments in computational reflection. In: ACM Conference on Object-Oriented Programming, Systems, Languages and Applications (OOPSLA'87), Orlando, FL USA, American Computer Machinery, ACM Press (1987)
2. Odell, J.: Meta-modeling. In: Proceedings of OOPSLA'95 Workshop on Metamodeling in Object-Orientation, ACM (1995)

3. Yoder, J.W., Balaguer, F., Johnson, R.: Architecture and design of adaptive object-models. SIGPLAN Not. **36**(12) (2001) 50–60
4. Bencomo, N., Blair, G.S., Coulson, G., Batista, T.: Towards a meta-modelling approach to configurable middleware. In: 2nd ECOOP2005 Workshop on Reflection, AOP and Meta-Data for Software Evolution, Glasgow, Scotland (July 2005)
5. Blair, G.S., Costa, F.M., Saikoski, K., Clarke, N.P.H.D.M.: The design and implementation of Open ORB version 2. IEEE Distributed Systems Online Journal **2**(6) (2001)
6. OMG: Meta Object Facility (MOF). Object Management Group, Needham, MA (2000) OMG Document formal/2000-04-03.
7. Budinsky, F., Steinberg, D., Merks, E., Ellersick, R., Grose, T.J.: Eclipse Modeling Framework. The Eclipse Series. Addison Wesley (2004)
8. Costa, F.M.: Combining Meta-Information Management and Reflection in an Architecture for Configurable and Reconfigurable Middleware. Ph.D. thesis, University of Lancaster, Lancaster, UK (September 2001) http://www.comp.lancs.ac.uk/computing/users/fmc/pubs/thesis.pdf.
9. Costa, F.M.: Meta-ORB: A highly configurable and adaptable reflective middleware platform. In: Proceedings of the 20th Brazilian Symposium on Computer Networks, Buxzios-RJ-Brazil, Brazilian Computer Society (2002) 735–750
10. Costa, F.M., Santos, B.S.: Structuring reflective middleware using meta-information management: The Meta-ORB approach and prototypes. Journal of the Brazilian Computer Society **10**(1) (2004) 43–58
11. OMG: The Common Object Request Broker: Architecture and Specification. Rev. 3.0 edn. Object Management Group, Needham, MA USA (2003)
12. Bencomo, N., Blair, G.: Genie: a domain-specific modeling tool for the generation of adaptive and reflective middleware families. In: The 6th OOPSLA Workshop on Domain-Specific Modeling, Portland, USA (October 2006)
13. Bencomo, N., Blair, G., Grace, P.: Models, reflective mechanisms and family-based systems to support dynamic configuration. In: Workshop on MOdel Driven Development for Middleware (MODDM), held with the 7th International Middleware Conference, Melbourne, Australia (November 2006)
14. Coulson, G., Blair, G.S., Grace, P., Joolia, A., Lee, K., Ueyama, J.: OpenCOM v2: A component model for building systems software. In: Proceedings of IASTED Software Engineering and Applications (SEA'04), Cambridge-MA, USA (November 2004)
15. OMG: MDA Guide Version 1.0.1. Object Management Group. (June 2003)
16. Schmidt, D.C.: Guest editor's introduction: Model-driven engineering. Computer **39**(2) (February 2006) 25–31
17. Bézivin, J.: In search of a basic principle for model driven engineering. The European Journal for the Informatics Professional **V**(2) (April 2004) 21–24
18. Capra, L., Emmerich, W., Mascolo, C.: CARISMA: Context-Aware Reflective mIddleware System for Mobile Applications. IEEE Transactions on Software Engineering **29**(10) (October 2003) 929–945
19. Costa, F.M., Blair, G.S.: Integrating reflection and meta-information management in middleware. In: Proceedings of the International Symposium on Distributed Objects and Applications (DOA'00), Antwerp, Belgium, IEEE, IEEE (2000)

Applying OMG D&C Specification and ECA Rules for Autonomous Distributed Component-Based Systems

Jérémy Dubus and Philippe Merle

INRIA Futurs, Jacquard Project
Laboratoire d'Informatique Fondamentale de Lille - UMR CNRS 8022
Université des Sciences et Technologies de Lille - Cité Scientifique
59655 Villeneuve d'Ascq Cedex France
Jeremy.Dubus@inria.fr, Philippe.Merle@inria.fr

Abstract. Manual administration of complex distributed applications is almost impossible to achieve. On the one side, work in autonomic computing focuses on systems that maintain themselves, driven by high-level policies. Such a self-administration relies on the concept of a control loop. The *autonomic computing control loop* involves an abstract representation of the system to analyze the situation and to adapt it properly. On the other side, models are currently used to ease design of complex distributed systems. Nevertheless, at runtime, models remain useless, because they are decoupled from the running system, which dynamically evolves. Our proposal, named DACAR, introduces models in the control loop. Using adequate models, it is possible to design and execute both the distributed systems and their autonomic policies. The metamodel suggested in this paper mixes both OMG Deployment and Configuration (OMG D&C) specification and the Event-Condition-Action (ECA) metamodels. This paper addresses the different concerns involved in the control loop and focuses on the metamodel concepts that are required to express entities of the control loop. This paper also gives an overview of our DACAR prototype and illustrates it on a ubiquitous application case study.

1 Introduction

While being more and more complex, business applications are also distributed on an increasing number of machines. The resulting heterogeneity of the *deployment domain* —*i.e.* the set of machines that host these applications— makes deployment and maintenance of these applications become critical tasks. In particular, with the emergence of grid and ubiquitous computing [5,14], human administration of applications is almost impossible to achieve, since the deployment domain is not statically known at deployment-time. Moreover, it can strongly evolve during runtime (*e.g.* nodes can appear or disappear dynamically). This statement led to the creation of a new research topic called *Autonomic Computing* [10]. Work in autonomic computing focuses on systems able to maintain

T. Kühne (Ed.): MoDELS 2006 Workshops, LNCS 4364, pp. 242–251, 2007.
© Springer-Verlag Berlin Heidelberg 2007

themselves during runtime, driven by high-level policies. In autonomic computing, the *control loop* is the core concept that helps in achieving autonomic management and reconfiguration of applications. This control loop involves an abstract representation of the system analyzing the situation and adapting the application properly. There is a causal link between the abstract representation of the system and the running system.

Models are widely employed to design distributed applications. The use of models allows the designer to only specify an abstract view of a system to be deployed. Using these abstract models, many approaches (*e.g.* the *Model-Driven Architecture* [7]) are able to generate a more concrete view of the system, and the task of the designer is drastically simplified. Unfortunately, the models of an application become useless once the system is deployed, since models and systems are decoupled and they evolve independently. However, introducing models as the abstract representation of a system in the autonomic computing control loop makes the use of models still relevant at runtime. The model is causally linked to the running system, and it evolves in the same way. Then autonomic computing can benefit from the use of models by having a complete abstract representation of the system to extract fine-grained information, and then apply the adequate reconfiguration.

DACAR (for *Distributed Autonomous Component-based ARchitectures*) is our proposal that consists in establishing a metamodel that mixes the OMG D&C specification [8] and ECA rules [3], in order to inject models as computation basis in autonomic computing.

The remainder of the paper is organized as follows. Section 2 presents the fundamental principles of autonomic computing as defined in [10]. Section 3 discusses the key research challenges to address the problem of introducing models in autonomic computing. Section 4 presents DACAR, our proposition for model-based autonomic computing. An illustrative ubiquitous example is detailled in Section 5. Section 6 discusses other work related to autonomic distributed component-based systems. Finally, Section 7 exposes our conclusions and perspectives.

2   Principles of Autonomic Computing

The essence of autonomic systems relies on the notion of *control loop* (represented in Figure 1) as defined in [10]. This loop consists of four phases: Monitoring the system, Analyzing the identified changes coming from the system, Planning the adequate reconfiguration actions, and Applying them. The analyzing and planning phases are relying on the Knowledge part information for computation. At runtime, this knowledge part must always be conform to the execution environment. It means that every change in the execution environment must lead to an update of the knowledge part, and *vice-versa*. Then, a *causal link* must be maintained between the knowledge part and the execution environment. We suggest to separate the architecture of the control loop into three parts:

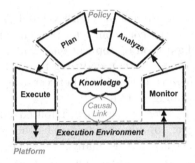

Fig. 1. The control loop of autonomic computing

● **The knowledge part** represents the abstract autonomous system. First, this representation must be complete in order to be aware of any information that may influence decisions to take. Additionally, it must be reconfigurable, because the abstract representation must evolve in the same way that the application deployed onto the domain. It must also be a high-level representation where only relevant information concerning the application must be represented, to avoid getting lost into details when computing a decision.

● **The policy part** groups the *Analyze* and *Plan* phases. They are responsible of exploiting the knowledge part to analyze situation and prepare adequate reconfigurations. The global autonomic policy is gathered here.

● **The platform part** encompasses the execution environment, and the *Monitor* and *Execute* parts. This part encompasses operations to deploy, reconfigure, and monitor the running system. Those operations depends on the underlying middleware technology used.

3   Key Research Challenges

This section discusses the key research challenges addressing the introduction of models into autonomic computing. Consequently, we try to answer the following questions: How models of autonomic applications should look like? How the control loop can be split? Which metamodels can be used to provide concepts to express entities of the control loop?

The control loop architecture has been split into three parts that represent the different concerns of an autonomic system.

First, the platform part of the control loop should be modelled. This platform should provide monitoring information about the running application as well as deployment operations to instantiate applications onto the deployment domain. Then, a unique metamodel can hardly be used to express any runtime platform model. Consequently, we decide to encapsulate the platform part into one software component with clearly defined interfaces providing the required operations. The details about the implementation of this component rely on the runtime platform chosen for executing applications. By employing a platform component, we maintain independence from the middleware layer running the applications (*e.g.* J2EE, CCM, SCA, etc.).

The second part is about the knowledge part. Which information about the application a knowledge model should encompass? This part must contain all the information relevant to analyze the system and to plan adequate reconfiguration actions. This model must provide the concepts to:

- Describe deployment domain entities —*i.e.* Computers available on the network, bandwidth of interconnections between these computers, etc. These concepts are needed since in the case of a ubiquitous or grid-tailored application, the knowledge about computer's appearance/disappearance is critical.

- Describe the components of the applications. This encompasses the component types, the interfaces they provide and require, the location of the binaries of these components, etc. This information is needed because the reconfiguration of running component instances requires the knowledge of their specification.

- Express the structure of the concerned applications, which we also call the *Deployment Plan*. It consists in information about the component instances to deploy, the computers hosting these instances must be deployed, and how these instances are bound together. This information about the system architecture is crucial. Without knowing this information, it is impossible to deploy and start the application. Moreover, autonomic management of applications often demands dynamical reconfiguration of the application structure.

To model application data such as component types, deployment plan, there are already existing solutions, like the *Architecture Description Languages* (ADL) [11]. However, most of the existing ADLs are specific to a given component model and the few that are generic do not provide concepts to express deployment domain entities. Nevertheless, the Object Management Group (OMG) has recently adopted a new specification called *Deployment and Configuration of Distributed Component-based Applications* [8]. This specification defines a metamodel with two parts, the *Component Data* part and the *Component Management* part. The first part describes the packaged components, with their typed interfaces and implementations, whereas the second part describes the deployment infrastructure and the way it handles data from the first part to execute the deployment process. The Component Data part of the OMG D&C specification provides the three parts of our knowledge metamodel: the *Types*, the *Domain* and the *Deployment Plan*. From this point of view, OMG D&C is a convenient knowledge metamodel to use.

However, using OMG D&C means forgetting some of the aspects of a running system. For instance, it is impossible to express components container policies, such as transactions, persistency or lifecycle concerns. Nevertheless, there exist extensions to specify extra-functional container policies, such as the CORBA Component Descriptors (CCD). Therefore, in order to reify and control every fine-grained concern of a component-based application, the OMG D&C metamodel should be extended.

The third part describes the high-level autonomic policy. This part must describe exhaustively the autonomic policies of an application. How should these policies be expressed? Which concepts can allow the designer to specify precisely the exhaustive autonomic policies of a distributed component-based application, knowing that the model at runtime should have sufficient information to analyze the situation and to take the right decision when needed?

There are three main concepts in order to express an autonomic policy. First, a *stimulus* part is an event that triggers the autonomic policy. This stimulus emerges in a certain *context*, which can be modelled as a set of properties of the application or the stimulus itself. Finally, there is an *execution* part which represents the actions to do in consequence. We argue that the ECA rule paradigm, well-known in the domain of active databases [3], fits well our needs for the expression of autonomic policies. The Event part represents the stimulus, the conditions of a rule are the context of this rule trigger, and the actions represent the execution part of the model.

Another issue to be raised concerning this part of the model is to decide whether the policy expression must be fine or coarse-grained. In other words, the question is about having an application-specific autonomic policy or composing generic fine-grained policies to build an application global policy. Our opinion is that by composing fine-grained policies, it will be possible to extract independent and reusable autonomic micro-policies. It is then possible to define policies by composing both independent and more application-specific policies. On the other way the well-known feature interactions defined in [13] (such as the *Shared Trigger Interaction*, the *Looping Interaction*, etc.) can be detected and resolved thanks to the fine granularity of our rules.

Using such fine-grained policies will increase the numbers of policies involved. Since rules can trigger each other, we are facing the threat of a combinatorial explosion of recursive rule triggers. But resolving *Looping Interaction* means no infinite loop is possible. Moreover, the execution of the policies is very fast since they are fine-grained. Finally, rule interaction can be statically known. Thus there are ways to control the explosion of rule interactions.

4   Our Dacar Prototype

DACAR (for *Distributed Autonomous Component-based ARchitectures*) is our prototype to build autonomic distributed CORBA component-based applications. We use the OpenCCM platform (http://openccm.objectweb.org) to deploy applications. The OMG D&C descriptors are reified into memory as a graph of Java objects that represents the executable model of the running applications. Currently, rules are not expressed using a model since our rule metamodel has to be completely defined. The rules are implemented as Fractal lightweight components (http://fractal.objectweb.org). Monitoring and reconfiguration execution parts are implemented using specific OpenCCM mechanisms [9].

We consider two sorts of events: The *endogenous* events are coming from the knowledge part (*e.g.*, a new instance description has been added in the domain part). The knowledge part must be a model that reacts to changes. It means that when a value or any concept is modified in the model, an event must be sent. This is possible using the design pattern *Observer* for example. Every change in the knowledge model must lead to the creation of an event.

The *exogenous* events are events coming from the execution platform (*e.g.*, a new node has been started in the deployment domain). The *condition* part of a rule represents conditions that event properties must fulfil in order to trigger the rule. The *action* part can affect either the knowledge part or the platform. Thus, we can classify rules in three categories (represented in Figure 2).

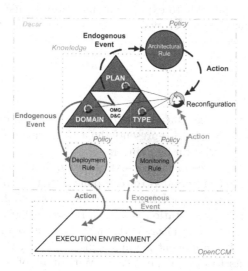

Fig. 2. The three types of rules involved in Dacar platform

The **Monitoring rules** are triggered by exogenous events. They perform actions on the knowledge part to update it in accordance with changes that occurred onto the running platform, *e.g.* When a new node is detected in the execution environment, add its description in the domain part of the knowledge part. These rules are generic and reusable across applications. The **Deployment rules** are triggered by endogenous events. They perform actions on the running platform to update it according to changes that occurred onto the knowledge part, *e.g.* When a new instance is declared in the deployment plan part of the knowledge part, prepare the deployment of this instance on the execution environment. These rules are also generic and reusable across applications. The **Architectural rules** are triggered by endogenous events. They perform actions on the knowledge part to update it according to properties that this knowledge part must fulfil, *e.g.* When a new `Client` instance is declared in the plan of the knowledge part, declare a binding between this `Client` component and a `Server` component instance existing in the plan. These rules are application specific.

Using these three categories of rules it is possible to ensure the causal link between the knowledge part and the application at runtime. The monitoring rules ensure that every change occurring in the execution environment leads to an update operation of the knowledge part. The deployment rules ensure that every concept declared in the plan of the knowledge part is prepared to be deployed on the execution environment. Both monitoring and deployment rules are the generic micropolicies enounced in Section 3. Finally, the architectural rules are the only specific part of the policy; they are responsible of the self-adaptation policy of the application. It refines the knowledge part according to changes emerging from the knowledge part itself. It is possible to express complete autonomic applications using our metamodel. DACAR has been evaluated on the design and execution of several autonomic CORBA component-based applications.

5   Case Study

This section illustrates the DACAR concepts through a simple scenario of autonomous application. Figure 4 represents the architecture of our scenario. More details about this scenario can be found in [4].

This example takes place in the context of a ubiquitous application. In a railway station, there is a `RailwayStation` component that can provide information about the trains on departure, relying on a `DataBaseTrainSchedule` component. Every person that enters the station and has a Personal Digital Assistant (PDA) must be able to request the `RailwayStation` component. In order to realize this, a dedicated `TrainGUI` component is implemented and must be deployed on every PDA that wants to obtain the service. With most of existing ADLs, it is impossible to specify that a `TrainGUI` component must be deployed on every PDA that enters the domain. Moreover, these deployed `TrainGUI` components must be bound to the `RailwayStation` instance.

We can first introduce the generic monitoring rule R_M, in charge of adding new node descriptions into the domain part of the autonomic computing knowledge. We can also give details about one generic deployment rule R_D that is in charge of deploying component instances declared in the plan. They are expressed on Figure 3.

Two architectural rules, described on the Figure 4, are required to implement autonomic behaviours of our simple ubiquitous example. This rule R1 ensures that every terminal that enters the domain gets an instance of `TrainGUI`. The second rule R2 ensures that every `TrainGUI` is connected to the `RailwayStation` component. With these only two rules, the architecture will be extended to take into account every PDA that enters the domain. These rules reuse generic deployment and monitoring rules that are in charge of applying the deployment operations when needed, and adding the description of new nodes into the knowledge model when it is detected, respectively.

The potential gains of our approach are numerous. First, the ECA rules represent a convenient and natural way to express reconfiguration policies, as well deployment and monitoring operations. Moreover, architectural rules can be

RULE R_M
EVENT
    A new node N is detected onto the Platform
CONDITION
    N.profile == PDA
ACTION
    knowledge.domain.addNode(N)

RULE R_D
EVENT
    A new instance I
    is declared in the knowledge.plan part
CONDITION
    true (no condition)
ACTION
    platform.deployInstance(I)

Fig. 3. The generic rules of the example

designed to factorize the description of very large and redundant applications, just like the simple example we gave in this section. Indeed in our example,

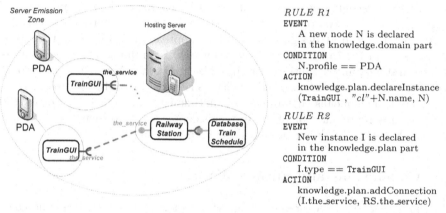

RULE R1
EVENT
    A new node N is declared
    in the knowledge.domain part
CONDITION
    N.profile == PDA
ACTION
    knowledge.plan.declareInstance
    (TrainGUI , "cl"+N.name, N)

RULE R2
EVENT
    New instance I is declared
    in the knowledge.plan part
CONDITION
    I.type == TrainGUI
ACTION
    knowledge.plan.addConnection
    (I.the_service, RS.the_service)

Fig. 4. An autonomic train service example and its specific adaptation rules

the same actions are repeated when new PDA enter the domain, but the two concise architectural rules factorize these actions. Finally for critical systems, there is no need to monitor the application and to manually interact with the system whenever a human intervention —that is also error-prone— is needed. Any arbitrary part of the application can be self-managed.

6   Related Works

In this section, we will discuss work addressing distributed autonomic applications, to justify the relevance of the metamodels we defined and the way we interpret models at runtime to deploy and execute autonomic applications.

JADE proposes a component-based implementation of a control loop to administrate J2EE applications on clusters [2]. The target platform and the application are modelled using Fractal components, in order to provide management interfaces. A *sensor* mechanism is employed to monitor the system and communicate the observations to the control loop. JADE allows the architectures to be reconfigured according to infrastructure context changes. It does not provide way to express architecture-specific adaptation mechanisms. Moreover the knowledge part of JADE consists only in a Fractal component assembly which is not as expressive as a real typed model defined by a metamodel.

CoSMIC is a model-driven generative programming tool-chain that permits efficient deployment and reconfiguration in Distributed Real-time Embedded (DRE) systems [6]. It is also based on the OMG D&C specification to specify deployment process. Nevertheless, CoSMIC only monitors Quality-of-Service results. Autonomous reconfigurations are then triggered by performance leaks in the system. This adaptation process is driven neither by the architecture nor by its deployment domain evolutions, by opposition to our approach.

Finally, PLASTIK is a meta-framework that provides mechanisms to manage runtime reconfigurations of component-based software, with *programmed changes* —*i.e.* foreseen reconfigurations at design-time— versus *ad hoc changes* —*i.e.* not foreseen at design-time [1]. This approach relies on reactive reconfigurations, in the same way that our approach. It proposes two layers, an architectural one, and a runtime one, just like in DACAR. Nevertheless, the only coherency supported between the two layers is from the ADL layer to the platform layer. This means that in case of runtime-level spontaneous changes, the architectural representation of the system is deprecated, and then useless. In our approach, a causal link is maintained between the two layers.

7   Conclusions and Future Work

In this paper, we have presented our vision of model-based autonomic computing in which a metamodel composed of three parts have been found out to express distributed component-based autonomic applications. This led to the implementation of DACAR, a framework to model autonomic component assemblies, following the vision of autonomic computing. DACAR reuses the OMG D&C architecture metamodel to build and manipulate the knowledge part of the control loop, and reuses the ECA rules paradigm to express the applicative adaptation policies. The first point of our future work will consist in establishing precisely the exhaustive metamodel used in DACAR, especially the rule metamodel. Then it will be possible to ensure properties expressed in the model and so to build safe autonomic architectures. We plan to use a metamodeling language such as KERMETA [12] in order to build and reconfigure real models of both architecture and adaptation policy.

References

1. Thais Batista, Ackbar Joolia, and Geoff Coulson. Managing Dynamic Reconfiguration in Component-based Systems. *Proceedings of the European Workshop on Software Architectures (EWSA'05)*, pages 1–18, June 2005. Pisa, Italy.

2. Sara Bouchenak, Fabienne Boyer, Emmanuel Cecchet, Sébastien Jean, Alan Schmitt, and Jean-Bernard Stefani. A Component-based Approach to Distributed System Management - A Use Case with Self-Manageable J2EE Clusters. In *11th ACM SIGOPS European Workshop*, Leuven, Belgium, September 2004.
3. Thierry Coupaye and Christine Collet. Denotational Semantics for an Active Rule Execution Model. *2nd International Workshop on Rules in Database Systems, Lecture Notes In Computer Science*, 985:36–50, 1995. London, United Kingdom.
4. Areski Flissi, Philippe Merle, and Christophe Gransart. A service discovery and automatic deployment component-based software infrastructure for Ubiquitous Computing. *Ubiquitous Mobile Information and Collaboration Systems, CAiSE Workshop, (UMICS 2005)*, June 2005. Porto, Portugal.
5. Ian Foster and Carl Kesserman. *The Grid: Blueprint for a New Computing Infrastructure*. 2004. ISBN: 1-55860-933-4.
6. Aniruddha Gokhale, Balachandran Natarajan, and Douglas C. Schmidt et al. CoSMIC : An MDA Generative Tool for Distributed Real-time and Embedded Component Middleware and Applications. In *Proceedings of the ACM OOPSLA 2002 Workshop on Generative Techniques in the Context of the Model Driven Architecture*, November 2002. Seattle, USA.
7. Object Management Group. Model Driven Architecture (MDA). Technical Report Document number ormsc/2001-07-01, Object Management Group, July 2001.
8. Object Management Group. Deployment and Configuration of Distributed Component-based Applications Specification. Available Specification, Version 4.0 formal/06-04-02, April 2006.
9. Andreas Hoffman, Tom Ritter, and Julia Reznik et al. Specification of the Deployment and Configuration. IST COACH deliverable document D2.4, IST COACH, July 2004. http://www.ist-coach.org.
10. Jeffrey Kephart and David Chess. The Vision of Autonomic Computing. Technical report, IBM Thomas J. Watson, January 2003. IEEE Computer Society.
11. Nenad Medvidovic and Richard N. Taylor. A Classification and Comparison Framework for Software Architecture Description Languages. *IEEE Transactions on Software Engineering*, 26, issue 1:70–93, January 2000.
12. Pierre-Alain Muller, Franck Fleurey, and Jean-Marc Jézéquel. Weaving Executability into Object-Oriented Meta-Languages. In *Proceedings of MODELS/UML'2005*, pages 264–278, October 2005. Montego Bay, Jamaica.
13. Stephan Reiff-Marganiec and Kenneth J. Turner. Feature Interaction in Policies. *Computer Networks 45*, pages 569—584, March 2004. Department of Computing Science and Mathematics, University of Stirling, United Kingdom.
14. Mark Weiser. The Computer for the 21st Century. *Scientific American*, pages 94–100, September 1991.

Summary of the Workshop on Multi-Paradigm Modeling: Concepts and Tools

Holger Giese[1], Tihamér Levendovszky[2], and Hans Vangheluwe[3]

[1] Department of Computer Science
University of Paderborn
D-33098 Paderborn, Germany
hg@upb.de

[2] Department of Automation and Applied Informatics
Budapest University of Technology and Economics
Budapest, Hungary
tihamer@aut.bme.hu

[3] Modelling, Simulation & Design Lab
School of Computer Science
McGill University
Montréal, Québec, Canada
hv@cs.mcgill.ca

Abstract. This paper reports on the findings of the first Workshop on Multi-Paradigm Modeling: Concepts and Tools. It contains an overview of the presented papers and of the results of three working groups which addressed multiple views, abstraction, and evolution. Besides this, a definition of the problem space, the main concepts, and an appropriate terminology for multi-paradigm modeling as presented and discussed during the workshop are provided.

Keywords: Modeling, Meta-modeling, Multi-Paradgim Modeling, Multi-Formalism.

1   Introduction

Complex software-based systems today often integrate different beforehand isolated subsystems. Thus, for their model-driven development multiple formalism at different levels of abstraction from possibly different domains have to be integrated. This is especially true when besides general purpose languages such as the UML also domain specific languages are employed. In this first workshop on Multi-Paradigm Modeling (MPM) at the MoDELS conference, a forum for researchers and practitioners to discuss the resulting problems and challenges has been set up.

An initial invited talk was given by Hans Vangheluwe in order to provide some generally agreed upon definitions of multi-paradigm modeling.

T. Kühne (Ed.): MoDELS 2006 Workshops, LNCS 4364, pp. 252–262, 2007.

The paper continues with a definition of the problem space, main concepts, and terminology for multi-paradigm modeling in Section 2. Then, the presented papers are located within the introduced problem space in Section 3 before we summarized the findings of the working groups which have been set up within the workshop in Section 4. Finally, a list of the program committee follows in Section 5.

2 Multi-Paradigm Modeling

In this section, the foundations of Multi-Paradigm Modeling (MPM) are presented. In particular, we introduce *meta-modeling* and *model transformation* as enablers for Multi-Paradigm Modeling. MPM encompasses both *multi-formalism* and *multi-abstraction* modeling of complex systems. To provide a framework for the above, the notion of a *modeling language* is first dissected. This leads quite naturally to the concept of meta-modeling as well as to the explicit modeling of model transformations. The notion of abstraction is explored in the working group results section 4.2.

Models are an *abstraction* of reality. The structure and behavior of systems that we wish to analyze or design can be represented by models. These models, at various *levels of abstraction*, are always described in some *formalism* or *modeling language*. To "model" modeling languages and ultimately synthesize visual modeling environments for those languages, we will break down a modeling language into its basic constituents [1]. The two main aspects of a model are its syntax (how it is represented) on the one hand and its semantics (what it means) on the other hand.

The syntax of modeling languages is traditionally partitioned into *concrete syntax* and *abstract syntax*. In textual languages for example, the concrete syntax is made up of sequences of *characters* taken from an *alphabet*. These characters are typically grouped into *words* or *tokens*. Certain sequences of words or *sentences* are considered valid (*i.e.,* belong to the language). The (possibly infinite) *set* of all valid sentences is said to make up the language. Costagliola et. al. [2] present a framework of visual language classes in which the analogy between textual and visual characters, words, and sentences becomes apparent. Visual languages are those languages whose concrete syntax is visual (graphical, geometrical, topological, . . .) as opposed to textual.

For practical reasons, models are often stripped of irrelevant concrete syntax information during syntax checking. This results in an "abstract" representation which captures the "essence" of the model. This is called the *abstract syntax*. Obviously, a single abstract syntax may be represented using multiple concrete syntaxes. In programming language compilers, abstract syntax of models (due to the nature of programs) is typically represented in *Abstract Syntax Trees* (ASTs). In the context of general modeling, where models are often graph-like, this representation can be generalized to *Abstract Syntax Graphs* (ASGs).

Once the syntactic correctness of a model has been established, its meaning must be specified. This meaning must be *unique* and *precise*. Meaning can be expressed by specifying a *semantic mapping function* which maps every model in a language onto an element in a *semantic domain*. For example, the meaning of a Causal Block Diagram can be specified by mapping onto an Ordinary Differential Equation. For practical reasons, semantic mapping is usually applied to the abstract rather than to the concrete syntax of a model. Note that the semantic domain is a modeling language in its own right which needs to be properly modeled (and so on, recursively). In practice, the semantic mapping function maps abstract syntax onto abstract syntax.

To continue the introduction of meta-modeling and model transformation concepts, languages will explictly be represented as (possibly infinite) sets as shown in Figure 1. In the figure, insideness denotes the sub-set relationship. The

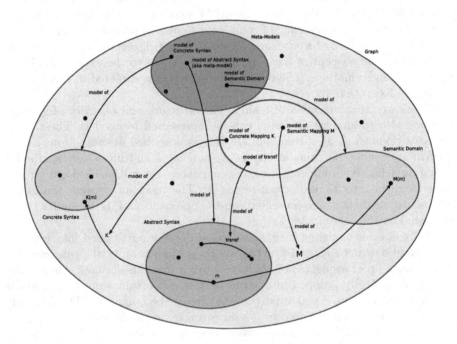

Fig. 1. Modeling Languages as Sets

dots represent model which are elements of the encompassing set(s).

As one can always, at some level of abstraction, represent a model as a graph structure, all models are shown as elements of the set of all graphs Graph. Though this restriction is not necessary, it is commonly used as it allows for the design, implementation and bootstrapping of (meta-)modeling environments. As such, any modeling language becomes a (possibly infinite) set of graphs. In the bottom centre of Figure 1 is the abstract syntax set A. It is a set of models stripped of their concrete syntax.

Meta-modeling is a heavily over-used term. Here, we will use it to denote the explicit description (in the form of a finite model in an appropriate meta-modeling language) of the Abstract Syntax set. Often, meta-modeling also covers a model of the concrete syntax. Semantics is, however, not covered. In the figure, the Abstract Syntax set is described by means of its meta-model. On the one hand, a meta-model can be used to *check* whether a general model (a graph) *belongs to* the Abstract Syntax set. On the other hand, one could, at least in principle, use a meta-model to *generate* all elements of the language. This explains why the term meta-model and grammar are often used inter-changeably.

Several languages are suitable to describe meta-models in. Two approaches are in common use:

1. A meta-model is a *type-graph*. Elements of the language described by the meta-model are instance graphs. There must be a *morphism* between an instance-graph (model) and a type-graph (meta-model) for the model to be in the language. Commonly used meta-modeling languages are Entity Relationship Diagrams (ERDs) and Class Diagrams (adding inheritance to ERDs). The expressive power of this approach is often not sufficient and a *constraint language* (such as the Object Constraint Language) specifying constraints over instances is used to further constrain the set of valid models in a language. This is the approach used by the OMG to specify the abstract syntax of the Unified Modeling Language (UML).
2. A more general approach specifies a meta-model as a transformation (in an appropriate formalism such as Graph Grammars) which, when applied to a model, verifies its membership of a formalism by *reduction*. This is similar to the syntax checking based on (context-free) grammars used in programming language compiler compilers. Note how this approach can be used to model type inferencing and other more sophisticated checks.

Both types of meta-models can be *interpreted* (for flexibility and dynamic modification) or *compiled* (for performance).

Note that when meta-modeling is used to synthesize interactive, possibly visual modeling environments, we need to model *when* to check whether a model belongs to a language. In *free-hand* modeling, checking is only done when explicitly requested. This means that it is possible to create, during modeling, syntactically incorrect models. In *syntax-directed* modeling, syntactic constraints are enforced at all times during editing to prevent a user from creating syntactically incorrect models. Note how the latter approach, though possibly more efficient, due to its incremental nature –of construction and consequently of checking– may render certain valid models in in the modeling language unreachable through incremental construction. Typically, syntax-directed modeling environments will be able to give suggestions to modelers whenever choices with a finite number of options present themselves.

The advantages of meta-modeling are numerous. Firstly, an *explicit* model of a modeling language can serve as *documentation* and as *specification*. Such a specification can be the basis for the *analysis* of properties of models in the language. From the meta-model, a modeling environment may be *automatically* generated. The flexibility of the approach is tremendous: new languages can be designed by simply *modifying* parts of a meta-model. As this modification is explicitly applied to models, the relationship between different variants of a modeling language is apparent. Above all, with an appropriate meta-modeling tool, modifying a meta-model and subsequently generating a possibly visual modeling tool is orders of magnitude *faster* than developing such a tool by hand. The tool synthesis is *repeatable* and *less error-prone* than hand-crafting.

As a meta-model is a model in an appropriate modeling language in its own right, one should be able to meta-model that language's abstract syntax too. Such a model of a meta-modeling language is called a *meta-meta-model*. It is noted that the notion of "meta-" is relative. In principle, one could continue the meta- hierarchy ad infinitum. Luckily, some modeling languages can be meta-modeled by means of a model in the language itself. This is called *meta-circularity* and it allows modeling tool and language compiler builders to *bootstrap* their systems.

A model in the Abstract Syntax set (see Figure 1) needs at least one concrete syntax. This implies that a concrete syntax mapping function κ is needed. κ maps an abstract syntax graph onto a concrete syntax model. Such a model could be textual (*e.g.,* an element of the set of all Strings), or visual (*e.g.,* an element of the set of all the 2D vector drawings). Note that the set of concrete models can be modeled in its own right. Also, concrete syntax sets will typically be re-used for different languages. Often, multiple concrete syntaxes will be defined for a single abstract syntax, depending on the user. If exchange between modeling tools is intended, an XML-based textual syntax is often used. If in such an exchange, space and performance is an issue, an binary format may be used instead. When the formalism is graph-like as in the case of a circuit diagram, a visual concrete syntax is often used for human consumption. The concrete syntax of complex languages is however rarely entirely visual. When, for example, equations need to be represented, a textual concrete syntax is more appropriate.

Finally, a model m in the Abstract Syntax set (see Figure 1) needs a unique and precise meaning. As previously discussed, this is achieved by providing a Semantic Domain and a semantic mapping function M. This mapping can be given informally in English, pragmatically with code or formally with model transformations. Natural languages are ambiguous and not very useful since they cannot be executed. Code is executable, but it is often hard to understand, analyze and maintain. It can be very hard to understand, manage and derive properties from code. This is why formalisms such as Graph Grammars are often used to specify semantic mapping functions in particular and model transformations in general. Graph Grammars are a visual formalism for specifying transformations. Graph Grammars are formally defined and at a higher level than code. Complex behavior can be expressed very intuitively with a few graphical rules. Furthermore, Graph Grammar models can be analyzed and executed. As efficient execution may be an issue, Graph Grammars can often be seen as an executable specification for manual coding. As such, they can be used to automatically generate transformation unit tests.

Within the context of Multi-Paradigm Modeling, we have chosen to use the following terminology.

- A *language* is the set of abstract syntax models. No meaning is given to these models.
- A *concrete language* comprises both the abstract syntax and a concrete syntax mapping function κ. Obviously, a single language may have several concrete languages associated with it.
- A *formalism* consists of a language, a semantic domain and a semantic mapping function giving meaning to model in the language.
- A *concrete formalism* comprises a formalism together with a concrete syntax mapping function.

This terminology will be used in the sequel.

3 Presented Papers

The paper [3] summarizes the main achievements with respect to Mechatronic UML and relates it to Multi-Paradigm Modeling. The approach combines control engineering, electrical engineering, mechanical engineering, and software engineering disciplines to describe and verify reconfigurable mechatronic systems. The multidisciplinary nature of Mechatronic UML gives a good case study for multiparadigm modeling: different parts of a mechatronic system are described by different formalisms, such as differential equations or timed automata.

The paper [4] presents a tool named Computer Aided Method Engineering (CAME). This approach uses hierarchical activity diagram to model an arbitrary software development process. To these process steps, models can be attached. The modeling languages are created with metamodeling techniques. The models created for different paradigms are assembled manually.

The popularity of block diagrams motivates the work [5], which offers a translational semantics for block diagrams by syntactically translating them into Haskell. The declarative notion of Haskell facilitates more rigorous specification as opposed to its imperative counterparts, such as C. The translation applies syntactic Haskell extensions developed by the authors.

The paper [6] uses an approach underpinned by abstract algebraic and categorical constructs. The main idea is to formalize the semantics by specifying the domains as lattices of coalgebras. Between the lattices, Galois connections can be established. If this connection is maintained during the abstractions or concretizations, the important properties are preserved. In order to check the consistency of distinct domains, pullback constructs are provided to derive a common specification. These results can be applied to formalize the composition of multi-paradigm applications.

The paper [7] proposes a formalism for modeling language composition with a low-level language. The low-level language referred to as L3 consists of three aspects: structural, descriptive and behavioral. The multi-paradigm composition technique is illustrated with two simplified UML diagrams, namely, the class and activity diagrams enhanced with OCL constraints.

The paper [8], which can be found in this volume, discusses a conceptual approach to define declarative model integration languages. The integration behavior is bound to the metamodel. Furthermore, the authors build a conceptual framework which realizes the complex integration operations on the global level to efficient and simple local operators.

4   Working Group Results

4.1   Multiple Views

The first working group addressed the topic of multi-view modelling. Multi-view modelling is concerned with the common practice of modelling a single system by means of a collection of view models. Each of these view models can possibly be represented in a different concrete formalisms. As discussed in Section 2, differences between concrete formalisms may be at the level of concrete syntax, abstract syntax, or even semantics. Together, the multiple views allow a modeller to express all relevant knowledge about a system under study. Allowing multiple views in multiple concrete formalisms allows the modeller to express different aspects of his knowledge in the most appropriate fashion, thereby minimizing accidental complexity.

Multi-view modelling does come at a price though. The different views should be consistent. In particular, if one view is modified, other views describing the same aspect of the system may need to be updated. Note that updating may be trivial if the views only differ in concrete syntax. In the worst case however, the semantics of the different formalisms in which the views are expressed may differ. In this case, formalism transformation may be required. It is noted that updating (in a Model-View-Controller fashion) is in principle always possible if update mappings are available between all views. For efficiency reasons, the quadratic (in the number of views) number of required mappings and the quadratic (in the number of view models) number of updates can be reduced to a linear number if it is possible to describe a single repository model of which all views are projections.

Also, one often needs to know whether a collection of views completely describes a system (given some notion of completeness). The issues mentioned above are exacerbated if different views describe the system at different levels of abstraction. The working group discussed abstraction at length and came to similar conclusions as those of the second working group (though not formalized). Hence, we refer to the next section for a treatment of this subject.

Jean-Marie Favre pointed out the existence of a mega-model of multi-view modelling in the reverse engineering community. This mega-model relates *views* which need to conform to *viewpoints*. Those in turn are used to cover *concerns*. Each of these may be described in an appropriate formalism.

4.2   Abstraction

The second working group worked on the topic of abstraction and how models of the same and different type (formalism) are related to each other during the model-driven development using abstraction and its opposite refinement in different forms.

As foundation for the notion of abstraction, the group started with defining the *information* contained in a model M as the different questions (properties) $P = I(M)$ which can be asked concerning the model ($|P|$ and $p, p' \in P : p \neq p'$) and either result in true or false ($M \models p$ or $M \not\models p$).

For a model, it holds in general that only a restricted set of questions (properties) are correctly addressed by the model w.r.t. the original matter. Thus, for example, questions concerning the color of a diagram or the layout of a text do not matter. These relevant questions (properties) and the related notion of a bit, then served also to define abstraction as well as several related relations.

A relation between two models M_1 and M_2 can have the character of an *abstraction, refinement,* or *equivalence* relative to a non empty set of questions (properties) P.

- In case of an *equivalence*, we require that for all $p \in P$ holds: $M_1 \models p \iff M_2 \models p$. We write $M_1 =_P M_2$.
- If M_1 is an *abstraction* of M_2 with respect to P it holds for all $p \in P$ holds: $M_1 \models p \Rightarrow M_2 \models p$. We write $M_1 \sqsupseteq_P M_2$.
- We further say that M_1 is a *refinement* of M_2 iff M_1 is an *abstraction* of M_2. We write $M_1 \sqsubseteq_P M_2$.

We also have a second case of abstraction and refinement when only comparing the scope given by the set of questions (properties) considered in two models M_1 and M_2:

- We have an *equivalent scope* if $I(M_1) = I(M_2)$. We write $M_1 =_I M_2$.
- We have a more *abstract* scope if $I(M_1) \subseteq I(M_2)$. We write $M_1 \sqsupseteq_I M_2$.
- We further say that M_1 has a *refined* scope of M_2 iff M_1 has an *abstracted* scope of M_2. We write $M_1 \sqsubseteq_I M_2$.

The group then employed this definition to describe the role of abstraction and refinement for some general development steps:

In case of a *analysis model*, a more abstract model M_a is derived from the concrete model M in order to prove or disprove that a certain set of properties P holds. If the abstract model provides all required information concerning P ($I(M_a) \supseteq P$) we can distinguish the case that (1) both models are equivalent ($M_a =_P M$) or M_a is an abstraction of M ($M_a \sqsupseteq_P M$):

(1) $\forall p \in P : M_a \models p \iff M \models p$ (2) $\forall p \in P : M_a \models p \Rightarrow M \models p$.

These facts can be used to transfer the fulfilment of p from M_a to M. Note that usually the verification or analysis of p is only feasible for M_a. The equivalence or abstraction between the models is then used to propagate the result for p. While in case of equivalence the full result can be propagated, for abstraction the check $M_a \models p$ is only sufficient to conclude $M \models p$. The propagation is not valid for $\neg p$ as there is $M_a \models \neg p$ is not necessary for $M \models \neg p$.

A typical development step in computer science is *model refinement*: A refined model M_2 is derived from the abstract model M_1 by adding details to the model. The considered set of properties P can be either fixed or extended in the refinement step $(I(M_2) \supseteq I(M_1) = P)$. Due to the definition of refinement for $M_2 \sqsubseteq_P M_1$ holds: $\forall p \in P : M_1 \models p \Rightarrow M_2 \models p$.

During the development the check $M_1 \models p$ is then used to determine that any refinement step preserves this property. Thus, we can characterize the strategy as a pessimistic *risk elimination* step which excludes solutions if it is not guaranteed that for all its valid implementations (refinements) also p must hold.

While refinement is common in computer science, in engineering and related disciplines the typical development step is *approximation* which is rather different. Approximation can be seen as refinement with respect to negated properties: $\forall \neg p \in P : M_1 \models \neg p \Rightarrow M_2 \models \neg p$.[1] This effectively means that approximation is an optimistic approach which only eliminates *impossible solutions*. If a property p has already been falsified for M_1 ($N_1 \models \neg p$), we refuse all solution M_2 which cannot fulfill p.

4.3   Model Evolution

One of the main problems for a wide scale acceptance of model engineering practices in industry is the lack or the immaturity of methods and tools that allow to confidently switch to a fully model driven software development process. In conventional software development, for instance, source code versioning systems are commonplace, whereas it is still largely unclear of how adequate versioning should be applied in a model driven context.

Another pressing problem that was the topic of group discussion is the evolution of metamodels representing the abstract syntax of modeling languages. Such an evolution would alter the metamodel and therefore possibly render all models conforming to the original metamodel obsolete.

Hence, support for migrating models from the original to the changed metamodels ought to be provided. Ideally, this would come in the form of transformations that could migrate models towards newer versions of metamodels. Such transformations could possibly be derived automatically.

It is still an open question how the actual evolution of metamodels could be carried out. Perhaps it is feasible to find certain recurring "evolution patterns" similar to refactoring operations, which would ease the derivation of migrating transformations. A second possibility would be to allow "free-hand editing" of metamodels, in which case tool support should allow to at least partially load models into newer versions of metamodels and - for further manual editing - provide a comprehensive list of model elements that do not match the new metamodel. In both cases, it is advisable to store traceability information, for instance to be able to provide backwards compatibility.

---

[1] In practice, M_1 is usually an idealization w,r,t. p where an approximation is only extremely likely.

Apart from discussing these more technical challenges that call for tool support, the discussion elaborated on what kinds of metamodel evolution there are, and what the needs for evolution might be.

We could identify two basic kinds of evolutions. The first would be a purely *syntactic evolution*, which would result in adding "syntactic sugar" to the metamodel, for purposes of making the modeling language more convenient to use and comprehend. One example would be to introduce model elements, that represent structures built of more basic model elements. As an example, the Business Process Execution Language (BPEL) offers convenient constructs such as Flow or Sequence, which could alternatively be modeled by linking up activities accordingly on a fine-grained level. Models expressed in either way, however, have the same semantics.

The second kind of evolution would be *semantic evolution*, where the semantics of the model elements are changed or new elements are introduced whose semantics have to be determined. This can take place through changing a metamodel and according to that changing its semantic mapping towards a semantic domain. An explicit mapping towards a semantic domain, however, does often not exist, but a code generator or interpreter is employed to make models executable. Changes to the generator would represent a change in the semantics of the language. Essentially this poses a challenge for appropriate configuration management to bind metamodels, models and their respective generators.

The purpose of such syntactic evolution could be to enhance the learnability or usability of a modeling language, whereas semantic evolution would go towards enhancing the appropriateness and expressivity of a modeling language.

The discussion concluded with the understanding that metamodel evolution should not simply be about providing means to arbitrarily alter metamodels, but be a way to continuously maintain the quality of metamodels by ensuring their fitness for task.

This would possibly require metrics for measuring the quality of metamodels and the appropriateness of the expressivity or usability of the respective modeling languages. Such metrics would indicate when a modeling language ought to actually undergo evolution, to avoid "uncontrolled" modifications that may introduce ambiguities or distort the understandability and hence the practical applicability of a modeling language.

5   Program Committee

Michael von der Beeck *BMW (DE)*
Jean Bézivin *Université de Nantes (FR)*
Heiko Dörr *DaimlerChrysler AG (DE)*
Jean-Marie Favre
    Institut d'Informatique et Mathématiques Appliquées de Grenoble (FR)
Reiko Heckel *University of Leicester (UK)*
Jozef Hooman *University of Nijmwegen (NL)*
Gabor Karsai *Vanderbilt University (US)*

Anneke Kleppe *University of Twente (NL)*
Ingolf H. Krüger *University of California, San Diego (US)*
Thomas Kühne *Technical University Darmstadt (DE)*
Juan de Lara *Universidad Autónoma de Madrid (ES)*
Jie Liu *Microsoft Research (US)*
Mark Minas *University of the Federal Armed Forces (DE)*
Oliver Niggemann *dSPACE GmbH (DE)*
Pieter Mosterman *The MathWorks (US)*
Bernhard Schätz *TU Munich (DE)*
Andy Schürr *Technical University Darmstadt (DE)*
Hans Vangheluwe *McGill University (CA)*
Bernhard Westfechtel *University of Bayreuth (DE)*

References

1. Harel, D., Rumpe, B.: Modeling languages: Syntax, semantics and all that stuff, part i: The basic stuff. Technical report, Jerusalem, Israel (2000)
2. Costagliola, G., Lucia, A.D., Orefice, S., Polese, G.: A classification framework to support the design of visual languages. J. Vis. Lang. Comput. **13** (2002) 573–600
3. Henkler, S., Hirsch, M.: A multi-paradigm modeling approach for reconfigurable mechatronic systems. Technical report, Budapest University of Technology and Economics, Dept. of Automation and Applied Informatics, Genova, Italy (2006)
4. Saeki, M., Kaiya, H.: Constructing multi-paradigm modeling methods based on method assembly. Technical report, Budapest University of Technology and Economics, Dept. of Automation and Applied Informatics, Genova, Italy (2006)
5. Denckla, B., Mosterman, P.J.: Block diagrams as a syntactic extension to haskell. Technical report, Budapest University of Technology and Economics, Dept. of Automation and Applied Informatics, Genova, Italy (2006)
6. Streb, J., Alexander, P.: Using a lattice of coalgebras for heterogeneous model composition. Technical report, Budapest University of Technology and Economics, Dept. of Automation and Applied Informatics, Genova, Italy (2006)
7. Braatz, B.: An integration concept for complex modelling techniques. Technical report, Budapest University of Technology and Economics, Dept. of Automation and Applied Informatics, Genova, Italy (2006)
8. Reiter, T., Kepler, J., Retschitzegger, W., Altmanninger, K.: Think global, act local: Implementing model management with domain-specific integration languages. In: Lecture Notes in Computer Science, Satellite Events at the MoDELS 2006 Conference, Genova, Italy (2006)

Think Global, Act Local: Implementing Model Management with Domain-Specific Integration Languages*

Thomas Reiter[1], Kerstin Altmanninger[2], and Werner Retschitzegger[1]

[1] Information Systems Group (IFS)
Johannes Kepler University Linz, Austria
{reiter,werner}@ifs.uni-linz.ac.at
[2] Department of Telecooperation (TK)
Johannes Kepler University Linz, Austria
kerstin.altmanninger@jku.at

Abstract. In recent years a number of model transformation languages have emerged that deal with fine-grained, local transformation specifications, commonly known as *programming in the small* [13]. To be able to develop complex transformation systems in a scalable way, mechanisms to work directly on the global model level are desirable, referred to as *programming in the large* [26]. In this paper we show how domain specific model integration languages can be defined, and how they can be composed in order to achieve complex model management tasks. Thereby, we base our approach on the definition of declarative model integration languages, of which implementing transformations are derived. We give a categorization of these transformations and rely on an object-oriented mechanism to realize complex model management tasks.

1 Introduction

Model-driven development (MDD) in general aims at raising the productivity and quality of software development by automatically deriving code artifacts from models. Even though an immediate model-to-code mechanism can yield tremendous benefits, it is commonly accepted that working model-to-model mechanisms are necessary [23] to achieve integration among multiple models describing a system and to make models first-class-citizens in MDD.

In recent years, therefore, a number of model transformation languages (MTLs) have emerged, which allow to specify transformations between metamodels. Such transformations are defined on a fine-grained, *local* level, upon elements of these metamodels. Albeit the advantages that MTLs bring in terms of manipulating models, it is quite clear that defining model transformations on a local level, only, can pose substantial scalability problems. Similarly, [9]

---

* This work has been partly funded by the Austrian Federal Ministry of Transport, Innovation and Technology (BMVIT) and FFG under grant FIT-IT-810806.

T. Kühne (Ed.): MoDELS 2006 Workshops, LNCS 4364, pp. 263–276, 2007.

emphasizes the need for establishing relationships between macroscopic entities like models and metamodels, for instance for the coordination of various domain-specific languages.

There are already first approaches trying to alleviate the above mentioned problem from two different angles (cf. also Section 5). The first category adheres to a bottom-up approach, meaning that existing general purpose MTLs are extended for special tasks like model merging [14] or model comparison [21]. Furthermore, mappings carrying special semantics can be established between metamodels and further on be derived into executable model transformations [6].

The second category of approaches is top-down-oriented and falls into the area of model management, where relationships between models are expressed on a coarse-grained, *global* level through generic model management operators. The aim of model management is to ease the development of metadata intensive applications, by factoring out common tasks in various application scenarios and by providing generic model management operators for these tasks. The operators' generality allows to make assumptions about, e.g., algebraic properties of model management operations, but does not necessarily make any specific assumptions about the operators' actual implementations. For instance, Rondo [5] is an implementation of such a system, oriented towards managing relational and XML schemata.

It is our opinion that both, bottom-up and top-down approaches are valuable contributions and should be considered as potentially complementing each other, as opposed to be thought of as two sides of a coin. One of model management's main contributions is to provide a conceptually well-founded framework guiding the actual implementation of model management operators, for which the capabilities of increasingly more powerful MTLs can be leveraged.

Therefore, this paper represents early work in drafting an approach that tries to build on the strengths of both paradigms. On the one hand, the model management rationale to make models first-class-citizens and to achieve complex model management tasks by assembling global operations on models, is followed. On the other hand, our approach relies on domain-specific languages (DSLs) developed atop general-purpose MTLs for locally handling fine-grained relationships between metamodels.

The proposed approach resides in the context of the ModelCVS [18][17] tool integration project, which aims at integrating various modeling tools via metamodels representing their modeling language. Concretely, the problems that need to be solved are finding efficient ways to integrate various metamodels on a local level, and solve common problems, for example metamodel evolution, on a global level.

The remainder of this paper is structured as follows. Section 2 discusses the rationale behind our approach. Section 3 deals with the composition of model management operators and classifies different kinds of transformations. Section 4 goes into detail about how domain specific integration languages can be defined. Section 5 discusses related work and Section 6 summarizes our approach.

2   Rationale for Our Approach

To better motivate the rationale underlying our approach, this section starts with an analogy referring to the definition of primitive recursive functions. Table 1 shows the various abstraction layers our approach is built on and introduces terms and concepts used throughout this paper. Referring to computability theory, using only the constant, successor, and projection functions, all primitive recursive functions, such as addition or subtraction operators, can be defined. Analogous to that, on top of existing *model transformation languages* residing on the local level, we define *integration operators* on the local composite level for handling fine-grained relationships between model elements. Algebraic as well as integration operators are then bundled up into sets representing algebras or *integration languages*, respectively. We refer to this level as intermediate, because the elements of algebras and integration languages act upon the local level, but are used to define transformations acting upon the global level. Hence, on the global level, complex functions and concrete realizations of model management operators are found. These algebras and languages are at a suitable level of abstraction and are commonly used to assemble algebraic terms or model management scripts [4]. After establishing a view across the abstraction layers, ranging from bottom-level MTLs to top-level model management scripts, we illustrate our approach in a top-down fashion in more detail.

Table 1. Analogy referring to the definition of primitive recursive functions

Level	Natural Numbers	Example	Proposed Approach	Example
Global Composite	Terms	power2(max(x,y))	Model Mgmt. Scripts	m''=translate(m.merge(m'))
Global	Complex Functions	power2(z),max(x,y)	Model Mgmt. Operators	Translation,PackageMerge
Intermediate	Algebras	{+,-,N},{*,/,N}	Integration Languages	FullEquivLang,MergeLang
Local Composite	Operators	+,-,*	Integration Operators	FullEquivClass,MergeClass
Local	Base Functions	succ(x),null()	MTL Expressions	ATLRule,OCLExpression

Global and Global Composite. As depicted in Figure 1, we believe it is helpful to view the composition of complex model management operations as an object-oriented (OO) meta-programming task [2], where models are understood as objects and transformations as methods acting upon these "objects". Consequently, we think that an integral part of defining a metamodel should be to specify *integration behavior* in the form of transformations (1) that are tied to that metamodel (e.g., merging state-machines). The composition of transformations can then be facilitated by writing model management scripts in an OO-style notation, which invokes transformations on models (2) just like methods on objects. Transformations representing actual realizations of model management operators are defined by languages (3) which we refer to as *domain specific integration languages* (DSIL).

Intermediate. A DSIL consists of operators that enable to locally handle fine-grained relationships between metamodels and is formalized as a weaving metamodel [7]. The domain specificity of a DSIL stems from the fact that a DSIL can only be applied to certain kinds of metamodels (4). For instance, a *Merge-Lang* may be used to specify a merge for metamodels representing structures (e.g., class diagrams). As behavioral integration poses a very different challenge than structural integration [25], a merge on a metamodel representing some kind of behavior (e.g., business process), would have to be specified in a *FlowMerge-Lang*, whose operators are specifically aimed towards metamodels representing flows [24]. Efforts to formalize a metamodel's domain (e.g., by mapping metamodels onto ontologies [19]), could help to check whether a metamodel falls into the domain of a certain DSIL. From our point of view, this still poses an open research question and the applicability of a DSIL on a metamodel ultimately requires a user's judgement.

Local and Local Composite. An *integration specification* in a DSIL is a *weaving* model that conforms to its *weaving metamodel*, which is a certain DSIL's metamodel (5). A weaving consists of a set of typed links between elements of a model or a metamodel. The types of links represent different kinds of *integration operators* (6), whose execution semantics are defined through a mapping towards an executable MTL. Thus, an integration specification is finally derived into an executable model transformation (7).

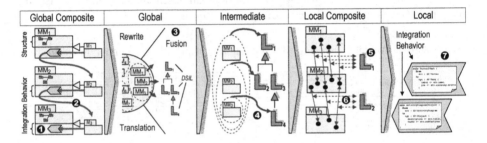

Fig. 1. Illustration of our approach's abstraction layers

Notably, our approach focuses on specifying integration between metamodels in a purely declarative way, as such a specification (which abstracts imperative implementations) is the basis for reasoning tasks like analysis or optimization.

3   Managing Models on a Global Level

This section discusses the two top-most layers of abstraction which have been previously introduced as *global* and *global composite*. The following subsection exemplifies transformation composition on the global composite layer through a model management script. Based on observations gained in the example, the global level is elaborated on in more detail by laying out a useful classification of transformations.

3.1   Model Manangement Scripts on the Global Composite Level

The following example deals with the merging of two domains represented by two metamodels, as depicted in Fig. 2. When these metamodels are merged, however, also their conforming models should be merged. We refer to such a model management task as an *exogenous merge*. A concrete application would be to merge previously modularized metamodels (e.g., a BPEL metamodel split into a structural and a behavioral part) or to extend a metamodel with a certain aspect (e.g., add "Marks" to a Petri-net metamodel) [20]. Throughout the example, however, for simplicity reasons and to emphasize the global perspective at this abstraction layer we will not go into detail about the makeup of the metamodels, which are simply referred to as A and B and their conforming models as a and as b, respectively.

There may be multiple ways to describe an *exogenous merge*. A straightforward way would be to program the whole task as one monolithic transformation in a general purpose transformation language. As already argued before, such ad-hoc approaches suffer poor scalability and reuse potential. Instead, a description of such complex tasks as a composition of global model management operations favors scalability and reuse: Firstly, one is not concerned with handling fine-grained relationships on the local model element level, and secondly, model management operations can be easily reused in order to assemble scripts for different tasks. Thinking of model management scripts as OO programs, as we propose to do, furthermore has the advantage that the code for this model management script does not need to be changed in order to work with other metamodels, as the actual transformations that are invoked, are *dynamically* bound depending on a model's metamodel.

Fig. 2 depicts the described setting and gives a listing of the according *exogenous merge* model management script. Details of the various steps in that script are discussed in the following.

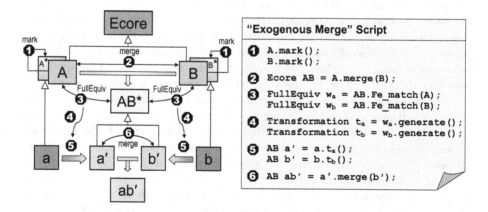

Fig. 2. Model management script for exogenous merge

In the first step (1) a *mark* transformation is run that tags all metamodel elements with a unique id by adding annotations. In the second step (2) a *merge* transformation is executed that unites the metamodels A and B as specified in the *merge* integration specification, for instance through overlapping the two metamodels on certain join points. This results in a new metamodel AB, which also contains the initially introduced markings. In the third step (3) a transformation creates a weaving between each of the original A and B metamodels and the newly created AB metamodel. A transformation creating such a weaving does a relatively easy job, as it can rely on the previously introduced traceability annotations to match model elements. The weavings created in our example comprise a certain integration specification, which in step (4) is derived into executable transformations, which are executed in (5) and migrate the models a and b towards models a' and b' that conform to the AB metamodel. Since these models now conform to the same metamodel, they can be overlapped in a *merge* transformation (6). We would like to mention, that also other ways of realizing traceability mechanisms exist, for instance through weaving a traceability aspect into a base transformation in an aspect-oriented fashion [16]. Embedding traceability information into a model through annotations, in our opinion has the advantage that a transformation producing a weaving can relatively easy create a trace weaving model. For further processing, the annotations could be easily pruned from the model.

3.2   Categorizing Transformations on the Global Level

After having discussed the composition of global model management operations, the following section will establish a better understanding of the transformations that were used in the previous example. However, this will not be done by discussing the behavior of these transformations in terms of how model elements are manipulated, as this is transparent on the global level and would differ for different kinds of metamodels. Rather, the global level requires to put thought on what *kinds of transformations* are being employed.

Hence, we classify our approach's DSILs used to define actual transformations, into certain categories. These categories reflect recurring kinds of transformations prevalent in model engineering. Such a categorization favors the definition of modular and comprehensible transformations and creates a mindset where one can think of solving complex model management tasks through composition of such modular transformations, as exemplified in the previous subsection. Another advantage of this approach is that for every category a generic toolset can be built that allows to manipulate languages falling into a certain category. Transformations producing weavings can all share a tool like the Atlas Model Weaver [7], whereas translating transformations, for instance, can benefit from tooling to capture execution traces.

A similar distinction is made in the area of generic model management [4]. However, we allow the distinction between different categories according to the kind of input (IMM) and output metamodels (OMM) (cf. Table 2) that the transformations act upon, as opposed to focus on making assumptions about the behavior or algebraic properties of transformations.

Table 2 gives an overview by showing a category's input/output characteristics, example transformations, a reference to similar operators proposed in literature, and a function signature being representative for a category's transformations. To put each of the example transformations in a concrete context, we refer to the previously used traceability mechanism in more detail now. First, the *containsAnnotations* transformation is called to check whether a model is free of traceability annotations. If so, with *addTraceAnnotations* traceability annotations are added to all model elements. Next, *translateWithAnnotations* or *mergeWithAnnotations* is called that produces an output model in which the traceability annotations are migrated from source to target model elements. Then, *matchByAnnotations* is invoked which establishes a weaving model representing traceability links according to the annotations contained in source and target model. In a final step, this traceability weaving is input to the *createReverseTranslation* transformation which produces a round-tripping translation transformation.

Table 2. Categories of transformations on the global level

Category	Arity	Output	Function Signatur	Example	Operators in Lit.
Check	1	Prim. Type	P p = check(M m);	containsAnnotations	Check-property [12]
Rewrite	1	OMM==IMM	M m' = rewrite(M m);	addTraceAnnotations	Refactorings [17]
Translation	1	OMM!=IMM	Mb mb = translate(Ma ma);	translateWithAnnotations	ModelGen [3]
Fusion	2	OMM==IMM	M m = fuse(M ma, M mb);	mergeWithAnnotations	Merge [12]
Relation	2	Weaving	W w = relate(Ma ma, Mb mb);	matchByAnnotations	Match [3]
Generation	1	Transform.	T t = generate(W w);	createReverseTranslation	GlueCodeGen [11]

Check. The first category deals with transformations that map models onto primitive value ranges, like booleans or natural numbers. This kind of functions allow to determine whether certain properties hold for models (consistency checks), or to evaluate certain criteria (e.g., number of inheritance relationships) of models.

Rewrite. This category encompasses transformations that modify a model but do not transform it into a model of another metamodel. This kind of transformations can be associated with editing or specialized refactoring operations [17], that do not require input from another model. An example language discussed later on is a language that allows to mark elements in a model with certain annotations.

Translation. A translating function maps concepts of one metamodel onto concepts of another metamodel and henceforth transforms a model conforming to one metamodel into a model conforming to another metamodel. A special case of a translating transformation would be if the source and target metamodels are the same, but nevertheless concepts are translated into other concepts. This would especially be the case when using UML, which, by means of stereotypes or tagged values offers a somewhat weaker mechanism than DSLs to represent concepts. Still we consider such transformations as part of this class, as the same translation language constructs can be of use, even though binding these needs some special effort.

Fusion. We classify a transformation as a fusion, if it takes two models as input and produces an output model taking into account each of the inputs. The input and output models thereby conform to the same metamodel. For instance, this class includes transformations that are usually associated with a merge or a diff [12], although domain specific realizations may potentially blend these two behaviors, by overlapping and clipping certain parts of the source models.

Relation. Transformations of this kind produce special kinds of models, which relate two other models. These models are referred to as weaving models [7] and consist of typed links between elements of left-hand side (LHS) and right-hand side (RHS) models. An example for a transformation creating a weaving could be carried out through a matcher, which heuristically establishes weaving links. Therefore, the creation of a weaving is often a task involving manual effort.

Generation. This kind of transformations generates other transformations. More precisely, they function as a compiler which turns weaving models into executable transformations. Typically this is either accomplished through a transformation whose target metamodel is the abstract syntax of a model transformation language or through a templating mechanism. It is important to note, that our view of a weaving is that a weaving model implicitly references its LHS and its RHS model, hence we omit these models in the above signature. Thus, we can still assume that the generation function has access to read the LHS and RHS models.

4   Integrating Models on the Local Level

The previous section has detailed the global composite and the global level. Hence, this subsection focuses on the remaining abstraction layers. As integration languages reside on the intermediate layer and this section makes use of a concrete example DSIL, the first subsection is dedicated to the *intermediate* level and to introducing the example language. The second subsection discusses the *local composite* level and discusses integration operators for the example DSIL. The *local* level is dealt with in the third subsection and focuses on the definition and extension of execution semantics for integration operators through a mapping towards MTL code.

4.1   An Example DSIL on the Intermediate Level

The abstract syntax of a DSIL is defined in a weaving metamodel [7], which is basically made up of meta-classes for the languages' integration operators. Furthermore, constraints are specified that enable to check whether a certain integration specification is valid. Such an analysis is comparable to static compile-time checking in traditional programming languages. In the following we will give an example for a basic language for the *translation* category. Due to space limitations we will not go into detail about languages of other categories, just as we are not claiming that the described integration operators are complete, as a precise definition is out of scope of this paper.

The setting for our example is depicted in Fig. 3, which shows a simple metamodel for activity diagrams (AD) as the LHS metamodel, and a Gantt-chart project plan (PP) metamodel as the RHS metamodel. An activity diagram consists of vertices and transitions in-between. A project consists of a number of tasks and every task has a reference to its previous task.

The intention is to transform ADs into PPs in a semantics preserving way. Instead of programming the transformation directly, a DSIL is used to specify a mapping that denotes the translation of concepts of the AD metamodel onto concepts of the PP metamodel. The code snippet on the right side of Fig. 3 shows the final transformation code that should be generated in an ATL-like[1] notation.

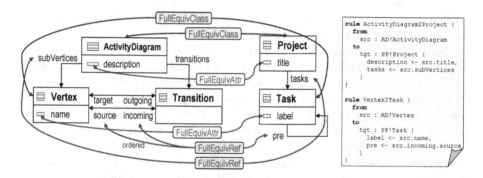

Fig. 3. Example integration specification in the *FullEquiv* language

4.2 Integration Operators on the Local Composite Level

The DSIL used is the so called *FullEquivalence* language, which can be seen as a basic language for the *translation* category. It consists of three operators, namely *FullEquivClass*, *FullEquivAttr*, and *FullEquivRef*, which in a pair-wise manner link classes, attributes, and references, respectively. During the definition of a DSIL, it is important to define how its operators relate to each other. In our example, for instance, the *FullEquivAttr* and the *FullEquivRef* operators have to stand in the context of the *FullEquivClass* operator, as the assignment of values and the setting of references needs to happen in the context of the model elements which these attributes and references belong to. Such a relationship is defined through containment in the metamodel of the *FullEquivalence* language by making the *FullEquivAttr* and the *FullEquivRef* operators children of the *FullEquivClass* parent. Relationships not inferable from structure (e.g., precedence rules) can be specified in a constraint language. An example for

---

[1] For simplicity reasons code snippets use simplified ATL syntax.

a constraint that should be enforced is that an attribute in a target model element cannot be referenced by more than one *FullEquivAttr* operator having the same *FullEquivClass* parent, as this would lead to ambiguity concerning which source attribute should be used to set the target attribute.

4.3   Mapping Integration Operators onto the Local Level

After describing the operators, in the following example it is shown how a generating function can derive an implementation in the form of MTL code. Furthermore, we will exemplify the extension of an existing operator's semantics. The execution semantics are expressed through a function, mapping integration specifications expressed as weaving models onto executable transformations. This is either achieved through a template producing MTL code, or through a transformation creating a transformation program encoded as a model (higher-order transformation). However, writing transformations that produce transformation programs can be a daunting task. Thus, for better understandability, our explanation uses an example template language, which allows to see the output in bits of concrete syntax more intuitively.

Depending on what kind of transformation engine is used, the semantics of the resulting transformations are for instance formalized as abstract state machines [15] or as graph-based formalisms, such as triple-graph-grammars [22].

Continuing the above example, the subsequent paragraphs concentrate on the execution semantics for each of the operators given in Fig. 3, by using ATL-like code templates. At compile-time, each operator is derived into a fragment of ATL-code, only. A weaving in a certain language, though, stands for a complete ATL transformation. The generator, therefore, needs to integrate all these fragments into a complete ATL transformation as shown in Fig. 3.

Fig. 4 depicts pseudo-template code to show how semantics of operators can be specified. The template code consists of target code (ATL) in plain text, and template code in angle brackets which is bound at compile-time against LHS and RHS model elements. Square brackets contain control-flow instructions for the generator. In the template body of the parenting *FullEquivClass* operator for instance, templates of children operators are invoked.

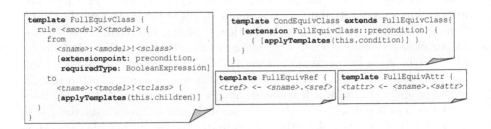

Fig. 4. Template code for integration operators

To enable the extension of existing operators, a plugin-mechanism can be used. Thereby, templates can offer extension-points, into which templates of more specialized operators can plug-in their contributions. In Fig. 4, the *FullEquivClass* template declares an extension point that requires the contribution of a boolean expression. An example for an extension is given by the template of the *CondEquivClass* operator, which itself invokes a template that returns a boolean expression bound to the operator's context. Through this inheritance-based reuse, a *CondEquivClass* operator can inherit all of *FullEquivClass'* behavior and additionally denote that a model element should be transformed if a certain condition holds, only.

5   Related Work

In this paper we have laid out an approach stretching across various abstraction layers, from global model management to local MTLs. As shown in Table 3, existing work typically focuses on certain abstraction levels, but, in our opinion, have not established a common understanding of how bottom-up approaches can be utilized for the implementation of top-down approaches in a scalable way. Furthermore, we compare related works on basis of certain key characteristics of our approach, like the employment of DSILs, OO-style model management scripts, the extensibility of operators and the explicit use of declarative integration specifications.

Table 3. Comparison of related work

Related Work	Key Characteristics				Abstraction Levels				
	DSIL	OO	Extensible	Declarative	Glob. Comp.	Glob.	Intermed.	Loc. Comp.	Loc.
MMgmt.	-	-	-	+	+	+	-	-	-
MOMENT	-	-	~	+	-	+	-	-	+
GGT	+	-	-	+	-	+	+	+	~
AMW	+	-	+	+	-	-	+	~	-
EOL	+	-	+	~	-	-	+	+	+
ATL	-	-	-	~	-	-	-	-	+

Model management as proposed by Bernstein et al. aims at applying operators on the model level [3] [12]. In [4] a language-independent semantics is established to guide the implementation of model management operators. Although our work embraces the ideas of model management operators, e.g., by categorizing transformations, we also extend the notion of model management scripts with OO-mechanisms and explicitly focus on providing for scalable implementations through DSILs.

MOMENT [10] realizes model management operators by defining their semantics in QVT relations [23] that are mapped onto the algebraic specification language Maude, which, through term rewriting, executes the defined transformations. Although we focus on supporting the implementation of model management operators, the justified intention behind MOMENT to study formal properties of transformations could complement our approach in the future.

However, our approach could potentially do this on the more abstract level of basically language independent integration operators and DSILs, as opposed to MOMENT, where Maude doubles as an execution environment as well as a testbed for proving formal properties.

The *Glue Generator Tool* (GGT) [8] aims at the reuse of existing MDA applications by specifying composition relationships between platform-independent models (PIMs), of which glue code for the integration of platform-specific models (PSMs) can be derived. Although rules similar to our integration operators are offered, our approach seems to be more flexible as we allow to extend the semantics of integration operators. Furthermore, the integration scenario described in GGT could be realized as a model management script carrying out the necessary transformations, which could allow for better modularity and maintainability of the overall approach.

The *Atlas Model Weaver* (AMW) [7] is a generic, extensible tool that aims at supporting modelers to establish semantic links between elements of arbitrary models or metamodels. The links are referred to as weavings and are formalized in a weaving metamodel, which can be extended to denote link types with special semantics. This extension mechanism is the basis for defining the syntax of integration operators and DSILs in our approach. Created weavings can then be subject to further processing like derivation of MTL code.

The *Epsilon Object Language* (EOL) is a language for managing models of arbitrary metamodels [21]. It can either be used as a standalone language for model navigation and comparison, or also as an infrastructure on which task-specific languages such as the *Epsilon Merging Language* (EML) or the *Epsilon Comparison Language* (ECL) can be built. Similarly, the *Atlas Transformation Language* (ATL) [1] is a hybrid (imperative/declarative) MTL based on the Eclipse Modeling Framework. In our opinion, both efforts present themselves as possible execution environments for our approach. Especially the definition of execution semantics for DSILs falling into categories like *Check* or *Fusion* could be conveniently accomplished relying on the expressiveness of languages like ECL or EML.

6   Conclusion and Future Work

In this paper we have proposed a conceptual approach which allows to define declarative model integration languages to implement model management operators, and to compose these into model management scripts. The distinction between local and global transformations fosters reuse of existing integration operators, and allows for sound composition of transformation functions. We have given a description of transformation categories and exemplified the composition of transformations into model management scripts. According to the understanding of transformations defining the *integration behavior* of metamodels, these scripts rely on an OO mechanism to invoke transformations which are dynamically bound depending on a metamodel's type. Furthermore, we discussed the syntax and the semantics of an example integration language and described a way to extend integration operators.

We think of the approach described in this paper as a step towards the realization of future transformation systems which operate on the global model level, as opposed to the local model-element level, only. To raise the level of abstraction, domain specific languages in the form of declarative integration specifications play a key part in our approach. These are built on existing general-purpose transformation languages and are basically technology neutral. We have experimented with the implementation of various weaving languages which consist of operators that form the language kernels for the proposed transformation categories. Current work deals with building a technical framework based on existing model engineering infrastructure supporting our approach and a generically reusable toolset for various transformation categories.

In the context of ModelCVS, besides the integration of modeling tools, a crucial issue is the support for language evolution through metamodel modification. Future work will investigate to what extent such metamodel extensions can have characteristics analogous to traditional OO sub-classing, which would allow transformations to be inherited towards extended versions of metamodels.

References

1. ATL Homepage, http://www.eclipse.org/gmt/atl/, 2006.
2. Batory, D., *Multilevel models in model-driven engineering, product lines, and metaprogramming.* IBM Systems Journal, VOL 45, NO 3, 2006.
3. Bernstein, P.A., *Applying Model Management to Classical Meta Data Problems.* In Proceedings of the Conference on Innovative Data Systems Research (CIDR), Asilomar, California, January 2003.
4. Bernstein, P.A., A.Y. Halevy, S. Melnik, and E. Rahm, *A Semantics for Model Management Operators.* Microsoft Technical Report, June 2004.
5. Bernstein, P.A., S. Melnik, and E. Rahm, *Rondo: A Programming Platform for Generic Model Management.* In Proceedings of the ACM SIGMOD International Conference on Management of Data, San Diego, California, USA, June 2003.
6. Bézivin et al., *Combining Preoccupations with Models.* 1st Workshop on Models and Aspects - Handling Crosscutting Concerns in MDSD at the 19th ECOOP, July 2005.
7. Bézivin, J., E. Breton, M. Didonet Del Fabro, G. Gueltas, and F. Jouault, *AMW: A Generic Model Weaver.* In Proceedings of the 1ère Journée sur l'Ingénierie Dirigée par les Modèles, Paris, France, 2005.
8. Bézivin, J., F. Jouault, D. Kolovos, I. Kurtev, and R.F. Paige, *A Canonical Scheme for Model Composition.* A. Rensink and J. Warmer (Eds.): ECMDA-FA 2006, LNCS 4066, pp. 346–360, 2006.
9. Bézivin, J., F. Jouault, P. Rosenthal, and P. Valduriez, *Modeling in the Large and Modeling in the Small.* LNCS, No. 3599, edited by Uwe Aßmann, Mehmet Aksit, Arend Rensink. Springer-Verlag GmbH, pp. 33–46, 2005.
10. Boronat, A., J.Á. Carsí, and I. Ramos, *Algebraic Specification of a Model Transformation Engine.* European Joint Conferences on Theory and Practice of Softwaere (ETAPS06), Vienna, March 2006.

11. Bouzitouna, S., M.P. Gervais, and X. Blanc, *Models Reuse in MDA*. In Proceedings of the International Conference on Software Engineering Research and Practice (SERP05), Las Vegas, USA, June 2005.

12. Brunet et al., *A Manifesto for Model Merging*. In Proceedings of the 1st International Workshop on Global Integrated Model Management (GaMMa2006), Shanghai, May 2006.

13. DeRemer, F., and H. Kron, *Programming-in-the-Large Versus Programming-in-the-Small*. IEEE Trans. on Soft. Eng. 2(2), 1976.

14. Engel, K.-D., D.S. Kolovos, and R.F. Paige, *Using a Model Merging Language for Reconciling Model Versions*. A. Rensink and J. Warmer (Eds.): ECMDA-FA 2006, LNCS 4066, pp. 143–157, 2006.

15. Gurevich, Y., P. Kutter, M. Odersky, and L. Thiele (eds.), *Abstract State Machines: Theory and Applications*. LNCS VOL 1912, Springer-Verlag, 2000.

16. Jouault, F., *Loosely Coupled Traceability for ATL*. In Proceedings of the European Conference on Model Driven Architecture (ECMDA) workshop on traceability, Nuremberg, Germany, 2005.

17. Kappel et al., *Lifting Metamodels to Ontologies: A Step to the Semantic Integration of Modeling Languages*. In Proceedings of the 9th International Conference on Model Driven Engineering Languages and Systems (MoDELS/UML), Genova, Italy, October 2006.

18. Kappel et al., *On Models and Ontologies - A Semantic Infrastructure Supporting Model Integration*. In Proceedings of Modellierung, Innsbruck, Tirol, Austria, March 2006.

19. Kappel et al., *Towards A Semantic Infrastructure Supporting Model-based Tool Integration*. In Proc. of the 1st Int. Workshop on Global integrated Model Management (GaMMa2006), Shanghai, May 2006.

20. Kapsammer, E., T. Reiter, W. Retschitzegger, and W. Schwinger, *Model Integration Through Mega Operations*. In Proc. of the Int. Workshop on Model-driven Web Engineering (MDWE), Sydney, July 2005.

21. Kolovos, D.S., R.F. Paige, and F.A.C. Polack, *The Epsilon Object Language (EOL)*. A. Rensink and J. Warmer (Eds.): ECMDA-FA 2006, LNCS 4066, pp. 128–142, 2006.

22. Königs, A., and A. Schürr *Specification of Graph Translators with Triple Graph Grammars*. In Proc. of Graph-Theoretic Concepts in Computer Science, 20th Int. Workshop, Herrsching, Germany, 1994.

23. Object Management Group (OMG), *MOF QVT Final Adopted Specification*. November 2005.

24. Reiter, T., W. Retschitzegger, W. Schwinger, and M. Stumptner, *A Generator Framework for Domain-Specific Model Transformation Languages*. In Proceedings of the 8th International Conference on Enterprise Information Systems (ICEIS), Paphos, Cyprus, May 2006.

25. Stumptner, M., M. Schrefl, and G. Grossmann, *On the Road to Behavior-Based Integration*. In Proceedings of Conceptual Modelling, First Asia-Pacific Conference on Conceptual Modelling (APCCM2004), Dunedin, New Zealand, January 2004.

26. Wiederhold, G., P. Wegner, and S. Ceri, *Toward megaprogramming*. CACM, Volume 35, Issue 11, pp. 89–99, November 1992.

MoDELS 2006 Doctoral Symposium

Gabriela Arévalo[1] and Robert Pettit[2]

[1] LIRMM – Université de Montpellier II, France
Gabriela.Arevalo@lirmm.fr
[2] The Aerospace Corporation, USA
rob.pettit@aero.org

Doctoral Symposium Overview

The Doctoral Symposium at the MoDELS conference provided an international forum for doctoral students to interact with other students and faculty mentors. The Doctoral Symposium sought to bring together PhD Students working in areas related to modeling and model-driven engineering. Selected students had the opportunity to present and to discuss their research goals, methods and results within a constructive and international atmosphere. The goal of the symposium was to provide useful guidance for completion of the dissertation research and initiation of a research career. The symposium was intended for students who have already settled on a specific research proposal and have some preliminary results, but still had enough time remaining before their final defense so that they could benefit from the Symposium discussions. Fifteen PhD students from different countries submitted papers to the symposium. Submissions were judged on originality, overall contribution, technical merit, presentation quality and relevance to the conference topics. Each submission was reviewed by one mentor from the senior program committee. Of the fifteen PhD submissions, seven students were invited to present their work at the symposium. To motivate the interaction between the participants, each student that was invited to attend was assigned a specific mentor to be in charge of leading the discussion after the student's presentation, and a specific mini-mentor (another PhD student) to contribute additional questions.

We would like to thank the members of the doctoral symposium panel for their work in reviewing the students' submissions, and for participating in the symposium and providing feedback to the students. The panel members were Hassan Gomaa (George Mason University), Jörg Kienzle (McGill University), Dorina Petriu (Carlton University) and Claudia Pons (Universidad Nacional de La Plata).

Gabriela Arévalo
Robert Pettit
MoDELS 2006 Doctoral Symposium Co-Chairs

T. Kühne (Ed.): MoDELS 2006 Workshops, LNCS 4364, p. 277, 2007.
© Springer-Verlag Berlin Heidelberg 2007

Model Driven Security Engineering for the Realization of Dynamic Security Requirements in Collaborative Systems

Muhammad Alam

Research Group Quality Engineering – Institut für Informatik
University of Innsbruck, Austria
muhammad.alam@uibk.ac.at

Abstract. Service Oriented Architectures with underlying technologies like web services and web services orchestration have opened the door to a wide range of novel application scenarios, especially in the context of inter-organizational cooperation. One of the remaining obstacles for a wide-spread use of these techniques is security. Companies and organizations open their systems and core business processes to partners only if a high level of trust can be guaranteed. The emergence of web services security standards provides a valuable and effective paradigm for addressing the security issues arising in the context of inter-organizational cooperation. The low level of abstraction of these standards is, however, still an unresolved issue which makes them inaccessible to the domain expert and remains a major obstacle when aligning security objectives with the customer needs. Their complexity makes implementation easily prone of error. This paper provides a bird eye view of a doctoral work, where an effort is made to develop a conceptual framework – called SECTET in order to apply model driven security engineering techniques for the realization of high-level security requirements.

1   Introduction

The emerging trend of globalization strongly characterizes the need for integration between business processes in order to attract broader audience to their services. It is widely accepted that business processes are still not mature along the path of having online integration. This can be attributed among other factors to the fact that a well defined trust management framework between the online partners located across geographical boundaries does not exist. Existing approaches for trust management are generally applicable to scenarios where the data is stored in a centralized repository. However, for cross-business processes, due to geographical and political reasons, a centralized repository is not always a viable option. In such scenarios, due to privacy, security and management reasons, every peer maintains its own set of data and has its own trust management requirements. Every peer has to comply with the trust management requirements of other peers in an online business scenario. Further, the use of

T. Kühne (Ed.): MoDELS 2006 Workshops, LNCS 4364, pp. 278–287, 2007.

different proprietary standards at different partner's sites for trust management also hinders successful B2B integration.

Service Oriented Architectures (SOAs) with underlying technologies like web services and web services orchestration have opened the door to a wide range of novel application scenarios, especially in the context of inter-organizational cooperation. By providing a solution to interoperability concerns, the advent of web services standards [22] have paved the way for the integration of business processes. Due to this flexibility, on the one hand, business partners having common business goals can connect their enterprise applications regardless of their platform or technology in use. On the other hand, this decentralized management has increased the exposure of enterprise applications and requires a thorough investigation of their security implications. Access control and privacy issues are always of major concern to distributed applications.

Applications built on web service technologies use plenty of standards like WS-Trust for trust negotiation, WS-security for the fulfilment of security requirements like confidentiality and integrity and eXtensbile Access Control Mark-up Language (XACML) for the specification of access policies to name a few. These open standards enable the agreement and inter-operability at the technical level, upon which different proprietary applications can be built. The low level of abstraction of these standards is, however, still an unresolved issue which makes them inaccessible to the domain expert and remains a major obstacle when aligning security objectives with the customer needs. Their complexity makes implementation easily prone of error. Further, these web services security standards have a distinct *inter-operability oriented* focus – that is, these standards abstract the heterogeneity of the underlying middleware platforms only rather than the *design intent* – which is, to model high-level security concepts in application domains. Enormous growth of these standards is also a vexing problem. The intricate inter-dependencies among these standards (e.g. dependencies among XPath, XQuery and XACML etc) require a considerable amount of time in mastering these standards which could be a daunting task. A pressing need is therefore, to develop techniques that can abstract the complexities of the underlying security architectures (based on web services security standards).

Moreover, in order to provide a satisfying alignment between the high-level security concepts in application domains and its corresponding implementation, all stakeholders involved in the realization of the distributed system – from the domain experts to the software engineers – must have a common understanding of the security requirements, each one at the appropriate level of abstraction. This means that the security concepts should not be confined only either to high-level descriptions or to low-level implementations. A very strong binding between the high-level security models and the underlying implementation is required and only abstraction techniques are not enough.

Over the years, an important goal of the software researchers is to develop techniques to model domain concepts in terms of their design intent rather than the underlying implementation environment. Effective complexity management techniques play a significantly important role in the development of accurate, reliable, and maintainable information systems which become increasingly larger, complex and distributed in nature. In this context, *Model-Driven Engineering* (MDE) is a promising approach 1) that treats models as an important artefact during software development; 2) that precisely envisages the problem and the solution domain at different level of abstractions and; 3) that defines methodologies for each level of abstraction and provides techniques to lower the level of abstraction by defining relationships between the participating models. The approach of MDE has two pillar aspects. The aspect *Domain Specific Language* (DSL) helps to model concepts in specific application domains such as online e-government, health-care services etc. Domain specific languages are formalized using metamodels which are used to describe relationships among concepts in a domain. The aspect *Transformation Engine* analyzes various aspects of the models in the problem domain and then synthesizes implementation artefacts from the models of the problem domain.

The software design framework from the OMG [13] – called *Model Driven Architecture* [11] – is considered as an implementation of the MDE [18]. Using the MDA framework, the software functionality is modelled with a standard modelling language (UML) as a *Platform Independent Model* (PIM) and then transformed to one or more *Platform Specific Models* (PSMs) or other PIMs. The MDA paradigm considers models an essential part of the definition of the software rather than a visual aid for understanding and communication. This makes it the most appropriate solution to abstract the complexities of the underlying platform while remaining expressive to model complex business scenarios.

We specialize the concept of MDE to *Model-Driven Security Engineering* (MDSE) by providing a framework in which security concepts in an application domain are modelled using UML and DSLs at the PIM abstraction level and are merged with business requirement models. These security enhanced PIMs are transformed to different open standard specifications (PSM) which in turn configure our component based reference architecture [6].

The rest of the paper is organized as follows: section 2 presents the conceptual foundations of our framework and the DSL in the context of a case study from the health-care domain. Section 3 summarizes the related work and finally in section 4 a conclusion is drawn with a focus on our contributions (section 4.1) and future work (section 4.2).

2 MDE for the Realization of Dynamic Security Requirements

The SECTET project cluster – a (model driven) security engineering framework – facilitates the design and implementation of secure inter-organizational workflows. Based on the SOA paradigm, the objective of the SECTET-framework is to design and implement inter-organizational workflows in a peer-to-peer environment – i.e. without central control. Case studies from the domain of health-care, e-government and education gave us the opportunity to the apply the SECTET-framework in real life scenarios [8,15,5,16,7,4,1]. The framework weaves the ideas about MDA, MDE and web services standards together in to an inter-organizational workflow conceptual framework that is more than the sum of its parts.

The framework caters the needs of a broader domain termed as *"Security Critical Inter-organizational workflows Scenarios"*. All component based application domains are under the scope of SECTET-framework broader domain. We believe that security concepts like authentication, authorization etc are fundamentally same for different application domains [9]. For example, the fundamental concept for authorization – called Role Based Access Control (RBAC) [17] is a general security concept and has been specialized in different application contexts. Similarly, SECTET represents a high-level repository of security concepts which are realized in specific, component based application domains. In this sense, the abstract languages defined within the SECTET-framework broader domain are termed as DSLs. Security requirements such as workflow security requirements, access control etc are modelled using DSLs at the design level and seamlessly integrated as security patterns in the business requirements models.

The **Trust Management** module within the SECTET-framework – the focus of my PhD thesis – deals with the realization of dynamic security requirements[1]. The module is composed of four major components. The **Analysis Component** employs the security use cases in order to capture dynamic security requirements. The security usecases are supported by a catalogue of constraint patterns which hosts a variety of positive and negative constraints patterns for dynamic security requirements. The constraint vocabulary defined through the catalogue helps to maintain a common understanding between all the stakeholders from the domain experts to the software engineers involved in the realization of distributed systems.

The objective of the **Modelling Component** within the Trust Management module is to make a clear separation of concerns at each appropriate level of abstraction and integrate them using appropriate modelling techniques. At the PIM abstraction level, the component models domain concepts with a UML profile called SECTET-UML. The profile is used to model business requirements such as data type and static security requirements such as roles and their respective hierarchies [17]. Within this classification schema, the *Document Model* (describing the data type view for the documents travelling between the partners and for the profiles of the users in the form of a UML class diagram) and the *Interface Model* (describing the abstract set of UML operations that each partner provides) are part of the business requirement models. The Role Model (describing role and their hierarchies in the form of a UML class diagram) and the *Privacy, Rights Delegation* and *Access Model* (describing conditions under which a role from the Role Model is allowed to access a (web) service from the Interface Model) are part of the access requirement models. In order to model

---

[1] Security requirements like access control, privacy and delegation of rights that are dependent on the calling subject profiles, accessed object attributes or current system state.

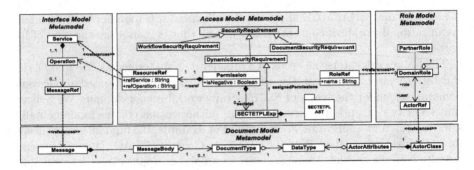

Fig. 1. Domain Model (Some Attributes are omitted for brevity)

dynamic security requirements, SECTET-UML is combined with a DSL – called SECTET-PL.

SECTET-PL [19,5] – a predicative language in OCL-style [21] – is tightly integrated with the UML – a de-facto standard for modelling. UML model property check at the PIM abstract level is the guiding principle for the design of SECTET-PL. Due to its restricted semantic scope, the generation of dynamic security policies from the abstract SECTET-PL specifications is very intuitive. Using the SECTET-PL predicates, positive and negative permissions can be specified with respect to any UML class diagram. Due to this flexibility, the dynamic security requirements specified via SECTET-PL can be transformed to any middle-ware, object-oriented security platform. SECTET-PL has been successfully applied (with some extensions) in multiple dynamic security requirement specification domains such as attribute-based delegation of rights [3] and privacy-enhanced access control [1].

The Modelling Component uses the MOF framework for the integration of business requirements (Document and Interface Model) with access control requirements (Role and Access Model) at the metalevel (cf. Fig 1). The metamodel – called *Domain Model* provides the integration between the business requirement models and the access requirement models with a focus on resolving model dependencies through proxy classes (such as `ActrorAttributeRef`, `AssociationEndRef` etc).

Figure 2a shows an instance of the Domain Model for an example dynamic security requirement from the medical domain. According to this example (cf. Fig 2b), *"A physician is only allowed to modify a medical record if he/she is a primary care physician"*. The `subject.map` function 1) abstracts the details of the authentication 2) assigns a role to the calling subject based on his/her credentials and 3) maps it to an internal representation in the *Document Model* (cf. Fig 2c – Physician). Figure 2 shows a simplified instance of the Domain Model (cf. Fig 1). According to this model, the instance of the positive `Permission` (`isNegative=false`) is associated with a SECTETPLExp and is assigned to the instance of the `RoleRef(PhysicianRole)`. The SECTETPLExp contains the abstract syntax tree for the SECTET-PL constraint. In this way, the Domain Model provides a common syntactical and semantic base for the SECTET-PL expressions.

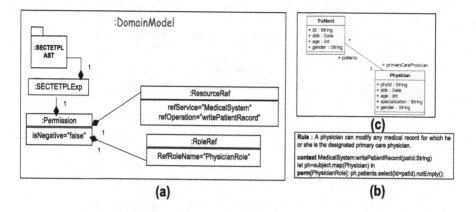

Fig. 2. A Simplified Instance of Domain Model

At the PSM abstraction level, the Modelling Component defines the domain specific web service security standard metamodels. For instance, the domain specific XACML [23] policy metamodel (cf. Fig 3) extends the general XACML policy model with a `RolePolicySet` (RPS) and a `PermissionPolicySet`(PPS). These policy sets define the structure that the XACML policies will have in our domain.

The **Transformation Component** within the Trust Management module incorporates two transformation patterns. The *Model-To-Model* (M2M) pattern deals with the transformation of high-level access requirement models to low-level XACML policy metamodel using the operational transformations of the *Query View Transformations* (QVT) [14] – an MDA standard. The *Model-To-Code* (M2C) pattern uses the XACML policy metamodel instances to generate XACML policy files. In order to transform the SECTET-PL expressions associated with the permission object (cf. Fig 2), we use the black box operations. According to QVT specification, black box operations can be considered as Java Native Interface (JNI) methods and are used to allow the domain specific libraries/algorithms to calculate complex model property values from the source model. The calculated values are then used to populate the target model elements. The black box operations can be coded in any programming language with MOF bindings. In this way, the specification of complex domain specific algorithms (such as syntax and semantic analysis of SECTET-PL expressions in our case) in their optimal languages can be done rather than in QVT transformation languages which are too general and therefore not best suited for coding these algorithms. Consequently, the complexity and length of the QVT scripts is reduced significantly and makes the implementation of some parts of the transformation opaque.

In the current project state, we use the Eclipse Modelling Framework (EMF) to generate domain specific instance models of the XACML metamodel. The XACML metamodel is drawn using Rational Rose and imported into the EMF. The imported metamodel is then populated with domain specific values and

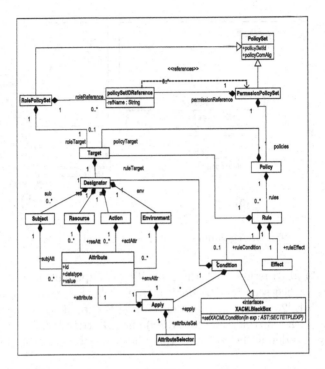

Fig. 3. XACML metamodel

transformed to XACML policy files using the OpenArchitectureWare's XPAND template language. For more information on how it is done, please refer to [12].

The **Reference Architecture** component within the Trust Management module – a web services enabled runtime environment realizes the security arte-facts generated from the M2C transformations. The Reference Architecture implemented as XACML dataflow model provides the backbone and the enabling technology for the artefacts defined at the model-level.

3   Related Work

Compared to other approaches that support a policy language for the specification of dynamic constraints, our primary goals are different from the existing approaches in that we intend to apply model-driven engineering techniques to advance aspects of access control. To the best of our knowledge, this is the first approach for model-to-model transformation of high-level access models to low-level web services models.

[10] presents an approach for the application of pattern-based software development to recurring problems in the domain of security. The basic idea of the approach is to capture expert-knowledge in the security domain and make it available to developers as a security pattern during software development.

The approach provides an in-depth view of security patterns, its development through an ontology based knowledge base and sorting out relationships between different existing security patterns. Although the author uses patterns to systematically capture knowledge about security issues at the model level, the semantics remain close to the technical level. The author does not address transformation in any way. The author in [2] has presented a verification framework for UML models enriched with security properties through a UML profile called UMLSec. The framework stores UMLSec models using XMI files format in a Meta Data Repository (MDR) which is then queried using Java Metadata Interfaces (JMI) by different analyzers. These analyzers perform static as well dynamic analysis on the UMLSec models for different security properties like confidentiality, integrity etc. Compared to these approaches, our framework is more domain specific and focused on the automatic generation of (standard) security artefacts specified during the early phases of software development. Further our objective is to develop high-level abstract languages through which executable security requirements of a distributed system can be specified at a higher level of abstraction. [20] proposes a UML based notation for access control using RBAC and provides code generation exclusively for object oriented platforms (J2EE or .NET). Our approach has the advantage that it can be used in any environment and also by using web services standards in our case, policy exchange and management across domain boundaries will be easier.

4   Conclusions

In this paper, we presented an overview of a doctoral work where an effort is made to develop a conceptual model driven security engineering framework for the realization of high-level dynamic security requirements. The framework – called SECTET particularly focus on the alignment of high-level security objectives of business services with the underlying implementation in the form of Privacy Security Trust (PST) technologies.

4.1   Contributions

In summary, our contributions include (1) focusing on the security concepts in a domain at the PIM abstraction level and making a clear separation between the security models and the underlying security architectures; (2) providing an abstract representation of the underlying security artefacts responsible for the configuration of security components rather than relying on direct code generation; (3) resolving model dependencies while integrating security models with the business requirement models not only at the model and application level but at the metamodel level as well and; (4) providing explicit high-level transformations for the platform independent DSL and its supporting models to platform specific security models.

4.2 Future Work

Currently, we are working along two lines. We are pushing an implementation of a model transformation engine based on MOF-QVT with the EMF for research purposes and extending our tool support [5,19] to perform visible QVT transformations. Secondly, we are extending SECTET-PL for the specification of rights delegation, obligation, information filtering and separation of duty constraints.

References

1. M. Alam, M. Hafner, and R. Breu. Modeling Authorization in a SOA based Application Scenario. IASTED Software Engineering 2006, ISBN: 0-88986-572-8.
2. J. Jürjens. Secure Systems Development with UML. ISBN: 3540007016.
3. M. Alam et al. A Framework for Modeling Restricted Delegation in Service Oriented Architecture. To Appear in TrustBus 2006.
4. M. Alam et al. Model Driven Security for Web Services (MDS4WS). INMIC 2004,Digi Obj Id 10.1109/INMIC.2004.1492930.
5. M. Alam et al. Modeling Permissions in a (U/X)ML World. IEEE ARES 2006, ISBN: 0-7695-2567-9.
6. M. Hafner et al. A Security Architecture For Inter-organizational Workflows-Putting WS Security Standards Together. ICEIS 2005, ISBN: 972-8865-19-8.
7. M. Hafner et al. Modeling Inter-organizational Workflow Security in a Peer-to-Peer Environment. IEEE ICWS 2005,ISBN: 0-7695-2409-5.
8. M. Hafner et al. SECTET An Extensible Framework for the Realization of Secure Inter-Organizational Workflows. Accepted for ICEIS 2006.
9. M. Hafner, M. Alam, R. Breu. A MOF/QVT-based Domain Architecture for Model Driven Security . To Appear in IEEE/ACM Models 2006.
10. M. Schumacher. Security Engineering with Patterns. LNCS 2754 ISBN: 3-540-40731-6, 2003.
11. Model Driven Architecture. http://www.omg.org/mda.
12. OAW For EMF Example available at. http://www.eclipse.org/gmt/oaw/doc/30_emfExample.pdf .
13. Object Management Group. http://www.omg.org.
14. Query View Transformation: OMG Adapted Specification available at. http://www.omg.org/docs/ptc/05-11-01.pdf.
15. R. Breu et al. Model Driven Security for Inter-Organizational Workflows in e-Government. TCGOV 2005, Proceedings. ISBN 3-540-25016-6.
16. R. Breu et al. Web service engineering - advancing a new software engineering discipline. ICWE 2005, LNCS 3579.
17. Role Based Access Control avialable at. http://csrc.nist.gov/rbac/.
18. S. Brahe and K. Osterbye. Business Process Modeling: Defining Domain Specific Modeling Languages by Use of UML Profiles. ECMDA-FA 2006, LNCS 4066, pp.241-255, 2006.
19. SECTETPL : A Predicative Language for the Specification of Access Rights available at. http://qe-informatik.uibk.ac.at/~muhammad/TechnicalReportSECTETPL.pdf.

20. T. Lodderstedt, D. Basin and J. Doser. A UML Based Modeling Language for Model-Driven Security . 5th international conference UML 2002 Dresden, Germany, 2002.
21. UML 2.0 OCL Specification available at. http://www.omg.org/docs/ptc/03-10-14.pdf.
22. Web service security specifications, available at.   http://www.oasis-open.org/specs/index.php.
23. XACML   2.0   Specification   Set.   http://www.oasis-open.org/committees/tc_home.php?wg_abbrev=xacml.

Educators' Symposium at MoDELS 2006

Ludwik Kuzniarz

Department of Software Engineering and Computer Science,
Blekinge University of Technology, Ronneby, Sweden
Ludwik.Kuzniarz@bth.se

Overview

Model-driven development approaches and technologies for software-based systems, in which development is centered round the manipulation of models, raise the level of abstraction and thus, improve our abilities to develop complex systems. Therefore, a number of approaches and tools have been proposed for the model-driven development (MDD) of software-based systems..

Putting the model-driven development vision into practice requires not only sophisticated modeling approaches and tools, but also considerable training and education efforts. To make people ready for model-driven development, its principles and applications need to be taught to practitioners in industry, incorporated in university curricula, and probably even introduced in schools.

Industry is striving to improve their practice of software development by adopting MDD. The adoption, nevertheless, is determined by the availability of skilled software engineers who have been educated and trained in modeling and model-driven development. On the other hand teaching model-driven development skills slowly influences the practices in industry as an increasing number of graduates might make realizing the vision of MDD possible.

The educator's symposium at MoDELS is intended as a forum in which educators and trainers can meet to discuss pedagogy, use of technology in the classroom, and share their experience pertaining to teaching modeling techniques and model-driven development.

The leading topic of this symposium was the synergy between industrial needs, influences on education and vice versa. A special emphasis will be put on the synergy between industrial needs and university education. In particular the following topics are encouraged:

- Designing of and experience from university courses at various levels with industrial needs in mind
- How to include industrial experiences into teaching modeling and MDD
- How to identify modeling-related topics to be undertaken while teaching modeling and MDD, which are of interests to industry
- How to ensure and assess industrial relevance of the contents of modeling courses
- How to assess industrial relevance of the teaching/learning process
- How the teaching of modeling techniques influences industrial practices
- Methodology issues (how to teach modeling or MDD) with industry in mind
- Integrating modeling and MDD into the software engineering curriculum

T. Kühne (Ed.): MoDELS 2006 Workshops, LNCS 4364, pp. 288–290, 2007.

- Teaching modeling, MDD and associated tools (requirements, available tools)
- Requirements from industry for university education in MDD
- Experiences from industry about education in MDD
- Case studies on required skills for realizing the vision of MDD.

Presentations

The presentations at the Educators' symposium leaned towards industrial relevance of modeling courses. The majority of papers considered the issues of industrial relevance of the education, which was one of the main topics of the symposium. In particular the papers addressed the following issues:

- experiences with teaching modeling throughout the software engineering curriculum
- using project-based learning as a vehicle for teaching modeling
- teaching modeling through student projects where parts of tools are implemented
- teaching modeling in the context of J2EE applications
- using an artificially created software development laboratory as a means of enhancing the motivation for learning modeling

All topics formed a basis for the discussion on subjects related to teaching the concepts of modeling and model-driven software development. All papers considered model-driven software development as the necessary skills for the future software developers.

The variety of authors from various countries from 2 continents provided an opportunity to compare the industrial views on modeling – from modeling being a desired skill in industry to modeling being only a surplus (while the desired competence was in the tools and technologies). These aspects led to two interesting discussion sections.

Discussions

The discussions during the symposium were concerned with two main aspects: maximizing students' chances of success on the global job market, building an experience exchange network between the student community and the teacher community. The following points were addressed during the discussion:

- Course content, in particular lectures and supplementary activities, such as exercises and laboratories,
- Process of teaching
- Format of the course, in particular, the distinction between education and training, as the latter seems to be more appreciated by industry
- Course support
  - training materials, such as textbooks, material from the web, Wiki – maintained by the students themselves,
  - Tools used during courses.

Main directions of the next symposium were also discussed. The first is industrial relevance from the students' learning perspectives. The next symposium is going to address the teaching process by observing elements important for students in order to be more competitive on the job market, to minimize the effort required to adjust to the company environment, and to maximize the benefits from the modeling skills.

Second, but not less important direction was that there is a need for a poster session where educational models are displayed and the educational aspects are highlighted.

There is also a suggestion to investigate a possibility of having a joint session with the doctoral symposium, as the doctoral students are a part of the intended audience of the courses given in modeling. In particular the joint session would be intended to acquire their opinions on the industrial relevance of the courses they had during their studies. Finally, the participants stressed the need to involve students from the university which is organizing the next MoDELS conference in the discussion sessions in the symposium.

A valuable contribution to the symposium was the invited presentation by Robert France on the basic ideas behind the repository of models for Model Driven development. The repository is being developed within the REMoDD project aimed at developing a community-driven repository that will contain artifacts whose use can significantly improve MDD, and enhance the learning experience of MDD students. The second aspect – teaching and learning perspective – has been later discussed. In particular, the questions of what should be included in the repository from teaching/learning perspective , how the access to its resources for teachers and students has to be arranged, and how to ensure the quality and didactic relevance of the artifacts in the repository. The description of the projects has been included as one of the symposium follow up materials.

Summary

The symposium presentations gave a representative treatment of the issues related to industrial relevance of model focused and driven education. The discussion tried to discuss and assess the teaching from both teacher and student perspectives and building an experience network.

Based on the discussion among the program committee and voting of the participants, two papers were nominated as the best papers:

- *If You're Not Modeling, You're Just Programming: Modeling throughout an Undergraduate Software Engineering Program*, by James Vallino, from Department of Software Engineering, Rochester Institute of Technology, USA, - describing a holistic approach to the introduction of modeling awareness in engineering practice in the overall software engineering curriculum.
- *Teaching software modeling in simulated software environment*, by Robert Szmurlo and Michal Smialek, from Warsaw University of Technology, Poland - presenting an attempt to show the students how to cope the real life problems of project development in a simulated environment.

If You're Not Modeling, You're Just Programming: Modeling Throughout an Undergraduate Software Engineering Program

James Vallino

Department of Software Engineering, Rochester Institute of Technology
Rochester, NY 14623-5608, USA
J.Vallino@se.rit.edu

Abstract. Modeling is a hallmark of the practice of engineering. Through centuries, engineers have used models ranging from informal "back of the envelope" scribbles to formal, verifiable mathematical models. Whether circuit models in electrical engineering, heat-transfer models in mechanical engineering, or queuing theory models in industrial engineering, modeling makes it possible to perform rigorous analysis that is the cornerstone of modern engineering. By considering software development as fundamentally an engineering endeavor, RIT's software engineering program strives to instill a culture of engineering practice by exposing our students to both formal and informal modeling of software systems throughout the entire curriculum. This paper describes how we have placed modeling in most aspects of our curriculum. The paper also details the specific pedagogy that we use in several courses to teach our students how to create, analyze and implement models of software systems.

1 Introduction

There has been much discussion of software development as an engineering profession and what changes are necessary in the undergraduate education of software professionals for the profession to move forward [1-3]. In 1993, Rochester Institute of Technology (RIT) began the design of a curriculum leading to the Bachelor of Science in Software Engineering [4, 5]. We developed our curriculum from the ground up rather than by adding a small set of software engineering courses to an established curriculum in computer science or computer engineering. We created software development to be primarily an engineering endeavor and

2 The Difficulty of Modeling Software Systems

A hallmark of engineering design is the use of models to explore the consequences of design decisions. Sometimes these models are physical prototypes or informal drawings, but the *sine qua non* of contemporary engineering practice is the use of

T. Kühne (Ed.): MoDELS 2006 Workshops, LNCS 4364, pp. 291–300, 2007.

formal, mathematical models of system structure and behavior. Unfortunately, the current practice in software engineering is such that rigorous models from which one could derive significant properties are either too rudimentary or so tedious to use that it is difficult to justify the incremental benefit in other than the most critical of systems. This reflects a key distinction between software and traditional engineering: whereas the latter builds on numerical computation, software is more appropriately modeled using aspects of discrete mathematics. The models stress relationships between software components, and numerical computation is the exception.

3   Modeling Throughout the Curriculum

We designed our curriculum to provide a focus on the principles and practices for the engineering of software systems through their entire life cycle. Our answer to the topical question, "How does modeling integrate into the software engineering curriculum?" is "It should be emphasized throughout the entire curriculum." Despite the difficulties described in the previous section, our curriculum stresses modeling throughout from more informal models expressed in the UML [6] to those expressed in mathematically rigorous languages such as Alloy [7] and FSP [8]. This emphasis on modeling is reflected in two of our ten program outcomes:

1. Model and analyze proposed and existing software systems, especially through the use of discrete mathematics and statistics.
2. Analyze and design complex software systems using contemporary analysis and design principles such as cohesion and coupling, abstraction and encapsulation, design patterns, frameworks and architectural styles.

Students develop their modeling skills starting with basic object-oriented design and progress through the remainder of the curriculum to higher levels of modeling abstractions in all areas of software engineering including architecture, requirements, verification and validation, and formal models. This paper describes how we incorporated modeling into most of the courses in our curriculum. Figure 1 shows the sequencing of courses this paper discusses. Except for the three courses within the box labeled "Design Electives" these are all required courses in our program. These software engineering courses are from the "design side" of our program. There are also required and elective courses on a "process side."

This paper first describes how we introduce our students to abstraction through modeling and move them from a programming view of software development to an engineering view. Next is a description of our use of mathematically formal models where our overall goals are three-fold: to acquaint our students with modern modeling tools, to connect the courses they take in discrete mathematics to real applications, and to persuade them that mathematics has much to offer to the engineering of quality software. In the context of these formal models we introduce our students to model-driven development. The paper concludes with a description of problems still to be solved and indications of success of modeling in a software engineering curriculum.

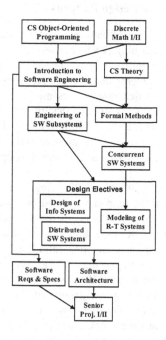

Fig. 1. Modeling in RIT's Software Engineering Design Courses

3.1 Basic Object-Oriented Modeling

The students in our program spend their first year studying the fundamentals of object-oriented programming. Three courses cover topics in basic programming, object-oriented technology, data structures, and algorithms with simple complexity analysis. Students are exposed to class diagrams in UML notation beginning in the middle of the first course. Modeling discussions stay at rather low levels, considering questions, such as, which nouns might represent objects in the system or state within the objects and which verbs are behaviors in an object. The design activity is mostly concerned with the design of single classes and interactions between pairs of classes.

Students in the three computing disciplines take an introduction to software engineering[9] during their second year. This is the first course taught by the Department of Software Engineering faculty. The main component of this course is a term-long team-based project using teams of 4 or 5 students. This course covers topics such as roles on a software development team, software development lifecycles, requirements specification, design principles, and user interface design. Each team develops a product from requirements through product iteration deliveries. For the first time, students are confronted with subtleties in the UML such as the distinctions between associations, aggregations and compositions. Teams must document their designs using UML class diagrams, sequence diagrams and statecharts. As they develop a larger system in this course, our students first begin to appreciate the importance of design modeling.

3.2 Modeling in a Course on Design Patterns

The next course, Engineering of Software Subsystems, covers most of the patterns in [10] using a problem-based learning (PBL) pedagogy. Instructors lecture for no more than 6 hours throughout the entire course. The traditional lecture time is replaced with active learning by the students doing class exercises and holding team meetings to discuss the project work which emphasizes modeling software systems using the patterns. The two team projects involve the design of a software system in the 2 to 3 kSLOC range. The team models its solution in the UML using class diagrams, sequence diagrams and statecharts. Discussions with the instructor center on the tradeoffs in various design approaches and the appropriateness of design pattern usage.

The first and the last assignments in the Engineering of Software Subsystems course particularly highlight the emphasis placed on modeling of designs. Students are confronted with a modeling challenge in the first class when they are given a design problem to solve using the modeling skills that they have developed through three quarters of computer science programming courses and one software engineering course. At the beginning of the second class each student will individually submit a first cut at a UML class model for the problem. The second class is divided into three parts. First, groups of three or four students will work together to create a consensus model incorporating the best aspects of the individual models. Next, teams present their models to the entire class. Finally, the instructor leads a discussion on ways in which groups of classes in these models relate to each other and to the solution of the problem pointing out where established patterns were used and the advantage of discussing the design at this subsystem level.

The last assignment challenges the students' modeling abilities in new ways. Each unit team is given the final code and documentation for a student project submitted for our introductory software engineering course. The first task is to reverse engineer the code to obtain a UML class model for the system and identify any, most likely inadvertent, design pattern usage. The team must capture dynamic models for the program by creating sequence diagrams for two significant program features. After gaining an understanding of the as-built system model each team will propose and implement a refactoring of the code base by following the principles that the course stresses and applying their newly gained knowledge of design patterns.

In design presentations throughout the course, teams must discuss how their modeling activities have considered design principles, such as, encapsulation, coupling, cohesion, and separation of concerns. As mentioned earlier, a cornerstone of modern engineering practice is the use of quantitative models to do early design analysis. In our assignments, we require students to manually compute some simple metrics, such as, class size and average class coupling from their design models. As part of the initial reverse engineering in the refactoring assignment, the teams use the Eclipse Metrics plug-in[11] to compute program metrics. Teams use this information to guide their refactoring efforts and work to improve on the project's metrics with their refactored implementation.

We have evidence that this approach to building modeling skills works. A quantitative comparison with a non-PBL version of the course matches the research on problem-based learning[12]. There is a statistically significant improvement in student satisfaction with and perceived learning from the course. The students also have a greater appreciation for the course textbook which they now must actually read because of the minimal lecture pedagogy used.

4   Formal Modeling

While the models discussed to this point have semantic definitions there is often disagreement between practitioners in their understanding of those semantics particularly when dealing with UML constructs. Disagreements, such as these, rarely exist when the models have a formal mathematical definition. The modeling is capturing logical interconnections and relationships between components using discrete mathematics rather than numerical attributes using continuous mathematics. The software engineering design models are difficult to analyze because of the complexity of the systems being designed and built. Despite these shortcomings, we believe it is important for our students to see that mathematical formalisms indeed undergird software design and provide benefits for engineering quality software.

4.1 "Theoretical" vs. "Practical" Modeling

We believe that the science of formal modeling is in the domain of the computer science and the engineering application of formal modeling is in the software engineering domain. Our approach begins with our students taking two courses in discrete mathematics followed by a computer science theory course, which includes the topics of languages, finite state machines, pushdown automata, Turing machines, and basic computability theory. We want the emphasis within software engineering to be on what we sometimes refer to as "practical" formal models. Our Formal Methods for Specification and Design course focuses on the development of mathematical models of software systems, and applying those models to the analysis of system properties, and to verifying design and implementation decisions. This course has used formalisms such as Z, VDM, and, most recently, Alloy[13] to capture system behavioral requirements, and uses simulation, and proof to analyze system properties. The assignments and projects are almost exclusively modeling and model checking exercises.

4.2 Finite State Process Modeling of Concurrent Systems

For a modeling methodology to be useful for the design of concurrent systems it should meet two criteria. First, the formalisms should be at a level that reduces the scale and complexity of the system sufficiently to allow the software engineer to analyze its important concurrent properties such as deadlock and progress checks. Second, there should be tool support available so that the analysis is done mechanically rather than by hand. The Finite State Process (FSP) modeling technique described by Magee and Kramer[8] satisfies both of these criteria and is the methodology emphasized in our Principles of Concurrent Software Systems[14]. Individual sequential FSP models use standard finite state machine semantics (mutually exclusive states, instantaneous execution of actions causing transitions) that our students easily grasp. Students do not have difficulty modeling non-concurrent FSPs. Modeling of concurrent systems is accomplished by composing multiple sequential FSPs into a single parallel composition. This is where students often struggle getting synchronization aspects of the model correct.

A tool called the Labeled Transition System Analyzer (LTSA) allows students to edit and analyze their FSP models. A major advantage of the LTSA is that with just a few hours of studio classroom time, students can do productive work within the LTSA environment. Model checking features provide analysis of deadlock, safety violations and progress failures.

Having mathematically proven that the model does not contain any anomalous behaviors, the intention is to keep the implementation as closely tied to the model as possible. To complete this model-driven development, it would be optimal to generate an implementation of the model via autocoding. The LTSA does not have an autocoding feature requiring students to do manual implementations. Students think about mappings from model elements to implementations. This yields a mechanical conversion to generate the code for the concurrency framework captured in the model.

When we initially taught this course, we did not explicitly cover the formal FSP semantics. We assumed that the students would recognize the application of discrete mathematics in the finite state machines that are the basis of the FSP semantics. We were quite surprised, then, when over 75% of the students answered "Not applicable" to the question, "How much did this course require you to demonstrate an ability to model and analyze proposed and existing software systems, especially through the use of discrete mathematics and statistics?" We added discussion of the formal semantics for each FSP feature. Students now recognize that while they may not be "doing discrete math" they are applying it in the design and analysis of concurrent systems.

Each of the projects we assign requires the team to use a model-driven development approach. One problem with FSP modeling is state-space explosion. The larger projects that we assign in this course will commonly have millions of states in the composite. While LTSA can handle systems of this size, a naïve approach to modeling will exceed the capacity of the tool. This aids student learning, in that it forces them to model the system at a level of abstraction that captures all the essential concurrency issues while fitting within the capacity of the LTSA.

4.3 Model-Driven Development

One course in our curriculum has model-driven development at its core. This elective course, Modeling of Real-Time Systems, is in our multi-disciplinary real-time and embedded systems course sequence[15]. The requirements and architectural design project has the team create a requirements specification for a small consumer device. The team does a UML use case analysis of the product followed by an architectural design and high-level class structural design. In the second project, the instructor provides a statement of requirements and the team models the behavioral requirements in a UML statechart, creates a class-level design and set of sequence diagrams, and implements the complete system. The third project is a complete model-driven development using statecharts for behavioral modeling of real-time and embedded systems. The students explore the code generation features of the Ilogix Rhapsody modeling tool they have been using throughout the course. The teams create a statechart-based definition of the system behavior and automatically generate C++ code for the application. A final individual project requires students to model a system, such as an auto power window controller, and reverse vending machine, with an identification of actors, a UML use case analysis, class structural design, and system dynamic modeling using sequence diagrams and statecharts.

5   Modeling in Other Design Areas

The previous sections described how our Engineering of Software Subsystems course sets the foundation for our students' use of design modeling and abstraction, and the way we present formal modeling to our students. This section describes how design-oriented courses throughout the rest of our program reinforce the software engineer's reliance on modeling and abstraction.

In the Principles of Distributed Software Systems course students work with the Concurrent Object Modeling and Architectural Design Method. This method follows the traditional UML approach, with a heavier emphasis placed on interaction models and communication diagrams.

Entity-Relationship-Diagrams, considered by some to have been a precursor to object-oriented class models, are the models that students develop and analyze in Principles of Information Systems Design. The course also requires teams to use J2EE Blueprints and enterprise-level patterns as abstractions in their information system designs.

In the Software Requirements and Specifications course our students see modeling techniques for expressing software requirements. Students model system requirements using UML activity diagrams and by applying analysis-level patterns. The course also exposes the students to Data Flow Diagrams and Nasi-Scheiderman diagrams as legacy modeling techniques that they may need to understand if they are required to work on older systems that had originally used those two methodologies.

In the Software Architecture course, students are challenged with understanding and developing models of software systems at the highest levels of abstraction. They must model the system from multiple architectural perspectives[16]. Views include, for example, structural, process, deployment, and concurrency. Systems are also assessed based on quality attributes in the areas of availability, modifiability, performance, security, testability, and usability. We also teach this course in a problem-based format. Assignments include preparing one-page executive summary memos that describe the effect a new technology will have on a product, and to advocate for a product line approach for a new development project. Case studies provide prominent examples of architectural analyses in the course. Teams select an open-source or well publicized architectural framework and perform their own architectural analysis of it.

6   Problems Still to Solve

This paper has discussed our approach to infuse software systems modeling throughout an undergraduate software engineering curriculum. This section will describe some of the problem areas that still remain.

6.1 Using a Consistent Subset of UML

We are not satisfied that we have chosen the right aspects of the UML to cover in each of our courses. We need additional emphasize on the semantics for basic UML class relationships. In several of our design-oriented courses we give a short UML quiz early in the term. There are many students who continue to have difficulty distinguishing the semantic differences between association, aggregation and composition.

We originally used use case analysis of requirements in our introductory course. The analyses that teams submitted were so poor that we questioned whether there was any educational benefit. In this case, we opted for an agile approach and switched to user stories to specify requirements. We felt that this was adequate for this introduction to software engineering, which is taken by students in computer science, computer engineering and software engineering, as long as the SE students saw full use case analysis in our Software Requirements and Specifications course.

6.2 Getting Students to Trust Their Models

Our students are comfortable with model-driven development when the models are class-based models. They still grapple with other abstraction models such as the concurrency models seen in Principles of Concurrent Software Systems. Students do not trust their FSP model and their ability to use the model to create a working implementation. We have observed, however, that the emphasis on modeling gives students an improved understanding of the system requirements and the thread synchronization points, which is a benefit even if they abandon the model during implementation.

7 Success of Modeling Throughout the Curriculum

RIT's traditional focus on career-oriented education means that almost all of our students enter the workforce upon graduation and their employers are a major stakeholder in the outcomes of the program. Discussions with campus recruiters and members of our Industrial Advisory Board have indicated an existing emphasis on or a strong move toward modeling using the UML. While we would not attribute the success of our students in their employment only to our program's emphasis on modeling, we do believe, however, that it is a prime factor that attracts employers to our students.

7.1 Preference for a Modeling-First Approach

A review of co-op employment evaluations provides anecdotal evidence of the value of our students' training to their employers. An engineering manager in an aerospace company, which has hired many of our students on co-op and in full-time positions, commented that the students have a strong focus on capturing requirements and system modeling. An engineering vice-president, who has hired several of our students and sponsored senior projects, commented that our graduates match up favorable against some software engineers who have been working for him for five years. A non-SE RIT faculty member, who manages interns for a health insurance provider, noted a significant difference in how software engineering students learn about a system. The SE students ask questions about components, architecture, and interactions between the components, preferring a higher-level and more abstract model-driven discussion. The computer science and information technology students tend to quickly ask for examples of working code and begin understanding the system from the bottom up. The SE students overwhelmingly believe they formed the base for this methodology in Engineering of Software Subsystems when they were forced to think abstractly about their projects using design patterns rather than code implementations.

7.2 Analysis of Formal Models

Even though the LTSA tool used in our concurrent systems course is not "industrial strength", one student used it on a co-op assignment. The student sensed that there was a problem in a protocol that he was asked to implement. The student remembered the features provided by LTSA; with an afternoon of effort he modeled the protocol, executed traces, and uncovered a progress failure that prevented the protocol from continuing to completion under certain circumstances. The model highlighted the exact problem that was latent in the system thus eliminating many hours of debugging and finger pointing between the hardware and software engineers.

8 Conclusions

The RIT undergraduate program in software engineering instills an engineering mindset in students. Our program exposes our students to both the informal modeling, which is more prevalent in software engineering practice, and formal modeling, which has benefits derived from its underlying mathematical rigor. Without the constraints of traditional computer science or computer engineering programs, we designed a curriculum in which modeling applied to software development is prominent throughout the curriculum. We believe that this emphasis on modeling is a distinguishing characteristic between the science and engineering of software development. As research in model-driven development progresses, we will adapt our curriculum to ensure that our students graduate with an ability to model complex software systems using state-of-the-art practices and abstractions.

References

[1] M. Shaw, "Prospects for an Engineering Discipline of Software." *IEEE Software*, v7, n6, Nov/Dec 1990, pp.15-24
[2] D. L. Parnas, "Software Engineering Programs Are Not Computer Science Programs." *IEEE Software*, Nov/Dec 1999, pp 19-30
[3] T. B. Hilburn, "Software engineering education: a modest proposal." *IEEE Software*, v14, n6, Nov/Dec. 1997, pp 44 – 48

[4] J. F. Naveda and M. J. Lutz, "Crafting a baccalaureate program in software engineering." *Proceedings of the Conference on Software Engineering Education & Training*, April 1997,.

[5] Department of Software Engineering, Rochester Institute of Technology, http://www.se.rit.edu.

[6] M. Blaha and J. Rumbaugh *Object-Oriented Modeling and Design with UML (Second Edition)*. Prentice-Hall, 2005.

[7] D. Jackson "Alloy: A Lightweight Object Modeling Notation." ACM Transactions on Software Engineering and Methodology (TOSEM) v11, n2, April 2002, pp. 256-290

[8] J. Magee and J. Kramer *Concurrency: State Models and Java Programs*. John Wiley & Sons, 1999.

[9] Ludi, S., Reichlmayr, T., and Natarajan, S. "An Introductory Software Engineering Course That Facilitates Active Learning," *Proceedings of ACM SIGCSE Conference*, St.Louis, MO. February, 2005.

[10] E. Gamma, R. Helm, R. Johnson, and J. Vlissides, *Design Patterns Elements of Reusable Object-Oriented Software*. Reading: Addison-Wesley, 1995.

[11] Eclipse Metrics Plug-in, http://metrics.sourceforge.net/.

[12] J. Vallino "Design Patterns: Evolving from Passive to Active Learning." *Proceedings of the Frontiers in Education Conference*. Boulder, CO. November 2003.

[13] M. Lutz "Exploratory Mathematics: Experiences With Alloy In Undergraduate Formal Methods," *Proceedings of 2006 American Society of Engineering Education Conference*, Chicago, IL. June 2006.

[14] M. Lutz and J. Vallino "Concurrent System Design: Applied Mathematics & Modeling in Software Engineering Education," *Proceedings of 2005 American Society of Engineering Education Conference*, Portland, OR. June 2005.

[15] J. Vallino and R. Czernikowski "Thinking Inside the Box: A Multi-Disciplinary Real-Time and Embedded Systems Course Sequence," *Proceedings of Frontiers in Education Conference*. Indianapolis, IN. October 2005.

[16] L. Bass, P. Clements, and R. Kazman *Software Architecture In Practice*. Addison-Wesley, 2003.

Teaching Software Modeling in a Simulated Project Environment

Robert Szmurło and Michał Śmiałek

Warsaw University of Technology, Warsaw, Poland
{szmurlor,smialek}@iem.pw.edu.pl

Abstract. Teaching software engineering in the academia always faces the problem of inability to show problems of real life development projects. The courses seem to be unable to properly show the need of using software modeling as important means of coping with complexity and handling communication within the project. The paper presents format of a course that tries to overcome this. It focuses on application of modeling tools in a realistic software engineering environment. The objective is to teach best practices of software design and implementation with the use of UML. The students can practice design and communication techniques based around CASE tools in teams of 12 to 14 people. The paper summarizes 5 years of experience in teaching modeling with CASE tools. Authors present a concept of how to simulate the roles of architects, designers and programmers as close to reality as possible. The paper also discusses the problems of organizing laboratory work for a large group of students. Authors present the tasks and their arrangement during the course.

Keywords: software modeling, education, CASE tools, project communication, UML.

1 Introduction

When teaching software engineering in the academia (and perhaps also in the industry) we face a very important problem of inability to show the reality of an actual software development project. Two elements seem to be important here: scale and communication. A typical project in the software industry produces tens or hundreds of thousands of lines of code which means hundreds or thousands of classes (in Java, C# or other OO language). Moreover, such a project involves many developers that play different roles (architects, designers, etc.) and need to communicate efficiently. On the other hand, typical group projects in the academia involve two to four students that together produce several hundred or perhaps several thousands of lines of code. With such a scale it is relatively easy to manage the code without any special models or modeling tools. With only a couple of students involved, the communication between them is relatively simple and can be accomplished through frequent "code analysis" meetings.

Problems in teaching scale and communication result in that the graduates coming to the industry are not prepared to participate in real scale projects. This

T. Kühne (Ed.): MoDELS 2006 Workshops, LNCS 4364, pp. 301–310, 2007.

seems to be one of important causes for not using modeling tools and applying in many projects a "code first, then document" approach. Many real projects seem to use the process of creating code similar to the one during courses, where students produce a couple of hundreds of lines of code.

Considering the above, there seems to be a very serious need to design a course where the students would learn how to apply modeling techniques in a realistic development environment [1,2]. This environment would need to be based on an assignment to create a significantly sized system in a team of more than 10 student developers. Such an environment would allow the students to apply the knowledge they gained about modeling and software lifecycle process during traditional lecture-oriented classes. It would also allow to apply modern CASE tools in an environment where such tools are really recommended.

When trying to design a format for such a course, several problems arise. The most important of them is how to organize students in larger groups. Large group contradicts "fairness" of marking as it allows poor students to "hide" behind those that really do the work. Another problem is communication in a large group of students. They normally don't meet regularly "at work", as people in real projects do. Yet another issue is how to divide responsibilities and distinguish between analysts, architects, developers, testers (and so on) [1].

In this paper we describe a course format designed by us which tries to take into account the above issues. The main goal was to teach the students how to use software modeling tools to organize their work in a realistically sized project. The idea here is that students should be organized in larger "project teams" (of more than 10 people). At the same time they need to be marked in smaller groups (of up to 3) and also individually. An important constraint for the course is the time assigned to it (30 hours for common lab work plus work at home). This necessitates certain simplifications of the development lifecycle. Finally, the goal of the course was to teach proper organization of group work around good quality architectural models that are consistent with precise requirements models. This makes it necessary to organize work around components with well defined interfaces. These components should be independent enough to prevent from a situation where a poorly performing group endangers other groups in the same project causing the whole project to fail and lower the marks significantly. This all should lead to a situation where the students would not hesitate to apply best modeling practices gained during the course in their real working environments after graduation.

2   Course Format

The course entitled "Object Oriented CASE Tools" is taught as part of an MSc degree in Computer Engineering at the Warsaw University of Technology. The students are assumed to have knowledge of software modeling in general and UML [3] in particular. Most of the students should have already taken a course in object oriented analysis and design or equivalent.

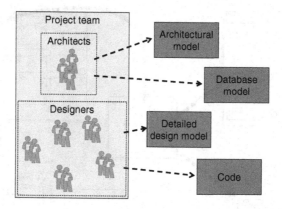

Fig. 1. Project team divided into sub-teams with assigned models and code

The presented course is taught for five years already. It consists of 30 hours of lab sessions plus student's work at home (individually and in groups). The students are suggested a wide range of textbooks for the course [3,4,5,6,7]. Throughout the years the course format had evolved, however the main concept remains unchanged. The assignments are based on larger groups of students (around 12-15 people). During one semester, several such groups (usually 5-6) are formed to constitute "project teams". These teams divide themselves into smaller sub-teams (architects + designers/programmers). This division is illustrated in Fig. 1. Usually, a sub-team of architects consists of three students. Designer sub-teams involve basically two students.

The project teams receive an assignment to write a small but complete software system according to a specific requirements specification. The teams have to design their systems by dividing them into components and then into classes. This is done under constant supervision of the teachers. Components forming the architectural model are managed by the architectural sub-team (see Fig. 1). Individual components are assigned to design sub-teams. These sub-teams have to design and then implement classes realizing interfaces of assigned components. The development efforts of design sub-teams are controlled by the architectural sub-team. Architects integrate the whole system and assure proper communication between other sub-teams to make this integration feasible.

All the development efforts in a project team are centered on the usage of a CASE tool. The teams have to produce three UML models: component model, design class model and interaction model (sequence diagrams). These design models are based on a use case model supplied by the teachers as part of the assignment. Moreover, the students have to write scenarios for the assigned use cases. Teachers assure that the models are consistent and strongly suggest the use of layered architecture. An important part of the work is to generate code from models and assure their synchronization. Detailed design models (class and interaction) are checked for compliance with the architectural model (component and interaction). Later code is checked for compliance with the detailed design.

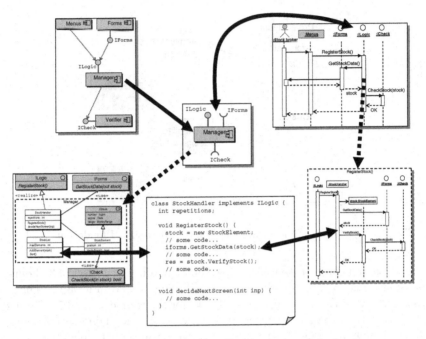

Fig. 2. Mappings between models and code produced during the course

The relationship of models produced during the course by project teams is illustrated on Fig. 2. The architects (in cooperation with designers) produce component diagrams and also design all the interfaces to these components. Use case scenarios are designed with architectural interaction diagrams compliant with the component model. The design sub-teams have their components assigned and then produce appropriate class diagrams that define the structure of each of the components. Architectural interaction diagrams are transformed into detailed design interaction diagrams. These describe the details of each of the interface operations, as to be implemented inside the considered component.

The project teams constitute themselves during the first meeting of the course which takes 2 hours. This time is also used by the teachers to explain all the details of the course format. After the initial meeting, the remaining time is divided into three phases. In the first phase (6 meetings), the students have to design the system. During the second phase (5 weeks) they implement it. Finally, the last phase (3 weeks) is devoted to testing.

The limited time the teams have to develop the system puts certain constraints on the size of the assignment. The system should be simple enough to be implemented by inexperienced developers in around 60-70 hours (800-900 man-hours). Having this limitation, the system should be quite small but non-trivial which we will discuss later. Additional constraint about the system is the ability to divide the project teams into sub-teams responsible for their parts (components). This constraint is necessary because the students work individually at home and they must be marked on an individual basis.

In order to cope with the above issues an appropriate choice for the assignment domain area is very important. In our experience with the course we have chosen four different domains for the applications to be built by the students. In the first year, the students had been creating a management system for an academic departmental library. In the second year the assignment was to design and implement the simulator of an intelligent building. In this assignment, the students were to design a home appliance control system (HACS). The system should had simulated such devices as automatic curtains, indoor/outdoor lights, gates, air conditioners, clocks, bells, security sensors, etc. (it was also used by others, see [1]). Here, the main focus was put on designing a distributed system of devices and a communication protocol between them. The central role in the architectural design played a message dispatcher module which was finally implemented by the architects.

In the third and fourth edition of the course, students were to design and implement a management system for the dean's office. In this project the system should support registering student candidates, promoting candidates into students, employing teachers, storing the students' final grades, etc. The requirements for the system included more than 20 use cases and proved to be too complex for the course. For the second time the assignment was modified. The students were explicitly asked to limit the number of implemented use cases before they started the work.

In the most recent edition of the course, we have simplified the project requirements and reduced the number of use cases in the assignment. In this project, the students had to design and implement an electronic ticketing system of a theme park. The requirements for the system contained just eight major use cases (with two extra for larger teams). Appropriate use case diagram is presented in Fig. 2a. Having such a functional requirements model, the system could be easily divided into four (or five) distributed application modules based on the involved actors. The presented use case model was communicated to the students through a model template file (see Fig. 2b - "Use cases" package). This file divided the model into the packages: Requirements, Architecture and Detailed Design (Components). The structure of the model and division into major packages is consistent with the project's lifecycle and facilitates communication based around requirements and architectural design.

The overall project timeline is divided into three phases: design, implementation and tests. Throughout the phases, the students can choose to play two different roles. In the first phase each designer/programmer sub-team creates the designs for the assigned use cases (two chosen from Fig. 2). The architects create an overall component diagram containing all the components of the system (including data access layer components) and design the structure of a database. During the second phase, the designed components, database and interfaces are implemented. Both roles have to accomplish different tasks, which are divided into individual and shared ones. The division is motivated by the need to grade individual sub-teams and and at the same time to give importance to group work character of the project.

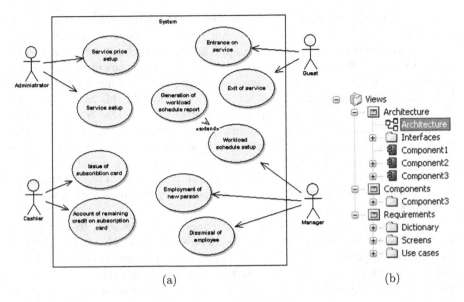

(a)   (b)

Fig. 3. (a) Use cases of the theme park project (b) Template model divided into packages

The design and implementation phases of the project are associated with a concept of exchanging designs between sub-teams. In the second part of the course every sub-team has to implement scenarios and components designed by another sub-team. The two sub-teams simply exchange their design models. Students have to explain their designs to members of the other sub-team. This approach allows to gain experience what kind of information should be included in the design models, and how properly present it. This is also a good way to illustrate various kinds of obvious mistakes and mis-designs that had been made. In the last phase of the course, the students have to design and run acceptance tests of the system. Within the described division of the course into design, implementation and testing, the course has several milestones, set to allow for marking of the students' progress and systematic work. Generally, half of the points is assigned for the quality of design and the rest - for the implementation and tests.

In the first editions of the course we have tried to simulate the iterative project lifecycle. However, the limited time did not allow us to simulate it properly. In the recent course, we have limited the lifecycle to just one "normal" iteration with a second "corrective" iteration. This allows us not to make the process shift into a pure waterfall (see eg.[8,9]). The second, short iteration allows us to simulate the iterative lifecycle [10] to some extend through a second deadline for acceptance tests. The first deadline simulates tests after an initial iteration in a project. Normally, the tests fail demonstrating to the students the problem with waterfall approach, where it is normal for the system not to pass the tests (for various reasons). In the "second" iteration the students do not produce new functionality but correct (or enhance) these parts of the system that caused the tests to fail. With this approach we can show to the students the need to organize their projects with "risk buffer" of an iterative process.

Important part of the course is devoted to the administrative aspects of a software development project. The students have to use a CASE tool available to them in the university's labs. For the purpose of this course we have used Enterprise Architect by Sparx Systems [11]. The tool allowed to integrate models made by individual sub-teams into a common model. This common model could be automatically published on a project team's web page. The web pages were used by the teams to communicate (including communication of changes in the architecture and interface implementation) and verify progress.

Apart from the CASE tool, the teams had to organize their implementation and testing environments. For this purpose, each team was given their own VMware virtual machine.The architects (in cooperation with other team members) could choose their own operating system and development environment in which they wanted to implement the system. The teams normally chose .NET or J2EE as their development frameworks. One of architects in each team was also responsible for maintenance and administration of the VMware machine. The other architects were personally responsible for database management, web page maintenance and keeping up-to-date the UML documentation of the whole system. They created their own websites which integrated the whole documentation of the project, most recent information and announcements. The website played a crucial role as the second communication medium between students in the team and complements the meetings during the classes. The website also constituted a report deliverable for the whole project.

3   Teaching Results

The teaching results can be divided into three aspects: quality of produced systems and team work, quality of produced designs and student's comprehension of modeling. The first two aspects can be judged by the quality of deliverables and generally by measuring how successful individual project teams were. To measure the third factor we have prepared a post-course questionnaire.

Five years of experience in teaching the course leads to a general conclusion that the proposed format proved to be quite successful. This success can be measured by the fact that out of 32 project teams (12-15 students each) only 1 (throughout the five years) did not succeed in delivering the assigned system. In all other cases the systems delivered were functional enough to pass most of the prepared functional tests. It has to be noted though that in the first three editions of the course, most of the teams did not deliver all of the required functionality. Nevertheless, the students managed to deliver fully operational systems with good user interface design.

The most important problem during classes was the organization of team work. This was caused by the fact that the students were really not prepared to work in a larger group. This was a totally new experience to them. For this reason, the course gained an opinion of a "hard one" - one necessitating more work from the students than an average course. Despite this, the students participating in the course have shown high commitment and motivation. They were additionally motivated to work by fellow students - project team members. The teachers could notice that the project teams became real teams with good interpersonal relationships. Only in some cases (2-3 teams out of 32) the team work did not succeed. This was especially the case when the architectural group did not perform well. It is thus crucial to have the architectural team being carefully chosen by the project team with the help of the teacher.

Another issue is associated with poorly performing design teams. The course format proved to be well suited to accommodate for such situations. None of the projects so far suffered because of one of the design teams did not do their job or did it too late. Vertical division of work made applications prepared by the students quite independent. Even without one of the modules, the applications could work simulating easily the lacking functionality.

Quality of team work is closely related to the quality of produced deliverables (models). In the initial editions of the course the students were to deliver systems with around 20 or more use cases. In the last two editions we have significantly limited the number of required use cases (to even less than 10). This was caused by noting that the students have sacrificed modeling when pressed by the deadlines, and concentrated mostly on coding. Lack of modeling caused poor quality of the systems and later problems with testing. In the last editions, the teachers have concentrated on enforcing proper modeling practices. This caused that the teams produced better designs leading to easier integration of systems and significantly less problems during testing.

A common problem in teaching modeling is how to motivate students to produce good quality models. Usually, they produce models that they later implement in code. The models are quite simple and the students feel that they could develop the system faster if they could get rid of the "unnecessary pictures" (which they have in their heads). To prevent this, in our course we have simulated the process of exchanging design information between separate sub-teams. In the second part of the course, the students were obliged to implement components designed by another sub-team. This forced them to present and explain their project to others. During this process both the presenting and the listening team (under the teacher's supervision) were gaining experience on the kind of information that has to be included in the design. Additionally, the students became aware of many obvious errors, mis-designs and shortcomings of their projects.

Another problem is associated with the usage of modeling (UML) tools. Very often, the students are taught to code the system first and then prepare the documentation. Such habits could be noticed during the described course. Some of the teams tried to reverse engineer their code in order to produce the required design models. The teachers tried to prevent such practices by frequent inspections of code and models. On the other hand, many of the teams did not need such inspections as they have noticed all the benefits of automatic code generation and kept code synchronized with the models without teacher's intervention.

The marking system developed for the course promotes the teams that keep their designs up-to-date. However, we have noticed that even with this system in place, the students needed additional motivation. This motivation was gained through a systematic use of the CASE tool. The students realized that the tool allows them to communicate design decisions and at the same time relieves from the burden of writing the "uninteresting" parts of code (the code structure).

To measure some of the teaching results of the course, associated with the student's comprehension of modeling practices, we have prepared a questionnaire to be filled by the students. In this voluntary, anonymous questionnaire, 75 students out of total 90, have participated. Students were to assign 1 to 5 points for each statement, where 1 point meant: 'I definitely disagree' and 5 points 'I definitely agree'.

Most students taking the course accepted the innovative form of the laboratory (4.0). The students had the opportunity of playing different roles in a realistic environment. During the course the students could find a role that suits them best. On the other hand, some of the students were quite sceptic about whether they would like to take more of such courses due to amount of work the course necessitates.

Answers to questions: "Good architecture design in UML helps to communicate during the process of system development" (4.2) and "Application of CASE tools is necessary in the process of software development" (4.2) have shown that the students really appreciate modeling and the role of CASE tools as an important element of software development. On the other hand, they seem to be more sceptic about applying the knowledge and experience they gained in real life ("The course will allow me to integrate faster with a team building a real system in the future", 3.6). This might be caused by their poor opinions on the quality of software development process in an average software house. Answers to question "The course have helped me to understand the process of system implementation with UML." (3.7) show that the students were not totally satisfied with the outcomes of the course. Their additional opinions expressed when discussing with the teachers show that they feel the course did not fully simulate a real project. They also felt that too little stress was put on transforming UML models into the technologies of their choice (.NET or J2EE).

4   Conclusions

Current curricula for software engineering courses seem to ignore the need to prepare students for work in a real-scale software project. It can be argued that this is caused by applying traditional approaches which concentrate on "fair" assessment of individual students. This however is in contrast to the needs of the industry. In the presented course we have tried to accommodate both the needs of academia and the needs of industry. We try to simulate a real industry project, at the same time introducing a system which allows for quite fair marking.

The course simulates just one (and a half) iteration of a real project. Experience shows that realistically, only up to 10 average use cases can be implemented. This is due to the fact that the course can simulate just below two weeks of full time work in a real project. Despite this limitation, the teams could produce a reasonable system. Even in this limited lifecycle, the students gain the capability to communicate with other members of their team through models. They also gain experience in conducting project meetings, organizing team work. Most importantly, the students really start appreciating modeling and the use of CASE tools - not only as means of documenting the system but also as facilitators of actual development process.

Acknowledgement

We wish to thank Sparx Systems for supplying us with their CASE tool system (Enterprise Architect) for the purpose of this course.

References

1. Cooper, K., Dong, J., Zhang, K., Chung, L.: Teaching experiences with UML at the University of Texas at Dallas. ACM / IEEE 8th International Conference on Model Driven Engineering Languages and Systems, Educators' Symposium (2005) 1–8
2. Filho, W.P.P.: A model-driven software process for course projects. ACM / IEEE 8th International Conference on Model Driven Engineering Languages and Systems, Educators' Symposium (2005) 33–40
3. Śmiałek, M.: Zrozumieć UML 2.0. Metody modelowania obiektowego. Helion (Poland) (2005)
4. Booch, G., Rumbaugh, J.: The unified modeling language user guide. WNT (2001)
5. Fowler, M., Scott, K.: UML distilled. WNT (2001)
6. Muller, R.J.: Database Design for Smarties: Using UML for Data Modeling. Mikom, Warsaw (2000)
7. Szyperski, C.: Component Oriented Programming. WNT (2001)
8. Huo, M., Verner, J., Zhu, L., Babar, M.A.: Software quality and agile methods. Proceedings of the 28th Annual International Computer Software and Applications Conference (COMPSAC 04) (2004)
9. Lewi, J., Steegmans, E., Man, J.D.: Object-oriented approach to software development, a walk through a number of topics. CompEuro 91 Advanced Computer Technology, Reliable Systems and Applications 5th Annual European Computer Conference. (1991) 626–633
10. Kuzniarz, L., Staron, M.: Best practices for teaching uml based software development. ACM / IEEE 8th International Conference on Model Driven Engineering Languages and Systems, Educators' Symposium (2005) 9–16
11. Enterprise Architect, Sparx Systems, http://www.sparxsystems.com.

Repository for Model Driven Development (ReMoDD)

Robert France[1], Jim Bieman[1], and Betty H.C. Cheng[2]

[1] Department of Computer Science and Engineering
Colorado State University
{france,bieman}@cs.colostate.edu,
http://www.cs.colostate.edu/{france,bieman}
[2] Department of Computer Science and Engineering
Michigan State University
East Lansing, Michigan
chengb@cse.msu.edu
http://www.cse.msu.edu/chengb

Abstract. The *Repository for MDD* (ReMoDD) project is concerned with developing a repository that will contain artifacts that support research and education in model-driven development (MDD). The ReMoDD platform will also provide interfaces and interchange mechanisms that will enable a variety of tools to retrieve artifacts from the repository and submit candidate artifacts to the repository. ReMoDD artifacts will include documented MDD case studies, examples of models reflecting good and bad modeling practices, reference models (including metamodels) that can be used as the basis for comparing and evaluating MDD techniques, generic models and transformation reflecting reusable modeling experience, descriptions of modeling techniques, practices and experiences, and modeling exercises and problems that can be used to develop classroom assignments and projects. In this paper we outline plans for developing ReMoDD.

1 Introduction

MDD research targets the complex problem of developing software systems that play critical roles in organizations and society. Researchers in the MDD community are developing techniques, methods, processes and tools that allow developers to raise the level of abstraction at which they conceive, analyze, implement and evolve complex software systems. The *Repository for Model Driven Development* (ReMoDD) project is concerned with developing a community-driven repository that will contain artifacts whose use can significantly improve MDD research productivity, improve industrial MDD productivity, and enhance the learning experience of MDD students. Artifacts will include detailed MDD case studies, examples of models reflecting good and poor modeling practices, semantic models for UML diagrams, reference models that can be used as points against which MDD techniques are compared and evaluated, model and specification patterns, generic models reflecting reusable modeling experience, model transformations, descriptions of modeling practices and experience, and modeling exercises and problems that can be used to develop classroom assignments and projects.

ReMoDD will publish an API (application program interface) that will allow a variety of tools to retrieve artifacts from the repository directly. For those who wish to use

T. Kühne (Ed.): MoDELS 2006 Workshops, LNCS 4364, pp. 311–317, 2007.

ReMoDD in a stand alone mode, we will develop web-based user interface software to make the artifacts easily and intuitively accessible, both in terms of performance and content. Specifically, we will develop software to present different views, browsing, and query interfaces to the user depending on their needs and objectives. For example, one type of user may be interested in finding all artifacts related to a specific domain (e.g., telecommunication systems). Another type of user may want to explore the available design patterns with sample implementations. And yet another user may want a general introduction to MDD and want to take a virtual tour through the different types of artifacts in the repository. We will need to investigate different types of storage media and structural organization of artifacts to best support these types of views and query needs.

The initial development of ReMoDD will be a collaborative effort involving researchers from Colorado State University (CSU) and Michigan State University (MSU). The team will also work with members of the MDD community to collect and evaluate candidate ReMoDD artifacts, as well as publicize the repository artifacts for dissemination purposes. An advisory board comprising MDD researchers and practitioners will provide the guidance needed to ensure that ReMoDD becomes a sustainable resource that significantly improves MDD research productivity and the quality and relevance of educational material.

2   Goals, Objectives, Targeted Activities

The objective of the project is to develop a community resource that provides a single point of access to shared artifacts reflecting high-quality MDD experience and knowledge from industry and academia. The aim is to facilitate sharing of relevant knowledge and experience that improve MDD research productivity and education.

We aim to collect and make available MDD artifacts from industry, academia, and other public domain sources (e.g., artifacts produced by open-source projects). Items in the repository will provide data for our research and will be a resource for the entire MDD research and education community. Initially, ReMoDD will support research in the following areas:

- Research on modeling languages and modeling approaches (e.g., research on aspect-oriented modeling, model semantics).
- Research on model transformations.
- Research on model analysis techniques.
- Research on evaluating the quality of modeling artifacts.
- Empirical studies of modeling phenomena.
- Research on reusable forms of modeling experience (e.g., work on developing and using domain-specific modeling languages, domain-specific modeling frameworks, and patterns).

In the long-term we envisage that the repository will consist of related living archives of software engineering artifacts including the MDD archive (ReMoDD) that will be developed in this research. For this reason, the repository infrastructure that will be developed to support ReMoDD will be architected so that it is not restricted to storing and manipulating only MDD artifacts.

Ensuring Relevance to the MDD Community. We will use two mechanisms to help ensure that the community resource we develop meets the needs of the MDD community: A project Advisory Board and a series of Repository Development Workshops (RDWs).

An Advisory Board comprising national and international MDD researchers and practitioners will provide the oversight needed to ensure that the repository provides the MDD artifacts that are highly relevant to the MDD community. Letters indicating the willingness of elected members to serve on the advisory board are included with this proposal (see Letters in Supplementation Section). By agreeing to serve on this board, means that a member is committing to providing feedback on the design of the repository, evaluating candidate artifacts, contributing artifacts, and publicizing the ReMoDD repository. The following is a list of persons who have agreed to serve on the Advisory Board:

Academia Members	
Joanne Atlee ,	University of Waterloo, Canada
Don Batory ,	Univ of Texas - Austin, USA
Jean Bezivin ,	University of Nantes, France
Lionel Briand,	Carleton University, Canada
Doris Carver ,	Louisiana State University, USA
David Garlan ,	Carnegie Mellon University, USA
Jeff Gray ,	University of Alabama at Birmingham, USA
Mark Harman ,	Kings College, UK
Jean-Marc Jezequel ,	IRISA/INRIA, France
Kevin Lano ,	Kings College, UK
Robyn Lutz ,	Iowa State University and NASA JPL, USA
Atif Memon ,	University of Maryland, USA
Spencer Rugaber ,	Georgia Tech, USA
Perdita Stevens ,	University of Edinburgh, UK
Industrial Members	
Michael Barnett ,	Microsoft Research, USA
Brian Berenbach ,	Siemens Corporate Research, Worldwide
Roger Burkhart ,	Deere & Company, USA
Alexander Egyed ,	Teknowledge, USA
Luis Pereira ,	Eaton Innovation Center, Worldwide
Bran Selic ,	IBM, Canada
Frank Weil ,	Motorola, Worldwide

Research Development Workshops (RDWs) will give members of the general MDD community opportunities to interact with the project team and thus influence the development of ReMoDD and its mission. The workshops will be held biannually at two major conferences: ICSE (International Conference on Software Engineering) and MoDELS (Model Engineering Languages and Systems). In the early phases of the project, the workshops will focus on eliciting requirements from the community (new and seasoned developers and researchers) and on reviewing the ReMoDD design. Later workshops will focus on (1) developing and discussing artifacts that will be used to seed the repository, (2) demonstrating how researchers and educators can interact with ReMoDD and (3) soliciting feedback that will be used to assess the effectiveness of ReMoDD and to improve the repository.

Impact of ReMoDD on Research and Education. ReMoDD will (1) provide research projects with artifacts such as models, model transformations, and code on which research products can be applied, (2) facilitate comparative analyses of experience related to MDD, (3) provide raw data on MDD artifacts, technologies, and practices to research programs, (4) support efforts related to collecting empirical data about modeling techniques, technologies and notations, and about implemented systems, (5) provide educators with materials that can be used in software engineering courses that cover MDD, and (6) be used to communicate MDD successes and failures to the software development community.

Impact on Standards Bodies. In addition, we envision that ReMoDD will also play a role with the standards bodies. The experience and knowledge captured by artifacts in the repository can be used by developers of MDD standards to shape standards and to illustrate application of the standards. The repository can also help promote use of standards through sharing of artifacts that conform to standards, and can help with the evolution of standards by providing information (e.g., experience reports, quality evaluations) that can be used to determine the effectiveness of the standards.

3   Project Description and Infrastructure

In this section we present our vision of the ReMoDD infrastructure. We anticipate that the initial view presented in this section will be modified and elaborated during the project based on results of a requirements analysis that will be carried out in the early phases of the project and on feedback we gather from the MDD community.

3.1   Core ReMoDD Content-Related Concepts

To support the short-term MDD-specific goals and the long-term software engineering repository goals we have based ReMoDD on the following content-related concepts: Artifact, artifact relationship, and artifact cluster. Basing ReMoDD on these generic concepts makes it possible to use the repository to store a variety of artifacts.

An *artifact* is an information item that can be retrieved from the repository. It can be simple or complex. A simple artifact is the smallest unit of information that can be accessed within the repository. It is a set of tightly-coupled elements that is stored and retrieved as non-decomposable unit in the repository. Examples of simple artifacts are UML class descriptions, UML relationships, Java programs, metamodels, test cases, and method descriptions. Each artifact has a type that contains metadata about the artifact and that specifies the kinds of manipulations that can be carried out on the artifact. The kinds of manipulations supported by an artifact can be described in terms of an interface that specifies allowable operations in terms of their signatures and constraints on their behavior. Users of the repository can use the metadata in artifact types to determine the quality of the artifacts and the tools needed to manipulate the artifacts once they are retrieved from the repository. For example, the type of a source code artifact can include metadata that gives the programming language used to express the artifact, the version and author of the artifact, and provides information on the quality of the code (e.g., complexity metrics). It can also contain specifications of interfaces for analyzing, compiling, testing, and executing the code. An artifact type can also specify data integrity and access control rules that are applicable to all artifacts of the type. These rules can restrict the form of the artifacts and how they are accessed within the repository.

3.2 The ReMoDD Development Plan

The ReMoDD project activities are structured into the following phases:

Project Startup: Activities in this phase will be primarily concerned with soliciting and analyzing detailed requirements from the MDD community and with developing a repository architecture that provides a balanced solution.

Repository Design and Implementation: The primary activities in this phase concern designing, implementing and testing the repository.

Repository Seeding: The primary activities in this phase concern collecting, packaging, and storing MDD research and education artifacts that will be shared via ReMoDD.

Repository Deployment: The activities in this phase are primarily concerned with making the repository available to the MDD community and training of potential users.

Repository Evaluation: The activities in this phase are primarily concerned with evaluating the effectiveness of the ReMoDD infrastructure and the use of its seed contents.

The Planning Grant will largely focus on the Project Startup and Repository Seeding efforts, both of which will be described in the Future Work section.

4 Evaluation

For the planning grant, the following evaluation activities are planned.

- **Evaluation of the software interface for the repository will be performed.** Prototype interfaces for the key elements of ReMoDD will be developed and made available to the Advisory Board members as well as our collaborators. The objective of this evaluation step is to determine what types of interactions will be most useful for ReMoDD users. An iterative process will be used to gather feedback and refine the interfaces appropriately. RDWs at ICSE and MoDELS conferences will be used to gather more concentrated feedback regarding the interfaces.
- **Evaluation of the artifacts in the repository.** As part of the seeding efforts, we will identify representative artifacts to be placed in ReMoDD. As part of the initial requirements phase, we are soliciting input from stakeholders as to what types

of artifacts are the most in demand for researchers and educators. Based on this feedback, we will collect appropriate artifacts from researchers, educators, and industrial collaborators. Once placed in a prototype repository with our prototype interfaces, we can then evaluate both the interfaces and the artifacts and determine what types of metadata are needed to make the artifacts the most useful.

5   Outreach

The inherent nature of the ReMoDD project is outreach to the research and educational communities. In addition to the Advisory Board members, we have a list of twenty collaborators from industry and universities who are interested in using and contributing to ReMoDD. To increase the scope of outreach, we are also working with several minority institutions to engage minority faculty and students in MDD research and education. The full proposal describes activities to leverage the contacts by the 3 PIs in HBCUs and other minority institutions to support underrepresented minority undergraduate students in MDD-related research projects. Special effort will be made to involve educational institutions with predominantly minority students in the development and use of the repository. The institutions with software engineering research and teaching faculty will be contacted directly and invited to participate in the Repository Development Workshops (RDWs). Finally, we have identified several global software companies who are enthusiastically interested in participating and contributing to ReMoDD. In many cases, the PIs have long-standing relationships with these companies, where industrial-strength data and projects have been shared with their respective universities. As such, the plan is to leverage these partners to gain additional industrial partners.

6   Future Activities

The planning grant is just now beginning. As such, our efforts will focus on the requirements elicitation for the project and the the preliminary seeding of the repository.

Project Startup. The following are the major activities in this phase:

– Establish the project Advisory Board.
– Elicit and analyze requirements for the repository.

At the start of the project we will hold a meeting with members of the Advisory Board to discuss initial project plans and to establish protocols that specify how the PIs will interact with the board. It is expected that the PIs will meet with the board members at least twice a year to discuss progress. These meetings will be held at the ICSE (May annually) and MoDELS (October annually) meetings. An online mailing list will also be set up to facilitate communication with board members.

Elicitation and analysis of repository requirements is the major activity in this phase. At the start of the project we will conduct a survey that will help us determine the types of artifacts that MDD researchers and educators would like to access in an open repository. We will use the mailing lists of the MoDELS conference, the OMG and other MDD related groups to distribute the survey, and provide online survey instruments.

To facilitate the elicitation activity the PIs will organize a Repository Development Workshop (RDW) at the MoDELS conference, which is due to take place shortly after the start of the project. The objective of the RDW would be to elicit requirements and discuss requirements with members of the MDD community. Members of the MDD community will present and discuss their requirements for the repository. The PIs will meet after these meetings to analyze the feedback and plan future requirements and early design activities.

Repository Seeding. The following are the major activities in this phase:

- Seed the repository from the MDD models used to develop ReMoDD.
- Seed the repository with artifacts from PIs projects.
- Seed the repository with artifacts from Advisory Board members.

This phase is intended to provide an initial population of the repository to assess how well the clusters we initially identified are suited to shareable artifacts. During this phase, we will also determine the types of manipulations that should be allowed on artifacts. This will help us determine the types of tools that should be either directly brought into the system or made pluggable into the client version of the system. For example, when browsing a collection of design patterns, should a user be able to click on a pattern, bring up the list of fields, and then pull up a UML diagram editor to begin editing one of the templates in the pattern?

The initial seeding of the repository will also help us to assess whether our criteria for simple and complex artifacts need to be modified, or whether we need another category of artifacts. Given that several of our advisory board members are from industry or work with industry, we will be able to explore scalability issues in terms of volume and complexity of artifacts. At the conclusion of the initial seeding phase, we will have examples of all the key types of artifacts that we plan to support (e.g., requirements, design, implementation, testing models, code for models, transformations, metamodels, and patterns). During the remainder of the project, we will continue to solicit additional artifacts from the community to submit to the repository. Our RDW will provide one means for soliciting artifacts. We will also send out announcements to the community soliciting additional artifacts. A software module will be developed to provide an easy means for users to submit candidate artifacts. All artifacts will be evaluated for their integrity by members of the ReMoDD team before being added to the repository.

2nd UML 2 Semantics Symposium: Formal Semantics for UML

Manfred Broy[1], Michelle L. Crane[2], Juergen Dingel[2],
Alan Hartman[3], Bernhard Rumpe[4], and Bran Selic[5]

[1] Technische Universität München, Germany
[2] Queen's University, Kingston, Ontario, Canada
[3] IBM Research, Israel
[4] Technische Universität Braunschweig, Germany
[5] IBM Rational Software, Canada
broy@in.tum.de, crane@cs.queensu.ca, dingel@cs.queensu.ca,
hartman@il.ibm.com, b.rumpe@tu-bs.de, bselic@ca.ibm.com
http://www.cs.queensu.ca/~stl/internal/uml2

Abstract. The purpose of this symposium, held in conjunction with MoDELS 2006, was to present the current state of research of the UML 2 Semantics Project. Equally important to receiving feedback from an audience of experts was the opportunity to invite researchers in the field to discuss their own work related to a formal semantics for the Unified Modeling Language. This symposium is a follow-on to our first workshop, held in conjunction with ECMDA 2005.

Keywords: UML, Formal Semantics.

1 Introduction

The UML 2 Semantics Project is an international collaboration, involving both academia and industry. Participants include IBM (Canada, Germany, and Israel), Queen's University (Kingston, Ontario, Canada), the Technical University of Munich (Germany), and the Technical University of Braunschweig (Germany). The main objective of this project is to develop a mathematically formalized semantics definition for the Unified Modeling Language (UML). The Project started in January 2005 and has achieved substantial results. That said, there is much work to be done and the project will likely continue for at least one more year.

The purpose of this symposium, held in conjunction with MoDELS 2006, was to present the current state of our research to an audience of experts. Equally important to receiving feedback on our research, this symposium was an opportunity to invite researchers in the field to discuss their own work. This symposium is a follow-on to our first workshop, held in conjunction with ECMDA 2005, in Nuremberg, November 2005.

T. Kühne (Ed.): MoDELS 2006 Workshops, LNCS 4364, pp. 318–323, 2007.

2 Motivation

UML has become the language of choice for modeling various aspects of software systems in academia and industry. UML is now widely adopted in academia and industry and has established itself as the dominant language for modeling software systems. UML 2 [12] is the latest major revision of UML and has been developed with the help of researchers and practitioners from numerous companies, universities, and government institutions. UML 2 addresses the shortcomings of the previous version and incorporates the advances distilled from a large body of research and practical experience. The current version of the standard specifically supports model-driven development (MDD), an approach to software development that has the proven potential to increase the productivity of industrial software development substantially. In short, MDD focuses on the construction of platform-independent, high-level models from which source code is automatically generated.

The current UML 2 specification is complex and uses a combination of semiformal diagrams, constraints, and informal natural language text. The imprecisions and ambiguities of natural language make it difficult to detect and correct subtle errors, incompleteness, and inconsistencies. These problems in turn complicate the development of tools supporting UML. For instance, tool builders may not find the amount of detail in the standard necessary, for the implementation of a particular analysis or translation. In addition, the interoperability between UML tools is compromised, because different tools may interpret the same artifact differently, such that the combined use of these tools may not yield consistent results. The high-level goal of this project is to overcome such problems, and to improve the standard and enhance the technical viability and benefits of MDD and UML.

The proposed formalization of UML will have several benefits. First, it will allow subtle errors in the current and future versions of the standard to be detected and suggestions for improvements to be made. Second, the formalization will have the potential to be of immediate, commercial utility to the companies developing tools supporting UML and MDD. For instance, it would enable tool vendors to develop tools that offer more powerful and effective testing, analysis, and model transformation functionality and better support the exchange of modeling artifacts between different tools.

3 The Semantics Architecture

The focus of the Project has been driven primarily by the concepts discussed in [13], especially the *semantics architecture*. Figure 1 identifies the key semantics areas covered by the current UML 2 standard.

At the highest level of abstraction, it is possible to distinguish three distinct layers of semantics. The foundation layer is structural, reflecting the premise that there is no disembodied behaviour in UML – all behaviour emanates from the actions of structural entities. This structural layer is represented by our *System Model*, discussed in Section 4.

The next layer is behavioural and provides the foundation for the semantic description of all higher-level behavioural formalisms. This layer is called the Behavioural Base and consists of three separate sub-areas arranged into two sub-layers. The bottom sub-layer consists of the inter-object behaviour base, which deals with how structural entities communicate with each other, and the intra-object behaviour base, which the relationship between structural entities (e.g., objects) and their behaviour. The system model also formalizes these concepts. The actions sub-layer is placed over these two; it defines the semantics of individual actions and the means by which actions are composed to form more complex behavioural specifications. Actions are the fundamental units of behaviour in UML and are used to define fine-grained behaviour. As discussed in Section 5, one current document in the project is dedicated to formalizing these actions in terms of the system model.

Actions are available to any of the higher-level formalisms to be used for describing detailed behaviours. The topmost layer in the semantics hierarchy defines the semantics of the higher-level behavioural formalisms of UML: activities, state machines, and interactions. These formalisms are dependent on the semantics provided by the lower layers. Currently, research is being done on formalizing activities and interactions in terms of the system model.

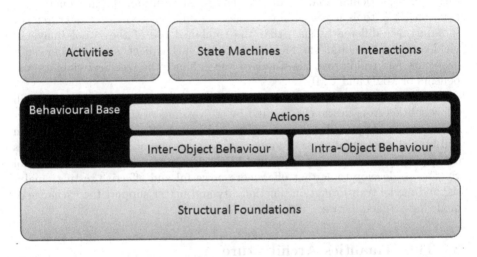

Fig. 1. The UML semantics layers: the Semantics Foundation consists of the bottom two layers – the Structural Foundations and the Behavioural Base [13]

4   System Model

The goal of the *System Model* is to provide a semantic domain into which UML specifications can be mapped [10]. In our case, the semantic domain is mathematics, specifically: numbers, sets, relations and functions. The notation is drawn from pure mathematics, as opposed to some other specialized, or invented, notation.

The system model defines a universe of interacting state machines that describe the behaviour of objects and their relationships with each other. It provides the means to define the semantics of any UML model. Intuitively, each state in the system model is composed of three parts, data store, control store and event store, and represents the states that the system being modelled moves through during its execution. Further information about the system model is detailed in the various documents listed in Section 5.

5 Status

Several major objectives were determined at the outset of the project:

1. To specify a definitive and complete formal semantics foundation for the UML 2 standard. At this point, approximately two-thirds of the semantics foundation has been finalized. This foundation, called the *System Model* is composed as follows:

   - Towards a System Model for UML: The Structural Data Model [3], which defines the structure part of the system model, including concepts such as class, reference, method, etc.
   - Towards a System Model for UML: The Control and Scheduling [2], which defines the control part of the system model, including concepts such as stack, frame, thread, message, etc.
   - Towards a System Model for UML: The State Transition System, which defines the dynamic behaviour of the system model.

   These three documents introduce a system model as the basis for a semantic model for UML 2. The system model forms the core and foundation of the UML semantics definition. Building upon this system model are several other documents:

   - Class Diagrams: Abstract Syntax and Mapping to System Model [5], which expresses a subset of UML class diagrams in terms of a tuple notation and then maps this structure to the system model.
   - Activity Diagrams: Abstract Syntax and Mapping to System Model [7], which expresses a subset of UML activity diagrams in terms of a tuple notation and then maps this structure to the system model.
   - Mapping Actions to the System Model [4], which examines several of the UML "primitive" actions, such as *CreateObjectAction*, *CallOperationAction*, etc. The behaviour of these actions is expressed in terms of changes to the system model.
   - Mapping Activities to the System Model [6], which examines the fundamental nature of activities, e.g., tokens, flow, how activities can be composed, etc. The result of activity execution is expressed in terms of the system model.

At this point in time, the documents listed above are available in unpublished format only. The most current version of each document may be found online [1].

2. To identify potential consistency flaws in the UML 2 standard and propose adequate corrections. Several subtle inconsistencies and flaws in the standard have been found over the past 18 months - these have been forwarded to the appropriate authors, who have raised issues when appropriate.
3. To identify analysis techniques that can be used to formally determine the correctness of UML 2 models. These techniques would enable tool vendors to develop tools that offer more powerful and effective testing, analysis, and model transformation functionality and better support the exchange of modeling artifacts between different tools. To date, that has been little progress on this objective, although it remains a high priority for future work.
4. To provide a strong foundation for the definition of a UML virtual machine that is capable of executing UML 2 models. Progress on this objective is being made on two fronts:
   - Dr. Alan Hartman's group at IBM Haifa, Israel has created a generic model execution engine [11] on top of which a UML simulator for activity diagrams and state machines has been implemented. The simulator allows modellers to step through their models in an interactive fashion and thus gain a better understanding of their behaviour.
   - Simultaneously, research is carried out to use the system model as the basis of an execution and analysis engine. The goal of this work is to refine the system model and to pave the way towards a more powerful analysis platform based directly on our formal semantics of UML.
   Cross-pollination between these two initiatives is expected to benefit both.

In addition to these primary objectives, research has been conducted on these related topics: clarification of complicated or new aspects of UML, e.g., associations [8], package merge [15,14], and generic model management [9].

6   Future Work

The original project mandate was for two years. We have made significant progress in that period of time. Although there is much more research to be done, we are anticipating the continuation of this project for at least one more year. Regardless, the majority of the system model is nearly complete and can be used in future research. More specifically, work on mapping the actions and activities to the system model will be continued.

Acknowledgments. This research is supported by Communications and Information Technology Ontario, the IBM Centers for Advanced Studies, the Technische Universität München, and IBM Germany.

References

1. UML 2 semantics project web page.
   `http://www.cs.queensu.ca/~stl/internal/uml2,2006.`
2. M. Broy, M.-V. Cengarle, and B. Rumpe. Towards a system model for UML: The control and scheduling model. Draft - Verson 0.7, Oct 2006.
3. M. Broy, M.-V. Cengarle, and B. Rumpe. Towards a system model for UML: The structural data model. Version 1.0, 4 June 2006.
4. M.L. Crane and J. Dingel. Mapping actions to the system model. Draft - Version 0.0, Oct 2006.
5. M.L. Crane, J. Dingel, and Z. Diskin. Class diagrams: Abstract syntax and mapping to system model. Draft - Version 1.7, Sep 2006.
6. M.L. Crane, J. Dingel, and Z. Diskin. Mapping activities to the system model. Draft - Version 0.0, Oct 2006.
7. J. Dingel, M.L. Crane, and Z. Diskin. Activity diagrams: Abstract syntax and mapping to system model. Draft - Version 0.0, Mar 2006.
8. Z. Diskin and J. Dingel. Mappings, maps and tables: Towards formal semantics for associations in UML2. In *Proceedings of the 9th International Conference on Model Driven Engineering Languages and Systems (MoDELS 2006)*, volume 4199 of *LNCS*, pages 230–244. Springer, 2006.
9. Z. Diskin and J. Dingel. A metamodel independent framework for model transformation: Towards generic model management patterns in reverse engineering. In *3rd International Workshop on Metamodels, Schemas, Grammars, and Ontologies for Reverse Engineering (ATEM 2006)*, 2006.
10. David Harel and Bernhard Rumpe. Meaningful modeling: What's the semantics of "semantics"? *IEEE Computer Magazine*, 37(10):64–72, 2004.
11. A. Kirshin, D. Moshkovich, and A. Hartman. A UML simulator based on a generic model execution engine. In *Proceedings of the 20th European Conference on Modelling and Simulation (ECMS 2006)*, 2006.
12. OMG. Unified Modeling Language: Superstructure version 2.0. Document formal/05-07-04, Object Management Group, 2005.
13. B. Selic. On the semantic foundations of standard UML 2.0. In M. Bernardo and F. Corradini, editors, *Formal Methods for the Design of Real-Time Systems (SFM-RT 2004)*, volume 3185 of *LNCS*, pages 181–199. Springer, 2004.
14. A. Zito and J. Dingel. Modeling UML2 package merge with Alloy. In *First Alloy Workshop*, Portland, Oregon, USA, November 2006. (to appear).
15. A. Zito, Z. Diskin, and J. Dingel. Package merge in UML 2: Practice vs. theory? In *Proceedings of the 9th International Conference on Model Driven Engineering Languages and Systems (MoDELS 2006)*, volume 4199 of *LNCS*, pages 185–199. Springer, 2006.

A UML Simulator Based on a Generic Model Execution Engine

Andrei Kirshin, Dolev Dotan, and Alan Hartman

IBM Haifa Research Lab, Haifa University Campus, Mount Carmel, Haifa, 31905, Israel
{kirshin, dotan, hartman}@il.ibm.com

Keywords: Model Execution, Model Simulator, Model Debugger, UML, State Machines, Activities.

We implemented a generic model execution engine. The engine provides mechanisms for the realization and the execution of behavioral semantics, and the control and observation of model behavior. We used this generic execution engine to implement a UML Model Simulator. It is designed as an extension to Rational Software Architect (RSA), adding execution and debugging capabilities.

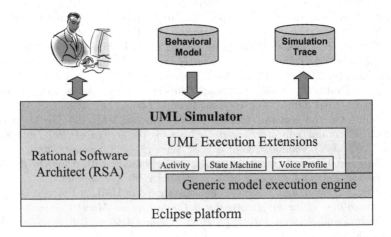

The current version of the UML Model Simulator supports UML classes and primitive data types, and focuses on the execution of activities and state machines. It also supports Java as an action language. Profiles can be used to add domain-specific behavior of a UML element, by applying stereotypes to UML elements. The tool can be extended to support the execution of models that conform to a specific profile.

The UML Model Simulator provides a wide range of debugging capabilities:

- It supports the most commonly used execution modes such as step-wise execution and run to breakpoint.

T. Kühne (Ed.): MoDELS 2006 Workshops, LNCS 4364, pp. 324–326, 2007.
© Springer-Verlag Berlin Heidelberg 2007

- It allows dynamic object creation. Object here can be an instance of a class, an activity, or a state machine. After the creation the user can execute behaviors and invoke operations.
- It allows run-time observation of an object's attribute values.
- It allows run-time observation of a behavior's state – visualization of the current state of a running state machine, currently enabled transitions, signals in the data pool, and activity token offers.

We extended RSA with a Model Debugging perspective that contains various views. **Model Explorer view**. This is the corresponding RSA view with the addition of two items to the popup-menu: *Debug Model* is used to start a model debugging session, and *Add Breakpoint* can be applied to any runnable element of the model. **Debug view**. This view is responsible for control of the execution process (starting, stopping, and step mode execution), object creation and destruction, observing the values of objects' attributes, and invoking the operations on the objects. **Call Stack view**. This view shows all running behaviors organized according to the call history. **Signal Pool view**. This view shows the signals waiting in the signal pool of each running behavior. **I/O view**. This view allows signals to be sent to running behaviors and shows the signals sent from the behaviors to the environment. **Ready view**. This view shows all elements that are ready for execution and all elements that have reached breakpoints. The user can select the next element for execution. **Breakpoints view**. This view lists all active breakpoints. **Diagram Animation**. This powerful feature builds a visual representation of the execution behavior.

When running an activity, the user can see which nodes are ready for execution (green), which edges pass tokens (blue), or which node provides the token (magenta).

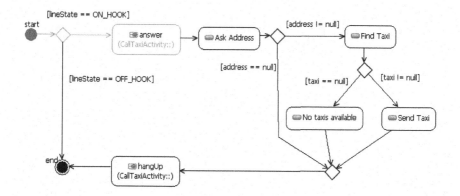

When running a state machine, the user can see the current state (magenta), and the enabled transitions (green).

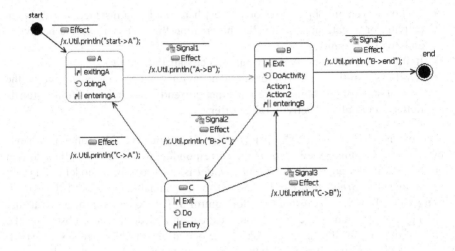

Queries and Constraints: A Comprehensive Semantic Model for UML2

Ingolf H. Krüger and Massimiliano Menarini

University of California San Diego
9500 Gilman Drive, MC 0404
La Jolla, CA 92093-0404, USA
{ikrueger,mmenarini}@ucsd.edu

Keywords: Semantics, UML, UML2, Model-based Development, Software Architecture, Programming Languages.

UML and UML2 are the de facto industry standards for model based software development. To deliver the benefits promised by model based development, including sophisticated synthesis and validation tool support, UML2 must have a precise and formally defined semantics. While there have been attempts at defining semantics for individual description techniques in the past, a unifying semantics approach covering the information represented by all UML2 description techniques has proven elusive so far. In this contribution we turn the picture around: we define a semantic core-model of distributed, reactive systems and interpret UML2's description techniques as queries and constraints at instantiations of this core model. A query selects the elements relevant for a specification. A constraint imposes structural and behavioral properties on the system under consideration.

The Abstract Specification Universe. To provide a unifying semantics for UML2 specifications we first need to define what the family of systems we intend to specify looks like. For this reason our first goal is to describe the core elements of the abstract universe that is the root of our semantic framework. We focus on the following elements: Entities, Channels, Messages, and Properties. This will allows us to talk about a clean and concise mathematical model for distributed, embedded, reactive, reconfigurable systems. Each system is made of two main elements capturing the structure of a system, namely Entities and Channels, and two elements capturing behavior, Messages and Properties. Entities have computational capabilities and can communicate with one another by means of channels. Channels connect arbitrary sets of entities. Entities connected to a given channel can send messages on it. All entities that are listening on the channel will receive these messages. Messages are the means of communication of our target system. The sequences of messages exchanged capture part of the behavior of the system. The other part of the behavior is captured by the sequence of values Properties assume during execution. In our model, Properties are named function parameters. Examples of Properties are: variables of a program code, sensor readings (such as the temperature read by a temperature sensor), and more complex system-level properties (such as the position of a train in the

T. Kühne (Ed.): MoDELS 2006 Workshops, LNCS 4364, pp. 327–328, 2007.

railroad system). Even system structure itself can be interpreted as a Property. Each Property can be used in function calls by the various Entities. At every instant it is possible to determine the value of a given Property in the context of a specific Entity by using the Property as a parameter for the Boolean functions it can appear in.

Queries and Constraints. The central idea of our semantic model for UML2 is that each specification (diagram or text) expressed in one of the UML2 languages can be understood as the contribution of two specification elements of our semantic framework: Queries and Constraints. A Query is a guard over the values of properties and the message history of channels; it determines if a particular Entity (of the execution space) is selected to be constrained by the respective UML2 artifact. A Constraint enforces a behavior of the system: it imposes that a message is or is not sent by the selected entity and it constrains the properties of the entity in the next system state. The semantic space of our model is, therefore, based on the notion of state that arises from the messages present on all communication channels at a given instant and from the valuation of all functions over the named Properties for each Entity. A sequence of states is a run of the system. The Query and Constraint semantics allows only runs such that for each state in which some Query is satisfied the next state fulfills the corresponding Constraints.

Mapping to UML2 Languages. The UML2 standard defines thirteen graphical and a textual languages. To show the power of the concept of Queries and Constraints as underlying semantic foundation for UML we sketch a possible interpretation of two of them. First let us examine how such an interpretation could be carried out for a language describing the behavior of a program: the state machine diagram. In this case the language is made of states, transitions, and operators (AND/OR). A suitable Query in such a case could use the state name, or would select all components that share a particular Property – to show shared state transitions in communication protocol, for instance. A Boolean function *stateis* having as parameter the state name returns true in case the current state is the one named in the parameter. A Constraint would be that the next value of the properties is such that *stateis* would return true only on the target state of an enabled transition for the current state. Another interesting example is the mapping of a deployment diagram. This time the constraints must enforce a particular structural arrangement of the target system. To achieve this goal we can simply encode the structure of the system using Properties. For instance, the programs to run on each node are identified by Properties encoding the program names. The behavior of each program is defined by having in each Query, used in the specification of the program, and additional guards on the program name (for instance *isrunning(ProgramName)*). The mapping is achieved by assigning the program name Properties to the entities representing network nodes. This strategy of specification has the additional benefit of allowing easy reconfiguration at runtime by means of changing Properties. Utilizing queries and constraints in this way yields significant flexibility in defining UML2 semantics.

Analysis of UML Activities with Dynamic Meta Modeling Techniques

Christian Soltenborn and Gregor Engels

Dept. of Computer Science, University of Paderborn,
Warburger Straße 100, 33098 Paderborn, Germany
{christian|engels}@uni-paderborn.de

Abstract. Based on a semantics of UML Activities specified with the Dynamic Meta Modeling approach, we analyze the dynamic semantics of Activities at modeling time.

Keywords: UML, semantics, behavior, verification, DMM.

1 Motivation and Background

Measuring the quality of models should be an important part of the model-driven approach (MDA): If models are treated as first-class elements, they obviously should not contain any serious flaws. However, manually analyzing complex models is not feasible. Therefore, the goal must be to provide tool support for the modeler which assists her in identifying errors, inconsistencies etc. within the model. One requirement for this is that the semantics of the modeling language is defined formally.

To define semantics for behavioral modeling languages like UML Activities, we propose the use of the *Dynamic Meta Modeling* (DMM) approach [1]. DMM was developed with two requirements in mind: A DMM based semantics specification should not only be formal, but also easily understandable. DMM fulfills both requirements by using *typed graphs* and *graph transformation rules* (GTRs)—which both have visual representations—as the underlying formalisms.

The idea of DMM is as follows: First, to be able to express states of execution, the meta model of the target language is enhanced with appropriate concepts (in the case of UML Activities, these are mainly a Token and an Offer class); instances of the enhanced meta model are then mapped to typed graphs. Second, GTRs are defined which describe how those typed graphs change in time (i.e., how tokens and offers flow through the Activity).

2 Analysis of DMM Based Semantics

A DMM specification yields a labeled state-transition-system (STS): A model instance (in our case, a concrete Activity) is mapped to the start state of the STS, and a transition occurs whenever a GTR can be applied to a state to derive a new state. That transition is labeled with the applied rule.

T. Kühne (Ed.): MoDELS 2006 Workshops, LNCS 4364, pp. 329–330, 2007.

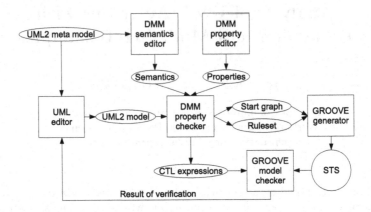

Fig. 1. Chain of tools

Dynamic properties of the diagram can then be verified by investigating the resulting STS. For this, we have utilized the GROOVE tool set [2], which provides not only a generator to compute an STS based on a start graph and a set of GTRs, but also a model checker for that STS.

Figure 1 shows the complete workflow: In a first step, the semantics of the language under consideration is defined, yielding an enhanced meta model. Using it, dynamic properties the modeler is interested in can be edited. The semantics definition and the properties are used at model time to translate a concrete UML model into a start graph, a set of GTRs and some CTL expressions. These fragments then serve as input for the GROOVE tool set. Finally, the result of the model checker can be used to improve the model. A more thorough description of the process can be found in [3].

3   Conclusion

The DMM approach in conjunction with the GROOVE tool set enables us to check dynamic properties of UML Activities at modeling time. Thus, our approach allows the formal definition of a UML semantics as well as the analysis of dynamic properties of UML diagrams.

References

1. Hausmann, J.H.: Dynamic Meta Modeling. PhD thesis, University of Paderborn (2005)
2. Rensink, A.: The GROOVE Simulator: A Tool for State Space Generation. In: Applications of Graph Transformations with Industrial Relevance (AGTIVE). Volume 3062 of Lecture Notes in Computer Science., Springer-Verlag (2004) 479–485
3. Soltenborn, C.: Analysis of UML Workflow Diagrams with Dynamic Meta Modeling techniques. Master's thesis, University of Paderborn (2006)

Author Index

Lecture Notes in Computer Science

For information about Vols. 1–4275

please contact your bookseller or Springer

Vol. 4320: R. Gotzhein, R. Reed (Eds.), System Analysis and Modeling: Language Profiles. X, 229 pages. 2006.

Vol. 4319: L.-W. Chang, W.-N. Lie (Eds.), Advances in Image and Video Technology. XXVI, 1347 pages. 2006.

Vol. 4318: H. Lipmaa, M. Yung, D. Lin (Eds.), Information Security and Cryptology. XI, 305 pages. 2006.

Vol. 4317: S.K. Madria, K.T. Claypool, R. Kannan, P. Uppuluri, M.M. Gore (Eds.), Distributed Computing and Internet Technology. XIX, 466 pages. 2006.

Vol. 4316: M.M. Dalkilic, S. Kim, J. Yang (Eds.), Data Mining and Bioinformatics. VIII, 197 pages. 2006. (Sublibrary LNBI).

Vol. 4313: T. Margaria, B. Steffen (Eds.), Leveraging Applications of Formal Methods. IX, 197 pages. 2006.

Vol. 4312: S. Sugimoto, J. Hunter, A. Rauber, A. Morishima (Eds.), Digital Libraries: Achievements, Challenges and Opportunities. XVIII, 571 pages. 2006.

Vol. 4311: K. Cho, P. Jacquet (Eds.), Technologies for Advanced Heterogeneous Networks II. XI, 253 pages. 2006.

Vol. 4309: P. Inverardi, M. Jazayeri (Eds.), Software Engineering Education in the Modern Age. VIII, 207 pages. 2006.

Vol. 4308: S. Chaudhuri, S.R. Das, H.S. Paul, S. Tirthapura (Eds.), Distributed Computing and Networking. XIX, 608 pages. 2006.

Vol. 4307: P. Ning, S. Qing, N. Li (Eds.), Information and Communications Security. XIV, 558 pages. 2006.

Vol. 4306: Y. Avrithis, Y. Kompatsiaris, S. Staab, N.E. O'Connor (Eds.), Semantic Multimedia. XII, 241 pages. 2006.

Vol. 4305: A.A. Shvartsman (Ed.), Principles of Distributed Systems. XIII, 441 pages. 2006.

Vol. 4304: A. Sattar, B.-H. Kang (Eds.), AI 2006: Advances in Artificial Intelligence. XXVII, 1303 pages. 2006. (Sublibrary LNAI).

Vol. 4303: A. Hoffmann, B.-H. Kang, D. Richards, S. Tsumoto (Eds.), Advances in Knowledge Acquisition and Management. XI, 259 pages. 2006. (Sublibrary LNAI).

Vol. 4302: J. Domingo-Ferrer, L. Franconi (Eds.), Privacy in Statistical Databases. XI, 383 pages. 2006.

Vol. 4301: D. Pointcheval, Y. Mu, K. Chen (Eds.), Cryptology and Network Security. XIII, 381 pages. 2006.

Vol. 4300: Y.Q. Shi (Ed.), Transactions on Data Hiding and Multimedia Security I. IX, 139 pages. 2006.

Vol. 4299: S. Renals, S. Bengio, J.G. Fiscus (Eds.), Machine Learning for Multimodal Interaction. XII, 470 pages. 2006.

Vol. 4297: Y. Robert, M. Parashar, R. Badrinath, V.K. Prasanna (Eds.), High Performance Computing - HiPC 2006. XXIV, 642 pages. 2006.

Vol. 4296: M.S. Rhee, B. Lee (Eds.), Information Security and Cryptology – ICISC 2006. XIII, 358 pages. 2006.

Vol. 4295: J.D. Carswell, T. Tezuka (Eds.), Web and Wireless Geographical Information Systems. XI, 269 pages. 2006.

Vol. 4294: A. Dan, W. Lamersdorf (Eds.), Service-Oriented Computing – ICSOC 2006. XIX, 653 pages. 2006.

Vol. 4293: A. Gelbukh, C.A. Reyes-Garcia (Eds.), MICAI 2006: Advances in Artificial Intelligence. XXVIII, 1232 pages. 2006. (Sublibrary LNAI).

Vol. 4292: G. Bebis, R. Boyle, B. Parvin, D. Koracin, P. Remagnino, A. Nefian, G. Meenakshisundaram, V. Pascucci, J. Zara, J. Molineros, H. Theisel, T. Malzbender (Eds.), Advances in Visual Computing, Part II. XXXII, 906 pages. 2006.

Vol. 4291: G. Bebis, R. Boyle, B. Parvin, D. Koracin, P. Remagnino, A. Nefian, G. Meenakshisundaram, V. Pascucci, J. Zara, J. Molineros, H. Theisel, T. Malzbender (Eds.), Advances in Visual Computing, Part I. XXXI, 916 pages. 2006.

Vol. 4290: M. van Steen, M. Henning (Eds.), Middleware 2006. XIII, 425 pages. 2006.

Vol. 4289: M. Ackermann, B. Berendt, M. Grobelnik, A. Hotho, D. Mladenič, G. Semeraro, M. Spiliopoulou, G. Stumme, V. Svátek, M. van Someren (Eds.), Semantics, Web and Mining. X, 197 pages. 2006. (Sublibrary LNAI).

Vol. 4288: T. Asano (Ed.), Algorithms and Computation. XX, 766 pages. 2006.

Vol. 4287: C. Mao, T. Yokomori (Eds.), DNA Computing. XII, 440 pages. 2006.

Vol. 4286: P.G. Spirakis, M. Mavronicolas, S.C. Kontogiannis (Eds.), Internet and Network Economics. XI, 401 pages. 2006.

Vol. 4285: Y. Matsumoto, R.W. Sproat, K.-F. Wong, M. Zhang (Eds.), Computer Processing of Oriental Languages. XVII, 544 pages. 2006. (Sublibrary LNAI).

Vol. 4284: X. Lai, K. Chen (Eds.), Advances in Cryptology – ASIACRYPT 2006. XIV, 468 pages. 2006.

Vol. 4283: Y.Q. Shi, B. Jeon (Eds.), Digital Watermarking. XII, 474 pages. 2006.

Vol. 4282: Z. Pan, A. Cheok, M. Haller, R.W.H. Lau, H. Saito, R. Liang (Eds.), Advances in Artificial Reality and Tele-Existence. XXIII, 1347 pages. 2006.

Vol. 4281: K. Barkaoui, A. Cavalcanti, A. Cerone (Eds.), Theoretical Aspects of Computing - ICTAC 2006. XV, 371 pages. 2006.

Vol. 4280: A.K. Datta, M. Gradinariu (Eds.), Stabilization, Safety, and Security of Distributed Systems. XVII, 590 pages. 2006.

Vol. 4279: N. Kobayashi (Ed.), Programming Languages and Systems. XI, 423 pages. 2006.

Vol. 4278: R. Meersman, Z. Tari, P. Herrero (Eds.), On the Move to Meaningful Internet Systems 2006: OTM 2006 Workshops, Part II. XLV, 1004 pages. 2006.

Vol. 4277: R. Meersman, Z. Tari, P. Herrero (Eds.), On the Move to Meaningful Internet Systems 2006: OTM 2006 Workshops, Part I. XLV, 1009 pages. 2006.

Vol. 4276: R. Meersman, Z. Tari (Eds.), On the Move to Meaningful Internet Systems 2006: CoopIS, DOA, GADA, and ODBASE, Part II. XXXII, 752 pages. 2006.